D0883634

The Concept of Cruel and Unusual Punishment

The Concept of Cruel and Unusual Punishment

Larry Charles Berkson
The University of Florida

Lexington Books
D.C. Heath and Company
Lexington, Massachusetts
Toronto   London

Library of Congress Cataloging in Publication Data

Berkson, Larry Charles.
    The concept of cruel and unusual punishment.

    Includes index.
    1. Punishment—United States. I. Title.
KF9225.B47   345'.73'077   75-16331
ISBN 0-669-00063-9

Published simultaneously in Canada

Printed in the United States of America

International Standard Book Number: 0-669-00063-9

Library of Congress Catalog Card Number: 75-16331

To My Parents

Table of Contents

List of Figure and Tables

Preface

Acknowledgments

Part I	**An Overview**	1
Chapter 1	Origins of the Concept	3
	English Antecedents	3
	Introduction of the Concept to North America	4
Chapter 2	Judicial Interpretation: An Overview	9
	1789-1910	9
	1910-74	10
Part II	**Legislative Action and Judicial Sentencing as Cruel and Unusual Punishment**	19
	A. Corporeal Punishments	19
Chapter 3	Challenging the Various Methods of Inflicting the Death Penalty	21
	Hanging	21
	Shooting	22
	Electrocution	23
	Gaseous Asphyxiation	29
Chapter 4	Challenging the Death Penalty as Excessive	33
	Robbery	33
	Arson, Kidnapping, and Espionage	35
	Assault	37

Rape   39
Murder   42

Chapter 5   Challenging the Death Penalty as Unconstitutional per se   43

People v. *Anderson*   44
Furman v. *Georgia*   45
Furman: Initial Reaction   49
Furman: The Impact   50

Chapter 6   Miscellaneous Chastisement   55

Whipping   55
Sterilization   56
Other Corporeal Punishments   58

B. *Incorporeal Punishments*   63

Chapter 7   The Doctrine of Excessiveness   65

Weems v. *United States*   66
Initial Reaction to *Weems*   67
Punishments Held Excessive Since *Weems*   71

Chapter 8   Other Challenges Based on the Doctrine of Excessiveness   75

Habitual Offender Statutes   75
Multiple Sentences in Single Prosecutions   80
Indeterminate Sentences   81
Unequal Sentences for Codefendants   83
Miscellaneous Sentences   84

Chapter 9   Deportation, Banishment, and Expatriation   87

Deportation   87
Banishment   87
Expatriation   92

Chapter 10 Status Statutes and Cruel and Unusual Punishment   97

To Be a Narcotic Addict   97
To Be an Alcoholic   101
To Be a Vagrant   102

To Be a Prostitute or Homosexual   104
To Be Mentally Ill or Insane   105

Part III.   **Administrative Action as Cruel and Unusual Punishment**   109

Chapter 11   Prison Rules and Practices   111

The Hands-Off Doctrine   111
Remedies   112
Challenges to Methods of Enforcing Prison Rules   115
Challenges to Specific Prison Rules and Practices   131
Challenges to Rules and Practices Found in Public
    Schools   137
Challenges to Rules and Practices Found in Other   139
    Governmental Agencies

Chapter 12   Total Prison Conditions   141

Chain Gangs   141
Jails   144
Penitentiaries   151
Juvenile Facilities   155

Part IV.   **Conclusion**   157

Chapter 13   Conclusion   159

Notes   165

Table of Cases   223

Index   247

About the Author   253

List of Figure and Tables

Figure

2-1   Cruel and Unusual Punishment Opinions Rendered: 1910-74   12

Table

2-1   Justice Brennan's Tests for Determining Cruel and Unusual
      Punishments   16
5-1   Aggravating and Mitigating Circumstances Affecting
      Imposition of the Death Penalty   52
8-1   Lengthy Sentences Upheld: 1789-1910   76
8-2   Lengthy Sentences Upheld: 1946-74   76
8-3   Multiple Sentences in Single Prosecutions Upheld: 1946-74   82
8-4   Indeterminate Sentences Upheld: 1946-74   84
8-5   Unequal Sentences Upheld for Codefendants: 1946-74   85
9-1   Acts Accruing Loss of Citizenship   93

Preface

The topic of "cruel and unusual punishment," generally neglected by legal scholars and historians alike, is ripe for serious and extended treatment. Most detailed research has been telescopic in thrust, focusing on a single aspect of the topic: its early history, particular methods of punishment, the degree of punishment, and particular cases. Oddly enough, there are books on most of the individual amendments in the Bill of Rights, but none on the Eighth Amendment. Few dissertations have been written on it. Most of the leading constitutional law books completely ignore the subject, mention it only briefly, or, at most, devote to it a page or two. Less than a half dozen journal articles deal with the concept in an even moderately comprehensive fashion. Moreover, articles on some subtopics, such as whipping and flogging, and administrative action as cruel and unusual punishment, are almost nonexistent in the contemporary literature.

Within the past few years a number of landmark court decisions have been rendered on Eighth Amendment grounds. Among these are decisions declaring environmental conditions in jails, and in two instances, whole penal systems, unconstitutional. The California Supreme Court recently ruled that the death penalty violated its state constitutional ban on cruel or unusual punishment. More recently, the United States Supreme Court ruled that, as applied, capital punishment violates the cruel and unusual punishment clause of the United States Constitution. No longer is the Eighth Amendment obscure and forgotten. Indeed, it has become one of the new frontiers of creative constitutional law.

The purpose of this book is to present a broad and comprehensive picture of the cruel and unusual punishment concept rather than to concentrate on any one aspect of the topic. The book is divided into four parts. The first presents an overview of the origins and development of the concept. Parts II and III separate legislative action and judicial sentencing from administrative action, as cruel and unusual punishment. Part II is divided into two main topics: corporeal and incorporeal punishments. Corporeal punishments are defined as those that inflict physical bodily harm. Incorporeal punishments inflict almost no physical bodily harm. Part III consists of two chapters. The first deals with administrative punishment levied for the violation of specific prison rules. The second deals with challenges to the total prison environment. Infliction of cruel and unusual punishment found in the former chapter is generally the result of some affirmative action on the part of administrative officials, while the latter is generally the result of negative action by legislatures. Part IV summarizes the basic findings and conclusions of the study.

Acknowledgements

I would like to extend a special note of thanks to Professor David Fellman of the University of Wisconsin for his thoughtful and constructive remarks on the original version of the manuscript. I am also indebted to Professor Ernest Bartley of the University of Florida for reading it in its entirety and for offering several helpful suggestions. Finally, I wish to thank Susan Carbon for her extensive editorial comments and the Division of Sponsored Research at the University of Florida for their aid in typing the final version.

Part I: An Overview

1

Origins of the Concept

English Antecedents

The American concept of cruel and unusual punishment is clearly traceable to early English history.[1] Many scholars argue that the phrase was meant to prevent torture and inhumane physical punishment. However, close examination of early English documents shows clearly that the clause was intended to prohibit excessive punishments rather than particular modes of inflicting them. For example, punishments in A.D. 900 were graduated to the offense. One law stated that if a person "knocks out another's eye, he shall pay 66 shillings, 6-1/3 pence." On the other hand, "if the eye is still in the head . . . one third of the payment shall be withheld."[2] A century later, the Laws of Edward the Confessor (1042-66) reputedly directed that "extreme punishment . . . shall be inflicted according to the nature and extent of the offense."[3] The Magna Carta (1215) contained three provisions dealing with the concept of disproportionate punishments. In essence, each permitted punishment only "in proportion to the measure of the offense."[4] Another great document of English liberty, the Petition of Right (1628), contained no mention of disproportionate punishments.[5] This is perhaps owing to the brevity of the document and the historical circumstances surrounding its adoption.[6] Nevertheless, a genuine concern over disproportionate sentences is evidenced by the fact that thirteen years later Parliament abolished Star Chamber. The Chamber, an executive tribunal, had become notorious for levying harsh punishments. Justifying the abolition, the statute in part stated that the judges had inflicted "heavier punishments than by any law is warranted."[7]

The present day language of the concept is first found in the English Bill of Rights (1689), which stated: "Excessive bail ought not be required, nor excessive fines imposed; nor cruel and unusual punishments inflicted."[8] At the time there was still no legal guarantee against inhumane and torturous punishment. Brutal penalties continued. As late as 1752, an act passed by Parliament empowered the judge to order a murderer dissected and gibbeted.[9] Not only were new statutes enacted; the harshest of the old ones were utilized as a basis for levying punishments. Radzinowicz offers a number of examples of women being burned at the stake during the 1770s and 1780s.[10] The last, Christian Murphy, was burned in 1789, the year in which the United States Constitution was adopted. Hanging in chains, or gibbeting, was another notorious method of punishment and is reported as late as 1792. The incredibly horrid penalty for high treason, that of drawing and quartering, was vigorously carried out with most of its grueling embellishments as late as 1817.

However, England did begin to abolish its most diabolical forms of punishment at an early date. During the reign of Edward VI, a cook by the name of Rose had poisoned a number of people, including the bishop of Rochester. In the uproar immediately thereafter, Parliament provided that one was to be boiled to death for such an offense.[11] Seventeen years later Parliament had second thoughts and repealed the law.

Despite this early retreat from cruelty, it was over two centuries before most of the brutal forms of punishment began to disappear.[12] In 1790 the burning of women was ended. In 1814, drawing and quartering was abolished. Twenty-seven years later, Parliament prohibited the whipping of women. Gibbeting was abolished in 1834, and pillorying in 1837. In 1870 beheading and quartering was prohibited. Finally, nearly all methods of extinguishing life were abolished by Parliament in 1965.[13]

Introduction of the Concept to North America

The first detailed enactment by a colonial legislature on the subject of human rights was the Massachusetts Body of Liberties. The concern of its author and ratifiers about torture, brutality, and punishment is reflected in the no less than six articles dealing with the subject.[14] Nonetheless, its adoption in 1641 did not precipitate an immediate landslide of legislative activity to restrict the imposition of cruel and unusual punishments. Indeed, not for another 135 years did a colonial legislature enact a statute directly relevant to the prohibition. Such a hiatus might superficially indicate a lack of concern with the concept. Closer investigation, however, shows this not to be the case. In the first place, English and colonial leaders had many problems more pressing than the rights of defendants and criminals. Second, and most important, actual punitive practices during the period show that the colonists were not entirely unconcerned with cruel and unusual punishment. There is little evidence that any significant number of persons were ever beheaded, drawn and quartered, boiled, gibbeted, or pressed to death.[15] There are few recorded instances of men being broken on the wheel.[16] Mutilation was rare. There were some brandings, and very early laws provided that the ears might be cut off or tongues bored through.[17] There is little to suggest, however, that these methods were used widely. Burning at the stake was also seldom used. None of the alleged witches in New England was ever burned.[18] Apparently, the only burnings occurred in pre-Revolutionary New York.[19]

Other forms of corporeal punishment practiced in England at the time were used more frequently. Paine's and Andrew's descriptions of the ducking stool, the collar of torment, the tumbrel or dung cart, and whipping in England, do not differ greatly from Earle's description of the same methods of punishment in the colonies.[20] Whipping was the most common form of corporeal punishment in early colonial days. Graphic accounts fill page after page of many books and articles on the subject.[21] With this exception, however, the infliction of corporeal punishments in the early colonial era was very restricted and became progressively more so.

Certain incorporeal punishments, however, were used extensively, perhaps as a partial alternative to corporeal punishments. Such humiliating devices as the pillory, stocks, scarlet letter and its variations, and public penance were utilized.[22] Physical harm often accompanied such punishment, as onlookers threw stones and other missiles at the helpless convicts, but such treatment was generally not part of the sentence.[23] Thus, on a comparative basis, corporeal punishments were relatively mild in colonial America in comparison with the same period in England.

With the adoption of the Virginia Declaration of Rights on June 12, 1776, a new era in the history of cruel and unusual punishment began. On May 15, 1776, a committee had been established to prepare a Declaration of Rights. The following day, James Madison, who eventually was to draft the federal Bill of Rights, was added to the committee. Two days later George Mason was appointed, and it was he who eventually wrote the Declaration. Article 9 stated: "Excessive bail ought not to be required, nor excessive fines imposed, nor cruel and unusual punishments inflicted."[24] Obviously, the phrase is an exact replication of the statement in the English Bill of Rights. But was the same meaning attached to it eighty-seven years later, on a different continent, by men of a somewhat different heritage? Did Mason, who wrote it, the delegates who ratified it, and those who were to recopy it later in other states view the clause as solely a prohibition against excessive punishments? Clearly, no. As Chief Justice Burger has stated: "From every indication, the framers of the Eighth Amendment intended to give the phrase a meaning far different from that of its English precursor."[25] By this time, the concept of cruel and unusual punishment was clearly interpreted much more broadly. There is no doubt whatsoever that in borrowing the language of the English Bill of Rights and in including it in the Eighth Amendment, our founding fathers intended to prohibit torture and other cruel punishments.[26]

Furthermore, there is little doubt that the concept was considered essential and fundamental. The prohibition, with its expanded meaning, became generally regarded as no less important than many of the liberties the United States Supreme Court today has elevated as "preferred" or "basic."

At the outset of the American Revolution each colony except Rhode Island organized conventions to draft and adopt constitutions.[27] Of the original thirteen states, eight adopted constitutions that contained *separate* bills of rights: Connecticut, Pennsylvania, Delaware, Virginia, North Carolina, Massachusetts, Maryland, and New Hampshire.[28] Of these, only Connecticut and Pennsylvania did not include prohibitions against cruel and unusual punishment. The omission by Connecticut is attributable to the brevity of the document. Pennsylvania's omission may have been simply an oversight, for in 1790 it adopted a clause containing the prohibition.[29]

Four states (New Jersey, Georgia, New York, and South Carolina) scattered individual rights *throughout* the main text of their constitutions rather than including separate bills of rights. The South Carolina Constitution included a statement directed at cruel and unusual punishment: "The penal laws as heretofore used, shall be reformed, and punishments made in some cases less sanguinary, and in general more proportionate to the crime."[30] Thus, in eight of the twelve states, freedom from cruel and unusual punishment was guaranteed, indicating that the concept was broadly recognized and considered very important by the founding fathers.

In 1777 the Continental Congress ratified the Articles of Confederation. The newly created Congress had very little power and consequently did little of importance. However, it did manage to organize the Northwest Territory. In 1783 a committee chaired by Thomas Jefferson had been appointed to prepare plans for temporary government of the area. The original plan did not contain provisions securing personal liberties, but as various committees subsequently considered the governing of the area, they began to suggest that certain fundamental rights be guaranteed. The final document of July 13, 1787 contained a bill of rights that stated: "No cruel or unusual punishments shall be inflicted."[31] For the first time, a national legislative body had seen fit to guarantee this right. The inclusion is impressive, because many other fundamental rights were not enumerated. For example, there is no reference to the freedoms of speech, press, and assembly, and there are no prohibitions against the quartering of troops, search and seizure, double jeopardy, and self-incrimination. This appears to be a clear indication of the high regard paid the concept by these early congressmen.

In 1787 the Constitutional Convention was held, but no bill of rights was attached to the proposed document.[32] When the new Constitution was presented to the Congress, Richard Henry Lee, the most outspoken opponent of an unamended constitution, offered a number of proposals.[33] Included was the provision that "cruel and unusual punishments should not be demanded or inflicted." However, the Congress rejected all of his proposals and submitted the Constitution to the states for ratification. Of the thirteen state conventions, six ratified the Constitution without recommending amendments.[34] In the Pennsylvania convention, however, Robert Whitehall of Cumberland County did propose a bill of rights, that included the inhibition that "cruel or unusual punishments ought not be inflicted."[35] However, over the objections of a sizable minority, the convention ratified the Constitution without recommending the amendments.

In the Virginia convention, Patrick Henry argued for inclusion of a prohibition against cruel and unusual punishment. He asserted:

In this business of legislation, your members of Congress will lose
the restriction of not imposing excessive fines, demanding excessive bail, and inflicting cruel and unusual punishments. These are
prohibited by your declaration of rights. What has distinguished
our ancestors? That they would not admit of tortures, of cruel
and barbarous punishment. If you will, like the Virginia government, give them knowledge of the extent of the rights retained
by the people; and the powers of themselves, they will, if they
be honest men, thank you for it.[36]

Subsequently, the Virginia convention heeded his advice and proposed that a
cruel and unusual punishment prohibition be included in the Constitution.
Therefore, North Carolina, New York, and Rhode Island proposed similar
amendments.[37]

The adoption of the Constitution commenced a new era in the history of
cruel and unusual punishment. Demands had begun at the ratifying conventions and continued to pour forth from political leaders and the general public
alike for protection against the newly created central government. On June 8,
1789, James Madison introduced the first draft of the federal Bill of Rights
into the United States House of Representatives. Part of his Fourth Article
stated: "Excessive bail *shall not* be required, nor excessive fines imposed,
nor cruel and unusual punishments inflicted."[38] One might legitimately
argue that the phrase was included as a matter of course, as it is very similar to the one in the English Bill of Rights, the Virginia Declaration of Rights,
and the amendments proposed by the Virginia ratifying convention, all of
which were identical. However, there is an important change in the wording of Madison's clause. The "ought not" found in the former documents
is replaced with "shall not." The substitution of the imperative "shall" for the
flaccid "ought" implies that the prohibition was considered so fundamental
that even stronger wording was required than that of previous documents.

The committee appointed to consider the proposals made no changes in
the phraseology of the clause. The final unchanged version of the amendment,
Article XIII, was sent, along with others, to the Senate on August 24, 1789.
Unfortunately, very little is known about the proceeding in the Senate, and
absolutely nothing about discussion focusing on the concept itself. The records
simply indicate that there was no substantive change in the amendment, but
that it was renumbered from Article XIII to Article X.[39] Because the Senate
amended some of the House's proposals, it was necessary to send the bill to
conference. Again, there is no record indicating any discussion of the concept.
The amendment was reported to the two legislative bodies unchanged. The
twelve amendments were accepted by the House on September 24 and by the
Senate on September 25, 1789, making it the second and third times that
national legislative bodies had seen fit to guarantee the right.[40] All eleven

states that ratified amendments, ratified the Tenth Amendment. Amendments One and Two were not ratified, and thus, on December 15, 1791 the cruel and unusual punishment clause became the Eighth Amendment and formally part of the law of the land.

Subsequently, other states not yet guaranteeing the right provided for it. In 1818, Connecticut adopted a constitution that stated: "Excessive fines [shall not be] imposed."[41] To this day, however, the constitution, along with that of Vermont, contains no prohibition against cruel and unusual punishment.[42] Rhode Island adopted its prohibition in 1842, New Jersey in 1844, New York in 1846, and Georgia in 1865.

Subsequent to Vermont (1791), thirty-six states have been admitted to the Union. Only two, Louisiana in 1812 and Arkansas in 1836, entered without a prohibition of some kind against cruel and unusual punishment. Each eventually rectified the omission.

2 Judicial Interpretation: An Overview

1789-1910

The first recorded judicial opinion in the United States on cruel and unusual punishment was rendered by the Supreme Court of Errors of Connecticut in 1811. Gibson Smith was convicted on two separate informations of distinct offenses and was sentenced to serve three years imprisonment on each, to run consecutively. He claimed that the "mode of accumulating the terms of imprisonment" was "novel, without precedent, cruel and illegal."[1] The court, however, promptly rejected his contention. Sandwiched between this and the *Weems* decision of 1910 were more than two hundred opinions dealing with the topic, many of which are reviewed in subsequent chapters.[2]

Prior to 1870, only twenty reported opinions dealt with the concept. They were decided, however, in fourteen different jurisdictions, indicating that the prohibition was widely recognized. During the 1870s more courts began dealing with the subject, and by 1910 thirty-eight different states had rendered such opinions. Only in Colorado, Delaware, Florida, Maine, Montana, Nevada, New Hampshire, and Utah were there none. A number of federal courts also rendered relevant opinions. Six courts clearly identified a violation of the prohibition.[3]

During the period there was a great deal of confusion as to which branch of government the inhibition applied. A majority of opinions held that the prohibition was directed to state legislatures and not to the courts. Toward the end of the period certain jurisdictions began holding that the prohibition restricted both the exercise of legislative and judicial power. This difference in viewpoint, however, had little importance with regard to the scope and meaning of the inhibition. In the first place, legislatures were universally perceived as being empowered with a great deal of discretion in the setting of punishments.[4] Statutes would not be held invalid unless the legislature provided a punishment so enormous that there was no doubt but that all discretion had been thrown aside, unless it was in clear and substantial conflict with the fundamental law, or was a punishment that disgraced the civilization of former ages and made one shudder with horror to read of it.[5] Moreover, punishments within statutory limits would not be held cruel and unusual unless the punishment was grossly and inordinately disproportionate to the offense so that the sentence was evidently dictated not by a sense of public duty, but by passion, prejudice, ill-will, or any other unworthy motive.[6] In the second place, trial courts were perceived as "particularly fitted" for the imposition of penalties; consequently, appeals

9

courts were hesitant to interfere with their discretion unless that discretion was "very grossly abused."[7] Sometimes opinions even suggested that the penalty could have, or perhaps should have, been harsher.[8] Finally, most jurisdictions held that severity should not be equated with cruelty.[9] Consequently, a severe punishment was not necessarily an unconstitutional one. Thus, no matter to which branch of government the inhibition was perceived as being directed, the legislature was almost unrestrained in its authority to levy punishments, and trial judges were relatively unhampered in setting sentences, provided they were within statutory limits.

Judicial decision-makers of the period, at all levels of the legal hierarchy, uniformly interpreted the clause as restricting certain modes of punishment. Moreover, there was a high degree of consensus as to which specific modes constituted cruel and unusual punishment. This is readily observed in the dicta of opinions written during the period.[10] Most refer to those of a barbarous or torturous character, unknown at the common law.[11] Others refer to degrading punishments that had become obsolete in every state when its existing constitution was adopted, to punishments that disgraced the civilization of former ages and made one shudder with horror to read of them, to those that shocked the mind of every man possessed of common feeling, and to those that caused a lingering death.[12] Specifically suggested as prohibited were such capital punishments as quartering, disembowelling alive, gibbeting (hanging in chains to starve to death), burning alive, crucifixion, breaking on the wheel, strangling to death, burying alive, boiling alive in water, oil or lead, and blowing from a cannon's mouth.[13] Such mutilations as dismemberment of limbs, ears and nose, slittings, and castration were also thought to be prohibited.[14] It is important to note that no cases involving any of these specific methods of punishment ever came before the courts. Beyond doubt, however, should any of these modes have been inflicted, they would immediately have been declared unconstitutional.

It is equally clear that among early jurists certain modes of punishment were perceived as not being prohibited. No one suggested, for example, that fines or imprisonment per se were cruel and unusual punishments. Indeed, the opposite conclusion was often advanced.[15] The death penalty was not prohibited, nor were various means of inflicting it, such as hanging, shooting, or electrocution. As Chief Justice Fuller stated in the *Kemmler* case, the prohibition clearly implied "something more than the mere extinguishment of life."[16]

1910-74

Since 1910 there have been 1798 opinions containing arguments dealing with cruel and unusual punishment.[17] Of that number, eighty-four, or 4.7 per cent, have held that a statute, punishment, or administrative action violated a cruel and unusual punishment inhibition. The propensity to litigate has increased sharply in recent years (Figure 2-1). This is primarily owing to the abandonment of the "hands-off" doctrine, which had earlier greatly restricted prisoners in contesting their grievances in federal courts.

There is regional variation in the extent to which the inhibition has been litigated. In terms of gross numbers, most litigation has been undertaken in the southeastern part of the country, while the least litigation has been initiated in the Northeast and Great Lakes areas. A disproportionate amount of litigation, in terms of population, has arisen in the Southwest, Plains, and Mountain states.

Most of the modes of punishment utilized at the end of the nineteenth century continued in use into the twentieth. Punishment by fine and imprisonment was constantly upheld as not being cruel and unusual punishment per se.[18] Hanging, shooting, and electrocution were continually upheld. To these methods was added the use of lethal gas. The continuing development of a liberal and humanitarian philosophy in the United States, however, insured that the modes of punishment already perceived as prohibited by the concept would not be reinstated. Indeed, the only new form of punishment approved was sterilization. With the exception of two rulings, this practice has been allowed to stand by making the subtle distinction between punitive and nonpunitive objectives.

Several developments took place during the period. The first was a mounting attack on the death penalty. Time and again the issue was raised, and time and again the courts ruled that it was not unconstitutional. Finally, in 1972 the California Supreme Court, for the first and only time to date, held the death penalty per se to be cruel and unusual punishment.[19] The United States Supreme Court several months later stopped short of this position, but did declare that "as applied" the death penalty was unconstitutional.[20]

The second development was a growing tendency by the courts to restrict various modes of punishment utilized by the *executive* branch of government.[21] Administrators of jails, prison farms, chain gangs, penitentiaries, and various social welfare institutions, such as rehabilitation centers and hospitals, have been prohibited from using certain forms of disciplinary action. Prior to 1910, there was only one instance when an incarcerate was granted relief on the ground that an administrator had inflicted a cruel and unusual punishment.[22] Subsequently, however, at least fifty-five decisions have so held. The modes of punishment held cruel and unusual ranged from certain types of solitary confinement and whippings through chaining a man to the walls, not providing exercise facilities, and denying adequate medical attention, to condemnation of the total environment of chain gangs, jails, and state penal systems.

The third development had to do with status crimes. During the previous period, the appeals court in Washington, D.C. had held invalid a conviction for "being a suspicious person."[23] Although this case was not cited, the United States Supreme Court in *Robinson* v. *California*[24] similarly held that any mode of punishment inflicted on a person because of his status was a cruel and unusual punishment. In this instance the inhibition was applied to the status of being a

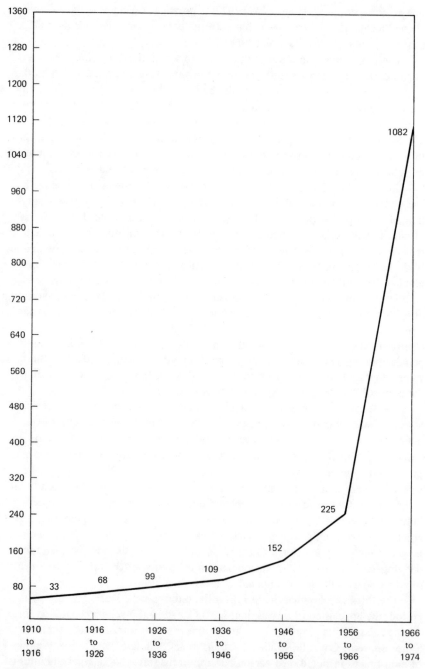

Figure 2-1. Cruel and Unusual Punishment Opinions Rendered: 1910-74

"narcotic addict." Such rationale has been extended to "being a vagrant" and "being an alcoholic." However, subtle distinctions between "status" and "overt acts" have restricted the utility of the doctrine.[25]

The fourth development was the tendency toward the abolition of banishment as a mode of punishment. In some opinions it is not clear whether banishment was considered a cruel and unusual punishment or simply a violation of "public policy."[26] In other cases there is little room for doubt. Some held that such a punishment was constitutional, while others did not. For example, a California court found Dear Wing Jung guilty of false representation in the naturalization proceedings of his wife. He was sentenced to serve six months in the penitentiary, but the imprisonment was to be suspended upon condition that he leave the country. The U.S. Court of Appeals for the Ninth Circuit considered the condition "equivalent to a 'banishment' from this country and from his wife and children, who will presumably remain here." The court continued: "This is either a 'cruel and unusual punishment' or a denial of due process of law. Be it one or the other the condition is unconstitutional."[27]

The fifth development was the limitation placed on the punishment of denationalization. A citizen may have his citizenship voided and declared never to have existed if he obtained it fraudulently. However, one may not be denationalized for desertion from the army, for remaining outside the United States for the purpose of avoiding induction into the military, or for voting in a foreign election.[28]

The sixth development during the period involved excessive degrees of punishment. Prior to 1910, 3.7 per cent of the opinions dealing with the inhibition held a penalty excessive. Subsequently, only twenty-two, or 1.2 per cent, have done so.

The seventh and final development during the period was the trend toward "incorporating" the Eighth Amendment into the due process clause of the Fourteenth Amendment. From the very beginning, the United States Supreme Court held that the Bill of Rights was a restriction on the national government and not on the states.[29] The Court specifically ruled a number of times that the Eighth Amendment did not apply to the states.[30] Federal appeals and district courts followed suit, and time and again held the prohibition applicable only to federal activity.[31] As early as 1824, a state court considered the provision "inapplicable to offenses against a state."[32] Nearly every state supreme court has issued similar rulings.[33] The first United States Supreme Court opinion to consider the relationship between the Eighth and Fourteenth Amendments was *In re Kemmler,* decided in 1890.[34] The primary rationale urged that the privileges and immunities clause protected citizens against the infliction of cruel and unusual punishment. Adhering closely to its previous decisions on the clause,[35] the Court distinguished between rights of state and rights of federal citizenship. The unanimous conclusion was that freedom from cruel and unusual punishment was not a national privilege. The Court stated that the Fourteenth Amendment "was not designed to interfere with the power of the State to protect the lives, liberties and property of citizens, and to promote their health, peace, morals, education and good order."[36] A secondary argument was based on the due process clause, but the Court did not consider it at any great length.

Two years later, the Court divided on the issue. Justice Field, in dissent, argued that the Bill of Rights declared the rights of citizens of the United States, and as such, the states could not abridge them. "If I am right in this view," stated Justice Field, "then every citizen of the United States is protected from punishments which are cruel and unusual."[37] Justices Harlan and Brewer concurred in his view, but the six-man majority disagreed.

Year after year, various courts continued to hold that the Eighth Amendment did not apply to the states. The first major change came in 1947. The argument was now based on a different rationale: reliance was not placed on the privileges and immunities clause but on the due process clause of the Fourteenth Amendment. By this time, much of the Bill of Rights had already been incorporated via the clause. In this instance, William Francis sought to prevent Louisiana from a second attempt at electrocuting him. The first had been unsuccessful due to mechanical failure. Justice Reed, writing for the majority, considered Francis' claim, "under the assumption, but without so deciding," that violation of the Eighth Amendment inhibition "would be violative of the Due Process Clause of the Fourteenth Amendment."[38] Justice Burton, writing in dessent, joined by Justices Douglas, Murphy, and Rutledge, also made it perfectly clear that he believed that the due process clause of the Fourteenth Amendment incorporated the cruel and unusual punishment provision of the Eighth Amendment.

Two years later, the Court of Appeals for the Third Circuit specifically held that the cruel and unusual punishment provision was incorporated into the due process clause. "We are of the opinion," stated the court, "that the right to be free from cruel and unusual punishment at the hands of a State is as 'basic' and 'fundamental' a one as the right of freedom of speech or freedom of religion."[39] That same year the U.S. District Court of New Jersey held that certain state practices, "in their composite," spelled out cruel and punishment in violation of the Fourteenth Amendment of the United States Constitution.[40] In 1950 a district court for the Southern District of California was very specific: "We entertain no doubt that the Fourteenth Amendment prohibits the infliction of cruel and unusual punishment by a state."[41] Two years later, Justice Douglas, in dissent, stated: "The infliction of 'cruel and unusual punishment' against the command of the Eighth Amendment is a violation of the Due Process Clause of the Fourteenth Amendment, whether that Clause be construed as incorporating the entire Bill of Rights or only some of its guarantees."[42] In 1958, Justice Frankfurter, a member of the majority in the *Francis* case, which had assumed, but not decided, that the prohibition was applicable to the states, suggested that "a cruelly disproportionate relation between what the law requires and the sanction for its disobedience may constitute a violation of the Eighth Amendment as a cruel and unusual punishment, *and in respect to the States* even offend the Due Process Clause of the Fourteenth Amendment."[43] This sentiment was concurred in by Justices Harlan and Whittaker.

With such precedent, it came as a shock to no one that in a 1962 decision the Supreme Court finally held that state statutes that inflict cruel and unusual punishments violate both the Eighth and Fourteenth Amendments to the United States Constitution.[44] No longer can state courts constitutionally dismiss excessive punishment allegations by simply asserting that the Eighth Amendment has no application to the state.

By applying the cruel and unusual punishment clause of the Eighth Amendment to the states, the United States Supreme Court imposed minimum standards on the states which the latter must follow. But just what are these standards? The answer is not much clearer today than it has been throughout the history of cruel and unusual punishment.[45] We know that both the federal government and states may not inflict certain modes of punishment, nor may either inflict excessive degrees of punishment. But the real question is: What guidelines does one follow to discover when a statute or punishment is unconstitutional in *kind* or *degree*? The simple answer is that there are few. The Supreme Court has consistently held that the concept of cruel and unusual punishment is constantly changing. For example, in *Weems,* Justice McKenna suggested: "Time works changes, brings into existence new conditions and purposes. Therefore, a principle to be vital must be capable of wider application than the mischief which gave it birth."[46] He further noted that the clause "may acquire meaning as public opinion becomes enlightened by a humane justice."[47] Forty-eight years later, Chief Justice Earl Warren affirmed the notion that the concept is "not precise," that its "scope is not static," and that it "must draw its meaning from evolving standards of decency that mark the progress of a maturing society."[48] The standard thus becomes one of decency versus indecency, very illusive terms to define. Indecency to a Mennonite may be simple fun to a New York stripper. Moreover, what is perceived as indecent to one generation may not be so perceived by the next. Thus, at best, any definition is good for only one period in time. The passing of a year or the substitution of a single Supreme Court justice may readily affect the outcome in any determination of decency.

Several tests have been proposed.[49] Most jurists either simply hold that any punishment is cruel and unusual if it "shock[s] the conscience of reasonable men,"[50] or utilize phrases of like import.[51] The obvious problem is that these tests are very ambiguous in application. By far the most systematic attempt to establish concrete standards by a Supreme Court justice is found in *Furman* v. *Georgia.* [52] Justice Brennan, in his concurring opinion, stated:

If a punishment is unusually severe, if there is a strong probability that
it is inflicted arbitrarily, if it is substantially rejected by contemporary society, and if there is no reason to believe that it serves any
penal purpose more effectively than some less severe punishment,
then the continued infliction of that punishment violates the command of the Clause that the State may not inflict inhuman and
uncivilized punishments upon those convicted of crimes.[53]

The essential underlying tenet of the four principles is that of human dignity.
A punishment simply must not be degrading. A reading of the three cases in
which the Supreme Court has declared a violation of the cruel and unusual
punishment concept, noted Brennan, shows that a punishment has not been
held fatally offensive under a single principle. The test, he observed, "will
ordinarily be a cumulative one."

When applying the above principles to the death penalty, Justice Brennan
suggested a number of specific tests (table 2-1). Assuming that this highly
sophisticated schema were accepted by a majority of the Court, it unfortunately
would not be of much greater help than the simpler ones alluded to earlier. The
justices are certain to disagree on the weight to be attached to each criteria and,
moreover, are sure to disagree about relevant facts upon which their conclusions
are based. How much pain is to be tolerated? How unique must a punishment
be to rule it out? What is the rate and frequency of infliction? And to what
levels must one drop before the infliction becomes unconstitutional? How far
has the historical trend progressed, and exactly what is the state of public thinking on the punishment? Will a lesser penalty serve the same objectives? These
are all questions over which men may legitimately disagree. Under these tests it

Table 2-1
Justice Brennan's Tests for Determining Cruel and Unusual Punishments

1. Degrading to human dignity

    a. pain is a factor (mental and physical)
    b. uniqueness

2. Arbitrary infliction

    a. rate of infliction
    b. frequency of infliction

3. Unacceptable to contemporary standards

    a. historical trends
    b. level of public controversy

4. Excessive in view of the purposes for which it was inflicted

    a. deterrent effect
    b. protection of society
    c. retributive purposes

appears that a number of punishments still utilized today are extremely suspect. Whipping and sterilization are obvious candidates for extinction. Lengthy penalties for "crimes without victims" are not far behind. But will all justices vote to rule out these penalties? Certainly not! For example, Justice Brennan found the death penalty per se cruel and unusual under these tests, while a majority did not.[54]

In conclusion, it is probably impossible to develop precise standards that will allow one to predict clearly when a punishment is cruel and unusual. If such standards were developed, they would probably not be acceptable to all the justices all of the time. Thus, with the appointment of a new justice, the standard might be overturned or substantially altered. Justices will ultimately revert to their own predispositions on which to base their decisions. About the most one can expect are some general guidelines, such as those suggested by Justice Brennan. Ultimately the fate of the clause rests on the multitude of variables that work on the justices, collectively and individually.

Part II: Legislative Action and Judicial Sentencing as Cruel and Unusual Punishment

A. *Corporeal Punishments*

3 Challenging the Various Methods of Inflicting the Death Penalty

As John Laurence has suggested: "A full, annotated bibliography of capital punishment alone would fill a volume."[1] One reason is that the topic has been a subject of controversy for centuries. For example, Dr. Benjamin Rush, a signer of the Declaration of Independence, is usually considered the father of the movement to abolish the penalty in the United States. Some writers have attempted to present objective histories of the penalty,[2] but most have either taken positive[3] or negative[4] stands on its abolition. The positions are based on a wide variety of propositions, ranging from theological, moralistic, and emotional justifications, through pragmatic, sociological, and legalistic ones. On constitutional grounds alone it has been attacked from several directions.[5]

Chronologically there have been three distinctly separate attacks on the death penalty. The first group believed in capital punishment but suggested that certain methods of inflicting it were unconstitutional. The second group objected to imposing the penalty for certain crimes, generally those other than murder. Members of the third and most recent group have challenged the death penalty as being per se unconstitutional. This chapter discusses the first attack, chapter 4 the second, and chapter 5 the last.

Literally dozens of methods of inflicting the death penalty have been invented by man.[6] Most have not been utilized in the United States. Only four methods have been sanctioned either directly or inferentially by the United States Supreme Court: hanging, shooting, electrocution, and gaseous asphyxiation. These same methods have been upheld in several state courts.

Hanging

Hanging is one of the oldest methods of inflicting capital punishment.[7] It is clearly traceable to biblical days. Although the common law prescribed no particular mode of inflicting the penalty, ordinarily it was hanging by the neck until dead. Indeed, it was the most popular mode of inflicting capital punishment in early America.[8] In 1967, Negley K. Teeters estimated that 16,000 persons had been hanged in this country alone.[9] Despite this, the United States Supreme Court has never been called upon directly to decide whether hanging is a cruel and unusual punishment. This is undoubtedly due to the method's long usage and wide acceptance. The Court has intimated time and again, however, that hanging is perfectly constitutional. Literally hundreds of times it has upheld death sentences by inference which were to be executed by means of the gallows.[10]

A number of state courts have ruled directly on the question. The Supreme Court of Maryland came very close to doing so in 1914.[11] Eight years later the Iowa Supreme Court left no room for doubt. "The infliction of the death penalty by hanging," stated the court, "is of ancient origin, and is not a cruel and unusual punishment, within the meaning of the Constitution."[12] This decision was followed shortly by similar holdings in Minnesota and Oregon.[13]

Shooting

The first serious challenge to a method of inflicting the death penalty came from the territory of Utah. Wallace Wilkerson was convicted in federal district court of the willful, malicious, and premeditated murder of William Baxter.[14] On November 28, 1877, he was sentenced to be "publically shot" until dead. He immediately appealed to the Supreme Court, territory of Utah. In 1876 the territorial legislature had revised its criminal code and had eliminated a section that provided that anyone sentenced to die should be "shot, hanged or beheaded, as the court may direct."[15] No similar statute was reenacted. Thus, Wilkerson contended that the court was not empowered with the discretion to select *any* mode of execution. The court, however, took the opposite view, relying heavily on *People* v. *Hartung* where similarly the mode of inflicting the punishment had been omitted from a New York statute.[16] Justice Boreman noted that such discretion was subject to limitation by the Eighth Amendment, but that there was no abuse in the present case. Further, the court implied that shooting as a means of execution was not cruel and unusual, because the army utilized it to enforce discipline and because it was practiced in other civilized nations. Justice Boreman noted that the mode had been used in the territory for a quarter of a century, and often criminals had chosen it over hanging and beheading. Consequently, he suggested, "that manner cannot be cruel which criminals prefer, and that cannot be unusual which is often adopted."[17]

On a writ of error the United States Supreme Court reviewed the decision.[18] No exception was taken to the proceedings in either lower court. The sole alleged error was the sentence of the trial court and affirmation by the appeals court, that Wilkerson be executed. The Court pointed out that Section 10 of the *Revised Penal Code* authorized the trial court "to pass sentence to determine and impose the punishment described," and construed this section as empowering trial courts to select the mode of punishment. Justice Clifford, writing for a unanimous Court, also noted that the Articles of War did not specify the mode of inflicting the death penalty, and that learned and expert writers on the subject agreed that "in the absence of statutory law . . . capital punishment [should] be inflicted by shooting or hanging."[19]

Although Wilkerson and his counsel did not contend that shooting as a mode of punishment was cruel and unusual, the Court as did the territorial court, discussed its constitutionality. In an oft-quoted passage, Justice Clifford noted:

> Difficulty would attend the effort to define with exactness the extent of the constitutional provision which provides that cruel and unusual punishments shall not be inflicted; but it is safe to affirm that punishments of torture . . . and all others in the same line of unnecessary cruelty, are forbidden by that amendment to the Constitution. . . . Concede all that and still it by no means follows that the sentence of the court in this case falls within that category.[20]

Justice Clifford also observed that other modes besides hanging were resorted to at the common law, and that, in fact, the common law did not even require the court to prescribe the mode of execution or fix the time or place for carrying it into effect.[21]

From the above dictum it is clear that the Court was of the opinion that shooting was not cruel and unusual punishment. Later, when Utah became a state, its legislature provided that a prisoner be given a choice between shooting and hanging.[22] This and similar statutes were never declared unconstitutional,[23] and as late as August 1971, the attorney general of the United States assumed this mode to be a proper means of inflicting the death penalty.[24]

Electrocution

In 1886, Governor David B. Hill of New York appointed a commission to seek out the best possible method of inflicting capital punishment.[25] As a result of its findings, the New York legislature enacted a statute that provided that anyone convicted of a capital crime committed after January 1, 1889, would be electrocuted rather than hung.[26] Shortly thereafter the new law faced its first challenge. William Kemmler, a twenty-eight-year-old fruit-peddler and wife-deserter had been living for some time with Matilda ("Tillie") Ziegler, who had similarly left her husband.[27] On Friday morning, March 29, 1889, William and Tillie had a prolonged fight. In a fit of jealous rage he beat her repeatedly with the blunt end of a hatchet.[28] She died the following day, and he was charged with first-degree murder.

The trial started on May 6, and lasted for four days. There was little doubt as to Kemmler's guilt. He confessed in jail, and several witnesses heard him admit that he had committed the crime. His principal defense was "mental irresponsibility," based on the fact that he was an habitual alcoholic. The jury quickly returned a verdict of guilty, and Judge Childs sentenced him, under the new statute, to suffer death by the application of electricity.[29] Charles S. Hatch,

Kemmler's attorney, contended that the sentence violated state and federal inhibitions against the infliction of cruel and unusual punishment. A stay of execution was granted by Charles C. Dwight, a judge of the New York Supreme Court. Hatch argued that he could prove the sentence constituted cruel and unusual punishment. Judge Dwight appointed Tracy C. Becker as referee to take testimony and make a report. At these hearings, Kemmler's lawyers, calling witness after witness, attempted to show that it was impossible to ascertain whether the victim would be killed in every case. Stories were related about the recovery of persons struck by lightning. The state, on the other hand, argued that accidental electrocution and experiments involving the killing of animals proved that the method was quick and painless. The final report contained 1025 pages of disputed testimony.

On October 9, 1889, Judge Day of the Cayuga County Court denied Kemmler's appeal. The judge noted that both sides argued on the grounds of mercy and humanity. He noted that the statute was passed "after much more than ordinary consideration and deliberation."[30] It was true that certain methods of inflicting the death penalty were deemed unconstitutional, but not death itself. Nor was death by gunshot or by hanging. In this instance, the legislature simply changed the method of inflicting it. "And can it be said," queried Judge Day, "that in this case it has been plainly and beyond doubt, established that electricity as a death-dealing agent is likely to prove less quick and sure in operation than the rope? I believe not."[31] Every presumption must be in favor of the statute, suggested Judge Day. Courts do not have the right to hold a statute invalid, he continued, unless its nullity and invalidity are beyond a reasonable doubt.

Kemmler immediately appealed Judge Day's refusal to grant relief to the Supreme Court of New York. Judge Dwight, who had earlier stayed his execution, wrote the decision for a three-man court. He noted that the state constitutional inhibition against cruel and unusual punishment restricted legislative authority, and that courts could and should strike down punishments such as burning at the stake, disembowelling, hanging in chains, and breaking on the wheel, "because they involve torture and lingering death."[32] The question, noted Judge Dwight, was whether the legislature had provided such a mode for taking life. He concluded that it clearly had not. The legislature had attempted to find the most humane method of inflicting death. The "burden of proof" was not successfully borne by Kemmler. In fact, Judge Dwight contended, the evidence suggested the opposite. Experiments on lower animals and accidental contacts by man tended to support the arguments of the state.

Kemmler again appealed. On March 21, 1890, Justice O'Brien of the New York Court of Appeals dashed Kemmler's hopes by affirming, on essentially the same grounds, the order of the lower court.[33] With all avenues of appeal exhausted at the state level, there was but one remaining hope: the United States Supreme Court. An application was made to Justice Blatchford for a writ of error, and he suggested that the full Court hear it. On May 21, 1890, the case was heard. Kemmler's principal contention was that the execution would violate the privileges and immunities clause of the Fourteenth Amendment, and secondarily, it would deny him life without due process of law. On May 23 the Court issued its opinion.[34]

After reviewing the history of the cruel and unusual punishment inhibition, Chief Justice Fuller concluded: "Punishments are cruel when they involve torture or a lingering death; but the punishment of death is not cruel within the meaning of that word as used in the Constitution. It implies there is something more than the mere extinguishment of life."[35] In that particular situation, he noted, the legislative objective was to adopt the most humane method known to modern science, not to inflict torture or a lingering death. Thus, the state had not abridged the privileges or immunities of the petitioner or deprived him of due process of law.[36]

With all avenues of appeal exhausted, the execution was set for Wednesday morning, August 6, 1890.[37] After several technical difficulties were resolved, Kemmler was executed, becoming the first criminal ever to die in the electric chair. The age of legal electrocution had been born.

The reaction to Kemmler's execution was mixed. Newspapers, magazines, and medical, electrical and legal journals published numerous articles on the subject. Several witnesses thought the execution a success.[38] An editorial in the *New York Times* suggested: "It would be absurd to talk of abandoning the law and going back to the barbarism of hanging."[39] Even before the execution, Elbridge Gerry had reviewed the history of hanging and had found numerous instances of broken ropes, decapitation, prolonged physical suffering because of well-developed necks, and even some authentic cases of subsequent resuscitation. His analysis led him to conclude that hanging, "while not unusual, may be, and too often is, cruel. Electricity, on the other hand, while not yet usual, has yet to be proven cruel; and as death whenever produced by it has been instantaneous, it is difficult to see how it can be shown to be cruel."[40]

However, there was much opposition to this new mode of punishment. Dr. E.C. Spitzka, who witnessed the execution and was one of the two doctors who performed the autopsy, is reported to have stated that the performance had satisfied him "that the electrical system of execution can in no way be regarded as a step [forward] in civilization. The guillotine," he continued, "is better than the gallows, the gallows is better than electrical execution."[41] Dr. Shrady, a renowned surgeon and witness, commented: "The death chair will yet be the pulpit from which the doctrine of the abolition of capital punishment will be preached."[42] An editorial in *The World* urged immediate repeal of the new statute. It strongly condemned this method of putting criminals to death as "very cruel and very shocking."[43] A note in the *Harvard Law Review* intimated some displeasure with the new mode of punishment by suggesting that the opinion of the Supreme Court "might well be changed in the light of subsequent experiment."[44] R.S. Morrison, writing in the *Central Law Journal,* also objected to this method.[45]

Despite these and other objections, electrocution became a very popular method of inflicting capital punishment. Ohio adopted it in 1889, Massachusetts in 1898, New Jersey in 1907, Virginia in 1908, North Carolina in 1909, and Kentucky in 1910.[46] Subsequently, over twenty states adopted this form of execution.[47] By 1910 Dr. E.A. Spitzka, a physician, professor, and expert on the brains of eminent men and criminals, was able to arrive at the unqualified conclusion that electrocution was the "most humane, decent and scientific method of inflicting the death penalty ever devised because of its efficiency, quickness and painlessness."[48]

All subsequent challenges to electrocution as a mode of inflicting death have been rejected. Three years after Massachusetts substituted the electric chair for hanging, its new statute was challenged as a violation of the cruel and unusual punishment inhibition found in the Massachusetts Declaration of Rights. The Supreme Judicial Court of Massachusetts, as had the United States Supreme Court, based its rationale mainly on the fact that the "intent" of the statute was to execute as "swiftly and painlessly" as possible. Furthermore, although the use of electricity had been a discovery of recent science and had never been heard of before, Chief Justice Holmes stated: "The word 'unusual' must be construed with the word 'cruel' and . . . [could not] be taken so broadly as to prohibit every humane improvement not previously known in Massachusetts."[49] Similarily, seven years later, the New Jersey Supreme Court held that its new statute represented "an effort by the lawmaking body to mitigate the pain and suffering of the convict" and was thus constitutional.[50] In 1915 the United States Supreme Court again intimated approval of this method of execution.[51] By 1921 the Virginia Supreme Court of Appeals was able to quickly cast aside the question "as well settled" and to conclude that death by electrocution "cannot in itself be regarded as a cruel or unusual punishment."[52] Subsequent challenges were made in Florida, Louisiana, and West Virginia, and all were rejected on similar grounds.[53] Nonetheless, as late as 1951 this mode of inflictting capital punishment was still being challenged as unconstitutional. Typically, however, the contention was rejected.[54]

One of the most unusual cases involving a legal electrocution took place in St. Martinville, Louisiana.[55] Willie Francis, an illiterate seventeen-year-old black convicted of murdering Andrew Thomas, a popular white druggist, was sentenced to be electrocuted. Unlike most states, Louisiana, at the time, did not execute its convicts in the state penitentiary. Instead it sent a portable, hardwood electric chair to the town in which the crime had been committed. Thus, on May 3, 1946, the date set for the execution, the portable chair was readied and Willie was led into the death cell. The switch was thrown, but the effect was delayed.[56] Francis then jumped, although it was apparent to all observers that something was wrong. Obviously in agony, Francis groaned: "Let me breathe." Two minutes after the switch had been turned on, the sheriff ordered the current terminated, and Francis was removed from the chair. He subsequently stated that he was unhurt, but that the electricity had "tickled" him.

The governor was called, and he decided to grant Francis a reprieve from an immediate second attempt. The date was moved to Friday, May 10. In the interim Bertrand de Blanc was obtained to defend Francis. He was initially granted a thirty-day stay of execution from the acting governor and then proceeded to seek a writ of habeas corpus in the court that had convicted Francis. Among other things, de Blanc contended that to put Francis through the agonizing experience again would be cruel and unusual and would therefore violate due process of law.[57] The petition was denied. He then filed four petitions with the Louisiana Supreme Court, all of which were turned down without hearing. The court had concluded that only the governor could grant a pardon or commute a sentence upon recommendation of the board of pardons.

De Blanc then directed his efforts toward the executive branch of government. He requested, and was granted, a special meeting of the board of pardons. On May 31 testimony was taken. The district attorney related a story about the legal and successful second attempt at electrocuting a man in the state of Texas. He further warned that lynching had often taken place in the past when guilty parties were freed. De Blanc argued: "Everything was done to electrocute this boy up to and including the pulling of the switch and the passing of electricity into his body."[58] He continually emphasized the mental and physical torture that Francis had been through. He also pointed to a number of instances when commutation had been granted after an attempt to execute had failed. Nonetheless, the board turned down his plea.

In the meantime, de Blanc had been working with J. Skelly Wright, later a federal appeals judge, in order to petition the United States Supreme Court. Upon application, the Court immediately issued a stay of execution. Because the term of Court was close to an end, oral argument was set for the following fall. The opinion was rendered on January 13, 1947.[59] By a five-to-four vote, the Court concluded that nothing that had taken place amounted to cruel and unusual punishment in a constitutional sense. To the suggestion that Francis should not be made to undergo the psychological strain of preparing for death a second time, Justice Reed reasoned: "Even the fact that the petitioner had already been subjected to a current of electricity . . . [does] not make his subsequent execution any more cruel in the constitutional sense than any other execution." He continued:

> The cruelty against which the Constitution protects a convicted man
> is cruelty inherent in the method of punishment, not the necessary
> suffering involved in any method employed to extinguish life
> humanely. The fact that an unforeseeable accident prevented the
> prompt consummation of the sentence cannot, it seems to us, add

an element of cruelty, to a subsequent execution. There is no purpose to inflict unnecessary pain nor any unnecessary pain involved in the proposed execution. The situation of the unfortunate victim of this accident is just as though he had suffered the identical amount of mental anguish and physical pain in any other occurrence, such as, for example, a fire in the cell block.[60]

Justice Frankfurter wrote a concurring opinion. He argued: "The Fourteenth Amendment did not withdraw the freedom of the State to enforce its own notions of fairness in the administration of criminal justice unless . . . 'in doing so it offend[ed] some principle of justice so routed in the traditions and conscience of our people as to be ranked as fundamental.' "[61] Without such a principle, he concluded, the "Court must abstain from interference with State action no matter how strong one's personal feelings of revulsion against a State's insistence on its pound of flesh."[62]

Justice Burton, joined by Justices Douglas, Murphy, and Rutledge, unequivocally dissented. "The capital case before us," he wrote, "presents an instance of the violation of constitutional due process that is more clear than would be presented by many lesser punishments prohibited by the Eighth Amendment or its state counterparts. Taking human life by unnecessarily cruel means shocks the most fundamental instincts of civilized man."[63] To illustrate that the proposed procedure was unconstitutional, Justice Burton juxtaposed it against a lawful electrocution. He noted that electrocution had been approved "only in a form that eliminates suffering."[64] In the present case, Francis may have actually received an electric shock, and thus a subsequent attempt at execution amounted to "death by installments." That the failure was unintentional did not impress Justice Burton. "The intent of the electrocutioner," he claimed, "cannot lessen the torture or excuse the result."[65] The Louisiana statute approved only "one continuous application of a lethal current," and the petition to the Supreme Court of Louisiana expressly stated that a current of electricity was caused to pass through Francis.

Having been denied relief by the United States Supreme Court, Francis' attorneys attempted several other legal manuevers to prevent the impending execution. None was successful, however, and ultimately Francis asked his attorneys to stop delaying the inevitable. On May 7, 1947, one year and six days after the first attempt, William Francis was sent to his death.

The Supreme Court decision received unprecedented coverage in the law journals. Some reviewers took no position on the legal questions involved and simply reported the decision.[66] At least one, however, strongly opposed the decision.[67] An article in the *Virginia Law Review* noted that "mental anxiety" is recognized as a part of punishment. Thus, a second attempt "would be cruel because the petitioner's mental anxiety would be doubled, and unusual because

in excess of punishment administered others similarly situated."[68]   Furthermore,
the article continued, Francis was "entitled to have the precise punishment meted
out to him which the law provides," and as the Louisiana statute called for one
application of electricity only, he had been entitled to relief.

On the whole, however, the legal community received the decision very favorably. Norman Schatz, taking a cue from Frankfurter's concurring opinion, suggested that the dissenters' opinion was "little more than an application of mere
personal standards."[69] Jacob Balick noted that the Court "was well within the
extensive limits set by previous opinions concerning 'due process.' "[70] Several
other scholars hinted that they favored the decision, but were not as explicit in
stating their rationale.[71]

Gaseous Asphyxiation

On March 28, 1931, Nevada became the first state in the Union to adopt
lethal gas as a mode of inflicting the death penalty.[72] As originally intended,
the condemned person was to be placed in a special cell within the limits of the
state prison, and sometime during a one-week period, when asleep, the air valves
were to be closed and others, admitting lethal gas, were to be opened. Thus, the
prisoner's life was to be taken without awakening him.[73] Referred to as the
"Humane Death Bill," it was not long before the statute was challenged as
inflicting cruel and unusual punishment. Gee Jon and Hughie Sing were convicted of the tong murder of Tom Quong Kee and sentenced to death under
the new statute. On appeal to the state supreme court they contended, among
other things, that use of gas was cruel and unusual primarily because the manner in which it was to be administered was indefinite and the formula to be
employed was uncertain. Using very familiar rationale, Justice Coleman, writing
the opinion of the court, rejected these contentions. He first noted that death
had always been the punishment for murder and that it had historically been
inflicted in many different ways. Utilizing the definition of cruel and unusual
punishment set forth in the *Kemmler* case,[74] Justice Coleman declared that the
court was "not prepared to say that the infliction of the death penalty by the
administration of lethal gas would of itself subject the victim to either pain or
torture."[75] He also took note of, but rejected, Jon's contention that scientific
knowledge of the subject established that the mode was cruel and unusual. He
pointed out that animals had been painlessly put to death by this method for
years. It was used by dental surgeons for extracting teeth painlessly. Justice
Coleman acknowledged the fact that gas might be administered so as to produce
suffering, but noted that hanging, shooting, and electrocution might be also.
Furthermore, he argued: "We must presume that the officials entrusted with
the infliction of the death penalty by use of gas will produce no such result."[76]

As in the past when new modes of inflicting the death penalty had been adopted, deference was paid to legislative judgment. It would be presumptuous and exceedingly bold on the part of the court, noted Justice Coleman, to substitute its judgment for that of the legislature. Consequently, the appeal was denied.

The state at this point had yet to develop plans for building a gas chamber.[77] Hurridly constructed, the cell was located in a separate building and lacked the rudimentary comforts found in most regular cells.[78] Instead, it contained a chair and a two-gallon jar filled with one quart of sulphuric acid and two parts water. Above the jar were tablets of cyanide of potassium suspended by a string extending into the next room. Gee Jon was led to the death cell, strapped into the chair, and the string was cut. Such an execution was a far cry from what some had envisioned. The Philadelphia *Record* called it "a piece of official barbarity."[79] Another Philadelphia paper, the *Public Ledger,* declared: "There is a terror in this thing that even Edgar Allan Poe could not equal." On the other hand, the Pittsburgh *Chronicle-Telegraph* withheld judgment primarily because at first execution by electricity had been challenged as not being a humanitarian advance, but later it had become "recognized as more merciful than hanging."

Reaction by the legal community was positive. Immediately after the Nevada Supreme Court handed down its decision, Robert Hartmann suggested that the opinion was a "very able exposition."[80] Apparently the only hesitation he had in giving unqualified support to the decision was that the statute did not provide for the type of gas to be used and therefore administrative officials might inadvertently use one that would inflict pain and suffering. He concluded, however, that if the statute was "modern and scientific" then "it should stand as a leader for future legislation of other States."[81]

With Nevada leading the way, several states followed suit.[82] Arizona substituted lethal gas for hanging in 1933 and was immediately followed by Colorado. In 1935, Wyoming adopted the method. That same year North Carolina became the first state east of the Mississippi to adopt it. Two years later California did so. With the passage of each new statute, controversy arose as to whether use of the new mode was morally and/or legally permissible. For example, Manuel Hernandez, a convicted murderer, argued, as had Gee Jon, that the new method adopted by Arizona inflicted cruel and unusual punishment. Justice McAlister, in refuting the assertion, relied heavily on the Nevada decision. "The fact that it [gaseous asphyxiation] is less painful and more humane than hanging" he asserted, " is all that is required to refute completely the charge that it constitutes cruel and unusual punishment."[83]

Adoption by North Carolina of the new method stirred considerable controversy. H.H. Honeycutt, warden of Central Prison and witness to over 160 executions by electricity, became an outspoken opponent of the method after observing a demonstration in which dogs were asphyxiated. He claimed to have heard them howl "piteously."[84] His arguments took on credibility when the first asphyxiation was botched miserably. Witnesses were appalled when the new gas chamber failed to function properly and Allen Foster remained conscious for at least three minutes. He did not finally expire for another seven.[85] Some observers suggested that the new method would be repealed by the next legislature. However,[86] the second asphyxiation was conducted very smoothly. Ed Jenkins, a convicted murderer, died within seven and one half minutes, and witnesses received the impression that he did not suffer.[87] In 1938, the North Carolina Supreme Court implied that death by asphyxiation was constitutionally permissible.[88]

Despite the well-established precedent, as late as 1953, Joseph A. Daugherty, convicted of the brutal murder of his wife, argued that a similar California statute inflicted cruel and unusual punishment because administrators "could use a lethal gas which would cause long and cruel suffering."[89] Justice Carter, relying on *State* v. *Gee Jon*,[90] suggested that it was doubtful the issue could be raised in the absence of a showing that such a gas had been used in the past or would be used in the future.

By 1970 ten states had adopted the use of lethal gas.[91] Although the United States Supreme Court has never ruled directly on the mode, it is obvious that it has passively accepted it. Perhaps otherwise it would not have denied certiorari in the *Daugherty* case.

4 Challenging the Death Penalty as Excessive

Historically, most jurisdictions in the United States have inflicted the death penalty for offenses other than murder. For example, in 1785, Massachusetts had nine separate capital crimes, and in 1837, North Carolina, about twenty-one.[1] In 1952, James A. McCafferty compiled a list of death penalty statutes found in every state, the federal government, and the District of Columbia. The list included murder, kidnapping, lynching, perjury in a capital case, dynamiting, armed robbery, arson, train robbery, burglary, killing a woman by abortion, and aggravated assault by a life prisoner. He also utilized a residual category, which included sixteen "other offenses."[2] In 1967, Hugo Adam Bedau compiled a similar list and enumerated these "other" offenses. They included insurrection, forcing a woman to marry, second conviction for selling narcotics to a minor, intentionally interfering with the war effort, committing any felony on a train after boarding with such intent, desecration of a grave, castration, attempting to kill the president or a foreign ambassador, instigation of a minor (by a relative or spouse) to commit a capital crime, destruction of vital property by a group during wartime, abducting anyone during a bank robbery, third conviction of any offense optionally punishable by death, piracy of interstate or foreign commercial aircraft, supplying heroin to a minor, and certain espionage violations of the Atomic Energy Act.[3] Despite the large number of possibilities, the death penalty has not been inflicted in recent times for most crimes on the list. For example, since 1930 capital punishment has been inflicted for only seven offenses: murder, rape, armed robbery, kidnapping, espionage, burglary, and assault by a life-term prisoner.[4]

Offenses for which the death penalty has been upheld other than murder include robbery, arson, kidnapping, espionage, assault, rape, and attempted rape.

Robbery

The first serious objection to the death penalty on the ground that it was excessive arose in the Territorial Court of New Mexico.[5] Thomas Ketchum was convicted of train robbery and sentenced to death by hanging. Although the challenge was made nine years before the *Weems* decision,[6] the court agreed to *assume* that courts could review the severity of punishment in extreme cases.[7] After noting the constitutionality of the death penalty and assessing its power to review legislative discretion, the court concluded that the penalty was not excessive. The statute providing the penalty had passed "unchallenged by the people of the territory" and had "evidently met with approval of the people."[8]   The court further noted that the robber shot a mail clerk through the face and a conductor through the arm. "Taking into consideration all the circumstances usually attending a train robbery," concluded the court, "we cannot say that we deem the death penalty in any degree excessive as compared with the gravity of the offense."[9]

Subsequent decisions were nearly all predicated on the rationale found in *Ketchum.* Courts usually noted that the death penalty itself was constitutional, that deference should be paid to legislative judgment in setting penalties, that the circumstances that might surround the commission of a robbery and the actual circumstances of the robbery should be considered, and finally, that the inherent nature of the offense was dastardly.[10]   In all but one instance, after these factors were considered, reviewing courts concluded that the death penalty for armed robbery was not cruel and unusual punishment.[11]   A case in Oklahoma provides the single possible exception. In *Brown* v. *State,*[12] the defendant was convicted of robbery with firearms and sentenced to death. The attorneys for the defendant, as well as the county prosecutor, recommended modification of the sentence. The criminal court of appeals, having been statutorily granted such power, modified the sentence to fifteen years imprisonment.

In several instances, challenges were made to the statutes themselves which allowed imposition of the death penalty for robbery. Universally such contentions were denied.[13]   Additionally, that the fruits of the crime were very small made little difference to the courts. For example, James Thompson was convicted of the robbery, with the use of a deadly weapon (an ax), of two dollars and some keys. "The amount of the property secured," reasoned the court, "is insignificant." The "motive which prompted the crime was evidently the hope of securing property of greater value."[14]

By 1948, the courts had so thoroughly accepted the constitutionality of the death penalty for armed robbery that the Kentucky Supreme Court, in rejecting an allegation of cruel and unusual punishment, simply stated that the argument was "so completely unfounded as to require no consideration, much less discussion."[15]   In 1964, James Cobert was executed for stealing a car.[16] In 1967 the Texas Court of Criminal Appeals refused to set aside a death sentence imposed on one Jesse Ellison. He had been convicted of robbing a liquor store with a deadly weapon (a knife).[17]   The following year the Supreme Court of Alabama similarly held that the death penalty imposed for five counts of armed robbery was not excessive, even though no one was killed.[18]   The court reasoned that robbery was one of the gravest crimes, and that the sentence was imposed at the common law. On appeal the United States Supreme Court avoided the Eighth Amendment issue and reversed on other grounds.[19]   As late as January 7, 1971, the Supreme Court of Georgia upheld the death sentence imposed on Robert Hart for armed robbery.[20]

Arson, Kidnapping, and Espionage

Georgia, North Carolina, Virginia, Alabama, and Arkansas have adopted various statutes inflicting the death penalty on arsonists. The Alabama statute imposed the supreme penalty only when maiming or death accompanied the arson. Twice in 1935 the statute was challenged as inflicting cruel and unusual punishment. The rationale utilized in upholding the death sentences in each is remarkably similar to that justifying the death penalty for armed robbery. In the first, *Ayers* v. *State,* the Alabama court noted: "The crime of arson is one of the most heinous in all the catalogue, and the statute, if anything, is too lenient."[21] In the other case, specific questions were certified to the Supreme Court of Alabama. James J. Lee had been convicted of arson in the first degree and thus was liable to the sentence of death. His objection was that the infliction of death "on one merely committing the offense of arson, with no *intention* to maim or kill," was cruel and unusual punishment. The court retorted, however, that the death penalty was "neither unusual or cruel, within the meaning of the Constitution, where the crime for which punishment imposed is manevolent and proximately causes the death of a human being, so long as the death inflicted is speedy, and without undue pain or torture."[22]

Kidnapping has been punishable by death in no less than thirty-three separate jurisdictions. Inflicting capital punishment on kidnappers has several times been challenged as constituting cruel and unusual punishment. As early as 1935, William E. Tanner, a convicted kidnapper upon whom the death penalty had been imposed, challenged the California statute. In typical fashion the court paid deference to the legislative power to set punishments, noting that it could not interfere unless the punishment "was clearly and manifestly cruel and unusual."[23] The court noted that kidnapping was a "heinous offense," and that train wrecking, treason, and assaults by life prisoners were also punishable by death. The validity of the statute, suggested the court, "appears to be unimpeachable."

In 1950, David Knowles, coconspirator with Caryl Chessman, again attacked the statute, and again the California court refused to set the penalty aside.[24] Eight years later the court similarly refused to set aside the death sentence imposed on Edward Wein. This time, however, the decision was accompanied by a long and eloquently reasoned dissent. Wein had actually been convicted of moving five persons from between four to seventy-five feet. Justice Carter, outraged that the death penalty had been imposed in such a case, asserted that "moving a person four feet does not justify taking life no matter what words describe the act."[25] He concluded that such a sentence could not "stand in the face of the constitutional mandate that cruel or unusual punishments may not be inflicted," because it was far too excessive.[26]

The United States Supreme Court has never directly ruled on the question of whether the death penalty imposed for kidnapping is cruel and unusual punishment. It has often denied certiorari, as in the *Knowles* case, and has thereby avoided direct confrontation with the issue.[27] The Court has also recently avoided the issue, after accepting certain cases, by reversing lower-court decisions on grounds other than cruel and unusual punishment.[28] It is clear, however, that the Court has in the past viewed the death penalty for kidnapping as constitutional. For example, in *Smith* v. *United States,* the Court, while in the process of upholding the federal Kidnapping Act, stated: "When an accused is charged . . . with transporting a kidnapping victim across state lines, he . . . *may* be punished by death."[29]

Inflicting the death penalty on traitors is a well-established practice. Perhaps the most famous case in recent American history came to national attention in the early 1950s. Julius and Ethel Rosenberg were convicted of selling secret information, relevant to both the Los Alamos Project and the atomic bomb, to Russia during World War II. Judge Irving Kaufman sentenced them to death, thus making the Rosenbergs the first peacetime victims of the death penalty for violation of the Espionage Act.[30] In 1952, the Court of Appeals for the Second Circuit was called upon to set aside the sentences.[31] Literally dozens of constitutional allegations were made, one of which was that the sentences imposed violated the Eighth Amendment. Essentialiy the Rosenbergs contended that their sentences were *cruel* because their acts were not those of traitors, but of foolish idealists who had sought to aid an ally, and that the sentences were *unusual* because others as guilty as they had received far lighter sentences.[32]

As the outset, Judge Frank noted that unless the court was "to overrule sixty years of undeviating federal precedents," it had no power to modify a sentence. He noted that most, if not all, courts had ruled that a sentence within the limits of a valid statute cannot amount to cruel and unusual punishment. Furthermore, he continued, even if the court assumed that it could issue such a ruling, given certain mitigating circumstances, it could not do so in this case, for no such circumstances existed. "The test of a 'cruel and unusual punishment' urged by the defendants—i.e., that 'it shocks the conscience and sense of justice of the people of the United States,' " he concluded, "is not met here."[33]

Another argument raised by the Rosenbergs was that although traditionally in this country courts have been authorized to impose the death penalty for *treason,* "to authorize such a sentence for a similar but less grave offense [espionage], in the trial of which there are omitted the guaranteed safeguards of a treason trial, is to permit 'cruel and unusual punishment' in violation of the Constitution."[34] Judge Frank rejected this contention, noting that it was based on the assumption that Congress would always authorize the death penalty for treason. Thus, if Congress set a maximum of twenty years for treason, under the preceding rationale, no greater penalty could be set for espionage, sedition or similar crimes, without constituting cruel and unusual punishment. Furthermore, he noted, in the case of *Ex parte Quirin,*[35] where citizen-saboteurs were sentenced to death for crimes other than treason, the United States Supreme Court "implicitly" rejected the cruel and unusual punishment argument when it allowed the decision to stand.[36] Judge Frank did note, however, that because the Supreme Court had not specifically discussed the cruel and unusual punishment inhibition in *Quirin,* that it might be desirable for the Supreme Court to review this part of the decision. It did not do so, however, and denied certiorari, although Justice Black dissented.[37] After several other unsuccessful appeals, the Rosenbergs were executed on June 19, 1953.

Assault

Various types of assault have been deemed punishable by death in certain states. Among these are assault with intent to rob, assault with intent to kill by a life-term prisoner, assault with a deadly weapon, and assault with intent to rape. Each has been challenged as excessive, thereby constituting cruel and unusual punishment. In every case, however, the statute has been upheld as constitutional.

Kentucky amended its criminal statutes in 1934 to make it the only state in the Union to provide the death penalty for assault with intent to rob.[38] The new statute was challenged in 1935.[39] John Tomlinson had been convicted of the offense, and although the death penalty had not been imposed, most likely because he was only sixteen at the time and had stolen only three dollars, he appealed, claiming that it was excessive. Chief Justice Clay, in a dictum, announced that the statute did not inflict cruel punishment.[40]

Statutes providing the death penalty for assault by a prisoner serving a life sentence have existed in Alabama, Arizona, California, Colorado, Pennsylvania and Utah. California courts have on several occasions upheld that state's statute, which provides:

> Every person undergoing a *life sentence* in a state prison of this state, who, *with malice aforethought,* commits an assault upon the person of another with a deadly weapon or instrument or by any means of force likely to produce great bodily injury, is *punishable with death.*[41]

The statute was first challenged by J.W. Finley, a life prisoner at Folsom Prison, who had been convicted of assault with a deadly weapon. Upon receiving the mandatory sentence, he appealed, alleging that the statute provided excessive punishment. Employing contemporary legal rationale (1905), the court noted that the determination of punishment was a matter of "legislative discretion," and that for the judicial department to interfere would be "an act of usurpation."[42] Only when the punishment was out of "all proportion" to the offense

might the courts interfere.[43]   The court noted that there was no other punishment for a prisoner serving a life sentence except the forfeit of his "physical
life." He was perceived as immune from any other human retribution, and
"under such circumstances he will be careless of other lives and all conse-
quences." Hence, those close to him must be protected.

Such rationale set the stage for future challenges. Only four years later,
the Supreme Court of California had occasion to hear a similar case. Jacob
Oppenheimer, a life prisoner at San Quentin, escaped from a cell in which he had
been incarcerated in solitary confinement for over eight years. Armed with a
portion of an iron window weight, he made his way to the dining room and
attacked a fellow inmate. In the ensuing fight he picked up a knife and stabbed
the inmate several times. Oppenheimer, however, was finally subdued. He was
found guilty of assault and was sentenced to death as required by law. The
court, relying heavily on its earlier decision in *People* v. *Finley*,[44] upheld the
sentence.[45]

In 1950, an even more remarkable case came before the California court.[46]
Wesley Wells, serving an indeterminate sentence of five years to life, had attacked
a prison guard. He was convicted and sentenced to death and on appeal contended that the imposition of the death penalty in such a case constituted cruel
and unusual punishment. The court ruled that an indeterminate sentence of
up to life was a life sentence within the meaning of the statute and, on the
basis of *People* v. *Oppenheimer*,[47] held that imposition of the death penalty
on a prisoner serving a life term for assault was not curel and unusual punishment. The statute was subsequently upheld by implication in 1960 and again
in 1969.[48]

The death penalty for assault with intent to commit rape has been variously
provided for in Maryland, Nevada, and Virginia. All challenges to these statutes
have been rejected. The first case arose in Maryland. James Dutton was convicted of the crime and was sentenced to be hung. The Court of Appeals of
Maryland, *without* considering, or even having knowledge of the facts of the
case, upheld the statute. The court's main rationale was that "under some circumstances the outrage upon the particular woman and upon society can scarcely
be said to be less because the defendant did not succeed in accomplishing his purpose than if he had."[49]   Thirty-two years later, the Maryland court reaffirmed
its position, even given a highly unusual situation.[50] The defendant was a "feeble-
minded illiterate" and medical experts uniformly urged leniency. The court, however, upheld the death penalty, citing *Dutton.*

The Virginia Supreme Court has similarly upheld its "assault with intent to
rape" statute. In *Hart* v. *Commonwealth*,[51] for example, a seventeen-year-old
black had assaulted young Virginia Garber, a white. Despite the fact that Hart
inflicted absolutely no bodily harm on her, the court held the penalty to be
constitutional. Again, traditional deference was paid to the legislative discretion and heinousness of the crime.

Rape

Rape has been punishable by death in at least eighteen different jurisdictions. It has long been recognized as one of the most heinous crimes, and time and again the courts have held that subjecting its perpetrator to the death penalty does not inflict cruel and unusual punishment. During the 1960s, however, a tremendous effort was made to encourage courts to declare that imposition of the penalty for rape was excessive, primarily for two reasons. First, unlike the other capital crimes previously mentioned, the death penalty for rape was actually levied on substantial numbers of defendants. Second, the punishment was inflicted disproportionately on one race of people.[52]

In 1963, the United States Supreme Court had occasion to review two rape cases involving the death penalty. Justice Goldberg, joined by Justices Douglas and Brennan, dissented from a refusal to grant certiorari.[53] In essence, he argued that the Court should hear the cases to determine whether the Eighth and Fourteenth Amendments permit the infliction of the death penalty on a convicted rapist when he has "neither taken nor endangered human life." Justice Goldberg set forth three questions he felt should be considered: first, does the penalty violate "evolving standards of decency"?; second, is the penalty excessive and disproportionate to the offenses charged?; and finally, can permissible aims of punishment be achieved by punishing rape less severely than by death?[54]

Because the three justices were in a minority, the death penalty continued to be imposed on rapists, whether or not life was taken or endangered. Reaction to the *Rudolph* dissent was threefold. Several lower-court opinions openly rejected it.[55] Others took cognizance of it but distinguished their cases on the ground that life was endangered.[56] For example, Judge Harry A. Blackmun, later appointed a justice of the United States Supreme Court, twice made this point.[57] In both instances, young illiterate blacks had raped white women, and in the process, physical harm had accompanied the attack. A third set of opinions pointed out that since the Supreme Court had denied certiorari in *Rudolph*, evidently it did not believe that the death penalty was unconstitutionally excessive for rape.[58]

During the decade of the 1960s alone, no less than thirteen jurisdictions upheld the death penalty for rape.[59] The rationale in each was quite traditional. The court usually paid deference to the legislature, noted the heinousness of the crime, and often pointed to the brutal circumstances surrounding the actual rape. The one major exception came in 1970. William Ralph, almost ten years before, had been convicted of rape and sentenced to death.[60] His conviction was affirmed by the Maryland Court of Appeals, and the United States Supreme Court denied certiorari.[61] He thereupon unsuccessfully filed five separate habeas corpus petitions for relief.[62] Taking a cue from the *Rudolph* dissent, he asserted that imposition of the death penalty for rape when life is neither taken nor endangered constituted cruel and unusual punishment. On appeal from his fifth denial, the Fourth Circuit Court of Appeals rendered its historic opinion. The court first took cognizance of relevant facts by noting that the victim was not of a tender age, and that the attending physician found "no outward evidence of injury or violence," or any unusual psychological trauma.[63] Judge Butzner, writing the opinion, quickly rejected the argument that abolishing the death penalty was solely a legislative function by asserting that the Eighth Amendment is a limitation on both the legislative and judicial branches of government. The court did note that there was no precedent for such a decision, and further, that the Supreme Court had by implication approved the death penalty several times, and that dicta in a few cases had suggested that capital punishment was constitutionally permissible. One case was cited, however, as suggesting that a state court had held the death penalty for rape, given the circumstances, so excessive as to violate the state inhibition against cruel and unusual punishment.[64]

In arriving at its decision the court relied on two principles. The first was drawn from *Weems* v. *United States*.[65] In that case, the United States Supreme Court maintained the Eighth Amendment required that punishment for crime be proportionate to the offense. The second was taken from another Supreme Court decision, *Trop* v. *Dulles*. There the Court emphasized that cruel and unusual punishment was partly defined in terms of "evolving standards of decency that mark the progress of a maturing society."[66] To determine whether these precepts had been violated, the court noted the legislative trend toward abolishing capital punishment for rape. It noted that Congress had recently abolished the penalty in the District of Columbia. Further, there had been only one year in the past forty when the federal government had executed anyone for rape. The National Commission on Reform of Federal Criminal Laws had recommended against it, as had the Model Penal Code. Furthermore, there was a worldwide trend away from the penalty for this crime, and the United States was one of only four nations retaining it. In this country thirty-four states allowed a maximum of life imprisonment, and none of the remaining sixteen made the death penalty mandatory in rape cases.[67] Furthermore, where the penalty did exist, it was infrequently applied. The disuse of the penalty, reasoned the court, is more important in ascertaining the evolving standards of decency than retention by the legislatures, for there is little public pressure to change a law that is seldom used. Thus, the court concluded: "When the victim's life is neither taken nor endangered the death penalty for rape violates the Eighth Amendment."[68] However, the court explicitly stopped short of declaring the death penalty unconstitutional for all rapes. Nor did the court conclude that infrequent impositions of the death penalty suggest that it was arbitrarily imposed because of race.

Outraged at the decision, the state reacted by petitioning for rehearing *en banc,* but was turned down. The state was again unsuccessful when the United States Supreme Court refused to grant certiorari.[69] Among the legal journals the reaction was mixed. Some simply reported the decision.[70] Others definitely opposed it.[71] One strongly questioned the selection of rationale.[72] Still others reacted very favorably.[73] Almost all raised questions about the decision. Objections appear to be twofold. First is the problem of how to determine when a life has been endangered. In many instances this may be almost impossible. Second is the danger of permitting the current trends to determine what punishment is cruel and unusual, for it is almost impossible to determine public opinion, and moreover, such a standard allows potential abuse by the majority over the minority.

It was hoped by some optimists that the decision would be expanded by other courts. They hoped to have the ruling extended to invalidate capital punishment for all rapes in which the victim was not killed. Some suggested that it might be extended to cover other capital crimes, such as robbery and assault. Still others suggested that the decision should be instrumental in eroding use of the death penalty altogether. Lower courts and other circuit courts of appeal, however, took no such position. Each time a statute inflicting death for rape was challenged as imposing cruel and unusual punishment, courts rejected the contention. Some simply ignored *Ralph*.[74] Those that did not rejected the contention primarily on two grounds. The first was that the *Ralph* decision, even though it was "entitled to respect," was not binding on the court reviewing the case.[75] The second was that the case under consideration was clearly distinguishable. For example, in *Bartholomey* v. *State,* the Maryland court reasoned that "the *Ralph* case applied only to rape which did not take or endanger the life of the victim, *and not to all rapes.*"[76]

Seemingly the strongest case to be presented after *Ralph* was that by A.J. Myers. Five young black men had raped a white girl. Myers was deemed guilty of a single rape, while some of the other assailants hit the girl, raped her several times, and forced her to commit unnatural sex acts. Their trials were severed; the four others pled guilty before a judge and were sentenced to life imprisonment. Myers was found guilty by a trial jury and was sentenced to death. On appeal he urged, among other things, that where the "victim had not been put in fear of life nor sustained serious bodily or psychological injury," the imposition of capital punishment constituted cruel and unusual punishment.[77] Although he cited *Ralph,* the Louisiana court rejected his argument simply because it had "consistently rejected contentions that the death penalty for aggravated rape constitutes cruel and unusual punishment where the victim's life was neither taken nor endangered."[78]

In conclusion, while the reaction among legal scholars to *Ralph* was mixed, its immediate impact on other courts was negligible. No lower court or other circuit court cited it approvingly. The challenge was finally presented to the United States Supreme Court in *Furman* v. *Georgia.*[79] The Court, however, did not come to grips with these issues and reversed the convictions on other grounds.[80]

Murder

Imposing the death penalty for murder has been challenged as excessive. In nearly every instance, however, the punishment itself has been attacked as well. For this reason, discussion of the topic is deferred until the next chapter.

5

Challenging the Death Penalty as Unconstitution Per Se

Just when and where the death penalty was first challenged as unconstitutional per se is unclear. During the present century the issue has been raised time and again. The 1960s brought an unprecedented flurry of activity, but did not result in a declaration that the death penalty is unconstitutional per se. Despite this, advocates of abolition were encouraged by a number of decisions that, by circuitous means, prevented the death penalty from being imposed.[1] In *Witherspoon* v. *Illinois*,[2] the Supreme Court held that individuals with conscientious scruples against capital punishment could not be automatically excluded from jury duty, as had earlier been the case.[3] In *United States* v. *Jackson*,[4] the Supreme Court held invalid the death penalty provision of the federal Kidnapping Act. In essence the act allowed the imposition of the death penalty if the defendant chose to be tried before a jury, but allowed a maximum of only life imprisonment if he waived the jury trial.[5] That same year the Supreme Court, relying on the *Jackson* decision, held the death provisions of the federal Bank Robbery Act unconstitutional.[6] Perhaps most encouraging to the abolitionists was the *Ralph* decision, discussed in the previous chapter.[7]

On the other hand, antiabolitionists could assert with equal confidence several reasons why the Supreme Court would and/or could never declare the death penalty unconstitutional per se. In the first place, the Court had, time and again, upheld various methods of inflicting the punishment. Each time it has implied that the penalty was constitutional. Moreover, between 1967 and 1972, no fewer than twenty-six state courts had held the death penalty constitutional when attacked as inflicting cruel and unusual punishment.[8] Furthermore, no federal court had ever held the death penalty unconstitutional per se.

Secondly, in the *Witherspoon, Jackson* and *Pope* decisions, the Court scrupulously avoided declaring the death penalty unconstitutional. Antiabolitionists could also point to the dictum of Chief Justice Warren in *Trop* v. *Dulles:*

> Whatever the arguments may be against capital punishment, both on moral grounds and in terms of accomplishing the purposes of punishment—and they are forceful—the death penalty has been employed throughout our history, and, in a day when it is still widely accepted, it cannot be said to violate the constitutional concept of cruelty.[9]

Advocates of this persuasion could also point to *McGautha* v. *California.*[10] In that case the practice of allowing a jury absolute discretion to impose or not to impose the death penalty was challenged as unconstitutional. In a five-to-four decision the Supreme Court upheld the practice.

People v. Anderson

After years of perseverance the abolitionists finally triumphed in the state of California. Robert Page Anderson was found guilty of first-degree murder and sentenced to death.[11] On appeal, the California Supreme Court affirmed his conviction.[12] In 1968, while in prison, he filed for a writ of habeas corpus, alleging among other things that the death penalty was per se unconstitutional.[13] In rejecting his claim, the court noted that numerous decisions had approved the assertion that the fixing of penalties was a legislative function, that the penalty had been used throughout history, and that it was still widely accepted. The court also rejected the contention that the wait on death row constituted cruel and unusual punishment because it often caused suicide and insanity. The majority noted that this contention had already been rejected in *People* v. *Chessman.*[14] However, the court reversed on other grounds and remanded for retrial. At the second trial the jury again imposed the death penalty, whereafter Anderson again appealed, contending that the death penalty was per se unconstitutional.[15] The state responded by noting that contemporary standards of decency were not offended by the penalty. The state pointed out that recent acts of the legislature provided for capital punishment, and that the death penalty had not been removed in most states. Further, it was argued that other provisions in the California Constitution recognized the death penalty, and that it served three legitimate goals of the state: retribution, isolation, and deterrence. Moreover, argued the state, the punishment was unconstitutional only if it were *both* cruel *and* unusual.

The court immediately took cognizance of the fact that the California inhibition utilized the disjunctive phrase "cruel *or* unusual." It noted that, as originally proposed, the conjuctive "and" was utilized and that only later was the disjunctive "or" substituted. Because of this, the court reasoned that the change "was purposeful" and concluded that the inhibition had been violated if the penalty were either cruel *or* unusual.[16]

The heart of the court's decision rested on its view of contemporary standards of decency. It recognized that forty-one states provided for the death penalty, that juries were willing to impose it, and that public opinion polls suggested that a majority of people favor its retention. However, the court distinguished between two groups of citizens: those "far removed" from the actual experience of capital punishment, and those who constitute an "informed public." "The infrequency of its actual application," stated the court, "suggests that among those persons called upon to actually impose or carry out the death penalty, it is being repudiated with an ever increasing frequency."[17] The steady decrease in the number of executions "persuasively demonstrates," asserted the court, "that capital punishment is unacceptable to society today."[18] Furthermore, it was noted that the associated lengthy terms of imprisonment prior to execution have dehumanizing effects and are often so degrading and brutalizing that they may be considered "psychological torture."

To the state's contention that capital punishment serves three legitimate objectives, the court retorted that the death penalty certainly could not be considered rehabilitative, that penalties are not sanctioned solely for retribution in California, that prisoners can be isolated by use of far less onerous means, and that the punishment is not necessarily a deterrent. Thus, it followed that the imposition of the death penalty was cruel. The court also noted that the punishment today is unusual. It is rarely imposed and more rarely carried out. Thus, the California Supreme Court in a nearly unanimous (six-to-one) decision, for the first and only time to date, held that the infliction of capital punishment per se constitutes cruel and unusual punishment.[19] Anderson's sentence was modified to life imprisonment.

The impact of this decision on the justices of the United States Supreme Court, who were deliberating the same question, probably cannot be gauged.[20] Nevertheless, the stage was set. A highly respected court of appeals had in effect declared that none of its prisoners on death row could be executed. With great anxiety prisoners in other states waited to see whether the United States Supreme Court would follow suit.

Furman v. Georgia

On June 29, 1972, just four months after the *Anderson* decision, the United States Supreme Court issued its long-awaited decision. As was typical of all previous decisions on the death penalty, except for *Anderson,* neither the abolitionists nor the antiabolitionists gained a clear-cut victory. In an all too brief per curiam opinion, the Court simply announced that in the cases before it, "the imposition and carrying out of the death penalty . . . constitutes cruel and unusual punishment in violation of the Eighth and Fourteenth Amendments."[21] Thus, the Court stopped far short of holding the death penalty unconstitutional per se. Nevertheless, the immediate effect was to free all prisoners on death row in the United States from fear of execution.

The decision itself consolidated three separate cases. William Furman, a twenty-six-year-old mentally deficient black, was convicted of the murder of a white householder. Lucious Jackson, a twenty-one-year-old black of average education and intelligence, was convicted of the rape of a white woman. To accomplish his objective he had held a scissors against her neck. During the struggle, she was bruised, but was not hospitalized. The Supreme Court of Georgia upheld both convictions and sentences.[22] The third case involved

Elmer Branch, a borderline mentally deficient black, who entered the rural home of a sixty-five-year-old white widow and raped her while holding his arm against her throat. The Texas Court of Appeals upheld the conviction and the death sentence.[23]

All nine justices wrote separate opinions in the five-to-four decision, representing a vast diversity of rationale on both the majority and minority sides. Only one basic rationale is found in all five majority opinions. All agreed that the death penalty had been applied in an arbitrary manner and thus constitutes cruel and unusual punishment.[24] Likewise, the minority agreed upon only one rationale: that judicial self-restraint should be exercised in the present case and that the ultimate determination should be made by the legislatures.

Justice Douglas, writing in the majority, relied almost exclusively on the idea that implicit in the Eighth Amendment is the concept of equal protection. Under the present laws, he noted, no standards are provided to govern the selection of the penalty by the jury. "People live or die," he asserted, "dependent on the whim of one man or of 12."[25] The discretion of judges and juries in imposing the death penalty enables the punishment to be applied selectively, thus allowing prejudice against the accused "if he is poor and despised, and lacking political clout, or if he is a member of a suspect or unpopular minority."[26] Similarly, Justice Brennan likened the situation to a "lottery system." He rejected the state's contention that the penalty was inflicted with "informed selectivity" only in "extreme" cases, by noting that if the *Furman* case was deemed "extreme," then nearly all murders fell into that category.[27] Consequently, to both Justices Douglas and Brennan, the sentences imposed were unconstitutional. Justices Stewart and White wrote very brief concurring opinions, differing little from the major thrust of Justice Douglas' arguments.

Perhaps somewhat surprisingly, Justice Douglas stopped short of declaring the death penalty per se unconstitutional. However, Justices Brennan and Marshall did not. The former unequivocally condemned the punishment. In an elaborate opinion, Justice Marshall constructed four standards against which to juxtapose the death penalty.[28] A penalty may be deemed cruel and unusual, he asserted, for any one of the following reasons: (1) if it involves so much physical pain and suffering that civilized people cannot tolerate it; (2) if it was previously unknown for a given offense; (3) if it is excessive and serves no valid legislative purpose; and (4) if it is abhorred by popular sentiment. While Justice Marshall quickly dismissed discussion of the first two standards, Justice Brennan eloquently took issue with the first.

Assertively, he argued that the death penalty does not comport with human dignity because of its unusually severe and degrading nature. "No other existing punishment," he stated, "is comparable to death in terms of physical and mental suffering."[29] In reaching that conclusion, he found the penalty unique and painful, and that it often constitutes psychological torture.[30]

Both Justices Marshall and Brennan condemned the penalty for its lack of valid legislative purpose. In painstaking detail, the former reviewed six conceivable purposes of the penalty (retribution, deterrence, prevention of repetitive criminal acts, encouragement of guilty pleas and confessions, eugenics, and economy), rejecting each in turn. "Retaliation, vengeance and retribution," noted Justice Marshall, "have been roundly condemned as intolerable aspirations for government in a free society."[31] As to the deterrent effect of the death penalty, it was pointed out that: (1) murders are not less frequent in states that have the death penalty, as opposed to states that do not; (2) that murders do not increase when the death penalty is abolished or decline when restored; and (3) that law enforcement officers are not safer from murderous attacks in states that have the death penalty than in those without it.[32] Thus, upon concluding that there is no correlation between the murder rate and the presence or absence of the capital sanction, Justice Marshall declared that the deterrence theory could not be used to justify the infliction of capital punishment.

Justices Marshall and Brennan both agreed that imprisonment was a sufficient means by which to prevent the criminal from committing further acts against society, thus rendering the death penalty unnecessary. They pointed out that the available evidence suggests that the threat of death has no greater deterrent effect than the threat of imprisonment. It was also pointed out that recidivism among murderers is extremely rare. For the most part they are first offenders and, when released from prison, are model citizens.

In quickly dismissing the last three purposes capital punishment might serve, Justice Marshall asserted: "If the death penalty is used to encourage guilty pleas and thus to deter suspects from exercising their rights under the Sixth Amendment to jury trials, it is unconstitutional."[33] Furthermore, "when all is said and done, there can be no doubt that it costs more to execute a man than to keep him in prison for life."[34] Therefore, he concluded, there is no rational basis for inflicting the death penalty.

Comparing capital punishment to his fourth standard, Justice Marshall rejected the penalty on the ground that today it is morally unacceptable to the people of the United States. As did Justice Wright in the *Anderson* decision, Justice Marshall distinguished between the public at large and the informed public.[35] If all were known about capital punishment, he claimed, the evidence would almost surely convince the average citizen that it is unwise and immoral. Perhaps anticipating objections to this extremely speculative assertion, Justice Marshall listed a number of reasons why he thought citizens *would* condemn the death penalty: (1) it is imposed discriminatorily against certain classes of people; (2) there is evidence that some people have been executed before their innocence can be established;[36] and (3) the death penalty wrecks havoc with our entire system of criminal justice.

The dissenters in *Furman* argued that the decision should be controlled by judicial self-restraint. In fact, Justices Blackmun and Rehnquist relied almost exclusively on this argument. While some justices were personally opposed to the death penalty and suggested that they might vote against it were they legislators, the underlying consensus was clear: it was not the prerogative of the judiciary to declare invalid laws enacted by the popular branches of government. Justice Blackmun, for example, noted that all of the reasons advanced to abolish the death penalty appeared reasonable to him, but "only in a legislative and executive way and not as a judicial expedient."[37]

Justices Brennan and White responded vehemently to this line of reasoning. The former noted that the right to be free from cruel and unusual punishment may not be submitted to popular vote. Therefore, judicial enforcement of the clause may not be evaded by arguing that legislatures have the power to prescribe punishments for crimes. "We must not, in the guise of 'judicial restraint,'" he suggested, "abdicate our fundamental responsibility to enforce the Bill of Rights."[38] Justice White further noted that judicial review by definition often involved a conflict between judicial and legislative judgment.[39] Interpreting the Eighth Amendment is no different than any other. The amendment, he contended, imposes an obligation on the judiciary to judge the constitutionality of the punishment.

Chief Justice Burger and Justice Powell raised various other issues in their dissents. Both dismissed the idea that capital punishment offends the conscience of society to such an extent that the Court should declare it unconstitutional. The chief justice noted that the penalty was authorized by forty states and the federal government. Four times within the last eleven years Congress had added capital punishment to its statutes. He further explained that public opinion polls "have shown nothing approximating the universal condemnation of capital punishment that might lead us to suspect that the legislatures in general have lost touch with current social values."[40]

Also rejected by these two justices was the notion that capital punishment is impermissible because it no longer serves any rational legislative interest. The chief justice viewed such a claim as one of policy determination, a dimension that should be left to the legislatures. Aside from this fundamental principle, he noted that there is no authority to suggest that the Eighth Amendment prevents society from seeking retribution. Furthermore, he noted, there is an "empirical stalemate" as to whether capital punishment is a deterrent.[41]

In summarizing the *Furman* opinions it may be suggested that the dissenters overreacted to the majority view. Essentially all that the latter did was to eliminate the death penalty as it was presently being (arbitrarily) applied. However, the dissenters, with the exception of Chief Justice Burger, wrote opinions as though the Court had abolished capital punishment per se.[42] Thus, they failed to seriously weaken the majority's case.

Chief Justice Burger, on the other hand, did attempt to refute the basic rationale of the majority. "This claim of arbitrariness," he asserted, "is not only lacking in empirical support, but it manifestly fails to establish that the death penalty is a 'cruel and unusual' punishment."[43] He later continued: "The very infrequency of the death penalties imposed by jurors attests their cautious and discriminating reservation of that penalty for the most extreme cases."[44]

The dissenters, like the majority, universally agreed upon one and only one rationale for upholding the penalty, that of judicial self-restraint. While Justices Brennan and White may be credited with discussing the issue, the majority as a whole, like the dissenters, did not adequately respond to the crux of their opponents' arguments.

Furman: Initial Reaction

To most observers the decision was quite unexpected. The New Republic hailed it as "one of the biggest surprises in its [the Court's] history." Even "the most zealous advocates of abolition," the article continued, "had resigned themselves to defeat."[45] The unexpected votes had come from Justices Stewart and White.[46]

Congressional reaction was mixed. Senator Edward Kennedy declared the decision to be "one of the great judicial milestones in American history" and asked that the opinions be printed in the Congressional Record.[47] On the other hand, James O. Eastland, chairman of the Senate Judiciary Committee, asserted that "the Supreme Court is again legislating and destroying our system of Government."[48] Within hours after the decision, Louis C. Wyman, representative from New Hampshire, and sixteen cosponsors in the House introduced a proposed constitutional amendment that would permit state legislatures to impose capital punishment "in cases involving deliberate and willful taking of human life."[49]

President Nixon's immediate reaction was one of caution. He told a news conference that he hoped the Court's ruling would not outlaw the death penalty for every offense.[50] Within nine months, however, he had taken decisive action to restore the penalty. On March 10, 1973, in a radio address, he spoke of "soft-headed judges" and announced that he had asked Attorney General Richard G. Kleindienst to draft a capital punishment law that would survive Supreme Court review. "Contrary to the views of some social scientists," he said, "I am convinced that the death penalty can be an effective deterrent against specific crimes."[51] On March 21, the attorney general sent to Congress a draft bill "to establish rational criteria for the mandatory imposition of the sentence of death."[52] A bill similar to the one the president offered was adopted by the Senate on March 14, 1974.[53] It provided for post-trial hearings to determine the existence or absence of specific aggravating or mitigating factors. However, a similar bill died in the House Judiciary Committee, thus eliminating any chance for reinstatement of the penalty in 1974.

The press was quick to note the importance of the decision. Every major newspaper in the country gave the story front-page headlines, a rare event in the history of judicial decisions. Public reaction was mixed. A poll by *Nation's Business* indicated that its readers were overwhelmingly opposed to the decision.[54] On the other hand, a number of well-known individuals hailed the ruling as bringing "us out of the dark ages."[55]

In California, plans to put the question of the death penalty on the ballot via initiative remained unchanged.[56] The original impetus for the action had come when the California Supreme Court in February had struck down the death penalty as per se constituting cruel and unusual punishment in violation of the state constitution. Eventually over one million persons signed petitions calling for the initiative, and on election day voters approved restoration of the punishment by a two-to-one margin.[57]

Reaction by the scholarly community has been extremely guarded. Most of the articles appearing in the journals to date have simply reported the decision[58] or have assessed its possible impact on the states.[59]

Furman: The Impact

The immediate impact of *Furman* was to spare the lives of 631 men and women on death row.[60] Nearly every state and federal statute calling for the death penalty was affected by the decision.[61]

The *Furman* decision directly affected the judiciary by overruling, *sub silentio,* the holding in *McGautha* v. *California,*[62] issued just thirteen months before. At that time the Court had held that the absence of standards to guide the jury's discretion in determining whether to impose or withhold the death penalty did not violate the Constitution. Justice Douglas, writing in *Furman,* immediately noted the incongruence between the two decisions. To him the "tension between them highlighted the correctness of Justice Brennan's dissent in the earlier [*McGautha*] decision."[63] Only Justice Stewart of those in the majority seemed to imply that *McGautha* was not overruled. A member of the majority in that decision, he made the distinction that in *McGautha,* only the due process and equal protection clauses of the Fourteenth Amendment were considered.[64] However, the *Furman* decision, he noted, was based on the Eighth Amendment.

Those dissenting in *Furman* also took cognizance of *McGautha.* Chief Justice Burger noted that the decision had upheld the prevailing system of sentencing in capital cases, and that all of the arguments and factual contentions presented and accepted in *Furman* had been rejected in *McGautha.* "If stare decisis means anything," he wrote, "that decision [*McGautha*] should be regarded as controlling pronouncement of law."[65] Like Justice Stewart, he noted that technically *McGautha* was decided on Fourteenth rather than Eighth Amendment grounds, but asserted that "it would be disingenuous to suggest that . . . the [*Furman*] ruling has done anything less than overrule

McGautha in the guise of an Eighth Amendment adjudication."[66] Justice
Powell agreed. In assessing the implications of *Furman* in light of *McGautha,*
he concluded that they "simply cannot be distinguished. These various opinions," he continued, "would, in fact, overrule that recent precedent."[67]
Similarly, Justice Blackmun noted that *Furman* was a turnabout.[68]

On the basis of *Furman* at least two state courts have struck down "mercy
statutes" as unconstitutional. A Delaware statute provided that "in all cases
where the penalty for crimes prescribed by the laws of this State is death, if
the jury, at the time of rendering their verdict, recommends the defendant to
the mercy of the court, the court may, if it seems proper to do so, impose
the sentence of life imprisonment instead of death."[69] The Supreme Court
of Delaware held that the mercy provision was unconstitutional under *Furman,*
but that it was severable from the rest of the statutory scheme providing for
the death penalty.[70] Standing alone, the statute providing for the punishment
was deemed constitutional, because it was mandatory and allowed no discretion.

Similarly, the North Carolina Supreme Court held its mercy statute severable from the state's statute mandating the death penalty for rape. Prospec-
tively, ruled the court, any defendant convicted of burglary and murder in the
first degree, arson, and rape must be sentenced to death.[71]

The decision stirred an unprecedented flurry of activity in the state legislatures. In nearly every state bills were introduced to reinstate the death
penalty in compliance with *Furman.* Over 115 proposals were submitted in
thirty-seven states alone.[72] The largest numbers were in North Carolina (15),
Missouri (12), and Maryland (10). Even in states where the death penalty was
previously prohibited, bills were introduced to reinstate it. For example, in
Wisconsin, where the penalty had been abolished for over 120 years, three
separate bills were introduced in the legislature. Quite expectedly, no fewer
than thirty-one states and Congress have reenacted death penalty statutes subsequent to the *Furman* decision.[73]

Oklahoma and Wyoming are among the states passing the harshest statutes.
Neither enumerates specific mitigating or aggravating circumstances, but simply
lists a long series of crimes for which the death penalty is mandatory. Georgia
and Montana list aggravating circumstances, but omit mitigating ones. Arizona,
Florida, Nebraska, Tennessee, Ohio, and Utah are among the states that list
both. Table 5-1 illustrates the types of aggravating and mitigating circumstances
found in the recently passed statutes. Most states, however, make no provision
as to how the court is to weigh the aggravating and mitigating circumstances.
This would appear to allow the courts great discretion in determining sentences.
Allowing such wide discretion obviously might fall within the ambit of the
Furman decision, and upon review by the United States Supreme Court, might
be declared unconstitutional.

While considering the merits of capital punishment, some legislatures have

Table 5-1

Aggravating and Mitigating Circumstances Affecting Imposition of the Death Penalty

A. Aggravating Circumstances

1. Prior conviction of a capital or life offense.
2. Prior conviction of a violent felony.
3. During commission of the offense, defendant knowingly created risk to others.
4. Received or was promised anything of pecuniary value.
5. The offense was committed in an especially heinous, cruel, or depraved manner.
6. Murder by a prison inmate.
7. Murder by a person committing or fleeing from the scene of a crime.
8. Murder committed to disrupt lawful exercise of any governmental function.
9. Murder committed to disrupt the enforcement of laws.
10. Murder of a judicial officer, former judicial officer, district attorney, former district attorney, solicitor, or former solicitor.
11. Directed another to commit murder.
12. Murder of any peace officer or fireman.
13. Committed by a person lying in wait or ambush.
14. Committed to conceal a crime.
15. More than one murder was committed.

B. Mitigating Circumstances

1. Defendant's capacity to appreciate the wrongfulness of his conduct was significantly impaired.
2. Defendant was under unusual and substantial duress.
3. Defendant was a principal in the offense committed by another but played a minor role.
4. Defendant could not have foreseen his conduct would cause grave risk to another.
5. Defendant has no significant history of prior criminal activity.
6. Victim was a participant in the defendant's conduct.
7. Defendant was under substantial domination of another person.
8. The tender age of the defendant at the time of the crime.
9. The murder was committed under circumstances which the defendant believed to provide a moral justification for his conduct.
10. The defendant was acting in the heat of passion.
11. Evidence upon which the defendant was convicted was entirely circumstantial.
12. Any other fact in mitigation of the penalty.

abolished the death penalty for certain crimes. Florida, for example, omitted from its capital offenses the "abominable, and detestable crime against nature." Georgia eliminated capital punishment for perjury causing the death of another. Nevada eliminated as capital offenses, treason, perjury resulting in a death, kidnapping with substantial bodily harm, forcible rape, battery with intent to commit rape, and dynamiting. Tennessee abolished the death penalty for rape and carnal knowledge.

Perhaps the most important change in the statutes is the fact that generally no longer may persons committing murder "in the heat of passion" be sentenced to death. Tennessee provided specifically that this was to be considered a mitigating circumstance. Most other states do not allow the death penalty for the murder of a wife or husband during a heated argument, or the murder of a participant in a bar room brawl. Undoubtedly this fact should decrease the number of persons sentenced to death in this country.[74]

In conclusion, the *Furman* decision has served as a catalyst, stimulating legislatures to reexamine the merits of inflicting the death penalty for certain crimes. Having done so, many states have eliminated the punishment for many of the less heinous offenses that formerly allowed the ultimate sanction. Nevertheless, the issue has not been settled. On April 21, 1975, the United States Supreme Court heard oral argument in yet another death penalty case.[75] The outcome will affect the lives of over two hundred prisoners currently under sentence of death.

6

Miscellaneous Chastisement

Whipping

At the time of the adoption of the United States Constitution, whipping was a very common punishment.[1] It was provided for by statute as a punishment for crime and deemed appropriate as a sanction for infractions of rules by prisoners in state institutions. Only the former is dealt with in this chapter.

Some early state courts specifically declared whipping constitutionally permissible.[2] For example, in 1828 the General Court of Virginia held: "The punishment of offenses by stripes is odious, but cannot be said to be *unusual*."[3] Other state courts simply assumed its constitutionality.[4] Later, during the second half of the nineteenth century, many state and territorial courts continued to hold that whipping was constitutionally permissible. For example in *Garcia* v. *Territory*,[5] the imposition of thirty lashes for larceny was upheld by the New Mexico Supreme Court on the grounds that deference should be paid to the lawmaking power of the legislature, that almost every state and territory had resorted to this mode of punishment, that its infliction had never before been held unconstitutional, that it was used in the army, and that the practice of whipping criminals convicted of theft had prevailed for over fifty years. The Maryland Court of Appeals, on similar grounds, upheld the imposition of seven lashes on a wife-beater in 1883.[6]

Despite these court decisions, whipping as a mode of punishment has historically been subject to constant attack. Beginning in about 1800, imprisonment began to be substituted for the "cat."[7] During the nineteenth century it fell into general disuse. Many scholars and jurists opposed its utilization altogether. Others, while not entirely opposing it, favored strict limitations on its use. In 1820, for example, Justice Taylor, writing an opinion for the North Carolina Supreme Court, asserted: "Public corporal punishment for any offense impresses an indelible stigma on the character and ought to be inflicted on those offenses only which are infamous in their nature."[8] Congress abolished the punishment for all federal courts in 1839.[9] In 1851, Justice Lipscomb of the Texas Supreme Court went so far as to assert: "Among all nations of civilized man, from the earliest ages, the infliction of stripes has been considered more degrading than death itself."[10] In 1893 the Indiana Supreme Court in a dictum suggested that the "whipping post" was cruel and unusual punishment.[11]

At the turn of the century and during the immediate decades that followed, a far-reaching debate erupted as to whether whipping was morally, socially, and/or legally acceptable in the United States.[12] Some writers advocated use of the whip in certain instances. For example, in 1889, the Reverend Hanaford A. Phebe, although opposed to the whipping of children, advocated whipping wife-beaters because of its deterrent effect.[13] For this reason, the Honorable Simon E. Baldwin in 1901 suggested using the whip on all sorts of criminals.[14] However, such a belief was clearly held by only a small minority at the time.[15]

Today the use of whipping as a punishment is extremely rare.[16] The only jurisdiction in the United States which allows it is the state of Delaware. On April 13, 1963, the constitutionality of that state's statute was certified to the Supreme Court of Delaware. The court recognized that constitutional provisions "are not static," but "grow and change" to meet the conditions of modern society. This did not mean, however, that the historical context could be completely discarded. Furthermore, it was not the duty of the court to abolish the punishment. It was up to the legislators, who were the representatives of the people. "What the weight of public opinion pro or con is," stated the court, "we have no way of knowing. . . . It is the province of the General Assembly in its widsom to give expression to the public will."[17] The trial court that had raised the question thereupon imposed a sentence of twenty lashes on Franklin Cannon, who had violated probation in an automobile theft case. Upon appeal, however, the Delaware Supreme Court remanded, instructing the lower court to examine the mental condition of the prisoner and to look for any potential unwarranted effects of whipping him.[18] Later that same year the Delaware Supreme Court reaffirmed its decision and upheld the imposition of twenty lashes on a convicted robber.[19] Again, however, the court reversed on other grounds. The United States Supreme Court did not review either decision. Today, however, it is highly questionable whether such an infliction could pass constitutional scrutiny. It is imposed in an extremely rare number of cases and, as such, under the rationale found in *Furman* v. *Georgia*,[20] it is probably levied in an arbitrary manner, thereby inflicting cruel and unusual punishment.

Sterilization

In 1907, Indiana enacted the world's first sterilization statute.[21] Subsequently, thirteen states adopted legislation specifically providing for the sterilization of criminals. The statutes generally provide for vasectomies on males and salpingectomies on females, and are aimed at sex offenders and habitual criminals. Additionally, twenty-eight states have provided for the sterilization of insane and feeble-minded persons.[22] No statutes provide for castration, and there is every reason to believe that if such a statute were adopted it would immediately be declared unconstitutional.[23]

Both types of statutes, those calling for the sterilization of criminals and those calling for the sterilization of the insane and feeble-minded, have been challenged as inflicting cruel and unusual punishment.[24] Today there is little question that the sterilization of the insane and feeble-minded is perfectly

constitutional. The controlling case was decided very early. Guardians of
Carrie Bell, a feeble-minded daughter of a feeble-minded mother and the mother
of a feeble-minded daughter, attacked a Virginia statute that allowed her
sterilization. Noting that the operation did not impair her general health or
interfere with her sexual desires or enjoyment, and that without the operation
she would be compelled to remain in an institution until she was "sterilized by
nature," the Virginia Supreme Court declared that the cruel and unusual
punishment inhibition had no application because the statute was not "penal"
in nature.[25] The United States Supreme Court heard the case on a writ of error,
Justice Holmes writing the opinion. Noting that the public welfare was para-
mount, he arrived at his widely quoted conclusion. "The principle that sustains
compulsory vaccination," he stated, "is broad enough to cover cutting the Fallo-
pian tubes. Three generations of imbeciles are enough."[26] In 1931, two state
supreme courts upheld statutes that imposed sterilization on feeble-minded
persons.[27] In 1933 the Oklahoma Supreme Court held constitutional the forced
sterilization of Samuel W. Main, who was afflicted with an hereditary form of
insanity.[28]

Despite the constitutionality of sterilizing the feeble-minded and insane,
there has been a strong movement to prevent such activity.[29] For example, the
Department of Health, Education and Welfare, under considerable pressure,
recently issued administrative policies to limit the use of federal funds to finance
sterilization.[30] Children under twenty-one who are unable to give their consent
for the operation are not to be sterilized unless a review committee and a court
of appropriate jurisdiction have granted approval.

There is today, however, some question as to whether sterilization of criminals is constitutionally permissible. For example, some courts have compared
sterilization to castration and mutilation, suggesting that the same purposes, the
same infliction of shame, humiliation, degradation and mental torture, are
involved in each.[31] One court went so far as to suggest that a rapist "might
regard it rather an advantage.... As a preventive of this crime," continued the
court, "vasectomy is without effect."[32]

On the other hand, several courts have upheld various sterilization statutes.
For example, Peter Feilen, who had been convicted of raping a ten-year-old girl,
claimed that a state statute providing for his sterilization inflicted cruel and
unusual punishment. The Washington Supreme Court noted, however, that
Feilen would not be subjected to "any marked degree of physical torture or
pain" and, further, that the statute was enacted "on the theory that modern
scientific investigation shows that . . . criminality . . . [is] congenital and hereditary."[33] In 1935 the Alabama Supreme Court, while issuing an advisory opinion, came to the same conclusion.[34]

In 1936 the California Court of Appeals upheld an unusual sentence
involving sterilization. A term of imprisonment in San Quentin had been
imposed on Harry Blankenship for the statutory rape of a thirteen-year-old

female. It was to be suspended, however, on condition that he submit to sterilization. There was some evidence to indicate that he had afflicted her with syphilis. Despite the fact that he could afford medical aid and could be cured, the court took the position that the state had the right to be "vitally interested in the health and welfare of its citizens" and thus held the sentence constitutional.[35]

Despite the controversy over whether criminals may be constitutionally sterilized, it now appears fairly clear that if a statute is viewed as eugenic, rather than punitive, it will be deemed constitutional.[36] The first bit of evidence for this conclusion is found in *Buck* v. *Bell.*[37] There Justice West of the Virginia Supreme Court, while upholding a sterilization statute, noted that it was not "penal." Four years later the Utah Supreme Court similarly noted that the Utah act was "in no sense penal" because its purpose was "eugenic and therapeutic."[38] The Oklahoma Court of Appeals perhaps recognized the distinction most clearly. "The decisive question," stated the court, "is whether the act under consideration is a penal statute or a eugenic measure."[39] In the case before it, the court found that the procedure was civil and not part of the conviction or sentence, and was therefore "a eugenic measure to improve the safety and general welfare of the race by preventing from being born persons who will probably become criminals."[40]

Today twenty-seven states provide for some type of sterilization.[41] All are professedly eugenic, except those in California and Nebraska. Enforcement is uneven, California accounting for almost one-third of all public sterilizations in the United States. Georgia, North Carolina, and Virginia also have high rates. During the past two decades eugenic sterilization in the United States has declined. In 1946 for example, 1512 persons were sterilized. In 1955 the figure had decreased to 1067 persons.[42]

Other Corporeal Punishments

Dicta in four opinions at the turn of the century made specific reference to pillorying.[43] Each made it quite clear that the punishment is cruel and unusual. For example, in *In re O'Shea,*[44] a California court categorized it with burning at the stake and breaking on the wheel.

The ducking or cucking stool probably enjoyed similar status. Two early opinions implied, but did not decide, that this form of punishment was within the prohibition. In the first, Nancy James was convicted in 1825 of being a "common scold" and sentenced to be placed in an "engine of correction" and plunged into the water three times.[45] She contended that this was a cruel and unusual punishment in violation of both the Pennsylvania and United States Constitutions. The court, after an exhaustive study, declared that it could find no record of the punishment being inflicted for more than one hundred years and concluded that it had been repealed not by positive law, but by the "voice of humanity." For this reason, and because the Supreme Court thought it unlikely that the followers of William Penn could have introduced such a punishment to Pennsylvania, the court declared that the punishment of ducking was not a part of the common law of Pennsylvania. The court stopped short, however, of declaring the punishment cruel and unusual. Indeed, it specifically held that the decision was not reached by considering the "humane provisions" of the state and federal constitutions relating to cruel and unusual punishments, except to "show the sense of the whole community."[46] The tone of the opinion indicates, however, that should the state legislature have statutorily allowed such a punishment, the court would have held the law unconstitutional. The righteous indignation against such a mode of punishment is clearly evident. "The city," stated the court, "is rescued from this ignominious and odious show, and the state from the opprobrium of the continuance of so barbarous an institution, which would pluck from the brow of our legislators, that diadem of humanity which the civilized would be awarded."[47]

The second case involving a ducking stool was decided in the District Court for the District of Columbia in 1829.[48] Ann Royall was convicted of being a common scold and fined ten dollars. She demanded a new trial on the ground that the only punishment for being a common scold was ducking, an obsolete mode of punishment, and one that was barbarous and unusual, and forbidden by the Bill of Rights. Further, if the punishment was obsolete, she contended, the offense was no longer indictable. Again the court refused to declare the ducking stool unconstitutional. Rather, it found that ducking was not the only common law punishment for being a common scold, and that even if part of the common law punishment had become obsolete, the only effect was to negate that part.[49]

Hard Labor

Although one might not generally regard hard labor as a corporeal punishment, it is included here because its imposition results in more physical strain than mental anxiety. Hard labor has been challenged as inflicting cruel and unusual punishment on several occasions, but these are primarily of historical interest. A few general rules may be derived from the early decisions. First, imprisonment in the penitentiary at hard labor is not of itself cruel and unusual punishment.[50] Second, its infliction is generally constitutional when applied to felons.[51] Third, the assigning of convicts to work on the public roads[52] or on chain gangs[53] is not per se violative of cruel and unusual punishment inhibitions. Fourth, despite the general constitutionality of hard labor as punishment, there are times when courts may inflict cruel and unusual punishment by imposing it. For example, in the absence of statutory authority, the penalty may not generally be levied on one convicted of a misdemeanor.[54] Some courts have

held that it may not be levied even on felons unless it is provided for by statute.[55] An extremely early decision went so far as to intimate that if the convict
had a physical infirmity and the imposition appeared to be inhumane, the hard
labor aspect of the sentence should be postponed.[56] The most recent decisions
have upheld the punishment. In *Wilson* v. *Kelley,* a federal district court specifically ruled that "work and labor on the part of prisoners is not in itself unconstitutional or unlawful."[57] In 1972 the Supreme Court of South Carolina
upheld a statute requiring the judge to sentence defendants "to hard labor on
the public work of the city . . . [or to] the county jail or State Penitentiary at
hard labor." Justice Littleton noted that there was "nothing in the record to
indicate that the appellant . . . performed any hard labor different from that
performed by a multitude of civilians engaged in certain types of employment."[58]

Solitary Confinement

Although one might legitimately argue that solitary confinement is not
"corporeal punishment," a great deal of physical discomfort accompanies such
incarceration. The imposition of solitary confinement by statute is a well-established tradition. The British provided for it in 1752.[59] A number of states have
enacted statutes imposing the penalty.[60] The most notable early challenge to
the punishment came in the famous *Kemmler* case.[61] The New York State legislature had provided that until a condemned prisoner was put to death, he was
to be placed in solitary confinement. Only officers of the prison, his counsel,
his physician, a priest or minister, and the members of his family were allowed
to see him. Kemmler contended that such conditions constituted cruel and
unusual punishment. The United States Supreme Court omitted discussion of
the issue and, hence, by implication decided otherwise.

Within two years the Supreme Court twice specifically upheld the constitutionality of solitary confinement.[62] State supreme courts followed suit.[63]
Massachusetts upheld its statute on the ground that the cell was "not intended
to prevent the presence of the prisoner in court."[64] The New Jersey Supreme
Court similarly held its statute constitutional on the ground that "a more
stringent provision for solitary confinement pending execution" was contained
in the Act of George II.[65]

On the other hand, courts have generally held that when a statute does not
prescribe solitary confinement, the levying of such a sentence by a judicial
officer constitutes cruel and unusual punishment. For example, in *Ex parte
Medley,*[66] the United States Supreme Court reasoned that an examination of
the history of solitary confinement revealed that it has been imposed as an
additional punishment for the worst crimes. As such, it could not be levied
on a condemned murderer unless provided for by statute. Similarly, the

Arkansas Supreme Court held unconstitutional a sentence imposing solitary confinement for contempt of court because no such punishment was known to the law. "In that sense," stated the court, "it is an unusual punishment which is expressly prohibited by the constitution of the State, which declares that cruel and unusual punishment shall not be inflicted."[67]

Some state statutes inflict solitary confinement on convicts who break prison rules. For example, a Tennessee statute levies thirty days solitary confinement for such infractions. Donald L. Hancock, an inmate of Tennessee State Prison, challenged the statute. Although he was granted relief because of the "exacerbated conditions of filth and discomfort," the federal district court specifically held that the use of solitary confinement called for by the statute was not per se unconstitutional.[68] More is said about the imposition of solitary confinement for infraction of prison rules in chapter 11.

Being placed in solitary confinement on death row has been challenged several times. Caryl Chessman, for example, spent eleven years there. The California Supreme Court in 1959 ruled that it was "unusual" and was attended by "mental suffering" but that it was not unconstitutional.[69] Several years earlier Ethel Rosenberg had challenged her confinement on death row at Sing Sing Prison, New York.[70] The Court noted that the cell was twelve feet long and four feet wide, and contained a bunk, chair, table, toilet, and wash stand. It was inspected regularly, was sanitary, and had plenty of light. Visitors were allowed. She was able to exercise in the yard. Further, the practice had a long history. Thus, it could not be deemed cruel and unusual punishment.

In 1971 a federal district court upheld the use of solitary confinement on death row, but granted the petitioner relief because adequate exercise facilities were not provided. "Confinement," stated the court, "for long periods of time without the opportunity for regular outdoor exercise does constitute cruel and unusual punishment in violation of the Eighth Amendment to the United States Constitution."[71] The following year the Supreme Court of Illinois again affirmed, however, that the imposition of solitary confinement per se did not inflict cruel and unusual punishment.[72]

Restricted Diets

There has been an extremely limited amount of litigation dealing with restricted diets. This is primarily due to the fact that very few statutes provide for them. The first major test case came in 1907.[73] A Wisconsin statute provided that a male abandoning and neglecting to support his wife should, upon conviction, be sentenced to one year in the state prison, or sentenced to between fifteen days and six months in the county jail, ten days of which "may in the discretion of the court be upon a diet of bread and water."[74]

Upon conviction, Sherman B. Spencer attacked the statute as inflicting cruel and unusual punishment, despite the fact that he was sentenced to serve one year in the state prison only. The court quickly noted that there were two separate punishments provided for in the statute, and that even if one was unconstitutional, this would not necessarily make the whole statute void. The court went even further however. "We are of the opinion," it was stated, "that the clause in question may well be justified as providing an appropriate punishment for an aggravated case of abandonment or failure to support."[75]

The second major challenge to restricted diets came in Nebraska. Thomas Nelson was convicted of unlawful possession of intoxicating liquor and was sentenced to imprisonment in the city jail for sixty days, the first and last twenty days of which were to be on a diet of bread and water. Nelson challenged the judgment imposed under the statute as "inhuman and oppressive," and unconstitutional as inflicting cruel and unusual punishment.[76] The court noted that similar statutes existed in many states. Relying on *Spencer* v. *State*,[77] it held that the imposition of a bread-and-water diet was not cruel and unusual punishment.

Imposition of restricted diets by administrators for the infraction of institutional rules is much more common than statutes providing for the punishment. This topic is discussed in detail in chapter 11.

Miscellaneous Punishments

The cutting of a Chinaman's cue has been declared an unconstitutional mode of punishment.[78] Ho Ah Kow, a Chinese national, was convicted of violating a city ordinance of San Francisco. Unable to pay the fine, he was sentenced to five days in the city jail. Pursuant to a local ordinance that provided that inmates' hair be "cut or clipped to a uniform length of one inch from the scalp," Nunan, the jailer, clipped off his cue. To a Chinese this meant disgrace. Among other things, Ho Ah Kow then sued for damages, Alleging that cruel and unusual punishment had been inflicted. The court reasoned that the ordinance could not be justified in terms of discipline or sanitary regulations, and that the clipping was undertaken to add severity to the punishment. "If adopted in consequence of the sentence," wrote Judge Field, "it is punishment in addition to that imposed by the court; if adopted without regard to the sentence it is wanton cruelty."[79] Thus, enforcement of the ordinance upon *Chinese prisoners,* as applied, was deemed a cruel and unusual punishment.

Finally, requiring a prisoner to carry a chain, suspended from ankle to wrist, is constitutionally impermissible.[80] However, the placement of seamen in irons for disobedience is constitutional.[81]

Part II: Legislative Action and Judicial Sentencing as Cruel and Unusual Punishment

B. Incorporeal Punishments

7

The Doctrine of Excessiveness

The inhibition against cruel and unusual punishment in the English Bill of Rights restricted the imposition of excessive degrees of punishment. Upon introduction to North America, the concept took on expanded meaning and emphasis was placed upon restricting the *kind* of punishment that might be imposed. Gradually the former idea became obscure and eventually was adjudged by many jurists to not be a part of the inhibition at all. The United States Supreme Court first had a chance to consider the issue in 1892.[1] John O'Neil had been found guilty by a justice of the peace in Vermont for selling intoxicating liquor unlawfully. He appealed to the county court and was tried before a jury, which found him guilty of 307 offenses and fined him $20 on each count, plus costs of prosecution and commitment. The total came to $6,638.72, and if not paid, he was to be imprisoned three days for each dollar. The total came to 19,914 days, or more than fifty-four years. On review the United States Supreme Court held that it would not rule on the cruel and unusual punishment allegation because it was not assigned as error, or raised in the brief of the appellant, and because the Eighth Amendment did not apply to the states.[2]

Justice Field, however, joined by Justices Harlan and Brewer, dissented. He argued that every citizen of the United States was protected from cruel and unusual punishment by the privileges and immunities clause of the Fourteenth Amendment, and thus, the Court had jurisdiction. Further, his reading of English history led him to conclude that the inhibition was directed "not only against punishment of the character mentioned, but against all punishments which by their excessive length of severity are greatly disproprotionate to the offenses charged. The whole inhibition," he continued, "is against that which is excessive either in the bail required, or fine imposed or punishment inflicted."[3] In the immediate case Justice Field found evidence to support O'Neil's contention that the punishment was excessive. He noted that the penalty was six times as great as could have been imposed for manslaughter, forgery, or perjury. Moreover, the punishment exceeded in severity anything he was able to find in the records of the Court during the entire century.

Eighteen years later the Supreme Court was again called upon to deal with an allegation that an excessive punishment had been inflicted.[4] None of the justices of the *O'Neil* majority remained on the Court.

Weems v. United States

Paul Weems, a disbursing officer for the Philippine Branch of the Bureau of Coast Guard and Transportation of the United States, had been indicted for falsifying records and a cashbook (padding the payroll) of the Captain of the Board of Manila. It was alleged that he intentionally entered as having been paid out in wages, 204 pesos and 408 pesos respectively, to employees at two lighthouses, Capul and Mata Bridge. He was found guilty under a statute that provided a minimum punishment of:

1. Twelve years and one day of *Cadena Temporal* (imprisonment in chains at "hard and painful" labor, which meant carrying a chain from wrist to ankle at all times).
2. Certain accessory penalties
    a. Civil interdiction (deprivation of rights of parental authority, guardianship of person or property, participation in family council, marital authority, administration of property, or the right to dispose of one's own property);
    b. Perpetual and absolute disqualification (permanent loss of right to vote, hold public office, receive retirement pay or honors);
    c. Subjection to official surveillance during life (keep authorities informed of domicile, observe rules of inspection, adopt some trade, art, industry or profession).
3. Fine of 1250 pesetos.[5]

After an unsuccessful appeal to the Supreme Court of the Islands, the case was brought to the United States Supreme Court, where for the first time in the case the cruel and unusual punishment issue was raised. This time the Court was willing to consider the issue, despite the fact that it had not been raised earlier. Moreover, because the case arose in federal jurisdiction, it could not be contended that the Eighth Amendment did not apply. Four justices, joining on both the procedural and substantive issues, determined the opinion of the Court.[6]

The rationale was very much the same as found in Justice Field's dissent in *O'Neil*. Justice McKenna, joined by Chief Justice Fuller, and Justices Harlan and Day, argued that the thrust of the English history as well as the intention of the founding fathers suggested that excessively severe punishments were restricted by the inhibition. "Their predominant political impulse was distrust of power," wrote Justice McKenna, "and they insisted on constitutional limitations against its abuse. But surely," he continued, "they intended *more than* to register a fear of the *forms* of abuse that went out of practice with the Stuarts."[7] The Court also noted that the clause was not meant "to prevent only an exact repetition of history." The constitutional principle was thus viewed as flexible. As Justice McKenna suggested: "Time works changes, brings into existence new conditions and purposes. Therefore a principle, to be vital, must be capable of wider application than the mischief which gave it birth."[8] If constitutional principles did not change, he argued, they would become "impotent and lifeless formulas."

Having determined that the Court had the authority to set aside disproportionate punishments, the Court then ruled that in the instant case the penalty was excessively severe. The thrust of the opinion was directed against the accessory penalties. The Court noted that Weems was subjected "to tormenting regulations that, if not so tangible as iron bars and stone walls, oppress as much by their continuity."[9] The penalties deprived him of essential liberty because they were for life. "No circumstance of degradation," wrote Justice McKenna, "is omitted. It may be that even the cruelty of pain is not omitted. He must bear a chain night and day." Moreover, "Such penalties for such offenses amaze those who . . . believe that it is a precept of justice that punishment for crime should be graduated and proportioned to [the] offense."[10]

Not only were the accessory penalties deemed cruel and unusual; Justice McKenna also noted that the punishment "is cruel in its *excess of imprisonment* and that which accompanies and follows imprisonment. It is unusual in its character. Its punishments come under the condemnation of the bill of rights, both on account of their degree and kind."[11] Thus, even the minimum penalty was repugnant to the Bill of Rights.

Justice White, writing in dissent, invoked the rationale of the majority opinion in the *O'Neil* case. He argued that the exception was not in the assignment of errors and, therefore, should not be considered. He further argued that his reading of English history led him to conclude that the inhibition was only meant to prevent the legislature "from authorizing or directing the infliction of . . . cruel bodily punishment."[12] However, except for these *kinds* of penalties, he reasoned, legislatures were free to fix the length of punishment. For the Court to hold otherwise, he argued, would be to interfere with the legislative powers of Congress.

Initial Reaction to *Weems*

Most scholars commenting on the case at the time appeared surprised, if not somewhat shocked, by the decision. For example, one contemporary scholar commented: "The *point* that was passed upon was so *novel,* and the subject matter so unusual, that even a layman stopped to read the comments he found in his daily paper."[13] Such phrases as "a very learned and exhaustive dissenting opinion," a "strong dissenting opinion," and "a very powerful dissenting opinion" were used to describe White's dissent, thereby suggesting that many scholars disagreed with the opinion of the Court.[14] One scholar did in fact state that Justice White's opinion was "more in accordance with public policy and the true intent of the framers of the Constitution,"[15] and another went so far as to claim that White's opinion "was altogether the better one."[16]

The contemporary reviews of the day give the distinct impression that most scholars felt the decision represented a point of departure in the general history of cruel and unusual punishment. To them, it was a beginning of a new era. This is clearly not the case. Rather than starting a new trend, *Weems* was the culmination of a long-existing one. Not only did it have a solid basis in English law, but there is much evidence that it was widely accepted in the United States as well.

In the first place, a large number of early opinions had stated that the pro-hibition was directed *not so much* against the amount or duration of the penalty, as against the character or kind of punishment levied.[17] Thus, there was appar-ently *some* latitude for punishments to be deemed excessive.

Second, a large number of opinions had held that any sentence within statutory limits was constitutional.[18] Implicit in such statements is the idea that sentences exceeding statutory limits might be deemed disproportionate to the offense committed.

Third, appellate courts in seven states had already been granted statutory authority to reduce or modify punishments they deemed excessive.[19] More-over, courts in several states without such statutes had similarly reduced certain sentences. For example, the Tennessee Supreme Court in 1881 declared invalid an excessive penalty imposed on W.F. Cornell, who had been convicted of assault and battery (whipping) on a prisoner.[20] Noting that the prisoner was being disciplined for smuggling whiskey into the jail, for holding a gun on the jailer, and for using abusive language, and further that Cornell believed that the form of punishment was authorized by the county court, the court determined that Cornell had acted only from a sense of duty. In such a situa-tion, the court concluded, the state does not demand "severity." The sentence was thereupon reduced to one cent and costs.[21]

Fourth, in several early cases, opinions had come extremely close to declar-ing particular sentences excessive in length. For example, in *Clellans* v. *Com-monwealth*,[22] the appellants were convicted of rioting and sentenced to three years of solitary confinement in the state penitentiary. The court declared that the three-quarters of a year already spent in the state penitentiary was "as severe a punishment as if they [the defendants] had been confined in the city jail, where they legitimately should have been sent, for two years."[23] Consequently, the defendants were discharged.[24]

Fifth, literally dozens of jurisdictions either inferentially or explicitly applied tests of proportionality, but once having done so, did not find a parti-cular sentence excessive and therefore cruel and unusual. Indeed, in many cases it was clear that if a sentence had been deemed excessive, it would have been declared in violation of a cruel and unusual prohibition. For example in *Ligan* v. *State,* a long term of imprisonment was challenged as excessive, but the Tennessee court held that "punishment *here* is neither cruel nor unusual."[25] The implication is obvious: on other facts the court might have found a punishment excessive.

The above example is just one representative instance where jurists have implied that excessive punishments might be declared cruel and unusual.[26] The implication becomes even more obvious when jurists examine, at length, the nature of the crime and conclude that the circumstances relating to it negate any claim that an excessive punishment has been levied. Two decisions are illustrative.[27] First, the Texas Court of Appeals, upon reviewing a sentence of twenty years for the arson of a house declared: "Such a man portrayed in this record should be punished to the full extent of the law."[28] The second is found in *People* v. *Clary,* where the California court reviewed a fifty-year sentence for robbery. "The manner of . . . [the robbery's] execution," stated the court, "was particularly outrageous."[29] Thus, the character of the man, in one instance, and the circumstances accompanying the offense, in the other, were deemed to justify the punishments inflicted. Presumably, had the man's character been of better standing or had the circumstances surrounding the commission of the crime been different, the courts might have held the respective punishments excessive as cruel and unusual.

Sixth, the claim was asserted over and over again in nearly every jurisdiction in the country.[30] Thus, a vast number of attorneys must have felt that the cruel and unusual inhibition restricted excessive degrees of punishment. Moreover, some of the more noted scholars of the period interpreted the concept in this manner. For example, Joel P. Bishop, surveying the history of cruel and unusual punishment clauses, stated that a punishment "though of a permissible kind, . . . may violate the Constitution by being excessive."[31] Similarly, Joseph Magrath, writing in the *American and English Encyclopedia of Law,* noted that not only were various "degrading punishments" unconstitutional, but that "punishments so disproportionate to the offense as to shock the sense of the community" were as well.[32]

Seventh, five state opinions were rendered before the *Weems* decision clearly declaring judicially imposed sentences excessive.[33] The first was written by the Supreme Court of Kentucky in 1820. Rhody Ely, a black, was sentenced by an inferior court to be whipped thirty lashes for raising his hand against a white person. The court noted that no matter how "severe, cruel and rigorous" the law, it must be upheld unless it contravenes the Constitution. "It would, however," continued the court, "be difficult to exempt this [statute] from the imputation of cruelty, within the meaning of the 15th section of the 10th article of the constitution." Moreover, "If a justice of the peace, or any other tribunal should under this act, inflict the stripes against a free person of color who lifted his hand to save him or herself from death or severe bodily harm all men must pronounce that punishment cruel indeed."[34] Thus, the mode of punishment (whipping) was not held violative of the prohibition per se, but rather the degree of punishment, under these specific circumstances, was held unduly severe.

Perhaps the clearest opinion declaring a sentence excessive was issued by the Supreme Court of Louisiana. John Garvey and others were convicted of destroying plants in a public square in New Orleans and were sentenced on seventy-two different counts. They were to pay a fine of $10 or, in default, be imprisoned in the parish prison for thirty days on each count. Thus, each defendant was to pay a total of $720 or spend 2160 days, or nearly six years, in jail. Among other claims, Garvey asserted that he had been subjected to excessive fines, and that the punishment was "cruel and unusual."[35] The court recognized that the state and federal constitutions prohibiting cruel and unusual punishments were identical, and took cognizance of the fact that the United States Supreme Court in *O'Neil* v. *Vermont*,[36] under similar circumstances, specifically stated: "The mere fact that cumulative punishments may be imposed for distinct offenses in the same prosecution is not material upon this question. If the penalty were unreasonably severe for a single offense, the constitutional question might be urged; but here the unreasonableness is only on the number of offenses which the respondent has committed."[37] The Louisiana court, however, noted Justice Field's dissent. Joined by three others, Justice Field was of the opinion that "the punishment imposed was one exceeding in severity, considering the offenses."[38] Similarly, the Louisiana Supreme Court held that because it considered the offense a continuing one, "the severity and unreasonableness of the punishment" was even more apparent than in the *O'Neil* case, because the defendants were found "guilty of seventy-two offenses within the space of one hour and forty minutes, each offense embracing only one and one-half minutes, and one offense following after the other immediately and consecutively."[39] The court noted further that if the punishment were upheld it would give a city magistrate the power to sentence an individual to an indefinite period of imprisonment in default of paying exorbitant fines. Thus, Garvey was entitled to relief because the sentence was excessive and in violation of the cruel and unusual inhibition in the state constitution.

In 1957, Professor David Fellman summarized the status of the Weems doctrine at that time. "Actually the great weight of authority," he wrote, "sustains the propriety of the court's inquiring into the severity of the sentence, so that a sentence which is clearly excessive is in most jurisdictions said to constitute a cruel and unusual punishment."[40] This conclusion is as accurate when applied in the period before *Weems* as it is for the ensuing period. Indeed, *Weems* v. *United States* was the finale, not the overture, in the history of excessiveness in the cruel and unusual punishment concept.

Despite the hopes of many scholars, the Weems doctrine has seldom been invoked successfully. One reason is that a decision by the United States Supreme

Court only six years later limited its scope tremendously. In *Badders* v. *United States*,[41] consecutive sentences of five years imprisonment and fines of $1000 on each of seven counts for placing seven letters, separately, in the mail to defraud were upheld. Justice Holmes, writing for a unanimous Court, refused to apply the comparative approach utilized by Justice McKenna in the *Weems* decision. He declared that there were no grounds for declaring the punishment unconstitutional, citing in particular *Howard* v. *Fleming*.[42] In that case the Court had concluded: "That for other offenses, which may be considered by most, if not all, of a more grievous character, less punishments have been inflicted does not make this sentence cruel."[43] Thus, as James Campbell has suggested, the decision did not weaken the principle that prohibits disproportionate punishments, but it did very much weaken the method of putting the principle into effect.[44] Consequently, the method of imposing the principle remained to a large degree abstract if not ambiguous. Lacking effective guidelines, courts simply reverted to the idea that any sentence within statutory limits was constitutional unless so disproportionate to the offense that it shocked the moral sense of all reasonable men.[45]

The second reason why the Weems doctrine has rarely been invoked successfully is that until 1962, the Eighth Amendment was continuously held by both federal and state courts not to be binding on the states. Thus, state courts until that time generally did not feel obliged to similarly interpret their own constitutional prohibitions against cruel and unusual punishment.

The third, and perhaps most important, reason has been that appellate judges still remained reluctant to substitute their personal judgment for that of others. The setting of penalties is still regarded as a legislative prerogative and, as such, a great deal of discretion is to be ascribed to legislators. Similarly, appellate courts remained hesitant about overturning penalties imposed by trial judges. The latter have been allowed broad discretion, ostensibly because they have the advantage of superior information and are able to view first hand the demeanor of defendants.

Punishments Held Excessive Since *Weems*

Despite the restricted application of the Weems principle, no fewer than nineteen decisions since 1910 have declared certain punishments or statutes excessive in violation of various cruel and unusual punishment inhibitions.[46] Five representative cases are discussed below.

In one case, Umberto Politano, a penniless, ignorant immigrant, had served two years, seven months imprisonment for nonpayment of alimony to his wife. The original award had been $12 a week, in default of which, he was sentenced to jail until he made payment. Oddly, the award was made despite the fact that his wife had a job and he did not. She had no children to care for, was

young, and was capable of earning her own living. While married for eleven
months, he spent his life savings of $3000 on her, and provided for his mother-
in-law and sister-in-law. The court noted that the nonpayment was not "willful" or because of "obstinacy." He simply could not pay the alimony. Speaking for the New York court, Justice Bonynge, obviously very irritated at the
situation, declared: "This carries the supposed rights of women to absurd, not
to say unconstitutional lengths."[47] Politano was ordered immediately discharged from prison.

One of the most extreme sentences was levied in Florida. John Nowling
was sentenced to three years imprisonment for concealing one gallon of whiskey.
In a per curiam opinion the Florida Supreme Court made short order of the
penalty by simply asserting that it was contrary to the Declaration of Rights
of Florida.[48]

In 1948 the Supreme Court of South Carolina overturned the sentence of
William Kimborough, who had been convicted of burglary and sentenced to
prison for thirty years. The court specifically noted that "punishment for a
crime, while not cruel and unusual in kind, may be so severe as to fall within
the meaning of this [the cruel and unusual punishment] provision."[49] The
court observed that the jury had recommended mercy, and consequently,
there was nothing "which would justify the [trial] court in disregarding the
recommendation made by the jury.... We are constrained to hold," continued
the court, "that the sentence imposed is manifestly too severe."[50]

Another interesting case was decided by the Supreme Court of Kentucky
in 1968.[51] Richard Workman, a boy of fourteen, was convicted of rape and
sentenced to life imprisonment without parole. He claimed that when the
statute was applied to juvenile offenders, it constituted cruel and unusual
punishment prohibited by both state and federal courts. Relying on an earlier
decision,[52] the court set up three tests by which to determine whether an
excessive punishment had been inflicted. The first was whether it shocked
"the general conscience" and violated "the principles of fundamental fairness,"
according to "developing concepts of elemental decency." The second test was
whether it was "greatly disproportionate" when placed against the offense. The
third test was whether it went "beyond what is necessary to achieve the aim of
the public interest as expressed by the legislative act." By applying these three
tests, the court found that the punishment shocked "the general conscience of
society . . . [and was] intolerable to fundamental fairness." The court reasoned
that the legislature must have had in mind "dangerous and incorrigible individuals who would be a constant threat to society." Incorrigibility, suggested the
court, is "inconsistent with youth." Thus, the court held that life *without
parole*, when applied to juveniles, constitutes cruel and unusual punishment.

A final example occurred in 1971. There the Michigan Supreme Court
declared unconstitutional a statute that made mandatory a minimum of twenty
years imprisonment for the sale of marijuana. Eric Lorentzen, a twenty-three-
year old employee of General Motors, who lived at home with his parents and

had no prior record, had been convicted of making an unlawful sale of marijuana. The court noted that the statute was equally applicable to a first-offender high school student as to a "wholesaling racketeer." It was further noted that the penalties for other harmful substances were much less harsh. For example, the penalty for selling drugs to induce abortions was ninety days, for selling adulterated food ninety days, explosives five years, and a machine gun five years. Manslaughter carried a maximum sentence of fifteen years. "Tested by the provisions of other Michigan statutes dealing with offenses involving the sale of various substances, or with offenses against persons or property," stated the court, "the present mandatory minimum sentence for the sale of marijuana of the Michigan statute here under consideration clearly fails to meet the test of proportionality."[53]

8

Other Challenges Based on the Doctrine of Excessiveness

In the previous chapter *successful* challenges to specific punishments were reviewed. Tables 8-1 and 8-2 illustrate some of the unsuccessful challenges to punishments that to some may appear disproportionately harsh.

Habitual Offender Statutes

Habitual offender statutes, variously known as increased sentence statutes, enhanced punishment statutes, recidivist statutes, and multiple offender statutes, have long existed in both English and American jurisdictions.[1] The legislative history of such statutes suggests that they were passed to deter recidivism by making the risks great and to isolate from society persons who simply could not be deterred.[2] Today such statutes exist in all but six states.[3] Some states permit or make mandatory life terms of imprisonment for habitual offenders. Others allow the imposition of sentences ranging from five to fifty years.

From the very outset habitual offender statutes were challenged as unconstitutional on several grounds. They have been held not to inflict double jeopardy, violate ex post facto clauses, or deny equal protection of the law.[4] As early as 1874, the California Supreme Court held that an habitual offender statute did not inflict cruel and unusual punishment. The primary rationale was that there were similar statutes in other states, and that nowhere had they been declared cruel and unusual. The court also noted that it was up to the legislature and not the judiciary to determine the severity of the punishment.[5] This rationale was to be repeated in nearly all subsequent cases involving habitual offender statutes. The Illinois Supreme Court issued a similar ruling in 1886, the Michigan Supreme Court in 1890, the Massachusetts Supreme Judicial Court and the North Dakota Supreme Court in 1893, and the Missouri Supreme Court in 1894.[6] The United States Supreme Court reviewed the latter decision the following year. Frank Moore had received a life term of imprisonment as a result of a second conviction for larceny. Chief Justice Fuller, in very cursory fashion, cited three cases where state courts had upheld habitual offender statutes and concluded that it was "quite impossible" for the Court to conclude that the Supreme Court of Missouri erred in holding that the punishment was constitutional.[7]

Subsequently, several other state supreme courts held that habitual offender statutes did not inflict cruel and unusual punishment.[8] The United States Supreme

Table 8-1
Lengthy Sentences Upheld: 1789-1910

Sentence	Offense	Case and Citation
3 years	arson of outhouse	Hester v. State, 17 Ga. 130 (1855)
3 years	adultery	State v. Hazen, 39 Iowa 648 (1874)
7 years	burglary of bottle of sherry and some cigars	Cummins v. People, 42 Mich. 142 (1879)
10 years	forgery ($18 promissory note)	State v. Durston, 52 Iowa 635 (1879)
20 years	assault with intent to rape	Dykes v. State, 64 Ga. 437 (1879)
2 years	fraud of $3	State v. Williams, 12 Mo. App. 415 (1882)
50 years	robbery of $500	People v. Clary, 72 Cal. 59 (1887)
5 years	receiving stolen property valued at $1	People v. Smith, 94 Mich. 644 (1893)
2 years	being a disorderly person	People v. Kelley, 99 Mich. 82 (1894)
3.75 years	larceny of two kegs of brandy valued at $23	State v. Hall, 97 Iowa 400 (1896)
50 years	manslaughter	Jones v. Territory, 4 Okla. 45 (1896)
30 years	burglary of two jars of black-berries	Handy v. State, 46 Tex. Cr. R. 406 (1904)

Table 8-2
Lengthy Sentences Upheld: 1946-74

Sentence	Offense	Case and Citation
	Narcotics Offenses	
6 years	attempted possession, control, and transportation	State v. Thomas, 224 La. 431 (1953)
90 years	possession .05 grams mari-juana	Trevino v. State, 380 S.W. 2d 118 (Tex. Cr. App. 1963)
50 years	possession 1.41 grams mari-juana	Parson v. State, 432 S.W. 2d 89 (Tex. Cr. App. 1968)
30 years	possession of one marijuana cigarette	Rener v. Beto, 447 F. 2d 20 (5th Cir. 1971)
25 years	possession of heroin by an addict	Griggs v. State, 451 S.W. 2d 481 (Tex. Cr. App. 1970)
30 years	sale of one marijuana ciga-rette	Johnson v. Beto, 337 F. Supp. 1371 (S.D. Tex. 1972)
15 years	sale of one half ounce mari-juana	Lovett v. State, 479 S.W. 2d 286 (Tex. Cr. App. 1972)
60 years	sale of marijuana	White v. State, 495 S.W. 2d 903 (Tex. Cr. App. 1973)

Table 8-2 (Continued)

Sentence	Offense	Case and Citation
	Nonviolent Sex Offenses	
10 years	exposing private parts	Pineda v. State, 157 Tex. Cr. App. 609 (1952)
30 years	sodomy	Hoard v. Dutton, 360 F. 2d 673 (5th Cir. 1966)
21 years	sodomy	Carter v. State, 500 S.W. 2d 368 (Ark. 1973)
8 years	sodomy in auto by unmarrieds although a married couple could receive only $300 fine and one year in jail	Carter v. State, 500 S.W. 2d 368 (Ark. 1973)
2 years	transporting women for prostitution	Perry v. United States, 209 F. Supp. 691 (W.D. Ark. 1962)
	Gambling Offenses	
5 years	lottery violation by seventy-five-year-old man	Alspaugh v. State, 133 So. 2d 587 (Fla. 1961)
5 years	violation of lottery laws	Hurwitz v. State, 200 Md. 578 (1952)
2 years	carrying on lottery	Delnegro v. State, 198 Md. 80 (1951)
	Offenses Against Persons	
40 years	assault with intent to ravish	Thompson v. State, 251 S.C. 593 (1968)
20 years	assault	Adair v. State, 231 Md. 255 (1963)
1 year to life	robbery of 25¢	People v. Williams, 4 Ill. 2d 440 (1954)
1000 years	robbery by assault	Sills v. State, 472 S.W. 2d 119 (Tex. Cr. App. 1971)
1500 years	rape	Callins v. State, 500 P. 2d 1333 (Okla. Cr. 1972)
199 years	rape	People v. Dixon, 400 Ill. 449 (1948)
100 years	murder in second degree	People v. Rodgers, 30 Mich. App. 582 (1971)
	Offenses Against Property	
5 years	writing check of $13.32 without sufficient funds	State v. Nance, 20 Utah 2d 372 (1968)
21 years	passing forged checks of $42, $68, and $68	Govt. of Virgin Islands v. Venzen, 424 F.2d 521 (3d Cir. 1970)
life	breaking and entering auto, amount stolen less than $1, for one with two similar convictions	Jones v. State, 482 S.W. 2d 634 (Tex. Cr. App. 1972)

Table 8-2 (Continued

Sentence	Offense	Case and Citation
8 years	breaking and entering with intent to steal	State v. Price, 8 N.C. App. 94 (1970)

Miscellaneous Offenses

4 years	felony to insult the flag	Deeds v. State, 474 S.W. 2d 718 (Tex. Cr. App. 1972)
2 years	public drunkenness	State v. Driver, 262 N.C. 92 (1964)
5 years	draft card mutilation	Cooper v. United States, 403 F.2d 71 (10th Cir. 1968)
10 years	possession burglar tools	State v. Pulley, 216 S.C. 552 (1950)

Court in 1912 again reviewed a case involving such a contention. James H. Graham had been sentenced to two years in the penitentiary for grand larceny. Later, under the name of John H. Ratliff, he was found guilty of burglary and sentenced to ten years imprisonment. Still later, under the former name of James H. Graham, he was again convicted of grand larceny and sentenced to five years imprisonment. Eventually it was found out that Ratliff and Graham were one in the same, and subsequently the jury made judgment and he was sentenced to life imprisonment under the state's habitual offender statute. The Supreme Court noted: "The propriety of inflicting severer punishment upon old offenders has long been recognized in this country and in England."[9] Moreover, the punishment had been uniformly sustained in the state courts. Such a statute simply did not inflict cruel and unusual punishment.

Since 1912 literally dozens of similar cases have come before the courts. In all but one instance, the claim that the statute in question inflicted cruel and unusual punishment has been summarily rejected after fairly limited discussion. For example, in *Oyler* v. *Boles,* the United States Supreme Court stated: "The practice of inflicting severer penalties upon habitual offenders is no longer open to serious challenge."[10] Since 1946 no less than twenty-one jurisdictions have upheld habitual offender statutes.[11] However, more recently such statutes have come under renewed attack. Daniel Katkin, for example, claims that nowhere has the issue been squarely faced. To him, the "mere recital of the legitimate objectives of a statute ought not be considered sufficient analysis to defeat a claim that the means used are not constitutionally permissible."[12] He believes that if the Supreme Court would reexamine the issue it would strike down habitual offender statutes because they are not an effective deterrent, they isolate from society only comparatively petty offenders, and because persistent offenders are neither violent nor efficiently organized professional criminals. Most important, he argues, these statutes "mandate or permit the imposition of sentences the severity of which is out of all proportion to the specific offense which 'trigger' them."[13] He notes that under federal law a judge is permitted to extend the sentence of a third-felony offender to twenty-five years. Yet there are forty felonies in the United States Code which limit the sentence to a maximum of two years. Thus, a third conviction for interstate transportation of lottery tickets could trigger a twenty-five-year sentence.

Others have stopped short of suggesting that such statutes are unconstitutional, but have suggested that they are unwise. In 1948, for example, Paul W. Tappan sent letters and questionnaires on the subject to state attorneys general. He concluded that the "main trend of reaction" was "unfavorable."[14] Another scholar has suggested that courts actually refuse to apply habitual offender statutes to recidivists in many instances.[15]

On July 13, 1973, the Fourth Circuit Court of Appeals became the first court to hold a sentence imposed under an habitual offender statute constitutionally impermissible.[16] Although the court did not declare the statute null and void on its face, it did declare the sentence to be disproportionate to the offenses committed and thus in violation of the Eighth Amendment. Dewey Hart had been sentenced to life imprisonment under West Virginia's recidivist statute. The mandatory sentence was based on three prior convictions: writing a check on insufficient funds for $50, transporting across state lines forged checks in the amount of $140, and perjury. The first offense had been committed in 1949[17] and the second in 1955. The perjury conviction resulted from testimony given at his son's murder trial in 1968. Judge Craven, writing the opinion, noted that the first offense was "very nearly trivial" and that even the most serious conviction, perjury, had forced Hart into a "moral dilemma," whether to choose to tell the truth or to protect his family. Moreover, none of the offenses involved violence or danger of violence to persons or property. Judge Craven noted that life imprisonment traditionally had been reserved for the most violent and dangerous persons. "Aside from the proportionality principle," he added, "there aren't enough prisons in America to hold all the Harts that afflict us."[18]

The court further held that the sentence was "unnecessary to accomplish the legislative purpose of protecting society." When compared to other state statutes, it was found to be among the nation's most severe. Further, a comparison of punishments available in the same jurisdiction for other offenses indicated that life imprisonment could be levied for only three other crimes. "Can it be rationally urged," queried Judge Craven, "that Hart is as dangerous to society and as deserving of punishment as the murderer, rapist, and kidnapper?"[19] To the court the answer was, certainly not. Hart had been subjected to "irrationally disparate treatment." With these considerations in mind, the court concluded that the sentence imposed upon Hart was "constitutionally excessive and wholly disproportionate to the nature of the offenses he committed, and not necessary to achieve any legitimate legislative purpose."[20]

Multiple Sentences in Single Prosecutions

Three possibilities exist whereby a defendant participating in a single activity may be sentenced to multiple terms of imprisonment. First, statutes may separate each step in a given process. For example, the federal statutory scheme dealing with counterfeiting allows prosecution for possessing plates, concealing, manufacturing and possessing counterfeit money as well as actually buying, selling, exchanging, transferring, receiving, delivering, or passing counterfeit money.[21] Second, statutes unrelated to each other may overlap and allow multiple sentences. For example, the Harrison Act allows prosecution for the purchase, sale, distribution, dispensation, exchange, or gift of narcotics.[22] The act also prohibits the purchase, sale, or concealment of illegally imported drugs as well as the importation itself.[23] Thus, a single sale usually results in convictions on several counts.[24] A third possibility whereby a defendant may be sentenced to multiple terms of imprisonment is when, as the result of a single act, more than one victim is involved.[25]

Lengthy terms of imprisonment have often been imposed to run consecutively in the situations outlined above. Many times these sentences have been challenged as violating the Constitution. Usually they are attacked as contravening the double jeopardy clause of the Fifth Amendment. In a substantial number of instances such sentences have been challenged as excessive and thereby in violation of a cruel and unusual punishment inhibition. As early as 1811, Gibson Smith, sentenced to three years on each of two counts of counterfeiting, raised the issue. He contended that the "mode of accumulating the terms of imprisonment" was novel, cruel, and illegal.[26] The Supreme Court of Errors of Connecticut replied that "no injustice" had been done to the prisoner, because the proceeding had precedent in the law and had been used for many years throughout the state.

Nearly three-quarters of a century later, the Texas Court of Criminal Appeals issued a similar ruling and upheld a sentence of five years imprisonment on each of two separate counts for horse stealing.[27] The court asserted that separate convictions were in harmony with the common law, and that the stealing of each horse was a separate and distinct crime.

The United States Supreme Court first heard extended arguments on the subject in *O'Neil* v. *Vermont*.[28] John O'Neil had been found guilty of selling intoxicating liquor and was convicted on 307 separate counts. He was fined $6140 ($20 for each offense) and costs. Justice Blatchford noted that the Vermont Supreme Court had declared the statute and sentence valid on the grounds that O'Neil had committed "a great many" offenses, and as such, he had "subjected himself to a severe penalty." He also noted that the Vermont Supreme Court had suggested that " if the penalty were unreasonably severe for a single offense, the constitutional question might be urged." In the case at hand, however, the Court continued, "the unreasonableness is only in the number of offenses which the respondent has committed."[29] Justice Field, in dissent,

argued that it did not matter "that by cumulative offenses . . . the period prescribed by the sentence was reached." The punishment, he continued, "was
greatly beyond anything required by any humane law for the offenses."[30]

Despite the fact that the *Weems* decision[31] ultimately overturned the major
thrust of *O'Neil,* this aspect of Field's dissent has never become law.[32] One
court, however, as previously observed, has held a sentence of this nature unconstitutional.[33] John Garvey and others were convicted on seventy-two separate
counts of destroying plants in a public square. The offenses all took place within
one hour and forty minutes. One offense followed another "immediately and
consecutively." Because of this fact, the Louisiana Supreme Court deemed the
offense a continuing one, rather than separate and distinct ones, and consequently declared the sentence excessive and therefore cruel and unusual.

In 1916 the United States Supreme Court was asked for a second time to
consider the question. The defendant had been convicted of placing letters in
the mail to defraud. Seven counts resulted from the placing of seven separate
letters into a mailbox. Defendant Badders was sentenced to five years imprisonment, to run concurrently, and a fine of $1000 on each count ($7000 in all).
He alleged that the sentence was cruel and unusual. The Court unanimously
rejected his contention by simply asserting: "There is no doubt that the law
may make each putting of a letter into the post office a separate offense."[34]
Since that time the question has been litigated frequently in various state and
federal courts. Each time the sentence has been upheld as not inflicting cruel
and unusual punishment. Table 8-3 summarizes some of the more unusual
cases arising between 1946 and 1974.

Indeterminate Sentences

Most indeterminate sentence statutes were adopted in the late nineteenth
century.[35] The first was enacted in 1877 in New York.[36] The idea was to
individualize punishment to better fit the needs of the prisoner and society.
The statutes are principally of four types.[37] Most provide for minimum and
maximum limits. Others set the minimum but allow the judge or jury to establish the maximum. A third type sets the maximum and allows the judge or jury
to set the minimum. The fourth type authorizes the judge or jury to fix both
the minimum and maximum. No jurisdiction, however, has provided for a truly
indeterminate sentence whereby the defendant is imprisoned until administrative officials determine that he is rehabilitated.[38]

The principal constitutional objections to these statutes have been that they
permit an unlawful delegation of judicial power to an administrative body, that
they interfere with the pardoning power of the executive, that they violate the
separation of powers doctrine, that they are void for uncertainty, and finally,
that they inflict cruel and unusual punishment.[39] A few cases have held that
in the absence of any authorizing statute an indeterminate sentence is unconstitutionally cruel.[40] However, all attacks on indeterminate sentences imposed

Table 8-3
Multiple Sentence in Single Prosecutions Upheld: 1946-74

Sentence	Case and Citation
5 years on each of six counts for violating the National Firearms Act	United States v. Fleish, 90 F. Supp. 273 (E.D. Mich. 1949)
12 years for forgery and 3 for uttering a forged check	State v. Teague, 215 Ore. 609 (1959)
20 years on each of two counts of bank robbery	Pependrea v. United States, 275 F.2d 325 (9th Cir. 1960)
40 years on each of two sales of marijuana	Anthony v. United States, 331 F.2d 687 (9th Cir. 1964)
2 life sentences for second-degree murder	State v. McNally, 152 Conn. 598 (1965)
52 years total resulting from three narcotics sales	Hendrick v. United States, 357 F.2d 121 (10th Cir. 1966)
10-20 years on each of five counts of burglary	United States ex rel. Darrah v. Brierly, 290 F. Supp. 960 (E.D. Pa. 1968)
10 years on each of two counts of transporting forged instruments	Boerngen v. United States, 326 F.2d 326 (5th Cir. 1969)
21 years on each of three counts of burglary and larceny	In re Lara, 82 Cal. Rptr. 628 (1969)
15-20 years on each of three robbery counts and 3-5 for escape	State v. Burrell, 106 Ariz. 100 (1970)
9-10 years on each of several counts of receiving stolen motor vehicles	Guerro v. Fitzpatrick, 436 F.2d 378 (1st Cir. 1971)
20 years on each of two counts of assault with intent to commit murder and 90 years for one count of robbery	Cole v. State, 262 So. 2d 902 (Fla. App. 1972)

under statutory authority, when challenged as inflicting cruel and unusual punishment, have been rejected. A brief review of some of the early cases will illustrate the rationale which was more often used in such decisions.

In 1883, the Missouri Supreme Court upheld a statute that provided a two-year minimum for fraud, but established no maximum.[41] Essentially, the court argued that because the actual sentence imposed was not excessive, the defendant could raise no legal objections. Three years later, the North Carolina Supreme Court held a similar statute valid on the ground that the discretion of the judge had not been abused.[42] That same year the Kentucky Supreme Court upheld a similar statute on identical grounds.[43]

In 1894 the Illinois Supreme Court upheld a statute that provided only a maximum term of imprisonment, but allowed a board of managers to determine the actual duration short of it.[44] The court reasoned that the length of imprisonment is a matter of legislative discretion, and the court would not interfere unless it was degrading, unknown to the common law, had become obsolete, or shocked the moral sense of the community. Similar rationale is found in a later West Virginia case.[45] There the Supreme Court of West Virginia held constitutional an indeterminate sentence of up to twenty-five years imprisonment which had been imposed for attempted armed robbery. The defendant's allegation, that the statute inflicted cruel and unusual punishment because no maximum term of imprisonment was provided for by the statute under which he was sentenced, was rejected on the grounds that such statutes have been held valid elsewhere and that "in the exercise of its police power," the legislature had the authority to prescribe the punishment.

In 1896, the Supreme Judicial Court of Massachusetts upheld a statute that provided minimum and maximum terms of imprisonment, by simply asserting that "such a form of sentence does not make the punishment more severe than it otherwise would have been."[46] A similar statute was challenged in Indiana two years later. The idea of placing the restoration of one's liberty in his own hands, the court noted, was widely approved. "To call these provisions 'cruel punishment,' " the opinion continued, "is to mock all humanizing efforts."[47]

Despite the undeviating precedent for rejecting the allegation that indeterminate sentences inflict cruel and unusual punishment, the claim has been constantly asserted in recent years. Table 8-4 summarizes some of the more notable indeterminate sentences held constitutional since 1946.

Unequal Sentences for Codefendants

Disparate sentences are often imposed on codefendants charged with the same offense. Generally, but not always, the most obvious disparities result when the trials are separated. The defendant receiving the longest sentence has often challenged his sentence as cruel and unusual. Never, however, has such an allegation been successful. Generally it is rejected on the grounds that the facts of the case justify the disparity or that the sentence was well within the statutory limits.[48] For example, in 1883, Wren Talbot and Tom Jones were each convicted of horse stealing. Talbot pled guilty and received five years, and Jones pled not guilty and received ten years. The latter appealed on the grounds that the verdict was "inequitable, unjust and excessive" and that it must have been imposed "from mere wantonness or caprice." The court ruled that "Jones took these chances when he made his fight" and that the "only question" the court would consider was whether "it exceeded the limits prescribed by law."[49] As that situation did not exist, the court ruled against Jones.

The United States Supreme Court made the same point in *Howard* v. *Fleming.*[50] There the Court rejected the contention of two defendants that their ten-year sentences were cruel and unusual because a third defendant received only seven years. "Doubtless there were sufficient reasons for giving to one of the conspirators a less term than the others," stated the Court. "At any rate," the opinion continued, "there is no such inequality as will justify us in setting aside the judgment against the two."[51]

Table 8-4
Indeterminate Sentences Upheld: 1946-74

Offense and Sentence	Case and Citation
1 day–life for second-degree assault with intent to commit sodomy	People v. Kaganovitch, 146 N.Y.S. 2d 565 (1955)
to life for contributing to the delinquency of a minor	Jensen v. Gladden, 231 Ore. 141 (1962)
to life for rape	State v. Dixon, 238 Ore. 121 (1964)
to 10 years for assault and battery	Washington v. State, 2 Md. App. 633 (1967)
10-25 years for robbery	Taylor v. State, 251 Ind. 236 (1968)
35-105 years for manslaughter	Helms v. State, 456 P. 2d 907 (Okla. App. (1969)
to 75 years for second-degree murder	Pulver v. State, 93 Ida. 687 (1970)
to 3 years for theft of two boxes of candy	Hanson v. State, 48 Wis. 2d 203 (1970)
to 25 years for armed robbery	Mallon v. State, 49 Wis. 2d 185 (1970)
revocation of drivers license for life following three convictions of drunk driving	Campbell v. State, 491 P.2d 1385 (Colo. 1971)

Table 8-5 summarizes some of the more extreme cases where codefendants received disparate sentences. In each instance they were upheld as not inflicting cruel and unusual punishment.

Miscellaneous Sentences

Forfeiture of property (money and licenses) and of civil rights has been levied as punishment. The rationale in cases challenging such penalties is often very unclear. Generally there is confusion as to whether the punishment is objected to because of its severity or because the mode is cruel and unusual. Generally the former rationale is advanced, and for this reason all such decisions are included for discussion here.

Statutes requiring forfeiture of licenses granted by the state have long been held constitutionally permissible. For example, in 1873 the Chicago and Alton Railroad, for violating a statute that attempted to prevent "unjust discriminations and extortion in the rates charged," was fined $1000 and attorneys' fees, and required to forfeit its franchise.[52] In brief fashion the Illinois Supreme Court simply declared that the forfeiture, as provided in the statute, was not disproportionate. Similarly, in 1905 the Louisiana Supreme Court upheld the forfeiture of a liquor license for selling liquor on Sunday.[53] The court noted that such a penalty was permissible under the "police power" and that other states had upheld revocation. Three years later the Supreme Court of Washington cursorily dismissed a case in which a license had been forfeited for selling

Table 8-5
Unequal Sentences Upheld for Codefendants: 1946-74

Sentence	Offense	Case and Citation
defendant—death, co-defendant—5 years	same murder	Saucier v. State, 156 Tex. Cr. App. 301 (1950)
defendant—life, co-defendant—5 years	armed robbery	State v. Eckenfels, 316 S.W. 2d 532 (Mo. 1958)
defendant—5-7 years codefendant—20-30	homosexual activity	Perkins v. State, 234 F. Supp. 333 (W.D. N.C. 1964)
defendant—5 years codefendant—5 mos.	false income tax return	Hendrick v. United States, 357 F. 2d 121 (10th Cir. 1966)
defendant—5 years codefendant—6 mos.	arson	McGowen v. State, 221 Tenn. 442 (1968)
defendant—7½ years codefendant—3 years	breaking and entering	United States v. Edmo, 456 F. 2d 240 (9th Cir. 1972)

liquor to minors. The court simply asserted that no merit existed in the plaintiff's case.[54] The following year the Nebraska Supreme Court upheld the forfeiture of a license to sell intoxicating liquor after hours, because "there is no vested right in a license to sell intoxicating liquors which the state may not take away at pleasure."[55]

The sole exception to the above holdings occurred in Michigan. In that instance the forfeiture of a license by a druggist for five years was deemed excessive. The court reasoned that any "fine or penalty is excessive which seriously impairs the capacity of gaining a business livelihood."[56] Obviously other jurisdictions at the time did not agree.

The forfeiture of money clearly does not constitute a cruel and unusual punishment, nor does the sacrifice of double forfeiture. For example, charged with a gambling violation, Benjamin Novak was ordered to pay $1300 (double what he had won illegally in a poker game). The Supreme Judicial Court of Massachusetts held: "The punishment was not cruel or unusual, nor the forfeiture imposed excessive."[57]

Several states have provided that persons convicted of certain crimes shall forfeit one or more of their civil rights.[58] Often statutes prohibit one who has been convicted from holding public office. One of the first challenges to these statutes arose in New York in 1824. Jacob Barker was convicted on four counts of violating the act to suppress dueling. As part of the judgment, he was prohibited from "holding or being elected to any post of profit, trust or emolument, civil or military, under the State of New York."[59] Barker appealed on the ground that the judgment inflicted cruel and unusual punishment in violation of the United States Constitution. The court, however, refused to rule on the question because the Eighth Amendment was "inapplicable to offenses against a state."[60] Four years later the Tennessee Supreme Court ruled directly on the question. A Tennessee statute required that anyone convicted of illegal gaming (lottery) was to be fined and disqualified from holding public office in the future.[61] Two defendants, Smith and Lane, were convicted under the statute, but fined only. The attorney general appealed the decision and demanded that disqualification be attached to the judgment. Smith and Lane contended that such an imposition would be excessively severe for their relatively minor offense. Justice Catron, writing for the Tennessee Supreme Court, disagreed. He noted that there was a need to prevent such people from losing state money. It was reasonable to believe that if such persons held office the public money would be endangered. The act sought to reduce the possibility of embezzlement.[62]

The only other decision in which disqualification was challenged as constituting cruel and unusual punishment involved the legal profession. A.M. Henry, an attorney, was convicted of "moral turpitude" and was disbarred in accordance with the law. On appeal he alleged that such a penalty inflicted cruel and unusual punishment. The Idaho Supreme Court held otherwise. "We are unable to find any authority of well-founded reason," stated the court, "for upholding that contention."[63]

It has been argued that sentencing one to prison for a specified period of time, with no possibility of parole, constitutes cruel and unusual punishment. Four recent decisions have rejected this contention. In 1957, John D. Green was convicted of murder and sentenced to death. Governor Rolph of California commuted the sentence to life imprisonment on the condition that he not be paroled. Green claimed that life without possibility of parole constituted cruel and unusual punishment. The Ninth Circuit Court of Appeals rejected his contention because he had "made no showing of a violation of his rights." The court also noted that other jurisdictions had allowed this practice.[64] The following year the Fifth Circuit Court of Appeals issued a similar ruling.[65] Sam Lathem, a druggist, was tried and convicted on three counts of the unlawful sale of morphine, in violation of the Narcotic Drug Act. He was sentenced to two years on each of the first two counts, to run concurrently, and five years on the third count. He asked for probation on the third count, but was denied because the act excluded parole or probation for first-time offenders. Latham alleged, among other things, that such a provision inflicted cruel and unusual punishment. The court in cursory fashion rejected this allegation, stating that the punishment of imprisonment "is usual." In a similar case the Ninth Circuit Court of Appeals reasoned that not allowing parole was constitutional, because the statute represented "an appropriate legislative appraisal of the seriousness of those offenses."[66] Further, such a determination was well within the discretion of the legislature.[67] In one recent case, however, the Kentucky Supreme Court ruled that to imprison for life, without parole, two fourteen-year-old youths for the rape of an elderly woman was excessive and in violation of the Kentucky Constitution.[68]

9

Deportation, Banishment, and Expatriation

Deportation

Deportation is defined as the expulsion of an undesirable from a country.[1] It differs from "exclusion" in that the latter denies entry into a nation, while the former deprives a person already residing within the nation continuation of that privilege.[2] Deportation is also different from banishment; the former expels aliens, while the latter expels citizens. Today neither the excluded nor the deported may assert that he has been subjected to cruel and unusual punishment and hope to be successful. The primary reason is that deportation is not recognized as *punishment for crime.* The basis for this rationale is found in the *Fong Yue Ting* decision.[3] In that case the United States Supreme Court held constitutional a federal statute that provided for the removal of Chinese aliens. It noted that an order of deportation is not the same as punishment for a crime and is not generally considered banishment in the traditional sense. The removal was viewed simply as a method of sending a person back to his own country if he had not complied with the conditions of his stay. Thus, the cruel and unusual punishment provision had "no application."

Fong Yue Ting has subsequently been reaffirmed time and again.[4] For example, in 1910 a federal district judge in Oregon ruled specifically that the cruel and unusal punishment inhibition did not apply to the deportation of a Chinese laborer who was in the United States without a certification of residence as required by law.[5] A more recent example occurred in 1946. In that year the Ninth Circuit Court of Appeals ruled on a case involving several persons who had been ordered deported to the Netherlands East Indies. It was conceded that proper and fair hearings had been held. The fear of the parties was that if returned, they would be arrested as "disloyal and traitorous" subjects and be liable to severe punishment and possible execution. The court summarily rejected their allegation by asserting: "There is no merit in the contention that appellants' deportation would be cruel and unusual punishment and hence a violation of the Constitution of the United States. Deportation," continued the court, "is not punishment."[6] Thus, deportation has consistently been held not to constitute cruel and unusual punishment per se.[7]

Banishment

The term banishment developed in early England from three distinct sets of practices. One was that of sanctuary and abjuration. This practice allowed a criminal to flee to a refuge, whereupon, if he confessed his guilt within forty days, he was free to leave the country provided that he not return without the king's permission.[8] Technically such banishment was not regarded as a punishment, but simply a condition of pardon.[9]

The second practice resulted when bills of attainder came into use during the fourteenth century. Parliament simply enacted legislation punishing persons, usually for political reasons, by exile rather than by death or imprisonment.

The third practice, transportation, forced common criminals to leave a particular territorial unit and directed them to another. Usually there was continued loss of liberty once the transport reached his destination. Often those transported were indentured as well. The practice was developed in England during the seventeenth century. Essentially it was the outgrowth of two factors. Before this time, criminals under sentence of death had often been sent to sea as galley slaves. As sailing power replaced the galley, such labor was not needed. At the same time, there was a marked increase in crime. The problem remained what to do with criminals. One alternative was to execute them, but as Barnes has written: "Even the barbarous authorities of those days could not bring themselves to a thoroughgoing application of the death penalty which was prescribed for the great majority of crimes at the period."[10] The logical alternative was to send them to the new colonies. Final legislation was enacted in 1717. Thus, punishment by transportation in England was wholly the creature of statutory regulation and not a part of the common law.[11]

It is quite clear that the American colonies, at the outset, condoned the punishment of banishment.[12] However, as time wore on, it is equally clear that the punishment became more and more repulsive to the inhabitants. By the dawn of the American Revolution, opposition was so strong that several state constitutions contained restrictions on the punishment. Some constitutions explicitly prohibited banishment,[13] while others utilized the terms "transportation,"[14] "exile,"[15] or "outlawry."[16] Nevertheless, banishment has not been uniformly condemned as a form of punishment. In fact, a number of state constitutions have, by implication, given it constitutional sanction. For example, several have prohibited the exile of a person "but by the judgment of his peers or by the law of the land."[17] Similarly, an Oklahoma provision allows transportation if consent is given, or if it is accomplished by due process of law.[18] Other states allow for persons to be outlawed, if done so by their peers.[19]

Statutorily, banishment apparently has been provided in only one jurisdiction, and this outside the territorial limits of the United States. In 1902 the Supreme Court of the Philippines reviewed a statute that provided that those sentenced to *destierro* be excluded from entering within a radius of from twenty-five to two-hundred-fifty kilometers of a certain designated place. The court noted the punishment was not new nor limited to Spanish law. Furthermore, the contention that it inflicted cruel and unusual punishment had no basis because of the conjunctive between the words cruel and unusual. As such, the punishment had to be both cruel and unusual. Banishment was not deemed cruel, because it was viewed as less harsh than a prison sentence. Consequently, the statute was deemed constitutional. To rule otherwise, reasoned the court, "would prohibit the introduction in the manner of penalties, of new ideas intended to ameliorate the condition of criminals."[20]

Banishment As Punishment

Jurists have generally agreed that banishment is not per se unconstitutional. Early decisions lend support to this proposition. For example, in 1800 the United States Supreme Court suggested: "The right to confiscate and banish . . . must belong to every government."[21] In 1824 the General Court of Virginia upheld a sentence that transported a free black beyond United States' limits.[22] Moreover, banishment itself has never been declared cruel and unusual punishment. One the contrary, most courts have upheld the practice. In *People* v. *Potter*,[23] a New York court did so specifically. In 1884, a federal court implied that banishment was constitutional when it asserted: "No citizen can be excluded from this country *except* in punishment for crime."[24] In 1902, the Supreme Court of the Philippines ruled that banishment "can not be claimed to be a cruel punishment."[25] This decision was cited approvingly by the Montana Supreme Court in 1935.[26] In 1905 two United States Supreme Court Justices, Brewer and Peckham, implied that banishment, though the severest kind of punishment, was constitutional.[27] The closest any court has come to explicity suggesting that banishment is constitutionally impermissible came in 1962. The Ninth Circuit Court of Appeals, reviewing a six-month penitentiary sentence that was to be suspended on the condition that the defendant leave the country, held that the condition was equivalent to banishment, and as such was "either a 'cruel and unusual' punishment or a denial of due process of law. Be it one or the other," continued the court, "the condition is unconstitutional."[28]

Banishment As a Condition of Release

Occasionally, judges have granted release or suspension of sentence if the defendant would agree to leave the territorial confines of the jurisdiction. Judges in North Carolina have been particularly active in this respect. In 1892, for example, Phillip Hatley and others were convicted of keeping a disorderly house and sentenced to a year in jail. The sentences were to be suspended if they left the state within thirty days. Hatley contended that banishment as a punishment was illegal.[29] However, the court stated that the sentence could not be fairly construed as one of banishment. The judgment was twelve months in jail, and the words "but if the defendants leave" were held not to constitute part of that sentence. Rather, they "were manifestly intended only as a note or memorandum directing the Clerk to postpone the period at which the sentence . . . [should] . . . go into execution."[30]   The court claimed that it would be "desirable and beneficial both to the community in which they were engaged in keeping a disorderly and disreputable house, and to the defendants, in giving them an opportunity to reform under new surroundings."[31] However, by 1953 the rationale was clearly outdated.[32] In *State* v. *Doughtie,* the Supreme Court of North Carolina held that a sentence suspended on the condition that the defendant leave the state for two years was for "all practical effect a sentence of banishment or exile for two years."[33] As such, it was void.

Chief executives (governors) have occasionally granted pardons on the condition that the defendant leave the state. In *State* v. *Smith,*[34] the defendant had been convicted of stealing a slave and was sentenced to death. The governor granted him a pardon on the condition that he leave the state and never return. He eventually returned, and the court ruled that the original sentence be executed. Smith alleged that the governor did not have the authority to banish him, because such a punishment was not part of the common law or provided for in the Constitution.[35] The court held otherwise, essentially on the ground that a punishment could be used even if it was not known in the common law.

One of the first cases involving a cruel and unusual punishment claim arose in 1846. George Potter was sentenced to five years imprisonment for grand larceny, but was pardoned by the governor on the condition that he leave the United States and never return. Eventually he did return and was resentenced. On appeal he alleged, among other things, that because banishment was unknown to the law of New York, its imposition as a condition of the pardon violated the state inhibition against the infliction of cruel and unusual punishments. "There is no doubt," stated the court, "that any immoral, impossible, or illegal condition would be void." However, the opinion continued, "banishment is neither [cruel or unusual]. It is sanctioned by authority, and has been inflicted, in this form, from the foundation of our government."[36]

Several other jurisdictions have upheld the practice, although generally the cruel and unusual punishment challenge has not been advanced. For example, in *Ex parte Snyder,*[37] a pardon on the condition that the defendant leave the state of Oklahoma for twenty years was upheld as lawful because it was voluntary. Today it is clear that the governor has the power to issue such conditional pardons.[38] In only one instance has banishment as a condition of pardon been declared void, and this decision was disapproved of a short time later.[39]

Banishment As a Public Policy

As a matter of public policy, it is clear that banishment in this country has always been suspect. Early evidence of this is reflected in the numerous decisions that disallowed banishment on the grounds that it was not provided for by statute. The North Carolina Supreme Court so ruled in 1892.[40] In 1900 the Supreme Court of South Carolina held that the trial judge did not possess the right to impose "such a sentence as is involved in the perpetual banishment of the defendant from the State."[41] In 1927, a California court of appeals issued a similar ruling. Marguerito Lopez was convicted of assault with a deadly weapon and sentenced to jail. Upon completion of his sentence he was to be deported to Mexico. The appeals court disallowed the deportation, noting that "without passing upon the question as to whether the state may properly enact such legislation it is sufficient that it has not."[42] Another California court held that a condition of banishment was unlawful because it was not provided for by statute.[43] One of the most recent cases arose in Ohio. A young man named Kasnett was found guilty of defiling the flag (wearing it on the seat of his pants) and sentenced to banishment from Athens County for two years. "We are of the opinion," stated the Court of Appeals of Ohio, "that that portion of the sentence relating to banishment is clearly illegal and that the imposition . . . was a mistaken use of discretion."[44]

Another series of cases holds specifically that banishment is contrary to general public policy. Perhaps most important among these is the case of *People v. Baum*.[45] Eva Baum was convicted of violating liquor laws and sentenced to leave the state for the period of her probation (five years). She contended that such a punishment was cruel and unusual. The Michigan Supreme Court noted specifically that banishment was not cruel and unusual at the common law. However, the court did flatly state: "Such a method of punishment is not authorized by statute, and is impliedly prohibited by public policy."[46] The rationale was predicted on the fact that one state should not dump its convicts on another, because the injured state might feel entitled to exercise its police and military power to repel the undesirables. Further, the practice would tend to incite dissension and "disturb that fundamental equity of political rights among the several States which is the basis of the Union itself."[47]

The North Carolina Supreme Court reiterated this sentiment in a 1953 case. Robert E. Doughtie was convicted of assault with a deadly weapon and sentenced to two years on the road, to be suspended if he left the state and did not return for the two years. The court noted that banishment "was beyond the power of the court to inflict," that it was not "consistent with the proper punishment for crime," and further, that it was "not sound public policy to make other states dumping grounds for criminals."[48] Similarly, in the *Kasnett* case referred to earlier, Justice Stephenson of the Ohio court, writing a concurring opinion, stated that he agreed with the majority when they held: "The imposition of banishment is illegal for the reason that such condition is contrary to public policy."[49]

The status of banishment today is somewhat uncertain. It clearly has never been in accord with general public policy. This is probably due to the late birth-

date of the United States, the bitterness instilled in the colonists by the English
system of transportation, and the general dislike for bills of attainder, which
were prohibited in the United States Constitution. Banishment as a direct
punishment probably is constitutionally impermissible. Although it has never
been directly declared unconstitutional by the United States Supreme Court,
the *Dear Wing Jung* case[50] probably reflects contemporary thinking. As it will
be recalled, the Court ruled that banishment was either a cruel and unusual
punishment or a violation of due process.

Equally suspect is the practice, occasionally utilized by judges, of releasing
convicts on condition that they leave the state. To date, many such sentences
have been vacated on the ground that the judge has exceeded his authority,
because the punishment is not provided for by law. However, it is quite clear
that governors have the authority to grant conditional pardons.[51] The practice
of granting pardons on condition of banishment extends well into the common
law. It can be traced to the practice of sanctuary and abjuration. Many courts
have noted that a pardon is an act of grace and mercy, and as such, the governor
may impose any condition he pleases as long as it is not immoral or impossible
to comply with. Others have taken the view that the convict is free to reject
the pardon, and therefore, it is permissible because it is voluntary. Finally,
others have argued that the separation of powers doctrine prohibits courts
from reviewing conditions of pardon offered by the executive.

Expatriation

Expatriation is defined as "the voluntary abandonment of nationality or
allegiance."[52] The United States Constitution makes no provision for either
voluntary or involuntary expatriation. However, the courts have consistently
upheld Congress' right to enact such legislation based upon its power to regulate
foreign relations.[53] Nevertheless, relatively few such statutes existed in the
United States until the twentieth century.[54] The three most comprehensive
statutes were passed in 1907, 1940, and 1954.[55] Contrary to the common law
practice, both Congress and the courts have long recognized the right of citizens
to expatriate themselves voluntarily.[56] It appears there have been few if any
constitutional objections to these procedures. Congress has also provided for
quasi-voluntary expatriation, whereby a citizen loses his citizenship if he per-
forms certain acts. Table 9-1 summarizes most of these. Many have been
attacked as unconstitutional. The only successful attack at the Supreme Court
level involving a cruel and unusual punishment inhibition came in 1958.[57]
Albert Trop, a twenty-year-old private, had been stationed in French Morocco
during World War II. For a breach of discipline he was confined to the local
military stockade. Finding conditions intolerable, he escaped but surrendered
himself the very next day to an American Army officer. During the interim he

Table 9-1
Acts Accruing Loss of Citizenship

Acts	Statute
Resumption of foreign residence by a naturalized citizen	34 Stat. 1228 (1907)
Marriage to an alien	34 Stat. 1228 (1907)
Naturalization by a foreign state	54 Stat. 1168 (1940)
Swearing allegiance to a foreign state	54 Stat. 1169 (1940)
Service in foreign armed forces	54 Stat. 1169 (1940)
Accepting foreign employment for nationals only	54 Stat. 1169 (1940)
Voting in a foreign election	54 Stat. 1169 (1940)
Dual national choosing another state at the age of majority	54 Stat. 1169 (1940)
Act of treason	54 Stat. 1169 (1940)
Six months residence abroad if a dual national	54 Stat. 1169 (1940)
Renunciation of United States	58 Stat. 677 (1944)
Loss by evading induction	58 Stat. 746 (1944)
Loss by desertion	54 Stat. 1169 (1946)

did not contact the enemy. For his offense he was convicted by a court-martial of desertion, and was sentenced to three years at hard labor, forfeiture of all pay and allowances, and was given a dishonorable discharge. In 1952 he applied for a passport, but was denied on the ground that he had lost his citizenship because of the conviction. In 1955 he sought a declaratory judgment stating that he was a citizen, but he was denied, as was his subsequent appeal.[58] The Supreme Court granted certiorari, and Chief Justice Warren wrote the opinion of the Court. He first noted that citizenship could be relinquished in two ways, either by "express language" or by "conduct that show[s] a renunciation of citizenship."[59] Since Trop had obviously not done the former, the real arguments revolved around the latter. The chief justice reasoned that by Trop's "conduct" he had not lost his citizenship, because desertion in wartime "does not necessarily signify allegiance to a foreign state."[60] Thus, the case at hand was considerably different from other cases the Court had recently decided. For example, in *Perez* v. *Brownell*,[61] decided the same day, the Court upheld the denationalization of a citizen who had voted in a foreign election. This was allowable, stated the Court, because voting in foreign elections might create international problems for the government. As such, Congress had, in the exercise of its foreign affairs power, the authority to prevent such a happenstance. In the *Trop* case, however, Chief Justice Warren noted, denationalization "is not even claimed to be a means of solving international problems. . . . Here the purpose is punishment, and therefore the statute is a penal law."[62]   In other words, expatriation for wartime desertion did not bear enough relation to the exercise of the war powers by Congress to hold the punishment valid.

Because the statute was deemed penal in nature, the question became: Did it abridge the Eighth Amendment? After noting that the Eighth Amendment was not "static" and that it must draw its meaning from the "evolving standards of decency that mark the progress of a maturing society," the chief justice concluded that the use of denaturalization as a punishment is barred by the Eighth Amendment. He noted that there is no "physical mistreatment" or "primitive torture," but instead there was "the total destruction of the individual's status in organized society. It is a form of punishment," he continued, "more primitive than torture, for it destroys for the individual the political existence that was centuries in the development."[63]

Justice Frankfurter, joined by Justices Burton, Clark and Harlan, dissented. After raising the timeworn objections to judicial activisim, he directly confronted the allegation based on the Eighth Amendment. Basic to his argument was the idea that denationalization was not really punishment "in any valid constitutional sense." It was viewed simply as a consequence of conduct that had elsewhere been made unlawful. It was no more of a punishment than was the "loss of civil rights as a result of conviction for a felony."[64] Furthermore, assuming *arguendo* that denationalization is a punishment, to insist that it is cruel and unusual punishment, Justice Frankfurter contended, "is to stretch that concept beyond the breaking point." Can it be "seriously urged," he later wrote, "that loss of citizenship is a fate worse than death?"[65]

Reaction to the decision was immediate. Newspapers noted the case, and articles appeared in many of the weekly magazines.[66] The law reviews were filled with an unprecedented number of critiques on the subject. Some went so far as to reprint the decision in its entirety.[67] Others simply reported the decision in an objective manner.[68] Some clearly favored the decision,[69] but none vigorously opposed it.

Two years later a case involving many of the same issues came before the federal district court in the District of Columbia. Joseph Cort, a citizen by birth, was declared to have lost his American citizenship because he had remained outside the United States, ostensibly to avoid military service. He had originally left the United States to work in England. In September 1953 he was ordered to report for induction. He then left for Czechoslovakia to work, as England at the time was under pressure not to renew his residency permit. In 1959 he applied for, but was denied, a passport on the ground that he had expatriated himself. Cort sought a declaratory judgment that he was a citizen, alleging that the statute inflicted cruel and unusual punishment. Judge Matthews noted that while the provision involved in *Trop* was somewhat different than in *Cort,* nevertheless, they were essentially alike: "The former decrees that conviction and dishonorable discharge for desertion in war time give rise to loss of citizenship," while "the latter decrees such loss for departing from or remaining outside the United States to avoid service in the armed forces during war time."[70] Thus, the court perceived "no substantial difference" between the cases, and as such, the *Trop* ruling was controlling and the statute was deemed unconstitutional.[71]

Six years later another district court became involved with the claim of an expatriate.[72] Beys Afroyim, a naturalized citizen, went to Israel in 1950 and voted in an election the following year. In 1960 he sought a passport to return to the United States, but was denied on the ground that he had expatriated himself. He claimed, among other things, that the statute inflicted cruel and unusual punishment. Judge Bryan, however, rejected the allegation. He carefully distinguished Afroyim's situation from Trop's. The cruel and unusual punishment inhibition was inapplicable in the present case, he contended, because the penalty is nonpenal in nature. It is exactly the situation that existed in *Perez*.[73] The statute was "designed to prevent international or unwitting interference with the foreign relations of the United States by an American citizen abroad."[74] Thus, the purpose of the statute was regulatory and not penal. The United States Court of Appeals for the Second Circuit affirmed the decision,[75] and the United States Supreme Court granted certiorari. Although the Eighth Amendment allegation was presented, the Court avoided discussing it, holding that the statute was unconstitutional because the Fourteenth Amendment prevents Congress from taking away citizenship without a citizen's assent.[76] The Court also specifically overruled *Perez*. A more recent case, *Rogers* v. *Bellei*,[77] considerably weakens the precedent of *Afroyim*. Again, however, although the Eighth Amendment allegation was raised, the Court simply ignored it in favor of other constitutional provisions.[78]

10 Status Statutes and Cruel and Unusual Punishment

Offenses have been traditionally defined in terms of acts or failures to act.[1] However, some offenses are defined in terms of *being* rather than in terms of *acting*. For example, many states have made it a crime *to be* a vagrant, a common prostitute, a common drunkard, a common gambler, or a beggar.[2] Some statutes make it a crime to be a narcotic addict.[3] Such statutes have long been attacked as unconstitutional, usually on the grounds that they excessively restrict liberty, are unconstitutionally vague, or are void because of overbreadth.

Prior to 1962 only one court had held that a "status statute" inflicted cruel and unusual punishment.[4] In *Stoutenburgh* v. *Frazier,*[5] the defendant was convicted of *being* a "suspicious person" and fined $40, in default of which he was to spend four months in the workhouse. The Court of Appeals for the District of Columbia stated: "It would be a cruel and unnatural punishment to impose fine and imprisonment upon a party, because he might happen to be regarded by some persons as a *suspicious person,* without anything more."[6] Judge Alvey noted that although many such laws existed in England, they had become "obsolete" because they imposed "severe restrictions upon the liberties of the people," and because such "cruel and unnatural punishments" had long since become inapplicable to modern society. Thus, the statute was held unconstitutional. It was not until 1962, however, that the United States Supreme Court rendered a decision of a similar nature.

To be a Narcotic Addict

One evening on a street in Los Angeles, Lawrence Robinson was stopped by a police officer, who noticed certain markings and discolorations on both of Robinson's arms.[7] Upon inquiry, Robinson admitted the occasional use of narcotics. He was taken to Central Jail in Los Angeles, and the next morning a member of the Narcotic Division of the Los Angeles Police Department examined him. It was the expert's opinion that the markings were caused by the injection of unsterile needles into the flesh several days before. He also noted that at the time Robinson *was not* under the influence of narcotics. Nevertheless, he was charged with violating the statute, which in part stated: "No person shall use, *or* be under the influence of narcotics."[8]

At the conclusion of the trial the jury was instructed that it was "a misdemeanor for a person 'either to use narcotics, or to be addicted to the use of

97

narcotics.' " The judge further instructed the jury that the defendant could be convicted under a general verdict if they agreed *either* that he was of the "status" *or* had committed the "act" denounced by the statute. Thus charged, the jury rendered a verdict of guilty, making no distinction as to which part of the statute Robinson had violated.

On appeal the United States Supreme Court reversed. After noting the facts of the case and discussing the state's police power, Justice Stewart, writing the opinion of the Court, turned a new page in the historical development of the Eighth Amendment. He noted that the statute did not punish a person for using, purchasing, selling, or possessing a narcotic, or for antisocial or disorderly behavior. Rather, it made the "status" of narcotic addiction a criminal offense, for which the offender may be prosecuted at any time before he reforms. Justice Stewart hypothesized that it was unlikely that a state would make it a criminal offense for a person to be mentally ill, or a leper, or to be afflicted with a venereal disease. Making a criminal offense of a disease, he asserted, "would doubtless be universally thought to be an infliction of cruel and unusual punishment in violation of the Eighth and Fourteenth Amendments."[9] He believed the statute in this case to be of the same category. Similarly, Justice Douglas concurring, wondered how *being an* addict could be punished as a crime, for "if addicts can be punished for their addition," he reasoned, "then the insane can also be punished for their insanity."[10]

Justices Clark and White dissented. The former viewed the entire system of narcotic prevention, control, and treatment as "comprehensive and enlightened." He noted that the majority conceded that a state might establish programs of compulsory treatment for these people, which would be civil in nature. Justice Clark believed that this is exactly what California had done. "The majority's error," he insisted, "is in instructing the California Legislature that hospitalization is the *only treatment* for narcotics addiction—that anything less is a punishment denying due process."[11] California found otherwise after extensive study, he asserted, and thus provided imprisonment for volitional addicts. The mere fact that the statute is labeled "criminal," he concluded, "seems irrelevant."

Justice White dissented, because he did not believe the appellant's conviction rested upon sheer status, condition, or illness. He believed Robinson's conviction resulted because of "regular, repeated or habitual use of narcotics immediately prior to his arrest."[12] As to the cruel and unusual punishment allegation, he found it "so novel" that he suspected that the Court was "hard put to find a way to ascribe to the Framers of the Constitution the result reached . . . rather than to its own notions of ordered liberty."[13]

The *Robinson* case inspired an unprecedented number of critiques in the law journals.[14] If any conclusion can be drawn, it is that the decision raised more questions than it answered. For example: Upon precisely what constitutional principle was the holding based?[15] What guidelines did the Court set forth for future litigation?[16] Did the opinion apply to other areas involving status, such as alcoholism?[17] Did the Court allow application of criminal sanctions to the *use* of narcotics? And was it the "imprisonment" which was cruel and unusual, or the "conviction"?[18] Nonetheless, there is general consensus that the Court declared narcotic addiction to be a disease, that states may civilly but not criminally confine addicts for treatment, and that statutes that make "status" a crime are unconstitutional because they inflict cruel and unusual punishment. There was further agreement that the case was purposefully written to be very restrictive and applied only to the specific case at hand involving a particular local law as construed by a particular state court.

One of the main objections to the opinion was that the Court utilized the wrong vehicle to arrive at its decision. For example, Robert Enloe pointed out that the statute could have been voided because of its vagueness, a well-established principle for nullifying state statutes.[19] Another writer suggested that the Court could have declared the statute unconstitutional, because it failed to require proof of an illegal act within the punishing jurisdiction.[20] Calvin E. Robinson suggested that the Court could have decided the case. without reaching the constitutional issue at all, by simply asserting that there are limits to state control, and the right of privacy is one of them.[21]

Perhaps the strongest attack came from Michael R. Asimow, writing in the *California Law Review.*[22] In his opinion the Court's rationale was questionable for two reasons. First, he noted that there is no reason to classify addiction exclusively as an illness. He suggested that the Court should have "balanced" the criminal, public policy, and medical aspects of the case, and that sometimes criminal penalties might outweigh the medical and psychological aspects.

Second, Asimow observed that not all addicts are "punished" in California. Borrowing from Justice Clark's dissenting opinion, he noted that the Court failed to take into account the various methods used in the state for treating those convicted under the statutes. These ranged "on a broad continuum from outright punishment through what could be deemed treatment."

A great deal of speculation was raised as to what the long-range impact of the decision would be. Those fearing a broad interpretation suggested that the decision might grow to include common drunks, tramps, beggars, prostitutes, habitual criminals, sexual deviants, pyromaniacs, and kleptomaniacs.[23] On the other hand, a number of scholars apparently hoped that the decision would make way for a reevaluation of criminal responsibility in cases involving insanity.[24] Others apparently hoped that the decision might apply to sterilization of the feeble-minded.[25] Still others apparently hoped that the decision might be extended to cover conduct that is but an incident of the disease.[26] Presumably, under this view, it might be claimed that making it a crime to steal money to support a habit would be unconstitutional.[27]

Enough time has passed to draw some general conclusions about the impact of *Robinson.* Generally speaking, the United States Supreme Court and the lower courts have taken a very restrictive view of the decision. In the first place, courts have made a distinction between civil and criminal commitment. For example, less than a year after *Robinson*, the California Supreme Court reviewed a case involving the same statute.[28] David De La O was convicted of "being addicted to drugs." Immediately after his conviction he was granted a hearing, and it was determined that he was an addict. The court then committed him to the California Rehabilitation Center. He applied for a writ of habeas corpus. The California Supreme Court denied his allegation that the whole process was unconstitutional under *Robinson,* basically because his final confinement was civil rather than criminal. The United States Supreme Court refused to grant certiorari, thereby giving a first indication that *Robinson* was not to be interpreted broadly.

Second, the courts have refused to extend the doctrine to overt acts. For example, the Wisconsin Supreme Court issued a ruling in 1964 upholding a statute that prohibited self-administration of a narcotic drug.[29] Similarly, in *Castle* v. *United States,*[30] the defendant had been convicted of purchasing drugs. The Circuit Court for the District of Columbia upheld the sentence, despite Castle's argument that *Robinson* prohibited conviction and sentence when the purchase was made to sustain his nonvolitional needs. Again, in *Hutchenson* v. *United States,*[31] the same circuit court upheld the conviction of a defendant for possessing drugs despite his argument that there was no meaningful difference between punishment for being an addict and punishing an addict for possession of drugs he requires.

The final means by which courts have restricted *Robinson* in the area of narcotics addiction has been to interpret statutes as applying to acts rather than status. In 1963, for example, a Louisiana statute quite similar to that of California was held constitutional on the ground that it applied to the actual "use" of narcotics.[32] Similarly, the New Jersey Supreme Court upheld the conviction of William Margo for being under the influence of drugs because this was not a status conviction, but a conviction for an act.[33]

There have been three exceptions to this general trend. In *People* v. *Davis,*[34] the Illinois Supreme Court rejected the argument that an Illinois statute, one almost identical with that found in *Robinson,* was meant to punish the "use" rather than the "status." As such, the statute was declared unconstitutional. Similarly, in Missouri, Walter Bridges was convicted of being addicted to a narcotic drug, and the State Supreme Court held unconstitutional that portion of the statute making mere addiction punishable by imprisonment.[35] Three years later the Supreme Court of Kentucky reviewed a statute that provided: "Any peace officer . . . who hears a person state that he is addicted to the use of narcotics, shall immediately arrest such person."[36] Construing the statute literally, the court reasoned that a person addicted to narcotics commits a crime the moment he sets foot within the state, even if he has entered for hospitalization. Thus, the statute was declared unconstitutional.

To Be an Alcoholic

One area in which the lower courts have been asked to enter as a result of *Robinson* is that of alcoholism. The first case that relied upon the decision was *Driver* v. *Hinnant.*[37] Joe B. Driver was convicted of violating a North Carolina statute making it a misdemeanor to appear in public in an intoxicated condition. Circuit Judge Bryan accepted his contention that this was cruel and unusual punishment under the Robinson doctrine and held the statute unconstitutional. He noted that Driver was beyond the shadow of a doubt a chronic alcoholic who was powerless to stop drinking, that his type of addiction was almost universally recognized as a disease, and "when that is the conduct for which he is criminally accused, there can be no judgment of criminal conviction passed upon him."[38] Thus, it was deemed unconstitutional to punish criminally persons for an act symptomatic of their disease.

The *Driver* decision was reinforced two months later in *Easter* v. *District of Columbia.*[39] Faced with the same problem, the District of Columbia court reversed a conviction for public drunkenness, holding chronic alcoholism to be a defense. Although the court did not specifically rely on *Robinson,* the case was cited several times.

Conversely, other lower courts immediately thereafter made the distinction between punishing drunkenness and punishing a drunk who appears in public. In *People* v. *Hoy,*[40] for example, Justice Quinn concluded that while prison is not the most appropriate place for chronic alcoholics, the court was not prepared to say it is cruel and unusual punishment to place them there for their own protection as well as that of the general public. Similarly, in *Seattle* v. *Hill,*[41] the Supreme Court of Washington held that while chronic alcoholism may be regarded as a disease for medical purposes, nonetheless, it does not immunize the defendant from prosecution for being drunk in public. "In the instant case," stated Justice Hale, "it was Mr. Hill's conduct, his actions in public while drunk, which caused his arrest and confinement, not his status or condition of being an alcoholic."[42]

The United States Supreme Court did not have an opportunity to review such cases until 1966. At that time a case did seem to present the Court with an opportunity to consider the problem. Nonetheless, certiorari was denied over the vigorous protest of Justices Fortas and Douglas.[43] The next year, however, the Court accepted a similar case.[44] In December of 1966, LeRoy Powell had been arrested and charged with violating a Texas statute that provided: "Whoever shall get drunk or be found in a state of intoxication in any place, or at any private house except his own, shall be fined not exceeding one hundred dollars."[45] Powell was convicted and fined twenty dollars. He appealed to the county court, contending that he was "afflicted with the disease of chronic alcoholism," and thus his appearance in public while drunk was not of his own volition. To punish him for such conduct, he contended, was to inflict cruel and unusual punishment.

The county judge ruled that as a matter of law, chronic alcoholism was not a defense to the charge. Powell thereupon appealed to the United States Supreme Court. Justice Marshall, joined by Chief Justice Warren and Justices Black, Harlan and White, wrote the opinion of the Court. He noted that on its face the statute did not fall within the Robinson holding. Powell was convicted, not for being a chronic alcoholic, but for being in public while drunk. Thus, Texas was not punishing mere status as California had done in *Robinson*. Behavior was being punished. "This seems a far cry," stated Justice Marshall, "from convicting one for being an addict, being a chronic alcoholic, being 'mentally ill, or a leper.' "[46] Furthermore, he later noted: "If LeRoy Powell cannot be convicted of public intoxication, it is difficult to see how a State can convict an individual for murder if that individual, while exhibiting normal behavior in all other respects, suffers from a 'compulsion' to kill, which is an 'exceedingly strong influence,' but 'not completely overpowering.' "[47]

Justice Black, joined by Justice Harlan, concurred in a separate opinion. He noted that the jailing of chronic alcoholics could be defended on therapeutic grounds. Such action, he contended, may prevent physical harm to themselves as well as to others. They are given food, clothing and shelter. Further, he alleged, civil commitment facilities might be no better than the jails they would replace.

Justice White concurred separately on essentially the same grounds, adding: "The alcoholic is like a person with small pox, who could be convicted for being on the street but not for being ill, or like the epileptic, who could be punished for driving a car but not for his disease."[48] He did intimate, however, that if it could be proven that Powell could not control his movements, and for that reason appeared in public, the punishment might be cruel and unusual. The record, however, was devoid of such evidence.

Justice Fortas, joined by Justices Douglas, Brennan and Stewart, dissented. He noted that Powell was afflicted with a chronic disease that had destroyed his power of self-control, and that his appearance in public was nonvolitional. The sole question, reasoned Justice Fortas, was "whether a criminal penalty may be imposed upon a person suffering the disease of 'chronic alcoholism' for a condition—being 'in a state of intoxication' in public."[49] In other words, to Justice Fortas, the Court was dealing with a statute that made the "mere condition of being intoxicated in public" a crime. Furthermore, he noted, the jailing of chronic alcoholics is punishment and, contrary to Justice Marshall's claim, it is not "therapeutic." The jails, he continued, are overcrowded and are not suited for such use. Thus, the statute was within the bounds of *Robinson*.[50]

To Be a Vagrant

Another area the courts have been asked to enter as a result of *Robinson* is vagrancy. The offense has been criminal, at one time or another, in virtually every state.[51] Many such statutes have been declared unconstitutional because of vagueness or overbreadth.[52] However, several recent cases involving vagrancy statutes have been challenged as inflicting cruel and unusual punishment.

The first hint that vagrancy statutes might be successfully challenged under the Robinson doctrine came in 1966. In a dissenting opinion, Justice Douglas exclaimed: "I do not see how economic or social status can be made a crime any more than being a drug addict can be."[53] The following year the Supreme Court of Nevada actually held two vagrancy statutes unconstitutional because they punished status.[54] In the first, a Reno ordinance prohibited persons of evil reputation (defined as anyone convicted of a felony, misdemeanor or gross misdemeanor involving moral turpitude, or anyone who had the general reputation in the community of being a prostitute, panderer, narcotics user, burglar or thief) from consorting for an unlawful purpose. Proof of "evil reputation" was prima facie evidence "that such consorting was for an unlawful purpose." After a conviction, and on subsequent appeal, it was contended that due process was denied, since the effect of the ordinance was to make status a crime. Although the court did not explicitly declare that the ordinance inflicted cruel and unusual punishment, it did declare that it was unconstitutional because on its face the effect was to make status a crime.

A short while later the same court declared a Las Vegas ordinance unconstitutional that made it a criminal offense to be a disorderly person.[55] A disorderly person was defined as one who had the physical ability to work, but had no visible means of support and was in a public place. Again, the court did not explicitly declare the ordinance unconstitutional for inflicting cruel and unusual punishment. However, the court did state that the ordinance could not be enforced because its effect was to make the status of poverty a crime. As such it violated due process.

In 1969 two cases came before federal district courts which dealt directly with vagrancy statutes and the Robinson doctrine. In *Goldman* v. *Knecht,*[56] the plaintiff was threatened with prosecution under a Colorado vagrancy statute. The statute defined a vagrant as "a person able to work an honest and respectable calling, who is found loitering or strolling about, frequenting public places where liquor is sold, begging or leading an idle, immoral or profligate course of life, or not having any visible means of support."[57] After declaring the statute unconstitutional because of overbreadth and vagueness, and because it denied equal protection, the court noted that the statute was vulnerable to a fourth attack: "The legislative effort to create a crime out of status or conditions as opposed to behavior."[58] The court noted that recent Supreme Court decisions had condemned legislative efforts of this kind, especially in *Robinson* v. *California.* "If addiction to narcotics is a status which the legislature cannot validly declare to be a crime under *Robinson,*" stated the court, "it follows that the Colorado attempt to declare idleness or indigency coupled with being able-bodied must also . . . be held beyond the power of the state legislative body."[59]

The second case, *Wheeler* v. *Goodman*,[60] involved twelve "hippies." Police in Charlotte, North Carolina apparently decided the youths were undesirable and systematically harassed them by making unlawful threats, interrogations, searches and seizures, by serving two unlawful eviction notices, and finally, by arresting eighteen people inside a house for vagrancy.[61] The court noted that "no overt act was required to convict for vagrancy—only indigency and idleness, coupled with ability to work." Further, the due process clause of the Fourteenth Amendment, the court continued, prohibits, as cruel and unusual, the punishment of status, and status, even that of a gambler or prostitute, may not be made criminal. Thus, the statute was unconstitutional.[62]

To Be a Prostitute or Homosexual

Another area the courts have been asked to enter as a result of *Robinson* has involved sexual offenses. In a case involving prostitution, Carole Anderson was indicted by a grand jury in the state of Minnesota for violation of a state statute.[63] She was found guilty and sentenced to a year in the Minneapolis workhouse. Appealing to the Minnesota Supreme Court, she alleged that the statute inflicted cruel and unusual punishment, essentially claiming that prostitution was a sickness and not a crime, and therefore should not be punished. The court rejected this allegation, claiming that it did not merit any discussion.

Several cases have arisen involving homosexuals. In 1964, Max D. Perkins and Robert E. McCorkle were convicted of "unlawfully, willfully, maliciously and feloniously committing the abominable and detestable crime against nature with each other." Perkins was sentenced to between twenty and thirty years imprisonment. He appealed the sentence on Eighth Amendment grounds. The court immediately noted that "imprisoning Perkins for his homosexual conduct is not unlike putting a person in jail for being addicted to the use of drugs, as was done in *Robinson* v. *California.*"[64] However, the court continued, *Robinson* dealt with status and here "Perkins was convicted of an overt *act.*" In other words, the court made the status/act distinction so often utilized in cases involving addicts and alcoholics.[65]

In several other instances, homosexuals have invoked the Robinson doctrine. In 1967 two cases arose in California. In one a defendant had been convicted of homosexual activity in a park's public rest room.[66] Upon review Justice Elkington rejected the contention as not being "reasonably applicable." In the other, George D. Frazier had been convicted of sodomy while incarcerated in prison.[67] He argued that further imprisonment for homosexual acts was "unreasonable and ineffective, and indeed cruel." Justice Draper, however, rejected his allegation, because no authority was cited and the court could find none. The following year the Michigan Court of Appeals reviewed the case of a defendant who had been convicted of indecent exposure and sentenced as a sexual delinquent person. The penalty for exposure by a nonsexual delinquent was a maximum of one year and by a sexual delinquent, up to life. The defendant claimed that the added penalty for "a sexual delinquent person constituted criminal punishment of a mental condition or status" and was therefore a cruel and unusual punishment. The court, however, rejected his claim. It did not view *Robinson* as controlling "for the reason that the sexual delinquent provision was not directed toward mental condition or status."[68] The court construed the provision as "excluding those persons who suffer from a mental disorder which is coupled with a propensity to the commission of sexual offenses."[69]

In 1969, the Illinois Supreme Court reviewed a case in which the defendant had been convicted of forcing a young boy to commit sodomy at knife point.[70] He claimed that his act was involuntary and arose from his homosexuality and therefore to punish him constituted cruel and unusual punishment. The court summarily rejected his allegation because his testimony did not *establish* that his acts were involuntary. In another case the Michigan Court of Appeals upheld the sentence of a defendant who had been convicted of sodomy with two boys, ages six and ten. The court reasoned that the statute did not "punish homosexuality or mental disease." It proscribed "overt conduct, not a particular mental condition or predisposition."[71] The sentence imposed was simply not cruel or unusual. Thus, in the cases involving sexual offenses courts have emphatically refused to expand the Robinson doctrine to acts symptomatic of a status.

To Be Mentally Ill or Insane

A final area of litigation that has developed as a result of *Robinson* is that of mental illness and insanity. In 1968 the Pennsylvania Supreme Court was asked to set aside a sentence imposed on several juveniles who had been adjudged "defective delinquents with criminal tendencies."[72] The juveniles contended that the statute punished them for the status of "being mentally defective," and as such, it inflicted cruel and unusual punishment. The court, however, made the usual distinction between status and action. They were not being punished for being mental defectives, asserted the court, but for antisocial conduct and specific criminal acts.

Four recent cases have involved insane persons. In one, Khalil Ben Maatallah was found insane and sent to the Nevada State Hospital for treatment. Two years later a district court directed his transfer to a state prison. He sought habeas corpus on two grounds: that he was no longer receiving treatment, and that he was confined as a criminal without having been convicted of a crime. The district court refused to take evidence and denied his petition. The Nevada Supreme Court reversed on the ground that mental illness is not a crime. Further, the court asserted: "Imprisonment for mental illness may be a cruel and inhuman punishment banned by the Eighth Amendment and by . . . the Nevada Constitution as well."[73] This opinion seems to be at odds with an earlier California decision. There defendant Thomas had been ordered committed as a mentally disordered sex offender not amenable to hospital treatment. He claimed that incarceration in a place other than a hospital or treatment facility under a civil commitment, without sentence on a criminal charge, constituted cruel and unusual punishment. The court noted that placing Thomas in a facility located in a prison where he did not benefit from further hospital treatment was "a drastic form of confinement."[74] However, stated the court, it does not offend the cruel and unusual punishment prohibition.

Another case involving insanity arose in New York. Alfred Curt von Wolfersdorf had been accused of kidnapping and killing a fourteen-year-old boy. An accomplice, who implicated him, was convicted and executed in 1953. Wolfersdorf at the time sought to take a polygraph test to prove his innocence, but this was disallowed because he was found to be insane. At the age of eighty-six, after having spent twenty years in Matteawan State Hospital for the criminally insane, he sought habeas corpus. He asked not to be set free, but to be sent to less disagreeable surroundings. He contended that he was not dangerous and was suitable for commitment to a civil hospital. The State Department of Mental Hygiene would gladly have transferred him, but a New York statute allowed civil commitment only for people not in confinement on a criminal charge. Judge Frankel was obviously agitated at the situation. He expressed amazement that the legal energies expended in the case had not produced the small mitigation Wolfersdorf sought for the last days of his life. "Cases like this," he continued, "could encourage the canard that Mr. Bumble was too generous by half when he suggested that 'the law is an ass.' "[75] He noted that the attorney general had admitted that Wolfersdorf could never be convicted, because the accuser was never cross-examined by attorneys and because most of the people who were involved had disappeared or died. The court noted that he was "locked away in a place more likely to drive men mad than to cure the 'insane.' "[76] In conclusion, the court stated that Wolfersdorf's "incarceration among the 'criminally insane' for twenty years because of *his status as an insane defendant* (presumed innocent) named in an untriable indictment violates his protection against cruel and unusual punishment."[77]

A similar case arose in Connecticut.[78] James Pardue was suspected of committing a number of robberies and bombings. He was caught and declared insane as a schizophrenic. He was admitted to the Medical Center for Federal Prisoners at Springfield, Missouri, but staff doctors recommended that he be transferred to a place where he could receive "adequate and appropriate" treatment. An arrangement was made to confine him in a Connecticut state hospital, but these plans never came to fruition, and Pardue was eventually sent to the federal prison in Danbury. At the time of the suit there were no plans to transfer him to a hospital. Judge Zampano noted: "The plain fact of the matter is that there are no federal facilities which offer appropriate psychiatric services and adequate security for the treatment of the defendant with a mental disorder not temporary in nature."[79] Pardue's confinement, he concluded, had reached and surpassed any reasonable time without being brought to trial. The delay in a final determination had been due to the court's vain efforts to find a satisfactory solution to the predicament. Thus, the court held, Pardue must be discharged from federal custody. However, the order was stayed thirty days to give state officials time to take custody if they so desired.

A more recent case involving a mentally ill person occurred in 1972.[80] Robert Myers, an alleged psychotic or paranoid schizophrenic, was convicted of murder. The jury, by its verdict, rejected the defense of insanity and mental irresponsibility. However, he argued that to punish him would inflict cruel and unusual punishment under the Robinson doctrine. The Washington Court of Appeals noted that the case was clearly distinguishable, as Myers was "not being punished because of his status as a chronic paranoid schizophrenic," but "for his criminal behavior determined to be responsibly undertaken on the basis of a test of insanity and mental irresponsibility accepted by a great majority of the states in this country."[81]

It should be clear that the impact of *Robinson* has been modest. Courts have generally made a distinction between "an act" and "a status." Statutes declaring acts committed by addicts, alcoholics, prostitutes and homosexuals, be they ever so slight, and no matter how closely related to a defendant's "disease," are generally considered constitutional. The only area in which the Robinson doctrine has apparently made some inroads has been in the area of vagrancy. However, it should be noted that this is probably due to the general trend toward declaring such statutes unconstitutional on due process grounds, rather than to any impetus supplied by the *Robinson* decision.

Part III: Administrative Action as Cruel and Unusual Punishment

11

Prison Rules and Practices

The Hands-Off Doctrine

Within the past decade a minor revolution has taken place in judicial attitudes toward court supervision of internal prison practices and regulations. Traditionally, federal courts have followed the policy of nonintervention, more popularly referred to as the hands-off doctrine. The euphemism, apparently first adopted in 1961,[1] is not a rule of law, but a behavioral description of judicial hesitancy to interfere with the internal operations of correctional institutions. The doctrine is grounded in three fundamental principles of American government. First is the separation of powers. From this perspective, the administration of prisons is viewed as falling exclusively within the executive branch of government. For example, in *Powell* v. *Hunter,* the Tenth Circuit Court of Appeals declared: "The prison system is under the administration of the Attorney General . . . and not the district court."[2] The Ninth Circuit Court of Appeals has perhaps best summarized the prevailing view. "It is well settled," concluded the court, "that it is not the function of the courts to superintend the treatment and discipline of prisoners in penitentiaries."[3] Support for this view is drawn from the fact that Congress delegated prison administration to the attorney general and not to the judiciary.[4] Similar arguments based on state statutes have been advanced by state courts.[5] Many times, for example, prisoners have been told that remedies must come from the parole board of corrections and not the judiciary.[6]

The second principle upon which the hands-off doctrine is based is federalism. It is argued that among the powers reserved to the states is the power to define criminal acts and provide subsequent punishment for the violation thereof. For example, in *Siegel* v. *Ragen,* Judge Finnegan asserted: "The government of the United States is not concerned with, nor has it the power to control or regulate the internal discipline of the penal institutions of its constituent states. All such powers are reserved to the individual states."[7]

The third principle upon which the hands-off doctrine is based is judicial self-restraint.[8] Several reasons have been advanced suggesting that this principle should be adhered to rigorously. First, it has been argued that because the exact rights of imprisoned convicts have not been finalized, the courts should be extremely reluctant to interfere with administrative determinations.[9] Second, it has been asserted that the judiciary lacks requisite expertise in penology upon which to base its decisions and, therefore, should avoid interfering

111

with rulings of prison administrators.[10] Poorly informed decisions, it has been argued, may create internal disciplinary problems and discourage experimentation with various innovative penological techniques.[11] Another reason often advanced has been that if courts allowed such petitions, the judiciary would be inundated with appeals, and consequently a breakdown in the judicial process might occur.[12] As the court noted in *McClosky* v. *Maryland*: "In the great mass of instances . . . the necessity for effective disciplinary controls is so impelling that judicial review of them is highly impractical and wholly unwarranted."[13] Finally, it has been argued that judicial self-restraint should be strictly followed, because in most instances prisoners have not exhausted their state remedies before appealing to federal courts for relief.[14]

Remedies

The failure of state legislatures and prison administrators to correct what can only be described as barbaric and deplorable conditions and practices has increasingly drawn the judiciary into the internal administration of certain penal institutions.[15] The result has been an expansion of the remedies available to convicts and the concurrent demise of the hands-off doctrine.[16]

Habeas Corpus Relief

Traditionally there were three limitations on the availability of the writ of habeas corpus:[17] (1) the proposition that the only relief that could be granted under the writ was total release;[18] (2) the proposition that administrative and state remedies had to be first exhausted before federal courts could hear such petitions;[19] and (3) the proposition that the writ could be used only to contest the legitimacy of one's confinement and not to test the mode or manner of that confinement.[20] The first limitation began eroding in 1944. In *Coffin* v. *Reichard*, the Sixth Circuit Court of Appeals ruled that habeas corpus relief is not limited solely to releasing the prisoner from confinement. The per curiam opinion asserted: "Any unlawful restraint may be inquired into on habeas corpus. . . . This rule applies although a person is in lawful custody. His conviction and incarceration deprive him only of such liberties as the law has ordained he shall suffer for his transgressions."[21]

The rule of exhaustion has also been considerably weakened. Traditionally, federal prisoners had to exhaust the administrative remedies established by the Federal Bureau of Prisons, and state prisoners had to exhaust state administrative and judicial remedies, to be eligible for the writ in state courts.[22] In 1957, however, the Second Circuit Court of Appeals held that a state prisoner, who was without sufficient funds to exhaust state remedies, could successfully apply for the writ in a federal court.[23] The decision was based on the fact that Section 2254 of the Judicial Code permits federal courts to hear habeas corpus petitions from state prisoners even though they have not exhausted state remedies "when there is either an absence of available State corrective process or the existence of circumstances rendering such process ineffective to protect the rights of the prisoner."[24]

The third limitation regarding confinement has also been eroded. In *Johnson* v. *Avery*,[25] for example, a state prisoner petitioned for habeas corpus, seeking to be released from solitary confinement. A federal district court in Tennessee granted relief and ordered the prisoner released from such confinement and returned to his status as an ordinary prisoner.[26] Today, if a constitutional right is asserted, the courts will carefully scrutinize the allegations of a convict applying for habeas corpus.[27]

Proceedings Under the Federal Civil Rights Act

Under the Civil Rights Act of 1871, any person "under color of law" who deprives any other person of his constitutional rights "shall be liable to the party injured in an action at law, suit in equity, or other proper proceeding for redress."[28] The act, however, applies only to convicts in state institutions, and not to federal prisoners. Convicts may sue for declaratory or injunctive relief,[29] as well as monetary damages.[30] The hands-off doctrine restricted many early suits,[31] but today if the prisoner shows that a federal right has been abridged, he will gain access to the courts.[32] Among the rights which have been asserted are freedom of religion,[33] freedom from cruel and unusual punishment,[34] and the rights of free access to the courts,[35] legal information,[36] and medical attention.[37]

The United States Supreme Court has declared that state remedies need not be exhausted before a prisoner may sue in federal courts under the act. "It is no answer," stated the Court in 1961, "that the State has a law which if enforced would give relief. The federal remedy is supplementary to the state remedy, and the latter need not be first sought and refused before the federal one is invoked."[38]

Other inroads into the hands-off doctrine have been made by courts hearing petitions under the Civil Rights Act of 1871. Several decisions, for example, have specifically rejected the rationale that because such petitions impede the smooth operation of the judicial process they should not be heard. As Judge Soberoff wrote in *Sewell* v. *Pegelow,* the courts "must not play fast and loose with basic constitutional rights in the interest of administrative efficiency."[39] The United States Supreme Court has also recognized that a prisoner's constitutional rights are not to be stifled by a defense of administrative expertise.[40]

Mandamus Proceedings

Prior to 1962 the only federal courts authorized to issue writs of mandamus on original jurisdiction were those in the District of Columbia.[41] In 1961 the Court of Appeals for the District, in *Fulwood* v. *Clemmer,* had made it clear that mandamus could be granted on request of a prisoner where constitutional rights were involved.[42] The following year all federal district courts were given the authority to "compel an officer or employee of the United States or any agency thereof to perform a duty owed to the plaintiff."[43] In 1966, the Fifth Circuit Court of Appeals held that mandamus could be used by a federal inmate to compel prison officials to perform a duty, and subsequently mandamus relief was granted.[44] The writ is also available to prisoners in state courts. For example, in *In the Matter of Brown* v. *McGinnis,*[45] an inmate successfully obtained a directive that the Commissioner of Corrections of New York extend to him certain religious rights and privileges.

Tort Actions

Tort actions against individual jailers have long been permitted.[46] However, suits against the United States under the federal Tort Claims Act were traditionally barred by the rationale that the congressional waiver of sovereign immunity did not extend to prisoners.[47] The main reasons advanced were based on the hands-off doctrine. It was argued that allowing prisoners to bring suits would have detrimental effects on discipline.[48] Further, it was noted that the waiver of immunity contained in the act expressly exempted claims based on discretionary acts (as opposed to ministerial ones). Two landmark decisions in 1962 removed these restrictions. A federal court held for the first time that prisoners may sue under the federal Tort Claims Act for negligent conduct by prison personnel.[49] The United States Supreme Court affirmed the lower-court decision the following year.[50] Between 1963 and 1967 more than eighty suits were brought by inmates of federal prisons under the act.[51] Similar relief is available to state prisoners under state tort claims acts.[52]

Contempt Proceedings

Another possible remedy is based upon the court's contempt power. In *Howard* v. *State,*[53] for example, the plaintiff argued that he was entitled to be released from solitary confinement because the orders committing him to prison did not provide for such incarceration. He asked that his jailers be held in contempt of court. The Supreme Court of Arizona, hearing the case on appeal, remanded with orders directing the lower court to investigate the allegations made and, if true, to hold the superintendent in contempt.

Summary

There is no doubt that the remedies available to prisoners have expanded during the past twenty years. At the same time, it is almost unanimously conceded that the hands-off doctrine has been considerably weakened.[54] However, the idea of nonintervention is far from dead.[55] For example, recently the Second Circuit Court of Appeals, in *Sostre* v. *McGinnis,* reversed a district court's decision that all solitary confinement exceeding fifteen days was unconstitutional. The stated ground was that "to place a punishment beyond the power of a state to impose on an inmate is a drastic interference with the state's free political and administrative processes."[56] For similar reasons, a federal district court in Illinois recently rejected the claim that segregated confinement constituted cruel and unusual punishment.[57] The court held that discipline was a matter of penological judgment which should be left to the experts in the field, and that wide discretion should be given penal authorities. It appears, in conclusion, that if a court does not deem a certain practice particularly reprehensible, it will simply invoke the long-standing hands-off doctrine, and avoid discussion of the substantive issues. On the other hand, if a court desires to alter or abolish a practice it deems particularly obnoxious, today it has sufficient precedent to support the casting aside of the hands-off doctrine. Having done so, it may then proceed to rectify the perceived wrong.

Challenges to Methods of Enforcing Prison Rules

Whipping, Chaining, and Miscellaneous Physical Punishments

As suggested earlier, whipping was commonly practiced at the time of the adoption of the Constitution. It was often provided for by statute. However, almost without exception the courts have historically held that in the absence of established rules and regulations, and legislative approval, whipping may not be levied by administrative officials. A long and well-reasoned opinion substantiating this proposition is found as early as 1881. In that year two prisoners in Tennessee were whipped for smuggling whiskey into the jail, for using insulting language, and for holding a gun on the jailer. The court noted that the prisoners were in clear violation of "duty and good order," and that the penalty was inflicted without anger. Nevertheless, the court held that whipping had "fallen under the ban of modern civilization, as tending to degrade the individual and destroy the sense of personal honor."[58] The court noted that whipping had been banished in the army and navy, and that "the tendency of legislation and public sentiment" in the state was against it. The jailer was convicted of assault and battery, but because he had acted in good faith on the assumption that he had authority to whip the prisoner, he was fined only one cent and costs.

Several North Carolina cases followed the Tennessee decision. In 1914, J.M. Nipper, who was in charge of convicts working on the roads, was found guilty of whipping an elderly prisoner on the "bare flesh" and was fined ten dollars plus costs. The court stated: "In view of the enlightenment of the age, and the progress which has been made in prison discipline, we have no difficulty in coming to the conclusion that corporal punishment by flogging is not reasonable, and cannot be sustained. That which degrades and embrutes a man cannot be either necessary or reasonable."[59] The court noted that only Russia allowed whipping for prison discipline. It had been abolished in thirty-two of the forty-eight states. Even in Maryland and Delaware, where flogging was still retained by statute, it was to be inflicted as punishment for crime and not to enforce prison discipline.

Two years later, E.W. Mincher, a convict guard, was found guilty of whipping prisoner Junius Potter and sentenced to twelve months in jail.[60] The North Carolina court, citing the *Nipper* case, noted that there were no rules allowing the application of corporal punishment.

Where statutory provisions and/or administrative rules and regulations are present, the whipping of prisoners has traditionally been upheld by the courts. For example, in 1927, the North Carolina Supreme Court held that L.E. Revis, superintendent of prison camps, who whipped prisoner Lee Cody, was innocent of charges brought against him. Revis had whipped Cody six lashes for violating prison rules. Two witnesses of "good moral character" were present, his clothes were left on, and the whipping was not done in a "cruel or unmerciful manner." The court, obviously displeased with the practice, held that the legislature had the power to allow such punishment regardless of the wisdom of the policy.[61]

One of the most important early decisions occurred in 1931. Lucas Candido sought a writ of habeas corpus on the ground that if unrestrained, the warden of the prison at Oahu, Hawaii would flog him with a cat-o-nine-tails. Such punishment, he claimed, was cruel and unusual. Warden Lane asserted that the board of prison inspectors authorized him to levy whipping as a punishment. The court noted that he had the power to supervise and discipline prisoners. The only perceived limitation on such power was the Constitution. After reviewing the history of the cruel and unusual punishment concept and the practice of whipping, the court ruled that "a form of punishment long used by the federal government and by some of the states does not become unusual simply because the federal government and some of these same states have discarded it."[62] Whipping, concluded the court, "is not barbarous and inhuman so as to shock all thinking persons."[63]

Even where state legislatures have explicitly prohibited corporal punishment of prisoners, in certain instances use of the whip or similar instruments has been upheld. For example, to quell a prison riot in California, guards repeatedly flogged forty prisoners with a rubber hose. The court noted: "There is a distinction between the deliberate infliction of corporal punishment for past offenses, and the use of a rubber hose or other weapon to suppress a threatened riot or to prevent a prisoner from doing bodily harm to an officer or to another inmate of the prison."[64]

Since World War II, whippings inflicted by prison officials have declined.[65] The courts have become more and more reluctant to allow such disciplinary measures.[66] Nevertheless, some have upheld the practice.[67] It was not until 1965 that the federal courts began taking decisive steps to curtail the use of the whip. In *Talley* v. *Stephens*,[68] Judge Henley enjoined further use of corporal punishment in the Arkansas State Penitentiary until appropriate safeguards could be established. He suggested that use of the whip must not be excessive and must be inflicted as dispassionately as possible by responsible people. Further, the convict should know in advance what conduct will be punishable by whipping. There was no appeal by either side.[69]

Two years later, three inmates of that same institution brought a suit against O.E. Bishop, the superintendent.[70] They claimed that the infliction of corporal punishment in any form was unconstitutional and in violation of the Eighth and Fourteenth Amendments. If, however, the court would not deem the punishment per se unconstitutional, whipping, nevertheless, still could not be imposed in the Arkansas prisons, because the rules controlling the use of corporal punishment did not protect prisoners from unconstitutional treatment. The court paid deference to the weakening hands-off doctrine, but noted that under "special circumstances" where constitutional rights are involved the courts could hear complaints. After reviewing the history of cruel and unusual punishment vis-à-vis whipping, the court concluded that the strap was not constitutionally forbidden. However, Judges Harris and Young did enjoin application of the punishment until proper and adequate safeguards surrounding its use could be established. The guidelines were to be submitted to the clerk of the court. Several suggestions were offered: (1) more than one person should be involved in the decision to administer corporal punishment; (2) rules should not be circumvented in times of anger; (3) the accusation by an inmate should not be summarily accepted; and (4) the superintendent should review the decisions. The court also issued an injunction permanently restricting any whipping on the bare skin of prisoners.

Although the prisoners had been partially successful, they nevertheless appealed to the Eighth Circuit Court of Appeals. This time their sole allegation was that use of the strap per se inflicted cruel and unusual punishment, in violation of the Eighth and Fourteenth Amendments. Again the court paid deference to the hands-off doctrine, but took the case because it involved "fundamental rights."[71] After reviewing the history of the Eighth Amendment, Judge Blackmun, citing *Trop* v. *Dulles*,[72] noted that it protected "nothing less than the dignity of man," and that determinations under it should be guided by civilized and evolving standards of decency. "The use of the strap in the penitentiaries of Arkansas," he concluded, "is punishment which, in the last third of the 20th century, runs afoul of the Eighth Amendment." The "strap's use, irrespective of any precautionary conditions which may be imposed," he continued, "offends contemporary concepts of decency and human dignity and precepts of civilization which we profess to possess, . . . [and] it also violates those standards of good conscience and fundamental fairness."[73] Judge Blackmun based his decision on nine considerations: (1) rules will not prevent abuse of the strap; (2) rules often go unobserved; (3) rules are easily circumvented; (4) rules are subject to abuse by the sadistic and unscrupulous; (5) rules are difficult to enforce in the lower hierarchy; (6) there are problems as to the size of the strap and quantity of infliction; (7) whipping generates hatred toward keepers, degrades the punisher and frustrates rehabilitative goals; (8) whipping makes adjustment to society more difficult; and (9) public opinion is adverse to the punishment. In conclusion he noted that the evidence of two expert penologists clearly demonstrated that use of the strap is "unusual." He encountered "no difficulty" in holding that its use was cruel, and thus restrained all personnel from "inflicting corporeal punishment, including use of the strap, as a disciplinary measure."[74]

Within the past few years there have been several instances in which courts have secured evidence of juveniles being subjected to constitutionally impermissible abuse. In the first case, District Judge Justice found widespread practices of beating, slapping, and kicking in the Texas juvenile facilities at Mountain View and Gatesville. He ruled that such practices violated the Eighth Amendment because they were "so severe as to degrade human dignity," were "inflicted in a wholly arbitrary manner," were "unacceptable to contemporary society," and finally, were "not justified as serving any necessary purpose."[75]

A second case came before Federal District Judge Grant, who granted injunctive and declaratory relief to inmates of the Indiana Boys School in Plainfield.[76] The juveniles had been subjected to supervised beatings with a thick board. No formalized rules guided the practice. Referring to *Jackson* v. *Bishop*,[77] Judge Grant failed to see "any distinction between the use of the strap and the use of a thick board" and ordered immediate cessation of the practice. On appeal, the Seventh Circuit Court of Appeals affirmed.[78] Although the court did not hold that all corporal punishment in juvenile institutions is per se cruel and unusual, it did hold that the beatings as presently administered were "unnecessary and therefore excessive."

In another case, Federal District Judge Webster held that the striking of a prisoner with a "slap jack" by the warden of the St. Louis Jail constituted cruel and unusual punishment.[79] He further ordered that no federal prisoner be subjected to corporal punishment.

The chaining of convicts by prison officials has always been disfavored in the United States. Perhaps the most famous judicial ruling during the nineteenth century dealing with the chaining of prisoners came from the District Court for the Southern District of Georgia. Judge Speer became aware of what he considered an "intolerable" circumstance while reading a local newspaper. He took it upon himself to investigate the situation and found that Nat Birdsong, the local jailer, had chained prisoner Joe Warren by the neck, to the grating of his cell. For over six hours it was impossible for Warren's heels to touch the floor. Judge Speer equated the "disciplinary measure" with pillorying and torture. He noted that death by strangulation was possible, and that it was "at best, an ignominious, cruel, and unusual punishment."[80] A suspended fine of fifty dollars and costs was levied on Birdsong.

A similar situation occurred in 1949. N.L. Carpenter, the warden of a North Carolina prison camp, ordered Clarence Lett to be handcuffed to the bars of his cell in such a manner that he could not sit or lie down. Lett remained there for seventy hours. Carpenter's defense was based on the fact that the mode of treatment was provided for by the administrative rules of the prison. The court, however, rejected this argument, noting that under the circumstances described, the punishment was harsh and went beyond the rule of law. "We express no approval of the regulation: . . ." stated the court, "or the mode of its enforcement."[81]

More recently, Judge Merhige of the Federal District Court for the Eastern District of Virginia held that chaining or handcuffing a man to his bars was "unconstitutionally excessive."[82] He noted in the case before him that prisoner Belvins was permanently scarred as a result of being so restrained, and that prisoner Johnson could not obtain adequate sleep and was subjected to prolonged physical pain. Further, neither man was allowed to "respond to a call of nature" or eat.

In another recent case, Judge Kaufman of the Federal District Court of Maryland held that contemporary medical standards no longer permit jailors to treat inmates suffering from epileptic seizures, delirium tremens, narcotic withdrawals, or mental disorders by routinely shackling them "with *iron or other* metal restraints to beds in the Jail infirmary."[83] In yet another case the Seventh Circuit Court of Appeals held that the tying of children spread-eagled to a bed for 77½ hours as punishment after an alleged consensual homosexual act was cruel and unusual punishment.[84]

Other physical punishments have been challenged as cruel and unusual. Allegedly, guards in the Arkansas state penitentiary system used such devices as the "crank telephone" and the "teeter board."[85] A federal district court issued an injunction permanently restraining such punishment, and the Eighth Circuit Court of Appeals upheld the ruling.[86]

In the aftermath of the prison riots at Attica State Prison in upstate New York, prisoners petitioned a federal district court for preliminary and permanent injunctions to prevent certain barbarous conduct on the part of the guards.

It was alleged that the convicts were subjected to beatings, physical abuse, torture, and the running of gantlets. The district court denied their application,
but on appeal the Second Circuit Court of Appeals reversed. The court noted
that such activity "was wholly beyond any force needed to maintain order"
and held that the mistreatment of inmates in the case at hand "amounted to
cruel and unusual punishment in violation of their Eighth Amendment
rights." Moreover, the opinion continued, "the district court was not justified in assuming, without further proof, that adequate steps would be taken
to protect the inmates against further reprisals, perhaps of a more sophisticated
and subtle nature. Under the circumstances, preliminary injunctive relief should
have been granted against further physical abuse, tortures, beatings or similar
conduct."[87]

In a similar case, William Bracey was awarded $2500 in damages by a federal
district court in Pennsylvania.[88] After a disturbance at the correctional institution at Camp Hill, two officials wrestled him to the floor, sprayed mace in his
face, and again threw him to the floor and beat him with night sticks. He was
then taken to another cell block where his clothes were ripped off and he was
beaten again. Subsequently he was pushed down a flight of stairs. During the
encounter he suffered a fractured nose, bloody right eye, swollen neck, knots
on his head, damaged ribs and an injured leg. He was hospitalized for eight days.
The court accepted Bracey's description because the state's witnesses' stories
were "shot through with internal inconsistencies." According to the court, the
best thing that could be said for the defendant-guard was that his memory had
"deteriorated to the point of no return." All of the beatings had occurred after
Bracey had been subdued. "Such excesses as were perpetrated on this plaintiff," concluded the court, "violate permissible boundaries of the Eighth and
Fourteenth Amendments."[89]

Despite the *Attica* and *Bracey* decisions, it is clear that during uprisings,
prison officials may constitutionally utilize riot control techniques to contain
recalcitrant inmates. For example, the use of fire hoses has been approved,
as well as tear gas.[90] Nevertheless, it is equally clear that the use of such devices
is limited to unusual circumstances and may not be inflicted on "nonthreaten-
ing inmates."[91]

Restricted Confinement

Solitary confinement[92] has a long history,[93] and today is used by nearly
every jurisdiction in the United States.[94] Until recently, the courts generally
refused to review cases brought by convicts challenging such incarceration on
the ground that to do so would violate the hands-off doctrine.[95] However, a
few inmates were successful. For example, in 1925 a convicted perjurer was
placed in a "dark cell or dungeon" on a diet of bread and water for thirty

days.[96] He alleged, in a court of original jurisdiction, that the superintendent of the prison should be held in contempt of court for violating commitment orders. The court refused to hear his complaint, and he appealed to the Supreme Court of Arizona. Justice Lockwood, writing the opinion, noted that a superintendent may only do what the commitment orders direct. If he does more, he is violating the law just as much as if he released a prisoner before his internment expired. The court also noted that a convict may be placed in stricter confinement for infraction of reasonable rules, but "that any prisoner who, while under sentence for crime, is subjected to unreasonable and harsh treatment without legal justification thereof, may appeal to the law for protection."[97] The court concluded that solitary confinement "inflicted upon one who has conducted himself in all respects as a quiet, tractable prisoner, obedient to the rules of his abode, and in the absence of any cause therefore, is *prima facie* harsh and unreasonable."[98] Consequently, the case was remanded to the lower court with orders to hold an investigation to determine whether the allegations were true.

Not until the 1960s, however, did federal courts begin with any regularity to review allegations that certain types of solitary confinement were in violation of the Eighth Amendment.[99] The first successful challenge was brought by T.X. Fulwood, a Black Muslim convict.[100] He preached a sermon condemning whites as liars, thieves, and murderers, in front of five or six guards and six or seven hundred inmates. A prison rule prohibited such activity because it might "tend to breach the peace." For the infraction, Fulwood was placed in a control cell described as a room with stone floors and walls, eight by twelve feet, with no windows, natural light, bed, washbasin, or furniture. He was allowed no exercise, visitors, mail, or reading matter. The light switch and mechanism for flushing the toilet were beyond his reach. He was allowed only 2000 calories a day, and only an occasional shower and shave. After thirteen days, Fulwood was removed to the special treatment unit, where he remained for eighteen days. He was then returned to the control cell, where he spent fifteen more days before being again released to the special treatment unit, where he remained for six months. While in that unit, he was required to eat in his cell, and consequently his food was always cold. He was not permitted to work, see movies, watch television, have visitors, or participate in rehabilitative programs. At the end of this period he was taken to the transient section of the jail, where he was allowed no money allowance, free letter privileges, or visitors. Further, he was denied many canteen privileges. In all, Fulwood had spent more than two years in solitary or restricted confinement.

Fulwood applied for a writ of habeas corpus. Judge Matthews noted that prison authorities could make proper rules and regulations to maintain discipline, but that "a prisoner may not be *unreasonably* punished for the infraction of a rule."[101] Relying on the *Weems* decision, he noted: "A punishment out of proportion to the violation may bring it within the bar against unreasonable

punishments."[102] In this instance, he concluded, the punishment Fulwood
received was "not reasonably related" to the rule infraction, and consequently
Fulwood was ordered returned to the general prison population.

In 1970 another district court held a term of incarceration in solitary
confinement to be excessive.[103] For failure to sign a "safety-sheet," Robert
Mosher received five months in solitary. Relying on expert testimony, Judge
Foley held that the confinement "was grossly disproportionate punishment
for the offense committed" and therefore violated Eighth and Fourteenth
Amendment rights. Injunctive relief was granted.

In the *Fulwood* and *Mosher* cases the district courts had held that particular durations of time in solitary confinement were excessive and therefore
constituted cruel and unusual punishment. Other decisions have held that
certain types of solitary confinement are unconstitutional per se. As early
as 1964 a circuit court of appeals implied that under certain circumstances
solitary confinement might be considered "cruel and inhuman."[104] That same
year the Idaho Supreme Court reviewed the denial of habeas corpus to a prisoner who contended that he had been forced to live for prolonged periods
of time in unsanitary conditions while in solitary confinement.[105] The court
found that, if true, the practices were "inexcusable and shocking" and went
well beyond mere prison discipline. The case was remanded for rehearing.

It was not until 1966 that a federal court specifically found the conditions surrounding solitary confinement unconstitutional.[106] Robert C. Jordan,
Jr., an inmate of the California Correctional Training Facility at Soledad, had
been confined for eleven days in a "strip cell." The cell was six by ten feet,
four inches, three sides of which were concrete. The fourth was covered by
steel bars and a metal screen. A second front wall, solid except for a barred
and screened window, was located two feet, ten inches from the barred wall.
The window could be closed off by a metal flap. The cell itself was devoid
of furnishings except for a toilet (or a hole in the floor depending on the
particular cell he was confined in) which could not be flushed from the inside.
There was no interior source of light. Jordan alleged that the flaps were kept
over the windows, the toilets were flushed only two times a day, and that
the cell was not cleaned while he was there, nor had it been for the previous
thirty days. He was not able to clean his hands, teeth, or body. He was
allowed no clothing for eight days and was required to sleep on a stiff canvas
mat on the cold concrete floor.[107] He further alleged that the cell was not
heated, and that he was denied adequate medical care. The court found his
testimony "clear and convincing" and substantiated by other witnesses. In
arriving at a decision, the court noted: "Requiring man or beast to live, eat and
sleep under the degrading conditions pointed out in the testimony creates a condition that inevitably does violence to the elemental concepts of decency."[108]
If penal institutions are to be permitted to continue the use of solitary confinement, stated the court, it "must be accompanied by supplying the basic requirements as may be necessary to maintain a degree of cleanliness compatible with

elemental decency."[109] The court offered guidelines to aid prison authorities
in complying with its decision. Such incarceration, suggested the court, must
be for short periods of time and must not be used for insane patients. Cells
should be evenly heated, adequately lighted, and well ventilated. They should
also meet high sanitary standards. Washbowls, toilets, bedding, and clothing
should be provided. Although the court did not award damages, it did grant
injunctive relief.[110]

The following year the Second Circuit Court of Appeals had the opportunity to review a similar claim.[111] Lawrence W. Wright, an inmate of Clinton
State Prison, New York, claimed that Warden McMann had placed him in a
dirty, unsanitary, and inadequately heated strip cell. Wright further alleged that
he was allowed no clothing for eleven days and was denied soap, towels, toilet
paper, toothbrush, and comb. The toilet was filthy and the windows were
opened to subfreezing temperatures. Wright was required to stand at military
attention each time a guard appeared. He was so confined for thirty-three days
one time and twenty-one days another. The district court had dismissed the
complaint.[112] The circuit court held that it had "no hesitancy in holding that
the debasing conditions to which Wright claim[ed] to have been subjected . . .
would if established, constitute cruel and unusual punishment in violation of
the Eighth Amendment."[113] The court reasoned that the "civilized standards
of human decency" simply did not permit such treatment. On remand, the
district court found the allegations to be true. "Such confinement," stated
the court, "in view of certain living conditions that existed then in the so-
called 'strip cell' and in a state of complete nudity was cruel and unusual infliction of punishment."[114] Wright was awarded $1500 compensatory damages,
costs, and expenses. The Second Circuit Court of Appeals affirmed this part
of Judge Foley's decision, and the United States Supreme Court denied
certiorari.

In 1969 a federal district court in Pennsylvania held that the placing of
two men in a single cell six by nine feet, containing no windows, articifical
light, bedding, soap, towels or toilet tissue, constituted cruel and unusual
punishment.[115] The case was affirmed by the Third Circuit Court of Appeals.

The following year a federal district court in New York held that fourteen-year-old Antoinette Lollis had been subjected to cruel and unusual punishment while incarcerated in solitary confinement. She had been placed in a
New York training school for girls because she was abused by her mother.
Antoinette allegedly started a fracas and as punishment was confined to the
"strip room." The barren room, containing only a wooden bench and a blanket,
was six by nine feet. She was kept there twenty-four hours a day and was
denied a request to see the psychiatrist. She was also denied tranquilizers,
which she was supposed to take regularly, was only allowed to wear pajamas,
and could not look out the window. Antoinette was released after two weeks
only upon the insistence of a judge who toured the facility. Relying on the
testimony of experts, Judge Lasker concluded that the "two-week confinement

of a fourteen-year-old girl in a stripped room in night clothes with no recreational facilities or even reading matter must be held to violate the Constitution's ban on cruel and unusual punishment."[116] He thereupon issued a preliminary injunction and enjoined the placement of anyone in isolation for an extended period of time. He ordered that standards be submitted to the court with regard to the maximum period of such confinement, the maximum number of times a year that one could be placed in such confinement, the facilities to be placed within such confinement, and the extent to which a child could join in common activities while so confined.

Three subsequent decisions have similarly held that certain conditions surrounding the solitary confinement of juveniles constitute cruel and unusual punishment. In 1972, Judge Pettine found unconstitutional the use of "bug-out" rooms in the Boys Training School of Rhode Island.[117] He found they contained nothing but a toilet and a mattress on the floor. Some cells at times did not have artificial lighting, and one cell had no open window. Juveniles were kept there from three to seven days, some wearing only underwear. The rooms were dark and cold and often the incarcerate was not given toilet paper, soap, sheets, or a change of clothes.

In another case, Federal Judge Grant of Indiana ruled that juveniles placed in solitary confinement must be told why they are being placed there, must be so confined only for a specific length of time, must be provided with continual treatment while there, must have reasonable access to his peers and the treatment staff, and must be provided with reading materials and the opportunity to exercise.[118] He was particularly offended by the fact that some boys had been placed in solitary confinement without these benefits for periods exceeding 150 days.

In a third case, Federal Judge Justice provided elaborate guidelines to be followed in determining whether or not a juvenile should be placed in solitary confinement.[119] Additionally, he held that while so incarcerated, the individual was to be visited by a case worker for a period of ten minutes each hour, except between the hours of 10:00 P.M. and 7:00 A.M. Further, it was required that a nurse visit the juvenile at least once a day, and if confinement was to exceed one day, a psychiatrist or psychologist was required to visit him on a daily basis.

One of the more recent cases involving solitary confinement arose in the Second Circuit Court of Appeals.[120] The court held that solitary confinement imposed in Connecticut's Correctional Institution at Somers was "below the irreducible minimum of decency required by the Eighth Amendment." Donald J. La Reau had spent five days in isolation for possession of a rope fashioned from towels. The cell was six by ten feet with concrete walls and floor. It contained no window, sink, water fountain, or commode. A "Chinese toilet" (merely a hole in the floor) served as a waste-disposing facility. He was allowed three meals a day, a mattress to sleep on, and blankets. However, he was not allowed to have reading materials (the cell was completely dark anyway), and was given no opportunity to exercise. He was allowed to talk to no one. It was Judge Timber's opinion that placing an inmate in a dark cell almost continuously day and night was a threat to his sanity. The court remanded with orders to frame an appropriate injunction against strip-cell conditions, and to determine what damages should be awarded to La Reau.

The following year District Judge Brown held the conditions surrounding the solitary confinement of Gary Poindexter and others in the Kansas State Penitentiary to be cruel and unusual.[121] They had been placed in "strip cells" without blankets, clothing, or personal hygiene materials. Furthermore, the doors to the cells had been welded shut. Similarly, the year before, Judge Keady of the Northern District Court of Mississippi had held that inmates at Parchman Prison had been subjected to cruel and unusual punishment.[122] They had been confined in a dark hole, naked, without any hygienic materials, bedding, adequate food, or heat.

It should be clear that no longer will the courts permit medieval dungeons to exist in modern society. However, a vast majority of all courts have held that solitary confinement is not per se unconstitutional.[123] In fact, many courts have upheld specific types of solitary confinement. For example, in 1970 Federal District Judge Seals upheld the practice of Texas institutions.[124] There, incorrigible inmates are placed in a clean cell which contains a toilet, washbasin, drinking fountain, and steel bunk absent mattress and blanket. The room is completely dark, but the prisoner is allowed a cloth gown, toothbrush and toothpaste, and may shower once a day. His diet is restricted to bread and water, but he is allowed a full meal every seventy-two hours. The maximum period of incarceration is fifteen days.[125]

Other courts have rejected specific allegations that certain types of solitary confinement constitute cruel and unusual punishment. Some note that the facts of the case simply do not support the allegations.[126] Others, paying at least minimal deference to the hands-off doctrine, assert that "solitary confinement, and the temporary inconveniences and discomforts which accompany it do not violate the eighth amendment."[127] Some note that the petitioners' complaints do not rise to the constitutional level, are frivolous, or are matters solely within the concern of the state.[128] Some note that prisoners are perfectly aware that infraction of prison rules will result in solitary confinement and therefore can avoid it, while others have held that if a prisoner can effect his own release, the confinement is constitutional.[129] For example, in *Winsley* v. *Walsh*,[130] Federal Judge David W. Williams held that Winsley's confinement in solitary for violating grooming regulations was constitutional. Winsley refused to cut his hair or beard, was warned, and subsequently placed in solitary. He was told that when he would comply with the regulations he would be removed to the general prison population. The judge ruled that he was not entitled to relief. Still other decisions have held that because the confinement has not been arbitrarily imposed, it does not constitute cruel and unusual punishment.[131]

Thus, despite the objections raised by prisoners and scholars, it should be perfectly clear that the punishment is quite permissible in the eyes of the courts.[132] As long as basic physical and mental health standards are maintained, and human dignity is not brutalized, the courts will simply not interfere with this sort of disciplining of inmates by administrative officials.

There are other types of incarceration that restrict the activities of inmates. These places have been variously referred to as segregated confinement units, maximum security units, segregation wings, control units, close confinement units, isolation units, and control cells. There are substantially fewer restrictions in these units than are found in solitary confinement. However, specific rules vary from institution to institution. For example, in some prisons, when an inmate is placed in segregated confinement, he cannot gain "good time" whereby the length of his incarceration is shortened by a few days each month.[133] In other prisons, "good time" days may be accumulated provided the inmate conducts himself in a proper fashion.[134] Generally, however, prisoners incarcerated in such units have contact with each other, are allowed to exercise, take correspondence courses, have mailing privileges, and receive visitors.[135] On the other hand, they are somewhat more restricted than the general inmate population and are totally isolated from them.[136]

The courts have heard numerous challenges to this mode of confinement and are unanimous in concluding that it does not inflict cruel and unusual punishment per se.[137] Generally, as long as prison officials have reasonable justification for placing an inmate in such a unit, the incarceration will be upheld.[138]

One of the reasons approved of by the courts is if the inmate is in constant violation of prison rules. For example, in *Evans* v. *Moseley*,[139] the Tenth Circuit Court of Appeals upheld a transfer from solitary confinement to a control unit because the prisoner continually tried to establish a chapter of the Black United Front against the wishes of prison authorities. The court noted that the action was not "arbitrary or capricious." In another case, the incarceration of Luther W. Miller in "B house lock-up" (a mode of segregation for hard-to-handle prisoners) in the Illinois State Penitentiary at Joliet was upheld because he had repeatedly broken rules, and represented a threat to prison security.[140]

A second reason approved of by the courts is to isolate particularly intractable convicts from the general population. Generally included among this group are inmates constantly involved in violent assaults on other inmates or guards, returned escapees, and highly potential escapees. In 1967, for example, the Tenth Circuit Court of Appeals upheld the confinement of a convict who had been continuously incarcerated in such a manner for over two years due to his participation in extreme violence on three separate occasions.[141] Such incarceration, stated the court, is not arbitrary.[142] In 1970, Gary S. Krist, infamous abductor of Miss Barbara Jane Mackle, whom he buried alive in a wooden box equipped with an air pump, claimed, among other things, that his segregated confinement constituted cruel and unusual punishment.[143] The court denied relief on the ground that such incarceration was reasonable. Krist had escaped a number of times before, and during one attempt, a fellow inmate was killed. Thus, there was a need to prevent further escapes and to protect other prisoners from his schemes. Perhaps a statement of the Vermont Supreme Court most clearly reflects the attitudes of administrators on the subject:

> Our prison officials should be commended rather than censured for segregating . . . the more hardened convicts. One of the principle purposes of imprisonment is reformation, and to that end first offenders, particularly those guilty of minor offenses, should be shielded from association with those who according to long experience, have a bad influence upon their fellows.[144]

A third reason approved of by the courts is to protect a convict from his fellow inmates in the general prison population. In *Smith* v. *Swenson*,[145] for example, an inmate, contrary to his wishes, was placed in segregated confinement. He had been threatened on several occasions, and his life was endangered. The court found absolutely no grounds for granting him relief. In a similar case, Nathan Breeden requested that he be placed in the maximum security unit for his own protection.[146] Once there, however, he objected to following the rules of the unit. He alleged that being subjected to the limited recreation, exercise, shaving, and bathing restrictions was cruel and unusual punishment. The court noted that he did not lose the opportunity for parole while so incarcerated, as did the other prisoners, and that being subjected to the other restrictions was not arbitrary or unreasonable. Moreover, he could leave the unit any time he so desired.

One of the most bitterly contested cases dealing with segregated confinement began in 1969. The Federal District Court for the Southern District of New York found sufficient justification to issue a preliminary injunction to restrain authorities from further incarcerating Martin Sostre in the punitive segregation unit at Green Haven prison.[147] In the unit, it was alleged, there was no work program, and no one was allowed access to the library, reading materials, motion pictures, television, or other recreational facilities. He was allowed to bathe and shave only once a week. Sostre also claimed that he remained in his cell for twenty-three hours a day, with only one hour of exercise. The light was regulated from outside the cell, and he was awakened at half-hour intervals during the night by the guards. Sostre was ultimately granted damages. The court found the practice "physically harsh, destructive of morale, dehumanizing in the sense that it is needlessly degrading and dangerous to the maintenance of sanity when continued for more than a short period of time which should certainly not exceed fifteen days."[148] Such punishment, the court later stated, "for any offense in prison is plainly cruel and unusual punishment."[149]

On appeal, however, Judge Irving R. Kaufman, writing the opinion for the Circuit Court, overruled the lower-court decision.[150] He concluded that although the conditions Sostre endured were severe, the appeals court could not agree with the district court that they were so foul and inhuman as to be violative of the basic concepts of decency. In reaching its conclusion, the court noted that the facts were not actually as Sostre had described them. The liberal diet, the items available in his cell, the opportunity for exercise, his participation in group therapy, the provisions for reading matter, and his communication with other prisoners "raised the quality of Sostre's segregated environment several notches above those truly barbarous and inhuman conditions heretofore condemned by ourselves and by other courts as 'cruel and unusual punishment.' "[151] However, the court did find that Sostre had been unlawfully placed there on account of political beliefs, and consequently, 124½ days of good time were restored.

Another case involving close confinement arose in Arkansas in 1969. Two types of convicts were placed in the isolation unit at Cummins Farm; those in protective custody, and those of a high-security, or escape, risk. The twelve-cell unit contained no windows and little furniture. The toilets could not be flushed from within the cells. Several inmates challenged their confinement. The court found their cells to be dirty, unsanitary, and pervaded by bad odors. There was great danger from the spreading of contagious diseases. Showers were allowed at most twice a week. The court found that the use of isolation units was necessary because administrative officials had been enjoined from utilizing the strap. Moreover, to be effective, such confinement had to be "rigorous, uncomfortable and unpleasant." However, the court noted, there are limits to the rigor and discomfort which a state may not constitutionally exceed. In this instance, the court ruled that the limits had been exceeded because the conditions were "mentally and emotionally traumatic as well as physically uncomfortable."[152] Further, such confinement was hazardous to health, degrading, debasing, and offended modern sensibilities. For these reasons, ruled the court, the confinement amounted to cruel and unusual punishment.

Having declared the practice unconstitutional, the court sought a remedy. Noting that finding a solution presented an extremely difficult and delicate situation, the court did not prescribe specific steps to be taken. Instead, it ordered the respondents to submit a report as to what they thought could be done to alleviate the problem.

The following year Angela Davis was successful in gaining release from "solitary facilities."[153] She was being held in the New York City Women's House of Detention pending extradition. An administrative decision was made to isolate her from the rest of the inmate population, allegedly because not doing so might lead to disruptions. The respondents claimed that she had become the center of attraction as well as an object of curiosity and had slowed down the movement of inmates in the clinical and dental areas. The court, however, rejected these arguments. It noted that there was no evidence that she had shown a propensity to cause disturbances in the past, and that "to sanction the isolation of the plaintiff merely because of the rubbernecking interest of her fellow prisoners would be to hold that all noted or notorious pretrial detainees would automatically be subjected to such a factual penalty for reasons beyond their control."[154] With regard to protecting her, the court noted that there were no facts or evidence to support the allegation that her safety was threatened. In conclusion, stated the court: "Nothing in the record indicates that the isolation of plaintiff has become necessary to ensure her appearance at the trial."[155] Thus, it was ordered that she be reinstated to the general inmate population and afforded the privileges enjoyed by them.

Two recent Illinois decisions have held particular periods of incarceration in punitive segregated confinement to be excessive. In the first, District Judge Foreman found that the plaintiff had been so confined for over sixteen months for offenses of a "relatively minor nature."[156] As such, the punishment was disproportionate, and all thirty-six prisoners involved were to be released to the general prison population. In the second case, Judge Carter ruled that a defendant was unconstitutionally incarcerated in B-Section, a segregated unit at San Quentin Prison.[157] O.C. Allen had been placed there following the death of a guard. Later, all charges against him were dropped, but he continued to be incarcerated in the unit. His stay there, the court held, had to have a reasonable relationship to a legitimate penal aim. Once the charges had been dropped, there was no such purpose. Thus, he had been unconstitutionally confined.

Additionally, two recent cases have held the conditions of confinement to be impermissible. In the first, James A. Castor had been placed in punitive segregation.[158] He was subjected to a bed check every thirty minutes or so around the clock, which made it impossible for him to sleep. He was awarded $100 in damages. The second case involved the incarceration of five pretrial detainees in the New Haven Correctional Center.[159] The cells were notably small, without sink, toilet, or running water. The prisoners were allowed out only fifteen minutes a day. Some inmates had been confined in this manner for sixty days. Judge Newman specifically noted that prisoners could be held in administrative segregation but that they must either be placed in cells with toilet facilities and running water or be permitted to use bathroom facilities at reasonable intervals. Further, they were to be provided with exercise out of their cells for at least one hour per day. Otherwise, the confinement would violate the basic concepts of decency and thus inflict cruel and unusual punishment.

It should be clear that placing an inmate in segregated confinement is perfectly permissible. Nevertheless, today the courts will carefully scrutinize the conditions surrounding such incarceration. The courts do recognize that the mental health of the prisoner is as important as his physical health, and although the courts have generally not placed time limitations on such incarceration, as some reformers have sought,[160] the judiciary will cast aside the hands-off doctrine to examine extreme conditions surrounding confinement in punitive segregation.

Restricted Diets

In an earlier chapter it was observed that both legislators and judicial officers have subjected convicts to diets of bread and water. Prison administrators have likewise imposed such diets on inmates for the infraction of rules.[161] Others have restricted the quantity of food. In 1962, for example, a convict challenged the practice of allowing him two small-portioned meals per day. A court of original jurisdiction in Utah found that the prisoner had not been provided with a sufficient quantity of food for sustenance and comfort, and issued a writ of habeas corpus on the ground that the practice violated the cruel and unusual punishment inhibition. On appeal, however, the Utah Supreme Court reversed and found that the evidence was insufficient to sustain the proposition.[162] Other allegations that sufficient quantities of food have not been provided have fallen victim to the hands-off doctrine.[163]

At least one federal district court has frontally attacked the idea of bread-and-water diets. In a class action, inmates incarcerated in prisons in Virginia alleged that such diets constituted cruel and unusual punishment. Judge Merhige agreed:

> Bread and water provides a daily intake of only 700 calories, whereas sedentary men on the average need 2000 calories or more to maintain continued health. . . .   The purpose and intended effect of such a diet is to discipline by debilitating him physically. Without food his strength and mental alertness begin to decline immediately. . . . Moreover, the pains of hunger constitute a dull, prolonged sort of corporal punishment. That marked physical effects ensue is evident from the numerous instances of substantial weight loss during solitary confinement.[164]

Judge Merhige found that such punishment is rarely used today and is generally disapproved of as obsolete. Furthermore, it is not essential to security. In conclusion, he found the restriction amounted to "an unnecessary infliction of pain . . . and [was] inconsistent with current minimum standards of respect for human dignity."[165]

Miscellaneous Methods

Most jurisdictions provide that a certain number of days shall be subtracted each month from a convict's total sentence if he abides by prison rules and regulations. Usually thirty days of good time result in the shortening of a sentence by five to ten days.[166] Taking away good time has rarely been challenged as inflicting cruel and unusual punishment.[167] Attempts to do so have generally been met with resistance in the form of the hands-off doctrine.[168]

In at least one instance the sacrifice of good time has been challenged as being excessive.[169] Patrick J. Sullivan was brought before the Good Time Forfeiture Board at the United States Medical Center at Springfield, Missouri. He pled guilty to the possession of four ounces of grain alcohol and as a result lost 365 days of good time. He claimed that the punishment was "not reasonably related to the infraction committed," but Judge Becker, a federal district judge, ruled that in light of the seriousness of the offense, the punishment was not cruel or unusual.

Parole revocation has also rarely been challenged as inflicting cruel and unusual punishment. As with good time determinations, deference has generally been paid to the hands-off doctrine. For example, Vernon C. O'Neill claimed that the United States Board of Parole was subjecting him to cruel and unusual punishment because it had postponed action on his parole. The court noted that parole is a matter of legislative grace rather than a right, and therefore it was not cruel and unusual punishment to deprive him of it.[170]

Another method often used to enforce prison regulations has been to subject inmates to work of a trivial nature. In one recent federal district court decision it was deemed cruel and unusual to require inmates to maintain silence during periods of the day or to require them to perform "repetitive, nonfunctional, degrading, and unnecessary tasks for many hours." Such activities as pulling grass without bending knees on a large tract of ground not intended for cultivation, or moving dirt with a shovel from one place on the ground to another and then back again, or buffing a small area of floor for a period of time exceeding that which is sufficiently required were singled out in particular.[171]

Challenges to Specific Prison Rules and Practices

Medical Treatment and Health Care

There is little question that today the intentional denial of needed medical treatment constitutes cruel and unusual punishment.[172] However, it is equally clear that improper or negligent medical treatment does not.[173] Judge Becker of the Federal District Court for the Western District of Missouri perhaps best summarized the present trend in legal thinking on the subject:

> Improper or inadequate medical treatment, in order to constitute cruel and unusual punishment within the proposition of the Eighth

> Amendment to the United States Constitution must be continuing,
> must not be supported by any competent, recognized school of
> medical practice and must amount to a denial of needed medical
> treatment.[174]

Thus, most decisions by medical specialists within the prison walls have been approved by the courts. Indeed, when medical expertise is involved, great deference is paid to the hands-off doctrine.[175] For example, decisions to permit unlicensed personnel to administer drugs,[176] to forcefully administer treatment when objected to,[177] to delay surgery until a specialist can be called,[178] to require the inmate to inform a guard as to the nature of his illness before being placed on the doctor's list,[179] to keep a prisoner in a hospital,[180] to use electric shock treatment,[181] to test for syphilis by performing a painful spinal tap,[182] and to wrap seriously nervous patients in cold sheets,[183] have all been upheld as not constituting cruel and unusual punishment. Further, decisions not to implant an artificial heart valve or to increase medication have been upheld when under similar attack.[184]

Despite the broad discretion given administrators, there have been several instances when courts have held particular practices unconstitutional.[185] In fact, Judge Northrop of the Federal District Court of Maryland claims that the issue of depriving prisoners of medical care has received more favorable consideration than any other as a basis for overcoming the usual defense that these matters involve questions of internal administration, and thus are not subject to judicial review.[186] In *Talley* v. *Stephens,* for example, Judge Henley reviewed a case in which two prisoners in ill health were required to perform heavy manual labor in the Arkansas penitentiary.

> In this connection, the court has no difficulty with the proposition
> that for prison officials knowingly to compel convicts to perform
> physical labor which is beyond their strength, or which constitutes
> a danger to their lives or health, or which is unduly painful consti-
> tutes an infliction of cruel and unusual punishment prohibited by
> the Eighth Amendment to the Constitution of the United States
> as included in the 14th Amendment.[187]

The court also held that the petitioners were entitled to demand proper medical care and attendance at "sick calls" at all reasonable times.

A second case involving health and work duties came before the Federal District Court for the Western District of Missouri in 1970. Aaron Black, incarcerated in the United States Medical Center at Springfield, sought to be released from work detail in the barber shop. Judge Becker noted that the respondent admitted that such work was "deleterious" to Black's health, and that although forced labor by convicts was not unconstitutional, "when the type of work to which the convict is assigned admittedly worsens a pathological condition, such

work must be deemed cruel and unusual punishment."[188]   Black was ordered
released from work in the barber shop.

In 1970 a rather unusual challenge came before the federal district court in
Nebraska. William Sawyer objected to the ingestion of his medication in crushed
form. He had emphysema and was required to take medicine three times a day.
Originally it was prescribed in pill form, but prison authorities subsequently
demanded that it be crushed. Sawyer claimed that he was so nauseated when
taking the medication in this manner that he had to wrap it in cigarette paper
in order to swallow it. This method was also banned by the authorities. Judge
Urbom noted that the doctor had recommended that the medicine be taken in
pill form, but had been overruled by the warden. He further noted that prison
officials should be "permitted to enforce reasonable regulations for the orderly
operation of a prison and for the safety and health of all prisoners, including
those directives reasonably designed to prevent abusive use of drugs."[189] However, in this case, he noted, no effort had been made to show that Sawyer had or
ever had any tendency to hoard narcotics. "In the absence of that kind of showing, . . ." Judge Urbom concluded, "requiring Sawyer to take his medication in a
form which results in nausea is sufficiently unusual, exceptional, and arbitrary to
constitute both cruel and inhuman punishment and a denial of adequate medical
treatment as required by the Eighth and Fourteenth Amendments."[190]

Three recent cases illustrate that the administration of drugs may impose
cruel and unusual punishment. A district court in Indiana held that injecting
juveniles intramuscularly with a tranquilizer for purposes of controlling excited
behavior had to be immediately stopped unless a licensed physician specifically
prescribed the dosage for the individual.[191] On appeal, the Seventh Circuit
Court of Appeals upheld the ruling because of the dangers involved in the
indiscriminate administration of drugs.[192] Judge Kiley noted that expert witnesses had testified that the practice could result in the collapse of the cardio-
vascular system, the closing of a patient's throat with consequent asphyxiation,
a depressant effect on the production of bone marrow, jaundice from an affected
liver, drowsiness, hematological disorders, sore throat, and ocular changes.

A third decision involved the intramuscular injection of opomorphine, a
drug that causes the patient to vomit.[193] Inmates at the Iowa Security Medical
Facility, a mental institution, were subjected to the "treatment" as part of a
behavior modification program. The injections were administered without
consent, by nurses, for such offenses as not getting up, smoking against orders,
or for talking, swearing or lying. The court noted that the testimony relating
to the medical acceptability of the treatment was "not conclusive." In fact,
the court found no evidence that the drug was used elsewhere in any other
state. Moreover, the fact that a great deal of pain accompanies vomiting was
noted. "The use of this unproven drug for this purpose on an involuntary
basis," concluded Judge Ross, "is, in our opinion, cruel and unusual punishment, prohibited by the eighth amendment."[194]

Perhaps the most extreme case of deprivation of medical treatment recently came before a federal district court in Alabama.[195] At the outset, Judge Johnson noted that the plaintiffs had presented substantial evidence that the prison authorities had abused their discretion in providing medical treatment to inmates. He noted, among other things, that the medical facilities were grossly understaffed and underequipped. The neglect of basic medical needs, he continued, could justly be called "barbarous" and "shocking to the conscience." At the Medical and Diagnostic Center there were only three part-time doctors to attend several hundred inmates. There was no registered nurse on duty at night or on weekends. The center had no administrator, dietitian, registered X-ray technician, medical records librarian, or civilian records clerk. Moreover, it was noted, the care at the center was far superior to that found elsewhere in the system. At the Atmore-Holman complex, some 150 miles from the center, there were approximately 1700 inmates. Only one part-time retired physician served these prisoners. Dental care was provided by a part-time dentist. Throughout the entire system there were no standards of procedure relating to fire control, sanitary conditions, record keeping, and safety. There was a chronic shortage of medical supplies, with rags often being substituted for gauze. Perhaps the most deplorable deprivation was the practice of not allowing inmates to attend sick call or making them wait extremely long periods of time before permitting them to do so.[196] A large majority of mentally disturbed prisoners received no treatment whatsoever.

Judge Johnson related several case histories to illustrate the gross neglect to which prisoners had been subjected. In one case a quadriplegic had spent months in the center's hospital and suffered bedsores. They had become open wounds because of lack of care, and they eventually became "infested with maggots." Days would pass without his bandages being changed, until the stench pervaded the entire ward. The month he died the bandages had been changed only once.

In concluding that the system represented a "willful and intentional violation of the rights of prisoners," the court held that the inmates had been subjected to cruel and unusual punishment. Judge Johnson issued a twenty-two-part decree restraining the Board of Corrections from failing or refusing to provide adequate medical care to each inmate. Among the specific provisions Judge Johnson required were that the medical facilities be brought up to the standards of the United States Department of Health, that the regulations of the Federal Bureau of Narcotics and Dangerous Drugs be followed, that a fire evacuation plan, approved by the state fire marshal, be adopted, that periodic inspections by the fire marshal be conducted, that a written statement of sanitation procedures be adopted, that regular inspection for general sanitation be instituted, that a report be filed within ninety days on the condition of equipment in the various facilities, that a study be undertaken to determine the minimum number of personnel needed to operate these facilities, that a minimum quantity of drugs and supplies be maintained, that eyeglasses, dentures, and other devices be provided, that a records system be maintained, and that physical examinations be given at regular intervals. It was further ordered that the defendants file a report with the court within six months detailing the implementation of each decree.

Prison Transfer

Prisoners often claim they are being subjected to cruel and unusual punishment when transferred from one institution to another. In 1969, for example, Fernando Rodriguez-Sandoval objected to being removed from a prison in Puerto Rico to the federal penitentiary in Atlanta, Georgia.[197] In 1971, Thomas Gallagher objected to being transferred from Sandstone Institution in Minnesota to the federal penitentiary at Terre Haute, Indiana, because he was afraid it would be more difficult to obtain early parole there.[198] In 1972, Melvin Lindsay objected to his transfer from Lewisburg, Pennsylvania, to the federal penitentiary at Atlanta, Georgia, because it denied him the opportunity to see his wife and family, who resided in Lewisburg.[199] In all three instances, courts upheld the transfers, utilizing rationale sounding very much like the hands-off doctrine. In *Rodriguez-Sandoval,* the court pointed out that Atlanta was the nearest federal penal institution for prisoners in his classification, and that "obviously, prisoners do not have a right to select their place of confinement."[200] In *Gallagher,* the court noted that prison transfer was not generally subject to judicial review, because the attorney general is given the authority to designate the place of incarceration. Further, the anticipation that he would not receive early parole was premature and hence not ripe for review. In *Lindsay,* the court simply stated that the lower court properly dismissed the case. Several courts, subsequently, have issued similar rulings.[201]

On the other hand, prisoners have often *sought* transfer on the ground that their present place of incarceration constituted cruel and unusual punishment. Generally, such allegations have been quickly dismissed. For example, in *Thogmartin* v. *Moseley,*[202] Vern Mac Thogmartin claimed that he was being subjected to cruel and unusual punishment by not being allowed a transfer to the Medical Center at Springfield, Missouri. He claimed that he was being denied the opportunity to rehabilitate himself. At the Medical Center, he claimed, he could receive advanced training as a medical technician. The court rejected his argument, asserting that the transfer of prisoners was an internal matter, and that the control and management of prisons was vested in the attorney general and not the courts. Judge Stanley noted that this was a clear example of when the hands-off doctrine should be followed. For similar reasons, Justice Conway refused to direct the transfer of Severe Hawthorne to an institution closer to New York City so that he could be near his family.[203]

A successful transfer was accomplished, however, by Alfred Curt von Wolfersdorf. It will be recalled that a court did order his transfer from one institution to another. His "incarceration among the 'criminally insane' for 20 years," concluded the court, "because of his status as an insane defendant (presumed innocent) named in an untriable indictment violates his protection against cruel and unusual punishment."[204] Similarly dictum in one opinion has suggested that it would be cruel and unusual punishment to confine a sane prisoner with mental defectives and insane persons. In such an instance, it was suggested, transferal might be constitutionally mandatory.[205]

Miscellaneous Practices

Several other institutional rules and practices have been challenged as inflicting cruel and unusual punishment. Foremost among these are the rules regulating personal grooming.[206] Rarely have such regulations been declared unconstitutional.[207] Generally they have been upheld on the grounds that the prisoner's right to wear a beard and long hair is outweighed by the interest of the state in maintaining sanitary conditions, discipline, and safety in prison facilities.[208] Courts have also upheld as not inflicting cruel and unusual punishment, the practices of prohibiting prisoners from having sexual relations with their wives,[209] and refusing, without explanation, to allow a prisoner to reenroll in college.[210] One court has held that the censorship and confiscation of manuscripts written by an unconvicted inmate at the United States Medical Center was an unconstitutional denial of his liberties.[211] It is not clear, however, whether the practice violated his First, Fourth, or Eighth Amendment rights.

Recently the practice of not providing rehabilitative treatment to the incarcerated juvenile has come under strong attack. In *Martarella* v. *Kelley,*[212] Judge Lasker found a clear constitutional right to such treatment under the Eighth Amendment. "Where the State," he held, "imposes . . . detention, it can meet the Constitution's requirement of due process and prohibition of cruel and unusual punishment if, and only if, it furnishes adequate treatment to the detainee."[213] Similarly, Judge Justice of the United States District Court for the Eastern District of Texas held that juveniles in six Texas facilities were entitled to rehabilitative treatment.[214] More recently, the Seventh Circuit Court of Appeals ruled that the " 'right to treatment' includes the right to minimum acceptable standards of care and treatment for juveniles and the right to *individualized* care and treatment."[215]

Another practice recently challenged is incarcerating young offenders with older ones. The practice was upheld by the Delaware Supreme Court in 1972.[216] Further, the practice of jointly incarcerating "Persons in Need of Supervision" (juveniles who have committed acts which would not constitute crimes if they were adults) with juvenile delinquents (juveniles who have committed adult crimes) has been held not to violate the Eighth Amendment.[217]

An extremely unusual case arose in Alabama in 1972.[218]   Defendant Brown had been sentenced to death by electrocution in Kilby Prison. Later the prison was razed and thus it became impossible to carry out the sentence. The court of criminal appeals had ruled that the penalty was simply suspended until the legislature could provide a new place for electrocution. The Alabama Supreme Court, however, noted that the result was to suspend Brown under a "molecular Sword of Damocles" which could fall, *if and whenever* the Legislature" acted. The "indefinite suspension," ruled Justice Cates, constituted cruel and unusual punishment. "Death by electrocution," he continued, "is to be swift. Here the bolt is swift but [the] wait is unknown."[219]   Further, the uncertainty constituted psychological cruelty. Moreover, it was obviously unusual. The sentence was changed to life imprisonment.

Challenges to Rules and Practices Found in Public Schools

Obviously, public schools are not penal institutions. However, rules established by school administrators are often challenged as inflicting cruel and unusual punishment.

Paddling Students

Corporal punishment for infraction of rules in public schools is as old as the educational system itself,[220] and every state except New Jersey and the District of Columbia permits its use.[221]   Recently, four cases challenging the practice as inflicting cruel and unusual punishment have reached federal courts. The first case arose in Texas. Douglas Ware, a student in the Dallas Public School System, contended that any corporal punishment is unconstitutional and in violation of the Eighth and Fourteenth Amendments because it is "arbitrary, capricious, and unrelated to any legitimate educational purpose."[222] He claimed specifically that he had been hit several times with a paddle two feet long, one fourth to one half inches thick, and six inches wide, that one time he was hit with a tennis shoe, that once he was knocked unconscious, and finally, that paddling took place without parental consent, contrary to administrative policy. Established procedure regulated the practice. Rules provided that it be undertaken in front of witnesses by a teacher after receiving written permission from the child's parents. The court noted that the evidence did show that the practice was abused by some, but that fact did not make it unconstitutional. There was a reasonable relationship between corporal punishment and the purposes of the educational function, explained the court. Judge Taylor, writing the memorandum opinion, did note, however, that it should be used sparingly, and only as a last resort. But paddling itself, he concluded, is simply not cruel and unusual punishment. The Fifth Circuit Court of Appeals affirmed the decision, and the United States Supreme Court denied certiorari.[223]

In a neighboring state, New Mexico, Zebediah Sims, a student in San Juan, sought an injunction against the use of corporal punishment on students by teachers.[224] Among other allegations, he claimed that the practice imposed cruel and unusual punishment, because it served no legitimate educational purpose, tended to inhibit learning, and retarded social growth. Judge Eubanks noted that the harm was only slight and that the facts were far different than those found in *Jackson* v. *Bishop*,[225] a case upon which Sims relied heavily. In language clearly consistent with the hands-off doctrine, he concluded that the court would "not act as a super school board to second guess the defendants."[226]

A third case arose in western Pennsylvania.[227] The school district of Northgate permitted corporal punishment under carefully controlled conditions. It was to be utilized only as a last resort after a conference between teacher and principal, the latter determining the time, place, and person to administer the punishment. The pupil had to be explained the seriousness of his offense and given the reasons for the punishment. The time between the offense and punishment was not to be so long as to cause undue anxiety. Further, it had to be administered in kindness, in the presence of another adult, and at a time and under conditions not calculated to subject the child to ridicule or shame. Paddling was to take place only on the buttocks, and only if no psychological damage would result. Despite the elaborate controls and safeguards, Bill Glaser and his parents contended that the practice inflicted cruel and unusual punishment. The court made short shrift of the allegation, noting that corporal punishment itself was not unconstitutional per se. In this instance, ruled Judge Weis, where only three "medium strokes" had been administered, it was not excessive. Citing approvingly the *Ware* and *Sims* decisions, he suggested that a school has the authority to discipline its students, and under these conditions, the court would not interfere.

A fourth such case arose in Vermont.[228] In that case a federal district court again upheld the paddling of students as authorized by state statute. The use of corporal punishment was deemed necessary to secure obedience and maintain order and thus did not offend the Eighth Amendment. In conclusion, it is evident that the infliction of corporal punishment on school children is not per se unconstitutional, and with appropriate safeguards, it may be administered without court interference.

Personal Appearance Codes

Public schools often regulate the length and style of students' hair. Generally the requirements are that the hair not hang below the collar line, over the ears, or below the eyebrows.[229] Such regulations have been attacked as unconstitutional from several directions. Some have alleged that the rules violate the First Amendment guarantee to freedom of expression,[230] the Fifth Amendment guarantee of liberty (usually to carry on an occupation such as playing in a band),[231] or the Fourteenth Amendment guarantee of due process.[232] Some have been successful,[233] while others have not.[234] The only case in which the cruel and unusual inhibition has been involved arose in South Carolina.[235] Stanley Rumler, a seventeen-year-old senior in Lexington High School, was suspended until he got a haircut pursuant to school regulations. He then contested the regulation as inflicting cruel and unusual punishment. The court, however, refused to consider the allegation a "real issue" and passed over it quickly without evaluation. Similarly, the Federal District Court for the Southern District of Texas cursorily rejected the allegation that expulsion from school for violating the dress code by wearing pantsuits constituted cruel and unusual punishment. The court noted that the assertion was raised "with more ingenuity than merit," and as the plaintiff had not been the subject of any criminal sanction and had not been abused, tortured, or otherwise brutalized, the suspension was "clearly not within the ambit of the Amendment."[236]

Challenges to Rules and Practices Found in Other Governmental Agencies

In 1972 the Court of Appeals of Ohio held that a social worker employed by the Bureau of Juvenile Placement was not subjected to cruel and unusual punishment when suspended for failing to comply with hair length regulations and a dress code.[237]

12 Total Prison Conditions

In the previous chapter challenges to the constitutionality of specific administrative rules and practices were reviewed. Attacking the constitutionality of a chain gang, prison farm, city or county jail, a state penitentiary, or an entire penal system is quite another thing. The idea, however, is not as new as some recent decisions imply. Most notable are the cases brought during the late 1940s and early 1950s alleging that chain gangs inflicted cruel and unusual punishment.

Chain Gangs

Seldom has as much controversy surrounded a series of cases as accompanied those started by Leon Johnson. In 1943, he and approximately 175 other convicts escaped from a Georgia chain gang and made their way into northern states.[1] He was arrested on an executive warrant issued by the governor of Pennsylvania at the request of the governor of Georgia. Johnson claimed that he had been subjected to cruel and unusual punishment while in the chain gang. He alleged that he received brutal treatment from the guards, who threatened to kill him, and that his life would be endangered if he were returned to Georgia. He was refused a writ of habeas corpus by both a county and a superior court in Pennsylvania, because the testimony was based on his "unsupported word" and was "without any corroboration."[2] Johnson then applied to a federal district court for a writ of habeas corpus, but was denied. The court did note that there was "evidence that Johnson received cruel treatment after he had been convicted and while he was serving his sentence." However, "such treatment" reasoned the court, "would not entitle him to his liberty as it does not constitute a custody of relator in violation of the Constitution or laws of the United States." The Eighth Amendment, continued Judge McVicar, "is not a limitation upon the States." Moreover, he stated, the allegation that Johnson's life would be endangered if returned "is not sustained by credible evidence."[3] Consequently, habeas corpus relief was refused.

The Third Circuit Court of Appeals, on review, reversed. The court noted that other witnesses had testified "that it was the custom of the Georgia authorities to treat chain gang prisoners with persistent and deliberate brutality at or about the time the petitioner was suffering punishment and for some years thereafter."[4] The court noted that both a November 1, 1943 issue of *Life*[5]

magazine, and a September 13, 1943 issue of *Time*[6] magazine were introduced
as evidence. Both articles revealed the horrors surrounding incarceration on
the chain gang. The *Time* article reviewed the testimony given by inmates to
a special investigating committee of the state legislature. It was reported that
the prisoners' diets consisted mainly of peas, beans, and syrup. They were
forced to work from sunup to sundown, and were beaten if they slackened
their pace. "Leg picks" were used to prevent escape.[7] Instances of whipping
with a rubber hose of up to fifty lashes were reported. Four inmates cut
their Achilles tendon, thus crippling themselves, to escape the work and beatings. The *Life* article reported many of the same facts. It also included several
very vivid photographs of what life on a chain gang was really like. There were
pictures of men wearing the traditional stripes, breaking rocks under the hot
sun. They were viewed eating cold fish lunches, wearing picks, and shown confined in filthy overcrowded cells. Additionally, the article reported beatings
with ax handles and the use of steaming "sweatboxes," a device in which a
prisoner had recently died. It told of "ignorant 'shotgun-men' " guards who
were politically chosen, but were paid only from $30 to $50 a month. Several
newspaper articles were also introduced.

Because the witnesses stated that the conditions described in these magazines were accurate, reasoned the court, their contents might be considered as
evidence. Furthermore, no witnesses were offered by Georgia to refute the
testimony. The court also held that the lower-court's statement, "there is
evidence that Johnson received cruel treatment," constituted a finding "that
Johnson had been subjected to cruel treatment following his conviction. It is
obvious also," continued the court, "that in using the phrase 'cruel treatment'
the court below was referring to the cruel and unusual punishment provision of
the Eighth Amendment."[8] Judge Biggs, writing the opinion, rejected the notion
that states were not prohibited from inflicting cruel and unusual punishment,
by holding that "where the right protected and guaranteed under the Bill of
Rights . . . is 'basic' and 'fundamental' to the rights of life and liberty, recognized and guaranteed by the Constitution of the United States, then the due
process clause of the Fourteenth Amendment prohibits a state from abridging
or denying the right in question."[9] The court did not, however, decide whether
the Eighth Amendment falls within the ambit of the Fourteenth Amendment.
Nevertheless, it entertained "no doubt that the Fourteenth Amendment prohibits the infliction of cruel and unusual punishment by a state."[10] To be free
from such punishment, ruled Judge Biggs, is a basic and fundamental right, one
which Johnson had clearly been denied.

> Indeed, no other conclusion would be possible, in view of the
> known facts concerning the working of the Georgia penal
> system at the time of the petitioner's sentence and in consid-
> eration of the circumstance that the State of Georgia offered

no testimony whatsoever in contradiction to that given by Johnson and his witnesses.[11]

   Thus, for the first time a federal court had declared that the environment
of an incarcerate inflicted cruel and unusual punishment.[12] The decision was
not well received and was harshly criticized in the law reviews.[13] Most analysts
argued that the case was wrongly decided,[14] many because they felt "the court
went beyond its jurisdiction in considering the treatment accorded Johnson on
the chain gang."[15] That same year the United States Supreme Court granted
certiorari and reversed the decision in a brief per curiam opinion.[16] The court
did not reach the substantive issues, but dismissed because Johnson had not
exhausted his state remedies.[17]
   Many opinions involving similar allegations following the *Johnson* decision
dealt almost exclusively with procedural questions.[18] However, a federal district
court in New Jersey did discuss the merits of the chain gang. Julius V. Harper,
being held for extradition to Alabama, alleged that while in a work camp at
Maplesville, Alabama, he was beaten by guards and the warden with sticks,
blackjacks and straps, was forced to eat unfit food, and was set upon by dogs.
As proof of his allegation, he showed scars said to have been inflicted by the
authorities. The court ruled that Harper had, in this instance, exhausted his
remedies, and proceeded to rule on the substantive issue. Judge Froman noted
that Harper had held up well under cross-examination by the attorney general,
and that there was no reason to doubt his word. "Although his testimony lacked
corroboration in many instances," he noted, "it carried conviction when fitted into
the pattern of the realities as they are known." Thus, "in their composite," he concluded, "they spell out cruel and unusual punishment within the scope of *Johnson
v. Dye* . . . and demonstrate a violation of his rights protected by the Fourteenth
Amendment of the United States Constitution."[19] Harper was ordered released.
   That same year Judge Froman again had an opportunity to review allegations concerning the cruel and unusual treatment of a prisoner.[20] This time,
however, he found that the facts did not support the allegations. The Richmond City Prison Farm in Georgia simply did not tolerate the treatment of
prisoners, he concluded, the way the state of Georgia did in the *Johnson* case.
   A similar conclusion was reached by Justice Hammer of the New York
Supreme Court.[21] Clarence Jackson, an escaped fugitive from Georgia, claimed
that he had lost the sight of his left eye, had broken his arm, and had scars on
his legs from the shackles used while imprisoned there. The court noted that
in 1946 Georgia had abolished all forms of corporal punishment and barred the
use of shackles, manacles, picks, leg irons, and chain gangs. There was no evidence that Jackson would be treated cruelly if returned to Georgia, he asserted,
and unlike Johnson, Jackson had no corroborating evidence or witnesses. On
appeal, the Second Circuit Court of Appeals affirmed, and the United States
Supreme Court denied certiorari.

The following year Sylvester Middlebrooks, Jr., was successful in gaining
release from California authorities who were holding him for extradition to
Georgia. His description of conditions on the chain gang are worthy of extensive quotation:

> 50 or 60 men were housed in one large room, 40 by 50 feet, with
> beds in tiers. No toilet facilities were available. . . . The prisoners
> worked from sun-up until sun-down. . . . The food, and vermin
> and filthy substances contained therein, caused the prisoners to
> become sick with nausea and dysentery. . . . The prisoners were
> often beaten and whipped. Double shackles were used, consisting
> of a band on each ankle and a chain 14 to 16 inches long in
> between. "Picks" were also used, consisting of long points ema-
> nating horizontally from the band on the ankle. . . . "Stocks"
> were used. . . . The prisoner was seated on the narrow edge of a
> 2 by 4, his wrists and ankles placed through holes in the stocks.
> His body thereby leaned forward at a 45 degree angle. A 2 by 4
> was wired across his knees to keep them pressed down. When a
> prisoner was removed from the stocks, even after one hour deten-
> tion, he often was unable to walk and had to be dragged to the bull
> pen. Sweat boxes were in use, consisting of small buildings 3 feet
> wide, 6 feet long without light or heat. . . . Shackles were kept on
> at night.[22]

Judge Carter declared that the right to be free from cruel and unusual punishment is basic and fundamental, and within the protection of the Fourteenth
Amendment. He found that Middlebrooks had been previously subjected to
cruel and unusual punishment and probably would be again if returned. By
holding Middlebrooks, he reasoned, California was an active participant in
again subjecting him to such punishment. Consequently, he was ordered
released.

From this brief review it should be obvious that northern courts were
extremely disenchanted with the practices accompanying imprisonment in
Southern chain gangs. Nevertheless, even today it is clear that the work camp,
chain gang, and hard labor are not per se unconstitutional.[23]

Jails

Historically, convicts have rarely challenged the constitutionality of their
environments. However, as most jails are extremely antiquated, the general
conditions surrounding incarceration are often deplorable. Many jails are
totally inadequate for the function they are to perform. The most horrifying

of stories have been told about the life of convicts incarcerated in these institutions.[24]

The first jail suit based on Eighth Amendment grounds was brought in 1904. George Ellis had been convicted of violating liquor laws and sentenced to the county jail for fifty-two months, fined $5200, and required to pay costs of $1300. He was to remain there until the fines and costs were paid. The county commissioners recognized that he was unable to do so, but refused to release him, even though he was in poor health and required medical attention. The jail was obviously outdated. The county judge, city attorney, and sheriff all testified that it was inadequate to accommodate the prisoner. It was poorly ventilated and provided no exercise program. To the suggestion that Ellis be set free on account of these conditions, the court replied: "It must be obvious . . . that we cannot order the petitioner released on account of the conditions of the jail. To do so would require us on similar applications to order the release of all prisoners confined there."[25]

Similar apprehension was expressed in a 1951 case in Alaska. Ernest Pickens alleged that being incarcerated in the city jail of Anchorage constituted cruel and unusual punishment. In the jail, forty prisoners were crowded into a room twenty-seven feet square. There was obviously little opportunity for recreation or exercise. Sleeping was accomplished in shifts. Young boys were mixed in with hardened criminals and mental patients. There was admittedly inadequate ventilation. The possibility of fire was great. Inadequate bathing and toilet facilities, coupled with general unsanitary conditions, facilitated the spread of contagious diseases. "Altogether," concluded the court, "the place is not fit for human habitation."[26] As in the *Ellis* case, however, the court recognized that if Pickens were released, the other thirty-nine prisoners would be certain to file similar petitions. This, noted the court, would "not add to the feeling of safety which every citizen ought to be able to enjoy."[27] Judge Diamond, writing the opinion, further noted that if the prisoners were discharged, they might never be brought to trial. It is obvious that he wanted to correct the horrid conditions, but at the same time, he could find no means by which to accomplish the task. Judge Diamond recognized that he could not order the marshal to furnish other quarters, because he had no funds to do so. Further, he could not order the house of representatives or the senate to appropriate the money. His ultimate solution was to note that the phrase "cruel and unusual punishment" is relative, and when comparing these conditions of incarceration with the conditions faced by the soldiers then fighting in Korea, the punishment, "while inexcusable and shocking to the sensibilities of all civilized persons, is not of such a nature as to come presently within the scope of the Eighth Amendment and to justify discharge of the petitioner at this time."[28]

In 1968, the Fifth Circuit Court of Appeals held that Willie Beard, an inmate at Altmore Prison Farm in Alabama, was entitled to have reviewed allegations that practices surrounding his incarceration went beyond matters of prison discipline and internal administration.[29] That same year inmates of the Cook County Jail in Chicago initiated action alleging that the physical conditions surrounding their imprisonment constituted cruel and unusual punishment.[30] The matter was settled out of court when the defendants attempted to remedy some of the more drastic conditions.[31]

It was not until 1970 that prisoners incarcerated in a jail were first successful in obtaining a declaration that their environment was unconstitutional. A New Mexico court held that conditions in the local jail were so intolerable that they inflicted cruel and unusual punishment.[32] A court order was issued limiting the total population of the jail to sixty inmates. The authorities were so stunned by the decision that they immediately released all inmates over that number, a course of action not demanded by the order.[33]

Later that same year a federal district judge in Louisiana ruled that the conditions in Orleans Parish Prison "so shocked the conscience as a matter of elemental decency" and were "so much more cruel than is necessary" to achieve legitimate penal aims, that such confinement constituted cruel and unusual punishment in violation of the Eighth and Fourteenth Amendments.[34] He had found as fact that the jail was built in 1929 to house 400-450 prisoners, and that at the time, 800-900 prisoners were incarcerated there. The cells were to hold four inmates, but at the time contained six to eight inmates.[35] The toilets were so badly rusted and corroded that cleanliness was impossible, and in some cells they had to be used as hand basins because the washbowls were not functioning properly. The cells had no interior lighting. The mattresses were never cleaned and were covered with vomit and urine. Many inmates slept on the floor, often with no sheets, pillows, or blankets. Ventilation was poor, making it extremely hot in the summer and very cold in the winter. The roof and walls leaked. The jail was infested with rats, mice, and roaches. Foul odors prevailed everywhere, and the kitchen was unsanitary. Bathing and exercise facilities were entirely inadequate. The threat of fire and of contamination by contagious diseases was great. Extremely dangerous prisoners were not placed in isolation, and there was easy access by everyone to materials from which to fashion deadly weapons. Security was inadequate, as were medical and hospital facilities. Judge Christenberry was fortunate in finding a remedy close at hand. He noted that a nearby jail was never filled to capacity and could hold many of the prisoners. Furthermore, two unfurnished floors of the other jail could be redesigned to accommodate more than 240 additional prisoners.

The following year several similar cases came before the courts. In one, five inmates of the Pulaski County Jail in Arkansas sought to have the conditions of their environment ameliorated.[36] The jail was used almost exclusively for persons awaiting trial and not for convicts. Judge Eisele made an inspection of the jail and found conditions similar to those in the New Orleans jail.

The defendants stipulated that the jail did not presently meet minimal standards, but argued that they were planning to build a new jail and would remedy the present conditions as fast as possible. The court issued an "interim order" directing the defendants to proceed with their plans. Both parties were ordered to submit reports reevaluating the progress of the defendants. In a subsequent report by the plaintiffs, certain improvements were acknowledged, but they alleged that many conditions had not been rectified. Among these, no new help had been hired to serve on the staff and thus help protect inmates from attack. No recreational programs had been instituted, the mail was still censored and restricted, and there were no improvements in ventilation, laundry facilities, cleaning, and bathing materials. Medical examinations were not given as promised, and rules and regulations of conduct were not constructed. The defendants' report disputed some of the allegations and pointed to the reasons for delays in implementing others. The court, in arriving at its conclusion, noted that it was not really appropriate to judge the constitutionality of the conditions by referring to the cruel and unusual punishment clause of the Eighth Amendment. After all, the incarcerates had been convicted of no crime. "The detainees," asserted the court, "should not have to suffer any 'punishment,' as such, whether 'cruel and unusual' or not."[37] Further, stated Judge Eisele, "inadequate resources can never be an adequate justification for the state's depriving any person of his constitutional rights. If the state cannot obtain the resources to detain prisoners awaiting trial in accordance with minimum constitutional standards," he continued, "then the state will not be permitted to detain such persons."[38]

The court was most concerned with the lack of adequate staffing. Attacks on inmates by fellow prisoners have become more and more visible in recent years. For example, in 1969 a case was brought before a federal district court in Mississippi. There an inmate was blinded and had received brain damage and other injuries as a result of being shot by a trusty inmate guard. Allegedly the guard shot the plaintiff to satisfy a grudge. The court noted that:

> Imprisonment under the extra hazardous conditions to which the plaintiff was needlessly exposed, and which culminated in permanently maiming and totally disabling him, was so severe and shocking to the conscience, and so utterly disproportionate to the crime [petty larceny for taking articles of the retail value of $2.11] as to constitute cruel and unusual punishment.[39]

The plaintiff was awarded damages. Other cases involving beatings and sexual attacks on inmates by fellow prisoners have appeared before the courts.[40] Generally, however, if the attack is an isolated incident, prison officials are not held responsible.[41]

With such cases constantly appearing before the courts, it does not appear unusual that Judge Eisele was particularly sensitive to the plight of the inmates in the Pulaski County Jail. To remedy the situation, he ordered that regardless of the number of qualified staff members, the prison population could not exceed 115 at any one time. Even less would be permitted if necessary paid personnel were not added to the staff immediately. He also ordered that at least one female "free world" staff member had to be present twenty-four hours a day to attend female inmates. Jailors would be permitted to work a maximum eight-hour shift, and at least two more guards had to be immediately added to the staff.

A second case arising in 1971 occurred in Ohio. The Lucas County Jail in 1971 was about seventy-six years old. Circumstances similar to those found in the earlier cases were present: overcrowding, and inadequate ventilation, illumination, plumbing, bathing facilities, toilets, clothing, bedding, food, exercise, and recreation facilities. There were few guards, and no attempt was made to segregate hardened convicts from those inmates awaiting trial. "If the constitutional provision against cruel and unusual punishment has any meaning," stated the court, "the evidence in this case shows that it has been violated. The cruelty is a refined sort," noted Judge Young, "much more comparable to the Chinese water torture than to such crudities as breaking on the wheel." Further, the evidence revealed that the punishment was unusual. "Most jails are bad," he continued, "but this one is unusually bad."[42] In a subsequent opinion, Judge Young wrestled with the problem of a remedy.[43] He noted that while the court could not order a new jail built, he did have the authority to issue an elaborate decree. In the first place, the sheriff was directed to reduce his policing and civil branch expenditures so that he could increase, without additional appropriations, the expenditures for the operation of the jail. The sheriff was also ordered to cease using jail space for the storage of confiscated property and other materials. The city carpenter and plumber were ordered to vacate the premises. The county commissioners were ordered to set up a bail program. The sheriff was given ninety days in which to reduce the inmate population (a maximum of two prisoners per cell). The defendants as a group were given thirty days to present a plan for correcting the interior lighting system. The sheriff was ordered to redeploy his forces so that properly trained guards were on duty at all times (two per floor). All jail personnel were required to begin immediately a course of programmed instruction prepared by the United States Bureau of Prisons. Successful completion was required for continued employment. In addition, the sheriff was required to submit within ninety days a comprehensive plan for the selection and in-service training of jail personnel. The defendants were ordered to take specific steps to ensure that food and food services met minimal standards. The sheriff was also ordered to submit, within thirty days, proposals for the classification of prisoners. It was further ordered that immediate steps be taken to effectuate an organized and supervised program of daily cleaning. In the area of medical services, certain standards were set. The sheriff was given thirty days to submit proposals for granting communications privileges, and to provide a place where inmate and counsel could meet. Prompt arrangements had to be made for library service. Nine specific repairs to the physical plant were ordered.

A third case in 1971 arose in Pennsylvania. Inmates in the Holmesburg Prison alleged that they were incarcerated in conditions that inflicted cruel and unusual punishment. The Superior Court of Philadelphia County had held that "the prison was a cruel, degrading and disgusting place, likely to bring out the worst in a man" and that after a riot on July 4, 1970, it was "a place ruled by cold blooded terror."[44] The court had ordered that plaintiff Bryant be transferred within forty-eight hours to "some other prison" or discharged from custody. To prevent an onslaught of petitions, the court had ordered a moratorium for thirty days to give the authorities an opportunity to remedy the situation. On appeal the Pennsylvania Supreme Court affirmed the lower court's decision. Justice Eagen, writing the opinion, noted: "The conditions at Holmesburg deprived the petitioners of the right to be free from cruel and unusual punishment, a right to which in their confinement they were legally entitled . . . and the deprivations of which made their imprisonment more onerous than the law allows."[45]

In 1972 the Philadelphia Court of Common Pleas reviewed another case brought by inmates incarcerated in that city.[46] The court, noting that it had already declared the Holmesburg Prison a "cruel, degrading and disgusting place," found the whole Philadelphia prison system to be a failure in almost every way. There were too many prisoners and too few guards. The health of the prisoners was in jeopardy. The cells were "not fit to live in." The kitchen and yard areas had problems with rats. Medical attention was inadequate. The prisoners received little if any counseling, job training, or education. The conditions in the Philadelphia prisons, concluded the court, violated both the United States and State Constitutions. The plaintiffs and defendants were ordered to submit, within ten days, recommendations with respect to the appointment of a master. Once appointed, they were to extend him "every reasonable assistance." The defendants were further ordered to correct certain practices immediately, and within thirty days, to submit a report of their accomplishments. On appeal the Pennsylvania Supreme Court affirmed.[47]

Another case arising in 1971 involved some rather bizarre circumstances.[48] In the fall of 1965, approximately 700 protesters in Natchez, Mississippi, were arrested for participating in an unlawful parade while attempting to publicize their grievances concerning racial discrimination. They were taken to the city auditorium, where many individuals were not permitted to make bond. None of them was brought before a magistrate. Late that night approximately 150 of them were transported by bus over 200 miles to the Mississippi State Penitentiary. They were placed in the maximum security unit and accorded the "standard" treatment given other inmates. The men were stripped naked and the women to their undergarments. All were forced to consume a laxative and were deprived of all personal belongings, including sanitary napkins and medicines. Up to eight persons were placed in the two-man cells, which contained neither mattresses, bedding, towels, soap, or toilet paper. The cells were extremely cold. While in the prison courtyard, many were kicked, pushed, cursed, and abused by the guards. On February 17, 1966, Katie R. Anderson brought a complaint on behalf of herself, sixty-eight adults, and eighty-four minors. She sought damages under the Civil Rights Act of 1871 on the grounds that they had been falsely imprisoned and subjected to cruel and unusual punishment. A jury returned a verdict for the defendants. Anderson appealed from the court's subsequent refusal to grant monetary damages notwithstanding the verdict, and its refusal to grant a new trial. On appeal the defendants urged invocation of the hands-off doctrine. They argued that the treatment of prisoners was "one of internal discipline," and not reviewable by the courts.[49] The court of appeals, however, noted that this did not mean that prison officials had "unfettered discretion" in handling prisoners. That the defendants admitted the prisoners were crowded into the cells with inadequate facilities, stripped naked, forced to take a laxative, and inspected and searched, "standing alone," was a violation of the Eighth Amendment, not to mention other unproven allegations, which were probably true. The treatment to which the plaintiffs were subjected, wrote Judge Goldberg, violated the "developing concepts of elemental decency" and was "greatly disproportionate to the offense" committed. The prisoners were not felons or hardened recidivists, he noted, "and confining them in the maximum security unit was totally unfounded. If similar treatment for convicted prisoners," he continued, "is universally condemned, which it is, that treatment has no place here. We deal with human beings," he concluded, "not dumb, driven cattle."[50] The lower-court decision was reversed, and the case was remanded for trial on the question of damages.

In 1972, Judge Zirpoli found the general environment in the Greystone section of the Santa Rita Rehabilitation Center in California "shocking and debasing" and unfit "for man or *beast*."[51] He found the conclusion "inescapable" that Greystone should be razed to the ground. Heating, ventilation, plumbing, and sanitation facilities were found to be "obviously and grossly substandard." The inmates were locked in dim, drably painted cells virtually twenty-four hours a day and thus were denied recreation, exercise, and vocational training. Perhaps most offensive to Judge Zirpoli was that the facility housed pretrial detainees and not convicted criminals. "The subhuman conditions . . . ," he concluded, "could not help but destroy the spirit and threaten the sanity of the men who had to endure them."[52]

The next year Judge Webster ruled that conditions in the St. Louis City Jail were "collectively" so inhumane that they imposed cruel and unusual punishment on federal pretrial detainees.[53] He ordered that Warden Al Lark not place more than two federal prisoners in any one cell or make use of "tier bosses" (inmate guards). The warden was also ordered not to inflict corporal punishment, place prisoners in segregation cells without following specific rules and regulations, or open out-going mail addressed to any court, attorney, elected official, or investigative agency. Further, the warden was to provide prisoners with clean mattress covers, blankets, towels, soap, water, and equipment for cleaning the cells at not less than weekly intervals.[54]

Penitentiaries

State penitentiaries are generally in no better condition than most jails. For example, in 1961 more than 100 prisons built before the Civil War were still in use. By 1967 a minimum of 11 percent of all prisons were over eighty years old.[55] The first successful challenge to an antiquated penal system took place in 1970.[56] Inmates of the Cummins Farm Unit and the Tucker Intermediate Reformatory in Arkansas brought a class action in behalf of the inmate population, alleging that the entire penal system inflicted cruel and unusual punishment.[57] The defendants admitted that they were not operating a "good" or "modern" prison system and conceded that unfortunate conditions existed. It was claimed, however, that the authorities were doing the best they could, given the limited funds with which they were provided. The court immediately noted that the use of the cruel and unusual punishment clause was not restricted to instances in which a particular inmate might attack a specific practice. "In the court's estimation," Chief Judge Henley wrote, "confinement itself within a given institution may amount to cruel and unusual punishment . . . where the confinement is characterized by conditions and practices so bad as to be shocking to the conscience of reasonably civilized people even though a particular inmate may never personally be subjected to any disciplinary action."[58]

After an extensive investigation, the court found that the system utilized few employees, used armed trusties to guard the rank and file, confined convicts when they were not working, required inmates to sleep at night in overcrowded, open dormitory-type barracks, and provided few if any programs of meaningful rehabilitation. The decision bitterly criticized the trusty system.[59] It was noted that the trusties at Cummins actually ran the prison. They performed 90 percent of the functions and could take over at any time they so desired. There were only two free world guards on duty at night. The court noted that the system of trusty guards is universally condemned by penologists because it is brutal, endangers lives, and is an open invitation to bribery, extortion, and smuggling. "In a very real sense," state Judge Henley, "trusty guards have the power of life and death over other inmates." Moreover, he continued, inmates "live in deadly fear of the guards and entertain deadly hatred for them, and their feelings are reciprocated fully."[60]

Similarly, the court noted that life in the open barracks was one of perpetual fear.[61] At night the two free world guards could not protect inmates from sexual or other attacks by fellow inmates. Many inmates, it was observed, possessed weapons. There had been seventeen stabbings within the previous eighteen months, four of which were fatal. Equally obnoxious were the overcrowded isolation cells. They were characterized as filthy, unsanitary, cold, and wet. At Tucker they were rat infested.

Lack of any rehabilitative program at Cummins also disturbed the court. Although he was not willing to declare confinement in a system with no rehabilitation program unconstitutional, Judge Henley did declare that the absence of such programs "may have constitutional significance where in the absence of such a program conditions and practices exist which actually militate against reform and rehabilitation."[62] The court found that such a situation did exist at Cummins and to a lesser extent at Tucker. Judge Henley also noted that the medical and dental facilities left much to be desired, and that unsanitary conditions existed in the kitchen at Cummins. Taken collectively, he concluded, "a sentence to the Arkansas Penitentiary today amounts to a banishment from civilized society to a dark and evil world completely alien to the free world, a world that is administered by criminals under unwritten rules and customs completely foreign to free world culture."[63] Such confinement was deemed inherently dangerous and consequently unconstitutional. "Apart from physical danger," noted Judge Henley, "confinement in the Penitentiary involves living under degrading and disgusting conditions. A man sentenced to life for murder may expect to fare better than a country boy with no serious record who is sentenced for two years for stealing a pig."[64]

Once having decided the unconstitutionality of prison life in Cummins and Tucker, the court was faced with the problem that Judge Diamond was forced to confront in the *Pickens* case.[65] With somewhat more ingenuity, Judge Henley ordered the respondents to make a prompt, reasonable, and vigorous start toward eliminating the conditions which made the system unconstitutional. "The handwriting is on the wall," he asserted, "and it ought to not to require a Daniel to read it. Unless conditions at the Penitentiary farms are brought up to a level of constitutional tolerability, the farms can no longer be used for the confinement of convicts."[66] The respondents were ordered to initiate a plan to rectify the situation. Judge Henley offered a few guidelines. Trusties were to be stripped of authority and phased out. Trusty guards were to be replaced with free world employees. The open barracks were to be subdivided, and isolation cells were to be controlled by free world employees. A final admonition was offered by the court.

> Let there be no mistake in the matter, the obligation of the Respondents to eliminate existing unconstitutionalities does not depend upon what the Legislature may do, or upon what the Governor may do, or, indeed upon what Respondents may actually be able to accomplish. If Arkansas is going

to operate a Penitentiary System it is going to have to be a system that is countenanced by the Constitution of the United States.[67]

Reaction to the decision was swift. The following day the *New York Times* carried an article approving the decision.[68] It was reported that John H. Haley, chairman of the State Board of Correction, and Robert Farber, Commissioner of Correction, both expected the results. They admitted that the conditions were as bad as Judge Henley had stated, and hoped that the decision would serve as an impetus to the legislature to approve the funds necessary to meet the judge's standards. "We've known that our prison conditions are considerably under national standards," Haley was reported as saying, "and national standards are nothing to be proud of." *The Nation*, a magazine that carried several articles on the barbaric conditions of the Arkansas penal system,[69] was "pleased to report the good news of Judge Henley's decision."[70]

Two weeks after the decision, a special session of the Arkansas General Assembly met at Little Rock. Naturally, one of the most pressing problems was that of prison reform. It is clear that the legislature paid heed to Judge Henley. It increased salary expenditures almost threefold, thereby allowing the hiring of additional guards. Furthermore, new salary scales and grades were established.[71] It was also provided that any monies remaining from uncollected salaries could be transferred to the maintenance and operating fund. An additional $180,000 was appropriated for renovations at Tucker. Act 7 of the Special Session provided an additional $200,000 in funds for the construction of a maximum security unit at Tucker.[72]

Despite the fact that Judge Henley's decision was highly acclaimed in both popular and scholarly journals,[73] the state appealed. The Eighth Circuit Court of Appeals, however, dashed the state's hopes by affirming the lower-court's decision. Stated Judge Van Oosterhout:

> We are convinced from an examination of the voluminous record, that Judge Henley's basic finding upon which the judgment and decree are predicated are supported by overwhelming substantial evidence and that such findings offered a firm basis for his determination that imprisonment of inmates at Cummins and Tucker units constitutes cruel and unusual punishment violative of the Eighth Amendment under conditions shown to have existed at the time of the decree.[74]

On October 20, 1972, the second major decision involving an entire state penal system was rendered.[75] A Mississippi federal district court ruled that the general conditions surrounding incarceration at the state prison in Parchman inflicted cruel and unusual punishment. The prison had been built in 1903 and had from that time maintained the practice of racial segregation. As at the

Cummins and Tucker institutions in Arkansas, armed inmates performed more of the guarding functions; civilian guards were simply too few. The trusty system was replete with payoffs, favoritism, extortion, and participation in illegal activities. Many of the armed trusties had been convicted of violent crimes, and 35 per cent of them had not been psychologically tested. Forty per cent of those tested were found to be mentally retarded, and 71 per cent of those tested were found to have personality disorders.

The buildings themselves were "in a deplorable state of maintenance and repair," resulting in "sub-human" conditions "unfit for human habitation under any modern concept of decency."[76] The electrical wiring was in a poor state of repair and presented safety hazards to the inmates. Furthermore, there was a lack of fire-fighting equipment. Broken windows were stuffed with rags for insulation against the elements. Bathroom facilities were lacking, and those that existed were poorly maintained. Kitchen facilities and food services were also "below par."

The disposal system for human and other waste at the outerlying camps was "shockingly inadequate" and a "health hazard" and in fact had been condemned by state health and pollution agencies. All fourteen water systems were deficient; the water available was about half that required for the inmate population.

The prison administrators had failed to classify inmates according to their propensity to commit violence. This was particularly acute because prisoners were placed in large, open-type cells and were thus easy targets for physical abuse. In other instances, the medical staff had failed to provide adequate care for the inmate population. Frequently state superintendents had allowed punishments that exceeded state law; some inmates had been kept in a dark hole for up to seventy-two hours. The rules and procedures relating to discipline were vague or unstated.

Finding these conditions and practices unconstitutional and in violation the Eighth Amendment, Judge Keady ordered that counsel prepare for a conference to discuss the terms of the injunctive relief. The prison administrators, the governor, and all employees were enjoined from continuing the unconstitutional practices. In terms of immediate relief, the court ordered that imposing any form of disciplinary punishment upon inmates was prohibited unless specified rules of the court were followed. An extensive list of excessive corporal punishments were deemed henceforth prohibited. Racial discrimination was also to be eliminated. Censorship of outgoing mail to local, state, or federal officials was to be discontinued. Medical facilities were to be elevated to meet minimal health care requirements. It was specifically ordered that the medical staff consist of at least three full-time physicians, two full-time dentists, two full-time trained medical assistants, six full-time nurses, one medical records librarian, and two medical clerical personnel. A classification system was to be established, taking into account the necessity for desegregation and adequate inmate protection. The open-type cells were to be divided to protect prisoners from attack.[77] Searches for weapons were to be conducted regularly, and the defendants were ordered to phase out the trusty system.

In terms of long-range relief, it was ordered that plans be developed for eliminating the unconstitutional conditions of inadequate housing, inadequate water and sewer facilities, inadequate fire-fighting equipment, and substandard hospital facilities.

Juvenile Facilities

Three recent decisions have examined the conditions surrounding incarceration in juvenile detention facilities.[78] In many respects the deficiencies and dehumanizing experiences challenged were extremely similar to those attacked by adults. In Rhode Island, Federal District Judge Pettine ordered that certain minimal conditions of confinement must be met.[79] He ordered that each inmate be provided with the basic necessities of sufficient clothing, blankets, mattresses, sheets and pillow cases, pillows, soap, towels, toothpaste, toothbrushes, and toilet paper. Moreover, daily showers were to be allowed as well as daily access to the medical facilities. Reading and writing materials were also to be provided, and the cells had to be equipped with lighting sufficient for such activities. Prescription eyeglasses were to be supplied, and general correspondence privileges were not to be curtailed. Additionally, administrators of the facility were ordered to submit plans, within thirty days, for the establishment of rehabilitation programs.

The second case arose in New York and involved three facilities.[80] Judge Lasker held that the general conditions in one, that of Manida, were constitutionally impermissible. The institution had been constructed in 1904 and was in a general state of decay. Its plaster was falling, paint was peeling, and there were cracks in the walls and ceilings. The showers were often unusable. Noting that injunctive relief should be "fashioned with deliberation," he ordered the parties involved to prepare for a conference to determine the scope and contents of the final order.

The third case involved the Texas Youth Council. Administrators of that department were ordered to provide each inmate with a bed, mattress, appropriate bedding, access to a toilet, one hour of large-muscle exercise per day, school books, and daily lesson plans.[81] It was further ordered that the authorities were not to enforce the so-called "silence rule" whereby inmates were prohibited from talking for long periods of time. Additionally, the authorities were enjoined from demanding repetitive, nonfunctional, degrading and unnecessary tasks, and disciplining inmates for sleeping during periods of the day.

It should be clear that *Pickens*[82] is no longer good precedent. Imaginative judges have found alternatives to setting prisoners free when inmates are confined in constitutionally impermissible environments. Judge Christenberry found another jail in which the convicts could be incarcerated.[83] Judge Eisele limited the number of inmates who could be held at any one time, and implicitly threatened to release prisoners if certain conditions were not met.[84] Justice Eagen ordered the transfer or release of a prisoner in such a manner as not to release all prisoners similarly incarcerated.[85] Judge Young showed a great deal of imagination in his attempt to rectify the horrid conditions in the Lucas County Jail.[86] In fact, since 1969, every case reaching state supreme courts or federal courts involving essentially the same issues has rejected the *Pickens* decision. This does not mean, however, that all such allegations have been, or will in the future be, successful. For example, in *Rhem* v. *McGrath*,[87] a federal district court held that confinement in the Manhattan House of Detention for Men, commonly known as "the Tombs," did not inflict cruel and unusual punishment. Similarly, in *State ex rel. Pingley* v. *Coiner*,[88] the West Virginia Supreme Court found that the environmental conditions at Moundsville Penitentiary did not inflict cruel and unusual punishment. The facts, reasoned the court, were clearly distinguishable from those in the *Holt*,[89] and *Bryant*[90] cases.

Part IV:
Conclusion

13 Conclusion

Tracing the historical development of the cruel and unusual punishment concept from King Alfred (A.D. 900) through the recent *Furman* decision[1] has been a long, involved, and at times complex process. The detailed discussion has made it relatively easy to overlook certain broad generalizations that can be derived from the study.

In Part I it was observed that the concept, as found in the United States, is clearly traceable to early English history. The inhibition was incorporated into the English Bill of Rights in order to restrict the degree of punishment, and not to restrict the mode of inflicting it. This is clearly established by an examination of early English documents and by analyzing the events immediately prior to and following its adoption in 1689. When the concept reached American shores, however, it took on a different meaning. From the very beginning, Americans expressed a great concern over cruel and unusual modes of punishment, as is illustrated in the Massachusetts Body of Liberties (1641). Many were rarely, if ever, utilized in the colonies. As the decades and centuries wore on, the notion that the phrase restricted the degree of punishment was deemphasized, while at the same time emphasis was placed on the idea that the phrase restricted the mode of punishment. This led many scholars and jurists to believe that the cruel and unusual punishment inhibition restricted *only* certain methods of punishment, as is evidenced in the nineteenth century decisions of both state and federal courts. Nevertheless, the idea that the prohibition restricted the degree as well was by no means dead. Attorneys insisted that the inhibition applied to disproportionate sentences. Many jurists vacillated in their positions when confronted with punishments they perceived as clearly excessive and at least five times overturned such sentences. The question remained open at the federal level until 1910, when the *Weems* decision[2] was handed down. In that case, the United States Supreme Court specifically held that disproportionate punishments violated the Eighth Amendment to the United States Constitution. Whether the state inhibitions restricted the imposition of excessive degrees of punishment, however, remained unclear. Actually, the *Weems* decision had a very limited effect on the state courts, and few of them subsequently held specific punishments disproportionate. The matter was finally settled when the United States Supreme Court held, in *Robinson* v. *California*,[3] that the due process clause of the Fourteenth Amendment incorporated the cruel and unusual punishment provision of the Eighth Amendment. The Court had already defined the inhibition as applying to both the mode and degree of punishment, and as such, the states were consequently forbidden to levy disproportionate sentences, even if their state constitutions permitted them to do so.

The exact meaning of the concept has vacillated from decade to decade, court to court, and place to place. It is clear that it is not static and must draw its meaning from evolving standards of decency. Just what decency is, is difficult to determine. The problem parallels Justice Potter Stewart's famous remark on obscenity. Although he could not define the concept, he asserted, "I know it when I see it."[4] The same appears to be true of the phrase "cruel and unusual punishment." One knows it when one sees it, but few can agree on what "it" is. Various tests have been suggested by scholars and jurists, the most elaborate being Justice Brennan's in *Furman* v. *Georgia.*[5]

The concept has become more and more important with the passing of each decade in the twentieth century. The propensity to litigate the issue has increased manyfold. If the present trend continues, nearly every state and federal appeals court can expect to be asked to consider the issue at least once a year. Many will be confronted with the issue dozens of times during any twelve-month period. The largest number of cases, in absolute terms, comes from the southeastern United States. Oddly enough, a disproportionate number of cases arise in the less populous areas of the Southwest, Plains, and Mountain states. The most recent surge of litigation has taken place in the federal district courts, owing to the demise of the hands-off doctrine. Prison rules and practices, levied and followed by executive administrators, are being challenged with regularity. Moreover, the rate of success by litigants has been far greater in this area than in any other.

Part II examined both corporeal and incorporeal punishments provided by legislatures or imposed by judges. In the first section, a great deal of effort was devoted to an examination of the death penalty. Early attacks focused on the mode of inflicting the punishment. Without exception, hanging, shooting electrocution, and gaseous asphyxiation were held constitutional. Failing to eliminate these methods of imposing the penalty, abolitionists then challenged the penalty as excessive when inflicted for the crimes of robbery, arson, kidnapping, espionage, assault and rape. Again, however, they had very little success. The once notable exception came in *Ralph* v. *Warden,*[6] in 1970. There the Fourth Circuit Court of Appeals held that to impose the death penalty for rape "when the victim's life is neither taken nor endangered" is to inflict cruel and unusual punishment.

In recent years a frontal assault has been launched on the death penalty. The abolitionists and antiabolitionists have been locked in a heated debate over whether the evolving standards of decency have now reached a point where the death penalty is per se unconstitutional. Both sides have strong and compelling arguments to support their cases. Until 1972, however, the antiabolitionists had clearly been victorious in the judicial system. The successes of the abolitionists had been limited to the repeal of the death penalty in a few states, and the fact that many governors continued to commute death sentences to life imprisonment. Indeed, no one had been executed in the United States for several years. In *People* v. *Anderson,*[7] however, the California Supreme Court, in a six-to-one decision, held that the death penalty was per se unconstitutional, in violation of the state prohibition against the infliction of cruel or unusual punishments.

Four months later, the United States Supreme Court delivered one of the most momentous decisions in the fight for equal application of the laws in the history of mankind. The decision, however, did not rule on the question of whether death for rape where life is neither taken nor endangered constitutes cruel and unusual punishment, or whether the death penalty is or is not per se unconstitutional. The Court held that, *as applied,* the penalty inflicted cruel and unusual punishment because it was imposed in an arbitrary manner, notably with more regularity on males, blacks, and the poor. Many states have redesigned death penalty statutes in an attempt to come within the Court's decision. Subsequent challenges to these new statutes will unquestionably be forthcoming. Indeed, the fight over the death penalty is far from over, and the United States Supreme Court will probably be asked to review many more such cases in the near future.

Other corporeal punishments were examined in Part II. Today, whipping exists on the statute books only in Delaware. Sterilization of the feeble-minded is viewed as constitutionally permissible. Hard labor, solitary confinement, and restricted diets are all permissible when imposed by statute or judge.

The second section of Part II examined incorporeal punishments. Numerous examples of extremely harsh sentences abound. It is a rarity, however, when a court declares a term of imprisonment disproportionate and, as such, cruel and unusual punishment. Habitual offender statutes have generally been upheld as constitutional, as have multiple sentences in single prosecutions, indeterminate sentences, and unequal sentences imposed on codefendants. Likewise, the deportation of aliens does not inflict cruel and unusual punishment. Banishment has generally not been considered per se unconstitutional. However, in recent years some courts have implied that it is, and others have held or suggested that it is contrary to public policy, and thus impermissible where not provided for by explicit statutory sanction. Similarly, in the past few decades, expatriation has become less and less popular as a mode of punishment. In *Trop* v. *Dulles,*[8] the United States Supreme Court refused to allow the expatriation of an army deserter in wartime.

Statutes that inflict punishment because of a person's status are clearly unconstitutional under the Robinson doctrine. However, a distinction has been made between the status of an individual and his actions. In *Powell* v. *Texas,*[9] the United States Supreme Court gave explicit sanction to the distinction and seemed to invite state courts to do the same. As a result, individuals may not be punished for being an addict, alcoholic, prostitute, homosexual, vagrant, or for being a mentally ill or insane person, but may be prosecuted for the acts of, or acts accompanying, addiction, alcoholism, prostitution, homosexuality, vagrancy, mental illness, or insanity.

Part III examined administrative action as cruel and unusual punishment. A number of prison rules and practices have been held to inflict cruel and unusual punishment. Today, for the most part, administrators may not legally whip prisoners or chain them to their cells. They may restrict the confinement of inmates, but only when explicit and carefully considered procedures are followed. Solitary confinement generally must be accompanied by a high level of sanitary conditions, adequate clothing, light and heat, recreation, and reading materials, and may not be unduly long. Diets must meet minimum nutritional standards set by experts in the area.

The intentional denial of medical care clearly comes within the purview of cruel and unusual punishment, and judges will carefully scrutinize such allegations. However, medical authorities within the penal system are given extremely broad discretion in establishing the means employed to cure patients of their infirmities. Transferring inmates from institution to institution is viewed as an internal matter to be decided by the executive branch of the government, and does not inflict cruel and unusual punishment. Further, administrative officials also have broad latitude in establishing personal appearance codes to maintain sanitary, safety, and diciplinary conditions in prisons.

Recently, a number of inmates have argued that the total penal environment to which they have been subjected inflicts cruel and unusual punishment. Such allegations are reminiscent of earlier attacks on the chain gang. The recent challenges have been directed at city or county jails and, in two instances, at entire penal systems. Generally the arguments are based on the fact that the institutions are outdated, reek of filth and stench, provide only inadequate bathing and health facilities, provide no rehabilitation or recreational facilities, provide inadequate diets, and offer inadequate protection from inmates and guards alike. The most notorious examples are clearly the horrendous situations that existed in the Arkansas and Mississippi penal systems. Hopefully the judiciary will continue to accept its responsibility of policing penal systems where conditions reach such subhuman levels.

Notes

Notes

Chapter 1
Origins of the Concept

1. Anthony F. Granucci, "Nor Cruel and Unusual Punishments Inflicted: The Original Meaning," *California Law Review* 57 (October 1969): 845.
2. Ibid.
3. See Boyd C. Barrington, *The Magna Charta and Other Great Charters of England* (Philadelphia: William J. Campbell, 1900), art. 41, p. 199. The authenticity is highly in doubt. See Barrington's discussion, pp. 181-82.
4. Richard L. Perry and John C. Cooper, *Sources of Our Liberties* (Rahway, N.J.: Quinn and Boden Co., Inc., 1959), p. 15.
5. Charles I, c. 1 (1628).
6. See Bernard Schwartz, *The Bill of Rights: A Documentary History* (New York: McGraw Hill Book Co., 1971), 1: 17-19.
7. Article I, sec. 9, Abolition of The Star Chamber, July 5, 1641. See Perry and Cooper, p. 139.
8. Schwartz, p. 41.
9. 25 Geo. 2, c. 37 (1752).
10. Leon Radzinowicz, *A History of English Criminal Law* (New York: Macmillan Co., 1948), pp. 209-13.
11. 22 Hen. 8, c. 9 (1530), repealed 1 Edw. 6, c. 12, ss. 2 and 13 (1547).
12. See 30 Geo. 3, c. 48 (1790); 54 Geo. 3, c. 146 (1814); 57 Geo. 3, c. 75 (1817); 4 & 5 Will. 4, c. 26 ss. 1 & 2 (1834); 7 Will. 4, 1 Vict. c. 23 (1837); and 33 & 34 Vict., c. 23, ss. 31 (1870).
13. See 5 Eliz. 2, c. 21; and 14 Eliz. 2, c. 71.
14. Article 1 (due process, dismemberment, banishment), 43 (whipping), 45 (torture), 46 (bodily punishments), 80 (women beating), and 92 (animal beating). See Zechariah Chafee, *Documents on Fundamental Human Rights* (New York: Atheneum, 1963), pp. 122-30.
15. There is one example, however, of a man being pressed to death, but not technically as punishment for crime. Giles Gorey refused to plead to a charge of witchcraft. He was ordered pressed until he entered a plea. He stubbornly refused and finally died under the tremendous weight. See Ernest G. Black, "Torture Under English Law," *University of Pennsylvania Law Review* 75 (February 1927): 348; and Leo Bonfanti, *The Witchcraft Hysteria of 1692* (Wakefield, Mass.: Pride Publications, Inc., 1971),

pp. 48-53. There is evidence that the sentence of drawing and quartering was imposed. See State v. Cannon, 55 Del. 587, 592, 190 A.2d 514 (1963); and Done v. People, 5 Parker 364, 383-84 (N.Y. 1863). There is some evidence that a man was gibbeted in New York. See Done v. People, and Negley K. Teeters, *Hang By the Neck* (Springfield, Ill.: Charles C. Thomas, 1967), c. II.

16. Alice M. Earle, *Curious Punishments of Bygone Days* (Detroit: The Singing Tree Press, 1968), p. 142; William Riddell, "Judicial Execution By Burning at the Stake in New York," *American Bar Association Journal* 15 (June 1929): 374; and Done v. People, 5 Parker 364, 384 (N.Y., 1863).

17. Earle, pp. 139-49.

18. Marquis Eaton, "Punitive Pain and Humiliation," *Journal of Criminal Law and Criminology* 6 (1916): 902.

19. William Riddell, "Post-Reformation Burning at the Stake of Heretics," *Journal of Law and Criminology* 21 (1930): 256. There is evidence that a single burning took place in Delaware. See State v. Cannon, 55 Del. 587, 592, 190 A.2d 514 (1963).

20. Wyatt Paine, "Jocular and Infamous Punishments," *Law Times* 114 (March 21, 1903): 479; and William Andrews, *Old-Time Punishments* (Detroit: Singing Tree Press, 1970); and Earle.

21. See Joseph Thompson, "Early Corporal Punishments," *Illinois Law Quarterly* 6 (December 1923): 39.

22. See Earle; and Eaton. Also see State v. Cannon, 55 Del. 587, 592, 190 A.2d 514 (1963).

23. In very early times corporeal punishments sometimes did accompany such a sentence. In Virginia, for example, a captain was sentenced to stand in the pillory with his ears nailed and to have them cut off unless he paid a fine. See Hans V. Hentig, "The Pillory: A Medieval Punishment," *Rocky Mountain Law Review* 11 (April 1939): 195.

24. Schwartz, 1: 235.

25. Furman v. Georgia, 408 U.S. 238, 377 (1972) (dissenting opinion).

26. Ibid., 322 (Marshall concurring opinion).

27. Rhode Island operated under its colonial charter until 1842.

28. The documents are conveniently compiled in Schwartz, 1: 231-79.

29. Constitution of Pennsylvania 1790, art. IX, sec. 13. See Benjamin Poor (ed.), *The Federal and State Constitutions, Colonial Charters and Other Organic Laws of the United States* (Washington: Government Printing Office, 1877), vols. I and II.

30. South Carolina, *Constitution,* 1778, art. XXXIX.

31. Ordinance of July 13, 1787, art. II. See Charles C. Tansill (ed.), *Documents Illustrative of the Formation of the Union of American States* (Washington: United States Government Printing Office, 1927), p. 52.

32. George Mason and Elbridge Gerry initiated action, but after Roger Sherman

suggested that the "State Declarations of Rights are not repealed by this Constitution; and being in force are sufficient," the proposal was rejected. Max Farrand, *The Records of the Federal Convention* (New Haven: Yale University Press, 1937), 2: 587-88.

33. James Curtis Ballagh, *Letters of Richard Henry Lee* (New York: DaCapo Press, 1970), 2: 442. For an illuminating analysis, see Edmund Cody Burnett, *The Continental Congress* (New York: W.W. Norton and Co., 1964). The proposal probably originated with Mason. As Burnett states: "The views of the two men so closely coincided, that not infrequently [Lee] appears to be the mouthpiece of Mason" (p. 698).

34. Delaware, Pennsylvania, New Jersey, Georgia, Connecticut, and Maryland. For convenient reference to all ratification documents, see Tansill, pp. 1009-59. The debates and proceedings of the conventions are collected in Jonathan Elliot, *The Debates* (Washington: Jonathan Elliot, 1828), vols. I, II, and III.

35. John Bach McMaster and Frederick D. Stone, *Pennsylvania and the Federal Convention* (Lancaster, Penna. Inquirer Printing and Publishing Co., 1888), p. 421.

36. Elliot, 3: 447.

37. Mr. Holmes, in the Massachusetts convention, did comment on the absence of the prohibition. "They [the Federal Congress] are nowhere restrained from inventing the most cruel and unheard of punishments, and there is no constitutional check on them, but that *racks* and *gibbets* may be amongst the most mild instruments of their discipline." This account was related in *Weems* v. *United States,* 217 U.S. 349, 396 (1910). See Elliot, 2: 111.

38. *Annals of Congress,* vol. I, column 434 (emphasis added).

39. *Journal of the Senate,* 121, 131.

40. See *Documentary History of the Constitution* (Washington: Department of State, 1894), 2: 321-24.

41. Art. I, sec. 13.

42. The Vermont Supreme Court has ruled, however, that the concept is part of the common law of the state. See State v. O'Brien, 106 Vt. 97, 107, 170 A. 98 (1934).

Chapter 2
Judicial Interpretation: An Overview

1. State v. Smith, 5 Day 175, 178, 7 Am. Dec. 132 (Conn. 1811).

2. An exact count is impossible because of the questionable rationale underlying the decision in some cases. The *Weems* case (May 2, 1910) is a natural dividing point in history, for it represents the first time the United States Supreme Court held that the federal clause prohibited excessive *degrees* of punishment.

3. Ho Ah Kow v. Nunan, 12 F. Cas. 252 (No. 6,546) (C.C. D. Cal. 1879); *In re* Birdsong, 39 Fed. 599 (1889); Ely v. Thompson, 10 Ky. (3 A.K. Marsh) 70 (1820); State *ex rel.* Garvey v. Whitaker, 48 La. Ann. 527, 19 So. 457 (1896); State v. Driver, 78 N.C. 423 (1878); and State v. Ross, 55 Ore. 450, 104 P. 596 (1909).

4. For example see *In re* O'Shea, 11 Cal. App. 568, 571, 105 P. 776 (1909); and Whitten v. State, 47 Ga. 297, 301 (1872).

5. State v. Manuel, 20 N.C. 20, 36 (1838); People v. Morris, 80 Mich. 634, 637, 45 N.W. 591 (1890); and Whitten v. State, 47 Ga. 297, 301 (1872).

6. See, e.g., Mitchell v. State, 82 Md. 527, 535, 34 A. 247 (1896).

7. Mallory v. State, 56 Ga. 545, 547 (1876); *accord.*, Peacock Distillery Company v. Commonwealth, 25 Ky. L. 1778, 1781, 78 S.W. 893 (1904); Godwin v. State, 123 Ga. 569, 51 S.E. 598 (1905); Siberry v. State, 149 Ind. 684, 705, 47 N.E. 458 (1897); Cornelison v. Commonwealth, 84 Ky. 583, 608, 2 S.W. 235 (1886); Lanasa v. State, 109 Md. 602, 612, 71 A. 1058 (1909); People v. Kelley, 99 Mich. 82, 86, 57 N.W. 1090 (1894); Weincke v. State, 34 Neb. 14, 25, 51 N.W. 307 (1892); State v. Reid, 106 N.C. 714, 716, 11 S.E. 315 (1890); Hendrix v. United States, 2 Okla. Cr. 240, 257, 101 P. 125 (1909); and State v. Sanders, 68 S.C. 138, 140, 47 S.E. 55 (1903).

8. See Sutton v. People, 145 Ill. 279, 290, 34 N.E. 420 (1893); and Bennett v. State, 32 Tex. Cr. R. 216, 22 S.W. 684 (1894).

9. Mitchell v. State, 82 Md. 527, 533, 34 A. 247 (1896); *accord.*, *In re* Tutt, 55 Kan. 705, 706, 41 P. 957 (1895); Lanasa v. State, 109 Md. 602, 612, 71 A. 1058 (1909); Toomer v. State 112 Md. 285, 295, 76 A. 118 (1910); Cummins v. People, 42 Mich. 142, 3 N.W. 305 (1879); State v. Stubblefield, 157 Mo. 360, 58 S.W. 337 (1900); State v. Hogan, 63 Ohio St. 202, 58 N.E. 572 (1900); and Commonwealth v. Wyatt, 27 Va. (6 Rand.) 694, 701 (1828).

10. Suggestions may also be found in the works of contemporary scholars. See Thomas M. Cooley, *A Treatise on Constitutional Limitations* (Boston: Little, Brown and Co., 1868), pp. 329-30; Joseph Magrath, "Cruel and Unusual Punishment," *American and English Encyclopedia of Law,* D. Garland and L. McGehee, eds., (New York: Edward Thompson Co., 1898), 8:436-42; and Joseph Story, *Commentaries on the Constitution of the United States* (Boston: Hilliard, Gray and Co., 1833, lst ed.), pp. 750-51.

11. Wilkerson v. Utah, 99 U.S. 130, 136 (1879); *In re* Kemmler, 136 U.S. 436, 447 (1890); *In re* O'Shea, 11 Cal. App. 568, 575, 105 P. 776 (1909); State v. McCauley, 15 Cal. 429, 455 (1860); State v. Williams, 77 Mo. 310, 312 (1883); Garcia v. Territory, 1 N.M. 415, 418. (1869); *Matter of* Bayard, 63 How. Pr. 73, 77 (N.Y. 1881); and People *ex rel.* Kemmler v. Durston, 7 N.Y.S. 813, 815, 55 Hun. 64 (1889).

12. *In re* O'Shea, 11 Cal. App. 568, 576, 105 P. 776 (1909); People v. Illinois State Reformatory, 148 Ill. 413, 421, 36 N.E. 78 (1894); *In re* Kemmler,

136 U.S. 436, 447 (1890); People *ex rel.* Kemmler v. Durston, 7 N.Y.S.
813, 815, 55 Hunt. 64 (1889); *Matter of* Bayard, 63 How. Pr. 73, 77
(N.Y. 1881); State v. Williams, 77 Mo. 310, 312 (1883); and *In re*
McDonald, 4 Wyo. 150, 161, 33 P. 18 (1893).

13. Wilkerson v. Utah, 99 U.S. 130, 135 (1879); *In re* Kemmler, 136 U.S. 436,
446 (1890); *In re* O'Shea, 11 Cal. App. 568, 575-76, 105 P. 776 (1909);
Whitten v. State, 47 Ga. 297, 301 (1872); Hobbs v. State, 133 Ind. 404,
409, 32 N.E. 1019 (1893); State v. Williams, 77 Mo. 310, 312 (1883); and
In re Kemmler, 7 N.Y.S. 145, 149 (1889).

14. *In re* O'Shea, 11 Cal. App. 568, 576, 105 P. 776 (1909); Whitten v. State,
47 Ga. 297, 301 (1872); State v. Williams, 77 Mo. 310, 312 (1883); *Matter
of* Bayard, 63 How. Pr. 73, 77 (N.Y. 1881); and *In re* Kemmler, 7 N.Y.S.
145, 150 (1889).

15. *In re* O'Shea, 11 Cal. App. 568, 575, 105 P. 776 (1909); State v. White,
44 Kan. 514, 520, 25 P. 33 (1890); State v. Borgstrom, 69 Minn. 508, 521,
72 N.W. 799 (1897); Hobbs v. State, 133 Ind. 404, 409, 32 N.E. 1019
(1893); and State v. Williams, 77 Mo. 310, 312 (1883). Also see Magrath,
n. 10.

16. *In re* Kemmler, 136 U.S. 436, 447 (1890).

17. See *West's American Digests* (St. Paul: West Publishing Co., 1910-present).
The terminal date of the *Digests* used was June 1974.

18. Bailey v. United States, 284 Fed. 126 (7th Cir. 1922); People v. Cruz, 113
Cal. App. 519, 298 P. 556 (1931); People v. Elliot, 272 Ill. 592, 112 N.E.
300 (1916); State v. Youman, 66 N.D. 204, 263 N.W. 477 (1935); State v.
Jochim, 55 N.D. 313, 213 N.W. 484 (1927); and State v. Sullivan 241 Wis.
276, 5 N.W. 2d 798 (1942).

19. People v. Anderson, 100 Cal. Rptr. 152, 6 Cal. 3d 628, 493 P.2d 880 (1972).

20. Furman v. Georgia, 408 U.S. 238 (1972).

21. Sometimes these punishments are declared excessive in degree as well as
kind. However, for the sake of simple classification, such punishments
will be discussed only under the category of modes.

22. *In re* Birdsong, 39 Fed. 599 (D.C. Georgia 1889).

23. Stoutenburgh v. Frazier, 16 App. D.C. 229 (1900).

24. 370 U.S. 660 (1962).

25. See Powell v. Texas, 392 U.S. 514 (1968); Hutchenson v. United States,
345 F.2d 964 (D.C. Cir 1965); Vick v. State, 453 P.2d 342 (Alaska 1969);
State *ex rel.* Blouin v. Walker, 244 La. 699, 154 So.2d 368 (1963); People
v. Hoy, 3 Mich. App. 666, 143 N.W.2d 577 (1966); State v. Margo, 40
N.J. 188, 191 A.2d 43 (1963); and City of Seattle v. Hill, 435 P.2d 692
(Wash. 1967).

26. People v. Baum, 251 Mich. 187, 189, 231 N.W. 95 (1930). But see David
Fellman, "Cruel and Unusual Punishments," *Journal of Politics* 19
(February 1957): 40-41.

27. Dear Wing Jung v. United States, 312 F.2d 73, 76 (9th Cir. 1962).
28. Trop v. Dulles, 356 U.S. 86 (1958); Cort v. Herter, 187 F. Supp. 683 (D.C.C. 1960); and Afroyim v. Rusk, 387 U.S. 253 (1967).
29. See, e.g., Livingston v. Moore, 32 U.S. (7 Pet.) 469 (1833); and Barron v. Baltimore, 32 U.S. (7 Pet.) 243 (1833).
30. See, e.g., Collins v. Johnson, 237 U.S. 502, 510-11 (1915); Ughbanks v. Armstrong, 208 U.S. 481, 487 (1908); O'Neil v. Vermont, 144 U.S. 323, 332 (1892); Eilenbecker v. Plymouth County, 134 U.S. 31, 35 (1890); and Pervear v. Commonwealth, 72 U.S. (5 Wall.) 475 (1866).
31. See, e.g., Johnson v. Dye, 175 F.2d 250, 254 (3d Cir. 1949); United States *ex rel.* Eggleston v. Snow, 219 F. Supp. 417, 418 (S.D. N.Y. 1963); Blythe v. Ellis, 194 F. Supp. 139, 140 (S.D. Tex. 1961); Bryant v. Harrelson, 187 F. Supp. 738, 740 (S.D. Tex. 1960); *Application of* Middlebrooks, 88 F. Supp. 943, 951 (S.D. Cal. 1950); Siegel v. Ragen, 88 F. Supp. 996, 999 (N.D. Ill. 1949); Johnson v. Dye, 71 F. Supp. 262, 265 (W.D. Pa. 1947); and Doss v. Lindsley, 53 F. Supp. 427, 433 (E.D. Ill. 1944).
32. Barker v. People, 3 Cow. (N.Y.) 686, 702 (1824).
33. See, e.g., Lee v. State, 227 Ala. 2, 4, 5, 150 So. 164 (1933); Johnson v. State, 214 Ark. 902, 908, 218 S.W.2d 687 (1949); People v. Cruz, 113 Cal. App. 519, 520, 298 P. 566 (1931); McCarthy v. Clancy, 110 Conn. 482, 500, 148 A. 551 (1930); Kinkaid v. Jackson, 66 Fla. 378, 380, 63 So. 706 (1913); Loeb v. Jennings, 133 Ga. 796, 801, 67 S.E. 101 (1910); People v. Elliot, 272 Ill. 592, 598, 112 N.E. 300 (1916); Gibson v. Commonwealth, 204 Ky. 748, 753, 265 S.W. 339 (1924); State v. Thomas, 224 La. 431, 435, 69 So.2d 738 (1953); Dutton v. State, 123 Md. 373, 385, 91 A. 417 (1914); McDonald v. Commonwealth, 173 Mass. 322, 328, 53 N.E. 874 (1899); People v. Harwood, 286 Mich. 96, 98, 281 N.W. 551 (1938); People v. Sly, 39 N.Y.S.2d 474, 478, 180 Misc. 96 (1942); State v. Blake, 157 N.C. 608, 611, 72 S.E. 1080 (1911); Commonwealth *ex rel.* Smith v. Banmiller, 194 Pa. Super, 566, 567-68 (1961); State v. Becker, 3 S.D. 29, 40, 51 N.W. 1018 (1892); State v. Hodgson, 66 Vt. 134, 156, 28 A. 1089 (1893); and Southern Express Company v. Commonwealth, 92 Va. 59, 67, 22 S.E. 809 (1895).
34. 136 U.S. 436 (1890).
35. See United States v. Cruikshank, 92 U.S. 542 (1875); and Slaughter-House Cases, 83 U.S. (16 Wall.) 36 (1872).
36. *In re* Kemmler, 136 U.S. 436, 449 (1890).
37. O'Neil v. Vermont, 144 U.S. 323, 363 (1892) (dissenting opinion).
38. Louisiana *ex rel.* Francis v. Resweber, 329 U.S. 459, 462 (1947).
39. Johnson v. Dye, 175 F.2d 250, 254, 255 (3rd Cir. 1949).
40. Harper v. Wall, 85 F. Supp. 783, 787 (D.N.J. 1949).
41. *Application of* Middlebrooks, 88 F. Supp. 943, 952 (S.D. Cal. 1950).
42. Sweeney v. Woodall, 344 U.S. 86, 93 (1952). He reiterated this thinking in 1959. NAACP v. Williams, 359 U.S. 550, 551 (1959).

43. Lambert v. California, 355 U.S. 225, 231 (1958) (dissenting opinion) (emphasis added).

44. Robinson v. California, 370 U.S. 660, 666 (1962). Stanley Mosk points out that the Court did not "unequivocally" hold that the Eighth Amendment applied to the states. Stanley Mosk, "The Eighth Amendment Rediscovered," *Loyola Universith Law Review* (L.A.) 1 (April 1968): 4, 8-9. However, that the present members of the Supreme Court take the view that *Robinson* applied the Eighth Amendment to the states via the Fourteenth, see *Furman* v. *Georgia,* 408 U.S. 238 (1972); Douglas at 241, Brennan at 305, Stewart at 309, White at 312, Marshall at 328, note 34, and Powell at 442, note 4 and 429.

45. It has been constantly suggested that the concept is not easy to define. See, e.g., Furman v. Georgia, 408 U.S. 238, 396 (1972); Wilkerson v. Utah, 99 U.S. 130 (1879); State v. Tomassi, 75 N.J.L. 739, 69 A. 214 (1908); Territory v. Ketchum, 10 N.M. 718, 65 P. 169 (1901); Ellis v. State, 54 Okla. Cr. 295, 190 P.2d 156 (1933); State v. Feilen, 70 Wash. 65, 126 P. 75 (1912); and State v. Woodward, 68 W. Va. 66, 69 S.E. 385 (1910).

46. Weems v. United States, 217 U.S. 349, 373 (1910).

47. Ibid., 378.

48. Trop v. Dulles, 356 U.S. 86, 100-01 (1958).

49. See Walter Gorski, "Eighth Amendment," *Connecticut Bar Journal* 40 (1966): 521-22; J.M. McWilliams, "Cruel and Unusual Punishment," *American Bar Association Journal* 53 (May 1967): 452-53; and Nancy-Nellis Warner, "Cruel and Unusual Punishment," *Catholic University Law Review* 3 (May 1953): 119-21.

50. See, e.g., State v. Evans, 73 Idaho 50, 58, 245 P.2d 788 (1952).

51. Louisiana *ex rel.* Francis v. Resweber, 329 U.S. 459, 471 (1947) (dissenting opinion) (repugnant to the conscience of mankind); Kasper v. Brittain, 245 F.2d 92, 96 (6th Cir. 1957) (shocking to the sense of justice); State v. Taylor, 82 Ariz. 289, 294, 312 P.2d 162 (1957) (shock the moral sense of the community); People v. Morris, 80 Mich. 634, 639, 45 N.W. 591 (1890) (shock the moral sense of the people); State v. Williams, 77 Mo. 310, 312 (1883) (shock the mind of every man possessed of common feeling); State v. Teague, 215 Ore. 609, 611, 336 P.2d 338 (1959) (shock the moral sense of all reasonable men as to what is right and proper under the circumstances); State v. Becker, 3 S.D. 29, 41, 51 N.W. 1018 (1892) (shock public sentiment and violate the judgment of reasonable people); and State v. Woodward, 68 W. Va. 66, 73, 69 S.E. 385 (1910) (shock our feelings of humanity, conscience, justice and mercy).

52. 408 U.S. 238 (1972).

53. Ibid., 282.

54. Only Justice Marshall agreed that the death penalty per se was unconstitutional. Justices Douglas, Stewart, and White did not go that far.

Chapter 3
Challenging the Various Methods of Inflicting
the Death Penalty

1. John Laurence, *A History of Capital Punishment* (New York: The Citadel Press, 1960), p. vii.

2. See, e.g., Leon Radzinowicz, *A History of English Criminal Law* (New York: The Macmillan Co., 1948); Thorsten Sellin (ed.), "Murder and the Penalty of Death," *The Annals* 284 (November 1952); and "The History of Capital Punishment," *Law Times* 158 (August 9, 1924): 116.

3. See, e.g., Harry Elmer Barnes, *The Story of Punishment* (Montclair, N.J.: Patterson Smith, 1972), pp. 248-64; Eugene Block, *And May God Have Mercy: The Case Against Capital Punishment* (San Francisco: Fearon Publishers, 1962); J.W. Garner, "On the Abolition of the Death Penalty," *Journal of Criminal Law and Criminology* 1 (November 1910): 626-27; Edward A. Kaplan, "A Case for the Abolition of Capital Punishment," *Louisiana Law Review* 29 (February 1969): 396-405; Lewis E. Lawes, *Man's Judgment of Death* (Montclair, N.J.: Patterson Smith, 1969); Maynard Shipley, "Does Capital Punishment Prevent Convictions?," *American Law Review* 43 (May-June 1909): 321-34; James H. Vahey, "Abolition of Capital Punishment," *The Green Bag* 19 (June 1907): 359-60; and E.W. White, "The Death Penalty," *Tennessee Law Review* 3 (November 1924): 22-25.

4. See, e.g., Jacques Barzun, "In Favor of Capital Punishment," *The American Scholar* 31 (Spring 1962): 181-91; and Ernest Van Den Haag, "On Deterrence and the Death Penalty," *Journal of Criminal Law, Criminology and Police Science* 60 (June 1969): 141-47.

5. See, e.g., "ACLU'S New Stand on Death Penalty," *Civil Liberties* 227 (June 1965): 2; Randolph Becker, "Eighth Amendment and Our Evolving Standards of Decency: A Tone for Re-evaluation," *Suffolk Law Review* 3 (Summer 1969): 616-27; Hugo Adam Bedau, "The Courts, the Constitution and Capital Punishment," *Utah Law Review* 1968 (May 1968): 201-39; and Jack Greenberg and Jack Himmelstein, "Varieties of Attack on the Death Penalty," *Crime and Delinquency* 15 (January 1969): 112-20.

6. Any list might include: beheading, self-destruction by poisoning, being pushed into a quagmire, stoning, hanging, crucifixion, throwing from a rock, pouring on molten lead, starving, tearing to death by red-hot pincers, sawing asunder (quartering), burning alive, burying alive, throwing into water in a sack with a dog, cock, viper and ape, beating to death, throat slitting, pressing to death (*peine forte et dure*), boiling to death, strangulating, tearing to pieces with horses, spearing to death, running the gauntlet, flogging to death, breaking on the wheel, flaying alive, and hitting on the head with a mallet (*mazzatello*).

7. See Arthur Koestler, *Reflections on Hanging* (New York: Macmillan Co., 1957); and John Deane Potter, *The Fatal Gallows Tree* (London: Elek Books, 1965).

8. By 1971 the number of states employing this mode of execution had been reduced to eight. See Bureau of Prisons, *National Prisoner Statistics* 46 (August 1971): p. 2.

9. *Hang By the Neck* (Springfield, Ill.: Charles C. Thomas, 1967), p. 4.

10. In particular, see *Ex parte* Medley, 134 U.S. 160 (1889).

11. Dutton v. State, 123 Md. 373, 91 A. 417 (1914).

12. State v. Burris, 194 Iowa 628, 639, 190 N.W. 38 (1922).

13. State v. Colcord, 170 Minn. 504, 508, 212 N.W. 735 (1927); and State v. Butchek, 121 Ore. 141, 253 P. 367 (1927).

14. People v. Wilkinson, 2 Utah 158 (1878). There is apparently some confusion over the exact spelling of Wallace's last name. The Utah court spelled it Wilk*in*son and the United States Supreme Court, Wilk*er*son. The latter will be used throughout this text.

15. Ibid., 160.

16. 22 N.Y. 95 (1860).

17. People v. Wilkinson, 2 Utah 158, 164 (1878).

18. Wilkerson v. Utah, 99 U.S. 130 (1879).

19. Ibid., 134.

20. Ibid., 135-36.

21. Ibid., 137.

22. Utah, *Compiled Laws* (1907), c. 38, sec. 4939. See *New York Times,* 29 March 1921, p. 9.

23. *New York Times,* 9 March 1930, p. 16.

24. Bureau of Prisons, p. 2.

25. For a lengthy history, see *New York Times,* 24 May 1890, p. 1.

26. New York, *Laws* (1888), c. 489, sec. 505.

27. For a fascinating and more detailed account, see Theodore Bernstein, " 'A Grand Success' ", *Institute of Electrical and Electronics Engineers* 10 (February 1973): 54-58.

28. People v. Kemmler, 119 N.Y. 569, 24 N.E. 6, 9 (1890).

29. *In re* Kemmler, 7 N.Y.S. 145 (1889).

30. Ibid., 149.

31. Ibid., 150.

32. People *ex rel.* Kemmler v. Durston, 55 Hun. 64, 7 N.Y.S. 813, 815 (1889).

33. People *ex rel.* Kemmler v. Durston, 119 N.Y.S. 569, 24 N.E. 6 (1890).

34. *In re* Kemmler, 136 U.S. 436 (1890).

35. Ibid., 447.

36. See also United States v. Cruikshank, 92 U.S. 542 (1875); and Slaughter-House Cases, 83 U.S. (16 Wall.) 36 (1872).

37. For a detailed account of the preparations and execution, see Bernstein.

See also Robert Elliott, *Agent of Death* (New York: E.P. Dutton and Co., Inc., 1940), pp. 24-29; George E. Fell, "The Influence of Electricity on Protoplasm," *The American Monthly Microscopical Journal* 11 (August 1890): 169-90; Lewis E. Lawes, *Life and Death in Sing Sing* (Garden City, N.Y.: Doubleday, Doran and Co., Inc., 1940), pp. 24-29; Carlos F. MacDonald, "The Infliction of the Death Penalty by Means of Electricity: Being a Report of Seven Cases," *Transactions of the Medical Society of New York* (1892), pp. 400-27, cited in Bernstein; *New York Times,* 8 August 1890, pp. 1-2; *New York Times,* 7 August 1890, p. 1; and *The Electrical World,* 16 August 1890, pp. 99-100.

38. Bernstein, p. 57.
39. Quoted in Elliott, p. 28.
40. Elbridge T. Gerry, "Capital Punishment by Electricity," *North American Review* 149 (September 1889): 324.
41. *New York Times,* 7 August 1890, p.2.
42. Ibid.
43. Quoted in Elliott, p. 28.
44. Note, *Harvard Law Review* 4 (January 1891): 287.
45. R.S. Morrison, "The Nullity of Protective Law," *Central Law Journal* 30 (February 14, 1890): 137-38.
46. See Malloy v. South Carolina, 237 U.S. 180, 185 (1915).
47. In 1971, twenty-three states had provisions authorizing the infliction of capital punishment by electricity. See Bureau of Prisons.
48. Reported by James W. Garner, "Infliction of the Death Penalty by Electricity," *Journal of Criminal Law and Criminology* 1 (November 1910): 626. Dr. Spitzka studied Fifty-four cases involving electrocution before arriving at his conclusion.
49. Storti v. Commonwealth, 178 Mass. 549, 553, 60 N.E. 210 (1901).
50. State v. Tomassi, 75 N.J.L. 739, 747, 69 A. 214 (1908).
51. Malloy v. South Carolina, 237 U.S. 180, 185 (1915).
52. Hart v. Commonwealth, 131 Va. 726, 743, 109 S.E. 582 (1921).
53. Ferguson v. State, 90 Fla. 105, 107, 105 So. 840 (1925); State v. Jones, 200 La. 809, 819-20, 9 So.2d 42 (1942); and State v. Painter, 135 W. Va. 106, 118, 63 S.E.2d 86 (1950).
54. State v. Burdette, 135 W. Va. 312, 340, 63 S.E. 2d 69 (1951).
55. For a detailed account, see Barrett Prettyman, Jr., *Death and the Supreme Court* (New York: Harcourt, Brace and World, Inc., 1957), pp. 90-128.
56. For another account, see "Sunday Heart," *Time,* 19 May 1947, p. 25.
57. The other central challenge was based on the double jeopardy clause of the Fifth Amendment.
58. Quoted in Prettyman, p. 106.
59. Louisiana *ex rel.* Francis v. Resweber, 329 U.S. 459 (1947).
60. Ibid. 464.

61. Ibid., 469 (concurring opinion).
62. Ibid., 470-71 (concurring opinion).
63. Ibid., 473 (dissenting opinion).
64. Ibid., 474 (dissenting opinion).
65. Ibid., 477 (dissenting opinion).
66. See Gerald D. Lenoir, "Double Jeopardy," *National Bar Journal* 6 (September 1948): 259-62; "Two Attempts at Electrocution of Death Sentence is Not Cruel and Unusual Punishment," *Loyola Law Review* 4 (June 1947): 84-85; and Fred Witty, "Right to Execute Death Sentence After First Attempt Fails," *Mississippi Law Journal* 19 (December 1947): 99-101.
67. An article by Paul Pigman also reflects an antidecision bias. See Paul O. H. Pigman, Note, *Tulane Law Review* 21 (March 1947): 480-86.
68. "Second Electrocution Attempt Not Violation of Constitutional Prohibition Against Cruel and Unusual Punishment," *Virginia Law Review* 33 (May 1947): 349.
69. Norman Schatz, "Cruel and Unusual Punishment by Electrocution," *Marquette Law Review* 31 (May 1947): 110.
70. Jacob Balick, "Cruel and Unusual Punishment," *Temple Law Quarterly* 20 (April 1947): 586.
71. See, e.g., Raymond J. McDonnell, "Second Electrocution After Failure of First Attempt," *St. John's Law Review* 22 (April 1948): 270-73.
72. Nevada, *Statutes* (1921), c. 246, secs. 418, 431.
73. *New York Times,* 29 March 1921, p. 9; and Robert A. Maurer, "Death By Lethal Gas," *Georgetown Law Journal* 9 (May 1921): 50-51.
74. *In re* Kemmler, 136 U.S. 436 (1890).
75. State v. Gee Jon, 46 Nev. 418, 436, 211 P. 676 (1923).
76. Ibid., 437.
77. *New York Times,* 7 January 1923, p. 3.
78. See "Nevada Gas House," *Outlook,* 15 June 1930, pp. 255-56; and P.J. Zisch, "Lethal Gas As A Means of Asphyxiating Capital Offenders," *Medico-Legal Journal* 48 (January-February 1931): 25-27.
79. Reported in "Execution by Gas," *The Literary Digest,* 1 March 1924, p. 17.
80. Raymond Hartmann, "The Use of Lethal Gas in Nevada Executions," *St. Louis University Law Review* 8 (1923): 167.
81. Ibid., 168.
82. Arizona, *Laws* (1933), p. 588 (See also *New York Times,* 5 March 1931, p. 14; and *New York Times,* 29 October 1933, p. 24); Colorado, *Session Laws* (1933), c. 61, p. 420. (The first asphyxiation in Colorado took place on June 22, 1934. See *New York Times,* 23 June 1934, p. 30. See also *New York Times,* 30 December 1933, p. 30); Wyoming, *Compiled Statutes* (1945), title 10, sec. 1704; (See also *New York Times,* 2 February 1935, p. 30); North Carolina, *Public Laws* (1935), c. 294, sec. 1; and California,

Statutes (1937), c. 172, sec. 172, sec. 1228. The latter came on the heels of a spirited debate between two wardens in the California state system. Warden Holohan thought the new method "more expeditious and more humane," while Warden Smith felt it was "two long, drawn out, too liable to bungling and much less humane than the rope" (*New York Times,* 4 December 1932, p. 6).

83. Hernandez v. Arizona, 43 Ariz. 424, 441, 32 P.2d 18 (1934).
84. *New York Times,* 8 December 1935, IV, p. 11.
85. *New York Times,* 2 February 1936, IV, p. 11.
86. See *New York Times,* 8 December 1935, IV, p. 11; and *New York Times,* 2 February 1936, IV, p. 11. Most similar statutes had little legislative opposition. For example, the vote in the Arizona House was 58-2. See *New York Times,* 5 March 1931, p. 14.
87. *New York Times,* 2 February 1936, IV, p. 11. See also *New York Times,* 1 February 1936, p. 3.
88. State v. Brice, 214 N.C. 34, 197 S.E. 690 (1938).
89. People v. Daugherty, 40 Cal.2d 876, 894, 256 P.2d 911, *cert. denied,* 346 U.S. 827 (1953).
90. State v. Gee Jon, 46 Nev. 418, 211 P. 676 (1923).
91. Bureau of Prisons.

Chapter 4
Challenging the Death Penalty as Excessive

1. Hugo Adam Bedau, *The Death Penalty in America: An Anthology* (Garden City, N.Y.: Doubleday and Co., Inc., 1967), pp. 6-7.
2. James A. McCafferty, "Capital Punishment in the United States: 1930-1952," (Unpublished Masters Thesis, Ohio State University, 1954), p. 26, cited by Walter C. Reckless, "The Use of the Death Penalty," *Crime and Delinquency* 15 (January 1969): 47.
3. Bedau, p. 45.
4. Ibid., p. 57.
5. Territory v. Ketchum, 10 N.M. 718, 65 P. 169 (1901). But see State v. Stubblefield, 157 Mo. 360, 58 S.W. 337 (1900).
6. Weems v. United States, 217 U.S. 349 (1910). See infra, chapt. 7.
7. Territory v. Ketchum, 10 N.M. 718, 723, 65 P. 169 (1901).
8. Ibid., 724.
9. Ibid., 725.
10. Boykin v. State, 281 Ala. 659, 207 So.2d 412 (1968); Workman v. Commonwealth, 309 Ky. 117, 216 S.W.2d 45 (1948); Gibson v. Commonwealth, 204 Ky. 748, 265 S.W. 339 (1924), *rev'd on other grounds,* 209 Ky. 101, 272 S.W. 43 (1925); Ellis v. State, 54 Okla. Cr. 295, 190 P.2d 156 (1933); Robards v.

State, 37 Okla. Cr. 371, 259 P. 166 (1927); Thompson v. State, 91 Tex. Cr. 234, 237 S.W. 926 (1922); and Brookman v. Commonwealth, 145 S.E. 358 (Va. 1928).

11. For an analysis of the statutes, see Norman Bierman, "Validity of the Death Penalty for Robbery," *St. Louis University Law Review* 14 (December 1928): 80-81. For arguments against the statutes, see *New York Times,* 21 February 1935, p. 15, and 22 February 1935, p. 20.

12. 266 P. 491 (Okla. 1928). That the decision did not serve as precedent elsewhere, see "Punishment by Death for Robbery By Violence," *Virginia Law Review* 15 (April 1929): 620.

13. See Evans v. State, 228 Ga. 867, 188 S.E.2d 861 (1972); State v. Stubblefield, 157 Mo. 360, 58 S.W. 337 (1900); and Robards v. State, 37 Okla. Cr. 371, 259 P. 166 (1927).

14. Thompson v. State, 91 Tex. Cr. 234, 236, 237 S.W. 726 (1922). See also Tomlinson v. Commonwealth, 261 Ky. 186, 87 S.W.2d 396 (1935) ($3); and Robards v. State, 37 Okla. Cr. 371, 259 P. 166 (1927) ($25).

15. Workman v. Commonwealth, 309 Ky. 117, 121, 216 S.W.2d 45 (1948).

16. Cobern v. Alabama, 273 Ala. 547, 142 So.2d 869 (1962). He was executed September 4, 1964. Murder, however, accompanied the theft.

17. Ellison v. State, 419 S.W.2d 849 (Tex. Cr. App. 1967). Kidnapping and rape were involved and admitted into evidence.

18. Boykin v. State, 281 Ala. 659, 207 So.2d 412 (1968). A woman was wounded in the leg.

19. Boykin v. Alabama, 395 U.S. 238 (1969). For comments, see "Due Process Requires An Affirmative Showing in the Trial Record That Defendant Has Entered His Guilty Plea Voluntarily and Understandingly," *Alabama Law Review* 22 (Fall 1969): 76-89; "Judicial Determination of Voluntariness of Guilty Pleas," *Harvard Law Review* 83 (November 1969); 181-87; Joseph T. McElveen, Jr., "Criminal Procedure," *South Carolina Law Review* 22 (1970); 141-45; Travis W. Moon, "Requirements for Acceptance of Guilty Pleas," *North Carolina Law Review* 48 (February 1969): 352-61; Libby E. Weiss, "Guilty Plea Must Be Affirmatively Shown to Have Been Given Intelligently and Voluntarily," *Temple Law Quarterly* 43 (February 1969): 94-97; and Rowland L. Young, "Review of Supreme Court Decisions," *American Bar Association Journal* 55 (September 1969): 869.

20. Hart v. State, 227 Ga. 171, 179 S.E.2d 346 (1971). Since 1930, twenty-three men have been executed for armed robbery: Alabama (five), Georgia (six), Kentucky (five), Mississippi (three), Oklahoma (one), and Texas (one). See *Citizens Against Legalized Murder Newsletter* 4 (December 1970): p. 4.

21. Ayers v. State, 25 Ala. App. 469, 470, 148 So. 875 (1933).

22. Lee v. State 227 Ala. 2, 4, 150 So. 164 (1933).

23. People v. Tanner, 3 Cal.2d 279, 298, 44 P.2d 324 (1935).

24. People v. Knowles, 35 Cal.2d 175, 217 P.2d 1. *cert. denied,* 340 U.S. 879 (1950).

25. People v. Wein, 50 Cal.2d 383, 427, 326 P.2d 457 (1958) (dissenting opinion).
26. Ibid., 428 (dissenting opinion).
27. People v. Knowles, 340 U.S. 879 (1950). See also United States v. Coon, 242 F. Supp. 483 (N.D. Iowa 1965), *aff'd.*, 360 F. 2d 550 (8th Cir. 1966), *cert. denied,* 385 U.S. 873 (1966).
28. See Jackson v. United States, 390 U.S. 570 (1968). For analysis, see Luther C. Nadler, "*United States* v. *Jackson*: Guilty Plea and Replacement Capital Punishment Provisions," *Cornell Law Review* 54 (February 1969): 448-58; Douglas A. Poe, "Capital Punishment Statutes in the Wake of *United States* v. *Jackson*: Some Unresolved Questions," *George Washington University Law Review* 37 (May 1969): 719-45; and "The Supreme Court, 1967 Term," *Harvard Law Review* 882 (November 1968): 156-62.
29. Smith v. United States, 360 U.S. 1, 8 (1959).
30. See "The Rosenberg Case: A Problem of Statutory Construction," *Northwestern University Law Review* 48 (January-February 1954): 751. See also "The Rosenberg Case: Some Reflections on Federal Criminal Law," *Columbia Law Review* 54 (February 1954): 238.
31. United States v. Rosenberg, 195 F.2d 583 (2d Cir.), *cert. denied,* 344 U.S. 838 (1952).
32. See "The Rosenberg Case: Some Reflections on Federal Criminal Law," 239-40 and n. 107.
33. United States v. Rosenberg, 195 F.2d 583, 608 (2d Cir.), *cert. denied,* 344 U.S. 838 (1952).
34. Ibid., 611.
35. 317 U.S. 1 (1942).
36. United States v. Rosenberg, 195 F.2d 583 (2d Cir.), *cert. denied,* 344 U.S. 838 (1952).
37. United States v. Rosenberg, 344 U.S. 838 (1952).
38. Kentucky, *Acts* (1934), c. 50.
39. Tomlinson v. Commonwealth, 261 Ky. 186, 87 S.W.2d 376 (1935).
40. He cited *Crutchfield* v. *Commonwealth,* 248 Ky. 707, 59 S.W.2d 983 (1933) as controlling. This was strange because *Crutchfield* upheld an earlier statute that provided five-to-twenty years imprisonment for violation of the offense, and not the death penalty.
41. California, *Penal Code,* sec. 246.
42. *In re* Finley, 1 Cal. App. 198, 201, 81 P. 1041 (1905).
43. Ibid., 202.
44. 153 Cal. 59, 94 P. 248 (1908).
45. People v. Oppenheimer, 156 Cal. 733, 106 P. 74 (1909).
46. *In re* Wells, 35 Cal.2d 889, 221 P.2d 947 (1950), *cert. denied,* 340 U.S. 937 (1951).
47. 156 Cal. 733, 106 P. 74 (1909).

48. People v. Harmon, 54 Cal.2d 9, 351 P.2d 329, 4 Cal. Rptr. 161 (1960); and People v. Vaughn, 78 Cal. Rptr. 186, 455 P.2d 122 (1969).

49. Dutton v. State, 123 Md. 373, 385, 91 A. 417 (1914).

50. Walker v. State, 186 Md. 440, 47 A.2d 47 (1946).

51. Hart v. Commonwealth, 131 Va. 726, 109 S.E. 582 (1921).

52. See Craig v. State, 179 So.2d 202, 206 (Fla. 1965) (dissenting opinion), *cert. denied,* 383 U.S. 959 (1966).

53. Snider v. Cunningham, 375 U.S. 889 (1963); and Rudolph v. Alabama, 375 U.S. 889 (1963).

54. Ibid., 889-91. For a thorough analysis, see Herbert L. Packer, "Making the Punishment Fit the Crime," *Harvard Law Review* 77 (April 1964): 1071-82.

55. See, e.g., Sims v. Balkcom, 220 Ga. 7, 11-12, 136 S.E.2d 766 (1964).

56. Harris v. Stephens, 361 F.2d 888 (8th Cir. 1966), *cert. denied,* 386 U.S. 964 (1967); Mitchell v. Stephens, 353 F.2d 129 (8th Cir. 1965), *cert. denied,* 384 U.S. 1019 (1966); and Maxwell v. Stephens, 348 F.2d 325 (8th Cir.), *cert. denied,* 382 U.S. 944 (1965).

57. Mitchell v. Stephens, 353 F.2d 129 (8th Cir. 1965), *cert. denied,* 384 U.S. 1019 (1966); and Maxwell v. Stephens, 348 F.2d 325 (8th Cir.), *cert. denied,* 382 U.S. 944 (1965).

58. See, e.g., Snider v. Peyton, 356 F.2d 626, 627 (4th Cir. 1966).

59. Harris v. Stephens, 361 F.2d 888 (8th Cir. 1966), *cert. denied,* 386 U.S. 964 (1967); Ralph v. Pepersack, 335 F.2d 128 (4th Cir. 1964), *cert. denied,* 380 U.S. 925 (1965); Rudolph v. State, 275 Ala. 115, 152 So.2d 662, *cert. denied,* 375 U.S. 889 (1963); Craig v. State, 179 So.2d 202 (Fla. 1965), *cert. denied,* 383 U.S. 959 (1966); Massey v. Smith, 224 Ga. 721, 164 S.E.2d 786 (1968); State v. Kilpatrick, 206 Kan. 6, 439 P.2d 99 (1968); State v. Crook, 253 La. 961, 221 So.2d 473 (1969); Jones v. State, 247 Md. 530, 233 A.2d 791 (1967); Gordon v. State, 160 So.2d 73 (Miss. 1964); State v. Rogers, 275 N.C. 411, 168 S.E.2d 345 (1969), *cert. denied,* 396 U.S. 1024 (1970); State v. Gamble, 249 S.C. 605, 155 S.E.2d 916 (1967), *cert. denied,* 390 U.S. 927 (1968); Branch v. State, 447 S.W.2d 932 (Tex. Cr. App. 1969); and Fogg v. Commonwealth, 208 Va. 541, 159 S.E.2d 616 (1968).

60. Ralph was convicted on January 18, 1961. See Jeffery L. Musman, "Death Penalty As Cruel and Unusual Punishment For Rape," *William and Mary Law Review* 12 (Spring 1971): 682.

61. Ralph v. State, 226 Md. 480, 174 A.2d 163 (1961), *cert. denied,* 369 U.S. 813 (1962).

62. Ralph v. Pepersack, 203 F. Supp. 752 (D.Md. 1962); Ralph v. Pepersack, 218 F. Supp. 932 (D.Md. 1963), *aff'd,* 335 F.2d 128 (4th Cir. 1964), *cert. denied,* 380 U.S. 925 (1965); Ralph v. Brough, 248 F. Supp. 334 (D.Md. 1965); and Ralph v. Warden, 264 F. Supp. 528 (D.Md.), *aff'd,* No. 11,549 (4th Cir. 1967) (mem.), *cert. denied,* 390 U.S. 992 (1968).

63. Ralph v. Warden, 438 F.2d 786, 788 (4th Cir. 1970).

64. Ibid., 789, citing Calhoun v. State, 85 Tex. Cr. App. 496, 214 S.W. 335 (1919). Such an interpretation of the rationale in this case appears questionable. See Note, *Minnesota Law Review* 56 (November 1971): 103, n. 54; and Sharon Cohen, Note, *George Washington Law Review* 40 (October 1971): 166, n. 50.

65. 217 U.S. 349 (1910).

66. 356 U.S. 86, 101 (1958).

67. But see "The Constitutionality of the Death Penalty for Non-Aggravated Rape," *Washington University Law Quarterly* 1972 (Winter 1972): 175.

68. Ralph v. Warden, 438 F.2d 786, 793 (4th Cir. 1970).

69. Warden v. Ralph, 408 U.S. 942 (1972).

70. Musman, n. 60; Note, *Minnesota Law Review* 56 (November 1971):95-110; and Note, *University of Richmond Law Review* 5 (Spring 1971): 392-400.

71. "The Constitutionality of the Death Penalty for Non-Aggravated Rape," 170-78.

72. Donald P. Butler, "The Imposition of the Death Penalty for Rape When the Victim's Life Has Been Neither Taken Nor Endangered Constitutes Cruel and Unusual Punishment Under Eighth Amendment," *Houston Law Review* 8 (March 1971): 807.

73. Cohen, 161-72; Charles E. McCartney, Jr., "The Limitated Application of the Eighth Amendment's Cruel and Unusual Punishment Clause to the Death Penalty," *Wake Forest Law Review* 7 (June 1971): 494-500; and Joseph F. McDowell, "Cruel and Unusual Punishment,"*Suffolk University Law Review* 5 (Winter 1971): 504-12.

74. Billingsley v. State, 287 Ala. 634, 254 So.2d 333 (1971); Liddell v. State, 287 Ala. 299, 251 So.2d 601 (1971); and State v. Chance, 279 N.C. 643, 185 S.E.2d 227 (1971).

75. Bartholomey v. State, 260 Md. 504, 521, 273 A.2d 164, 173 (1971). See also, State v. Barber, 278 N.C. 268, 274, 179 S.E.2d 404, (1971); and State v. Atkinson, 278 N.C. 168, 178, 179 S.E.2d 410 (1971).

76. Ibid. See also State v. Myers, 261 La. 100, 259 S.2d 27 (1972); and State v. Atkinson, 278 N.C. 168, 178, 179 S.E.2d 410 (1971).

77. State v. Myers, 261 La. 100, 103, 259 So.2d 27 (1972).

78. Ibid.

79. 408 U.S. 238 (1972).

80. But see Justice Powell's dissent (ibid., 456-61).

Chapter 5
Challenging the Death Penalty as
Unconstitutional Per Se

1. For scholars of this persuasion, see Randolph Kip Becker, "Eighth Amendment and Our Evolving Standards of Decency: A Tone for Re-evaluation,"

Suffolk University Law Review 3 (Summer 1969): 616-27; Hugo Adam Bedau, "The Courts, The Constitution and Capital Punishment," *Utah Law Review* 1968 (May 1968): 201-39; Arthur J. Goldberg and Alan M. Dershowitz, "Declaring the Death Penalty Unconstitutional," *Harvard Law Review* 83 (June 1970): 1773-1819; Gerald H. Gottleib, "Testing the Death Penalty," *Southern California Law Review* 34 (Winter 1961): 268-81; Jack Greenburg and Jack Himmelstein, "Varieties of Attack on the Death Penalty," *Crime and Delinquency* 15 (January 1969): 112-20; Michael H. Marcus and David S. Weissbrodt, "The Death Penalty Cases," *California Law Review* 56 (October 1968): 1268-1490; and Sol Rubin, "The Supreme Court, Cruel and Unusual Punishment, and the Death Penalty," *Crime and Delinquency* 15 (January 1969): 121-31.

2. 391 U.S. 510 (1968).
3. See Gregory J. Leisse, "The Supreme Court and Capital Punishment—From Wilkerson to Witherspoon and Beyond," *St. Louis University Law Review* 14 (1970): 463-85; Note, *Harvard Law Review* 82 (November 1968): 162-72; and *Time*, 14 June 1968, p. 78.
4. 390 U.S. 570 (1968).
5. 18 U.S.C., sec. 1201 (a) (1964).
6. Pope v. United States, 392 U.S. 651 (1968) (*per curiam*).
7. Ralph v. Warden, 438 F.2d 786 (4th Cir. 1970).
8. Furman v. Georgia, 408 U.S. 238, 442, n. 37 (1972) (dissenting opinion).
9. Trop v. Dulles, 356 U.S. 86, 99 (1958).
10. 402 U.S. 183 (1971).
11. For details, see Ronald I. Bell, "Cruel or Unusual Punishment: The Death Penalty," *Suffolk University Law Review* 6 (Summer 1972): 1045-61.
12. People v. Anderson, 64 Cal.2d 633, 51 Cal. Rptr. 238, 414 P.2d 366 (1966).
13. *In re* Anderson, 69 Cal.2d 613, 73 Cal. Rptr. 21, 447 P.2d 117 (1968).
14. 52 Cal.2d 467, 341 P.2d 679 (1959).
15. People v. Anderson, 100 Cal. Rptr. 152, 6 Cal.3d 628, 493 P2d. 880 (1972). He also contended that the death penalty violated the federal inhibition. The California Supreme Court did not consider this question because it was presently before the United States Supreme Court.
16. Ibid., 155. This fact made little difference, for the Court found capital punishment *both* cruel *and* unusual (ibid., 163).
17. Ibid., 166.
18. Ibid.
19. For other analyses, see Edward L. Barrett, Jr., "Anderson and the Judicial Function," *Southern California Law Review* 45 (Summer 1972): 739-49; and Scott Brice, "Anderson and the Adequate State Ground," *Southern California Law Review* 45 (Summer 1972): 750-66.
20. Justice Blackmun apparently felt that the Supreme Court was influenced by the *Anderson* decision. See Furman v. Georgia, 408 U.S. 238, 411 (1972) (dissenting opinion).

21. Furman v. Georgia, 408 U.S. 239-40 (1972).

22. Furman v. State, 225 Ga. 253, 167 S.E.2d 628 (1969); and Jackson v. State, 225 Ga. 790, 171 S.E.2d 501 (1969).

23. Branch v. State, 447 S.W.2d 932 (Tex. Cr. App. 1969).

24. Furman v. Georgia, 408 U.S. 238 (1972); Douglas at 256-57; Brennan at 305; Stewart at 309-10; White at 313; and Marshall at 364-66.

25. Ibid., 253.

26. Ibid., 255.

27. Furman, while backing up, tripped over a wire, fell down, and the gun discharged. His victim was on the other side of the door, and Furman did not know of the murder until arrested (ibid., 294, n. 48).

28. Ibid., 330-32.

29. Ibid., 287.

30. Ibid., 288, quoting People v. Anderson, 6 Cal.3d 628, 649, 493 P.2d 880, 894 (1972). For an especially illuminating article on this subject, see "Mental Suffering Under Sentence of Death: A Cruel and Unusual Punishment," *Iowa Law Review* 57 (February 1972): 814-33.

31. Ibid., 343.

32. Ibid., 349.

33. Ibid., 355.

34. Ibid., 358.

35. Ibid., 362.

36. For an interesting case, see James C. Jenkins, "A Most Extraordinary Case," *Case and Commentary* 24 (August 1917): 222-24. See also Edwin M. Borchard, *Convicting the Innocent* (New York: DaCapo Press, 1970).

37. Furman v. Georgia, 408 U.S. 238, 410 (dissenting opinion).

38. Ibid., 269, quoting Weems v. United States, 217 U.S. 349, 379 (1910).

39. Ibid., 313.

40. Ibid., 386.

41. Ibid., 395. For an interesting although early article suggesting that the death penalty is a deterrent, see Note, *Irish Law Times* 11 (June 9, 1899): 278-79.

42. See Justice Burger's remarks (ibid., 396).

43. Ibid., 399.

44. Ibid., 402.

45. "Mixed Reviews: Supreme Court Rulings," *New Republic,* 15 July 1972, p. 7. See also "Closing Death Row," *Time,* 10 July 1972, p. 37.

46. Both had voted in the majority in *McGautha* v. *California,* 402 U.S. 183 (1971). See infra, "*Furman*: The Impact."

47. U.S., Congressional Record, 92d Cong., 2d sess., June 29, 1972, S. 10662.

48. "End to Death Row? What Supreme Court Ruled?," *United States News and World Report,* 10 July 1972, p. 26.

49. *Capital Times* (Madison, Wisconsin), *30 June 1972, p. 6.*

50. *New York Times,* 30 June 1972, p. 2.

51. *New York Times,* 11 March 1973, pp. 1 and 55. See also *Capital Times* Madison, Wisconsin), 10 March 1973, p. 1; and *Wisconsin State Journal* (Madison), 11 March 1973, pp. 1-2.

52. From a copy of the bill. See *Chicago Sun Times,* 22 March 1973.

53. See *Congressional Quarterly,* 16 March 1974, pp. 712-13.

54. "Resounding Vote For The Death Penalty," *Nation's Business,* April 1973, pp. 20-21.

55. *Capital Times,* 30 June 1972.

56. *New York Times,* 30 June 1972, p. 6.

57. "Rebirth of Death?," *Newsweek,* 18 December 1972, pp. 23-24. See also *New York Times,* 11 March 1973.

58. See William G. Baker, "The Death Penalty—The Alternatives Left After *Furman* v. *Georgia,*" *Albany Law Review* 37 (1973): 344-64; "Five-to-Four Vote Kills Capital Punishment—Almost," *American Bar Association Journal* 58 (September 1972): 972-73; Michael G. Kohn, "The Death Penalty As Presently Administered Under Discretionary Sentencing Statutes is Cruel and Unusual Punishment," *Seton Hall Law Review* 4 (Fall-Winter 1972): 244-63; and "The Supreme Court, 1971 Term," *Harvard Law Review* 86 (November 1972): 76-85.

59. See Jerry D. Cluff, "Footnote to *Furman:* Failing Justification for the Capital Case Exception to the Right to Bail After Abolition of the Death Penalty," *San Diego Law Review* 10 (February 1973): 349-79; Charles W. Ehrhardt, et al., "The Aftermath of *Furman:* The Florida Experience," *Journal of Criminal Law and Criminology* 64 (March 1973): 2-21; Ross Parker, "Florida Statute 775.082: Ex post Facto, Bill of Attainder, and Policy Aspects of a Sentence of No-Parole Life Imprisonment," *University of Pittsburgh Law Review* 34 (Winter 1972): 290-302; and S. Cass Weiland and Greg Jones, "Federal Procedural Implications of *Furman* v. *Georgia:* What Rights for the Formerly Capital Offender," *American Journal of Criminal Law* 1 (October 1972): 107-47.

60. *Capital Times* (Madison, Wisconsin), 29 June 1972.

61. Some state statutes call for mandatory infliction of the death penalty and therefore are unaffected. See, e.g., Rhode Island, *General Laws Annotated,* sec. 11-23-2 (1970). For a complete list, see Baker, 359, n. 136. With only one exception, however, capital punishment under the Uniform Code of Military Justice will be the same.

62. 402 U.S. 183 (1971).

63. Furman v. Georgia, 408 U.S. 238, 248, n. 11 (1972).

64. Ibid., 310, n. 12.

65. Ibid., 400 (dissenting opinion).

66. Ibid.

67. Ibid., 427, n. 11.

68. Ibid., 408.

69. Delaware, *Code,* sec. 3901.
70. State v. Dickerson, 298 A.2d 761 (Del. 1973).
71. State v. Wadell, 194 S.E.2d 19 (N.C. 1973). For further analysis, see Raymond A. Parker, II, "The Current Status of the Death Penalty in North Carolina," *Wake Forest Law Review* 9 (December 1972): 135-41. By December 23, 1973 North Carolina had sent eighteen persons to death row to await the gas chamber. See *News and Observer* (Raleigh, N.C.), 23 December 1973.
72. On March 30, 1973, letters of inquiry were sent to each of the state governors. Responses were not received from Alaska, Arkansas, Idaho, Indiana, Louisiana, New Jersey, Pennsylvania, and Rhode Island. The following information is taken from the responses as well as information found in "The Death Penalty Gets A Push," *United States News and World Report,* 26 March 1973, p. 70; "Moves to Restore the Death Penalty," *United States News and World Report,* 4 December 1972, p. 60; and *Wisconsin State Journal* 9 May 1973, p. 10. No proposals were submitted to the Legislatures of Delaware, Kentucky, Minnesota, New York, and North Dakota.
73. *Gainesville Sun Times* (Florida), 4 March 1975.
74. See John B. Martin, "Crime of Passion," *Saturday Evening Post,* 30 July 1960.
75. *Gainesville Sun Times* (Florida), 4 March 1975. For details see *Gainesville Sun Times,* (Florida), 4 March 1975, p. 12A.

Chapter 6
Miscellaneous Chastisement

1. See, e.g., Alice M. Earle, *Curious Punishments of Bygone Days* (Detroit: Singing Tree Press, 1968), chapt. 6.
2. See, e.g., Aldridge v. Commonwealth, 4 Va. Cas. 447 (1824), Foote v. State, 59 Md. 264 (1883); Cornell v. State, 74 Tenn. 624; 629 (1881); and Commonwealth v. Wyatt, 27 Va. (6 Rand.) 694 (1828). See also United States v. Collins, 25 Fed. Cas. 545 (D.C. R.I. 1854).
3. Commonwealth v. Wyatt, 27 Va. (6 Rand.) 694, 701 (1828).
4. See, e.g., Werner v. State, 44 Ark. 122 (1884); and Ely v. Thompson, 10 Ky. (3 A.K. Marsh) 70 (1820).
5. 1 N.M. 415 (1869).
6. Foote v. State, 59 Md. 264 (1883).
7. Harry E. Barnes, *The Story of Punishment* (Montclair, N.J.: Patterson Smith, 1972), p. 57.
8. State v. Kearney, 8 N.C. 53, 54 (1820).
9. Act of Feb. 28, 1839, 5 Stat. 322, c. 36, sec. 5.

10. Herber v. State, 7 Tex. 69, 73 (1851).

11. Hobbs v. State, 133 Ind. 404, 409, 32 N.E. 1019 (1893).

12. See, e.g., "Flogging," *Canada Law Journal* 44 (June 1908): 441-43; Thomas Hopkins, "The Commissioners and the 'Cat'," *Law Times* 116 (December 19, 1903): 158; W.D. Morrison, "Corporal Punishment," *Law Magazine and Review* 25 (February 1900): 261-65; "The 'Cat' as an Effective Punishment," *The Solicitor's Journal and Weekly Reporter* 70 (January 2, 1926): 253; "The Court and the 'Cat'," *American Bar Association Journal* 8 (April 1922): 260; and "The Law As to Whipping," *The Solicitor's Journal and Weekly Reporter* 70 (January 16, 1926): 294. For more recent articles, see "Corporal Punishment in South Australia," *Adelaide Law Review* 2 (June 1963): 83-91; A.M. Kirkpatrick, "Corporal Punishment," *Criminal Law Quarterly* 10 (May 1968): 320-28; Graham E. Parker, "Corporal Punishment in Canada," *Criminal Law Quarterly* 7 (August 1964): 193-211; and A.J.W. Taylor, "Corporal Punishment and the Courts," *New Zealand Law Journal* (July 1963), 407-11.

13. Phebe A. Hanaford, "The Whipping Post for Wife Beaters," *Medico-Legal Journal* 17 (1889): 108-13.

14. Simon E. Baldwin, "The Restoration of Whipping As A Punishment for Crime," *Green Bag* 13 (January 1901): 65-67. See also Clark Bell, "The Cat as a Deterrent for Crime," *Journal of Law and Criminology* 3 (March 1913): 945-47; and "Whipping and Castration as Punishments for Crime," *Yale Law Journal* 8 (June 1899): 371-87.

15. See, e.g., Duane Mowry, "Whipping as Punishment for Crime; A Reply," *Green Bag* 13 (December 1901): 553-56.

16. It is still employed in Canada, Great Britain, and some Continental and Asiatic lands. See Barnes, p. 57. For brief summary of its use in Delaware, see *Washington Post,* 30 June 1972.

17. State v. Cannon, 55 Del. 587, 595, 190 A.2d 514 (1963). For an analysis, see Joel M. Feldman, "Constitutional Law—Cruel and Unusual Punishment," *Georgia Bar Journal* 26 (November 1963): 216-20.

18. Cannon v. State, 55 Del. 597, 401, 196 A.2d 399 (1963).

19. Balser v. State, 57 Del. 206, 195 A.2d 757 (1963).

20. 408 U.S. 238 (1972).

21. For a bibliography of many early periodical articles on the subject, see James W. Gardner, "Sterilization of Criminals," *Journal of Criminal Law and Criminology* 1 (November 1910): 623-24. For leading scholarly articles other than those cited in the following discussion, see Charles A. Boston, "A Protest Against Laws Authorizing the Sterilization of Criminals and Imbeciles," *Journal of Criminal Law and Criminology* 4 (1913): 326-58; "Constitutionality of the Iowa Sterilization Statute," *Iowa Law Review* 11 (April 1926): 262-68; John B. Gest, "Eugenic Sterilization: Justice Holmes v. Natural Law," *Temple Law Quarterly* 23 (April 1950): 306-12;

Marie E. Kopp, "Surgical Treatment As Sex Crime Prevention Measure," *Journal of Criminal Law and Criminology* 28 (January-February 1938): 692-706; J.H. Landman, "The History of Human Sterilization in the United States—Theory, Statute, Adjudication," *American Law Review* 63 (January-February 1929): 48-71; Richard S. Leftwich, "Eugenic Sterilization Statutes," *Virginia Law Review* 12 (March 1926): 419-22; Lester B. Orfield, Note, *Nebraska Law Review* 10 (July 1931): 164-69; Clarence J. Ruddy, "Compulsory Sterilization: An Unwarranted Extention of the Powers of Government," *The Notre Dame Lawyer* 3 (October 1927): 1-16; George T. Skinner, "A Sterilization Statute for Kentucky?" *Kentucky Law Journal* 23 (November 1934): 168-74; and William R. Warnock, "Sterilization of Mental Defectives," *Michigan Law Review* 61 (May 1963): 1359-64.

22. See generally Grant H. Morris and James F. Breithaupt, "Compulsory Sterilization of Criminals—Perversion in the Law," *Syracuse Law Review* 15 (Summer 1964): 739.

23. See ibid., 741. Also see Davis v. Berry, 216 Fed. 413, 417 (E.D. Iowa 1914), *rev'd as moot*, 242 U.S. 468 (1917); and Whitten v. State, 47 Ga. 297, 301 (1872).

24. They have been challenged on several other grounds as well. See Morris and Breithaupt; and James B. O'Hara and Howland Sanks, "Eugenic Sterilization," *Georgetown Law Journal* 45 (Fall 1956): 20-44.

25. Buck v. Bell, 143 Va. 310, 318, 130 S.E. 516 (1925).

26. Buck v. Bell, 274 U.S. 200, 207 (1927).

27. State v. Troutman, 50 Ida. 673, 299 P. 668 (1931); and *In re* Clayton, 120 Neb. 680, 234 N.W. 630 (1931).

28. *In re* Main, 162 Okla. 65, 19 P.2d 153 (1933). See also *In re* Simpson, 180 N.E.2d 206 (Ohio, 1962).

29. See *Time*, 23 July 1973, p. 50.

30. United States, *Federal Register* 38, no. 149 (August 3, 1973): 20930-31.

31. Davis v. Berry, 216 Fed. 413 (E.D. Iowa 1914), *rev'd. as moot*, 242 U.S. 468 (1917); and Mickle v. Henrichs, 262 Fed. 687 (D. Nev. 1918).

32. Mickle v. Henrichs, 262 Fed. 687, 688 (D. Nev. 1918).

33. State v. Feilen, 70 Wash. 65, 68, 126 P. 75 (1912). For a comment, see Stevenson Smith, "Is Vasectomy A Cruel and Unusual Punishment?," *Journal of Criminal Law and Criminology* 3 (January 1913): 783-86.

34. *In re* Opinion of Justices, 230 Ala. 543, 162 So. 123 (1935).

35. People v. Blankenship, 16 Cal. App.2d 606, 609-10, 61 P.2d 352 (1936).

36. See Joseph E. Browdy and Robert J. Saltzman, Note, *New York University Law Review* 36 (April 1961): 855-56; and 24 C.J.S., sec. 1978, p. 550.

37. 143 Va. 310, S.E. 516 (1925).

38. Davis v. Watton, 74 Utah 80, 85, 276 P. 921 (1929).

39. Skinner v. State *ex rel.* Williamson, 189 Okla. 235, 237, 115 P.2d 123 (1941), *rev'd on other grounds*, 316 U.S. 535 (1942).

40. Ibid.

41. The following information was drawn from the appendices in O'Hara and Sanks, 42-44.

42. The total estimated through 1968 was nearly 65,000. See Julius Paul, "The Return of Punitive Sterilization Proposals," *Law and Society Review* 3 (August 1968): 78.

43. *In re* O'Shea, 11 Cal. App. 568, 575, 105 P. 776 (1909); Hobbs v. State, 133 Ind. 404, 409, 32 N.E. 1019 (1893); *Matter of* Bayard, 63 How. Pr. 73, 77 (N.Y. 1881); and *In re* McDonald, 4 Wyo. 150, 161, 33 P. 18 (1893).

44. 11 Cal. App. 568, 105 P. 776 (1909).

45. James v. Commonwealth, 12 Serg. and Rawle 220 (Pa. 1825).

46. Ibid., 235.

47. Ibid., 235-36.

48. United States v. Royall, 27 F. Cas. 906 (No. 16,202) (C.C. D.C. 1829).

49. The court did hold that the punishment "*may* have become obsolete." Ibid., 910 (emphasis added).

50. See, e.g., Wilson v. Kelley, 294 F. Supp. 1005, 1012 (N.D. Ga. 1968); State v. White, 44 Kan. 514, 520-21 (1890); People v. Hanrahan, 75 Mich. 611, 621, 42 N.W. 1124 (1889); State v. Hogan, 63 Ohio St. 202, 218, 58 N.E. 572 (1900); State v. Huffstetler, 213 S.C. 313, 323, 49 S.E.2d 585 (1948); and State v. Durham, 89 Tenn. 723, 733, 18 S.W. 74 (1891).

51. See, e.g., Pervear v. Commonwealth, 72 U.S. (5 Wall.) 475 (1866) (illegal sale of intoxicating liquor); Plain v. State, 60 Ga. 284 (1878); State v. Gillmore, 88 Kan. 835, 845, 129 P. 1123 (1913) (desertion); State v. Gros, 208 La. 135, 142, 23 So.2d 24 (1945) (shooting with intent to kill); State v. Williams, 12 Mo. App. 415, 422 (1882) (obtaining money by fraudulent means); State v. LePard, 270 N.C. 157, 158, 153 S.E.2d 875 (1967) (robbery with firearms); and State v. Griffin, 190 N.C. 133, 138, 129 S.E. 410 (1925) (malicious castration). But see State v. Kimbrough, 212 S.C. 348, 46 S.E.2d 273 (1948) (thirty years at hard labor for burglary was excessive, thus unconstitutional).

52. Loeb v. Jennings, 133 Ga. 796, 801, 67 S.E. 101 (1920); Pearson v. Wimbish, 124 Ga. 701, 52 S.E. 751 (1905); State v. Farrington, 141 N.C. 844, 53 S.E. 954 (1906); and State v. Apple, 121 N.C. 584, 28 S.E. 469 (1897). But see State v. Williams, 40 S.C. 373, 382, 19 S.E. 5 (1894). See also State v. McCauley, 15 Cal. 429 (1860); and State v. Manuel, 20 N.C. 20 (1838).

53. Chain gangs themselves have never been declared unconstitutional. However, specific punishments and/or general environmental conditions imposed on such prisoners by administrators have been declared cruel and unusual. This subject is discussed in greater detail in chapter 12.

54. See, e.g., *Ex parte* Wong Lung, 17 Haw. 168 (1905); and People v. Adorno, 17 Puerto Rico 1059 (1911).

55. *Ex parte* Arras, 78 Cal. 304, 20 P. 683 (1889); and Eldridge v. Commonwealth,

87 Ky. 365, 367, 8 S.W. 892 (1888). But see Morgan v. State, 47 Ala. 34, 37 (1872); and Done v. People, 5 Parker 364, 389 (N.Y. 1863).

56. State v. Smith, 5 Day 175, 179 (Conn. 1811).

57. 294 F. Supp. 1005, 1012 (N.D. Ga. 1968).

58. McLamore v. South Carolina, 257 S.C. 413, 420, 186 S.E.2d 250 (1972), *cert. denied,* 409 U.S. 934 (1972). Justice Douglas dissented from the denial. He was of the opinion that the Court should determine whether the chain gang fits into our current concept of penology or whether it violates the Eighth Amendment. (ibid., 934-37).

59 25 Geo. II, c. 37 (1752). The act was repealed 6 & 7 Will. IV, c. 30 (1836).

60. See, e.g., New Jersey, *Acts* (1906), c. 79; New York, *Laws* (1888), c. 489; and Massachusetts, *Laws* (1887), c. 435.

61. *In re* Kemmler, 136 U.S. 436, 437 (1890).

62. McElvaine v. Brush, 142 U.S. 155, 158 (1891); and Trezza v. Brush, 142 U.S. 160, 161 (1891). For a commentary on *McElvaine,* see Note, *Harvard Law Review* 5 (March 1892): 409.

63. For an interesting earlier case, see Done v. People, 5 Parker 364 (N.Y. 1863).

64. Storti v. Commonwealth, 178 Mass. 549, 554, 60 N.E. 210 (1901). See also Sturtevant v. Commonwealth, 158 Mass. 598, 33 N.E. 648 (1893).

65. State v. Tomassi, 75 N.J.L. 739, 747, 69 A. 214 (1908). The court overlooked the fact that the Act of George II had already been repealed.

66. 134 U.S. 160 (1889).

67. Williams v. State, 125 Ark. 287, 290, 188 S.W. 826 (1916).

68. Hancock v. Avery, 301 F. Supp. 786, 792 (M.D. Tenn. 1969).

69. People v. Chessman, 52 Cal.2d 467, 341 P.2d 679 (1959).

70. Rosenberg v. Carroll, 99 F. Supp. 630 (S.D. N.Y. 1951).

71. Sinclair v. Henderson, 331 F. Supp. 1123, 1131 (E.D. La. 1971).

72. Shack v. State, 288 N.E.2d 155 (Ind. 1972).

73. Spencer v. State, 132 Wis. 509, 112 N.W. 462 (1907). Also see Commonwealth v. Wyatt, 27 Va. (6 Rand.) 694 (1828); and Johnson v. Waukesha, 64 Wis. 281 (1885).

74. Wisconsin, *Statutes* (1899-1906), c. 186, sec. 4587c.

75. Spencer v. State, 132 Wis. 509, 520, 112 N.W. 462 (1907).

76. State *ex rel.* Nelson v. Smith, 114 Nev. 653, 209 N.W. 328 (1926). For comment, see "Cruel and Unusual Punishment," *Iowa Law Review* 12 (December 1926): 88-89. See also The John and Winthrop, 182 Fed. 380 (9th Cir. 1910) (upheld a federal statute allowing imposition of bread-and-water diet as a punishment).

77. 132 Wis. 509, 112 N.W. 462 (1907).

78. Ho Ah Kow v. Nunan, 12 F. Cas. 252 (No. 6,546) (C.C.D. Cal. 1879).

79. Ibid., 254.

80. Weems v. United States, 217 U.S. 349 (1910). See chapter 7.

81. The John and Winthrop, 182 Fed. 380 (9th Cir. 1910).

Chapter 7
The Doctrine of Excessiveness

1. O'Neil v. Vermont, 144 U.S. 323 (1892).

2. Ibid., 331-32.

3. Ibid., 339-40 (dissenting opinion).

4. Weems v. U.S., 217 U.S. 349 (1910).

5. Ibid., 364-65.

6. The case was argued before eight justices, Justice Moody being absent on account of illness. Justice Brewer died before the opinion was rendered, and Justice Lurton had not yet taken his seat. Thus, only seven justices were involved in the final determination.

7. Weems v. United States, 217 U.S. 349, 372 (1910) (emphasis added).

8. Ibid., 373.

9. Ibid., 366.

10. Ibid., 336-67.

11. Ibid., 377 (emphasis added).

12. Ibid., 397 (dissenting opinion).

13. H. Friedman, "Comment on Recent Judicial Dicisions," *Journal of Criminal Law and Criminology* 1 (November 1910): 612.

14. "Cruel and Unusual Punishment," *Virginia Law Register* 16 (July 1910): 223; G.H.B., "Cruel and Unusual Punishment," *University of Pennsylvania Law Review* 59 (October 1910): 45; and Friedman, 613.

15. G.H.B. 46.

16. Henry Schofield, "Cruel and Unusual Punishment," *Illinois Law Review* 5 (January 1911): 321, 322. Others, however, remained neutral. See Note, *American Law Review* 44 (September-October 1910): 780; Note, *Central Law Journal* 71 (September 2, 1910): 161; Note, *Harvard Law Review* 24 (November 1910): 54; and Note, *The Green Bag* 22 (June 1910): 361. See also Eugene Wambaugh, "Constitutional Law in 1909-1910," *American Political Science Review* 4 (November 1910): 483, 492.

17. Raymond v. United States, 25 App. D.C. 555, 561 (1905); *Ex parte* Brady, 70 Ark. 376, 68 S.W. 34 (1902); State v. White, 44 Kan. 514, 520-21, 25 P. 33 (1890); Mitchell v. State, 82 Md. 527, 533, 34 A. 246 (1896); State v. Rodman, 58 Minn. 393, 402, 59 N.W. 1098 (1894); State v. Gedicke, 14 N.J.L. 86 (1881); Aldridge v. Commonwealth, 4 Va. Cas. 447, 450 (1824); and Fisher v. McDaniel, 9 Wyo. 457, 64 P. 1056 (1901).

18. See, e.g., Dykes v. State, 64 Ga. 437 (1879).

19. Arkansas, Idaho, Iowa, Nebraska, New York, Oklahoma, and Pennsylvania. See Livingston Hall, "Reduction of Criminal Sentences on Appeal I," *Columbia Law Review* 37 (April 1937): 522-23.

20. Cornell v. State, 74 Tenn. 624 (1881).

21. Other jurisdictions simply reversed and remanded. See Chambless v. State, 46 Tex. Cr. R. 1, 79 S.W. 577 (1904).

22. 8 Pa. 223 (1848).

23. Ibid., 229.

24. For other examples, see Brown v. People, 39 Mich. 57 (1878); Robison v. Miner and Haug, 68 Mich. 549, 37 N.W. 21 (1888); and People v. Murray, 72 Mich. 10, 17 N.W. 29 (1888).

25. 3 Heis. 159, 164 (Tenn. 1871) (emphasis added).

26. For others, see Jackson v. United States, 102 Fed. 473 (9th Cir. 1900); Rinker v. United States, 151 Fed. 755 (8th Cir. 1907); *Ex parte* Miller, 89 Cal. 41, 26 P. 620 (1891); Griffin v. State, 83 Conn. 1, 74 A. 1068 (1910); Loeb v. Jennings, 133 Ga. 796, 67 S.E. 101 (1910); People v. Illinois State Reformatory, 148 Ill. 413, 36 N.E. 78 (1894); Hobbs v. State, 133 Ind. 404, 32 N.E. 1019 (1893); State v. Duff, 144 Iowa 142, 122 N.W. 829 (1909); Harper v. Commonwealth, 93 Ky. 290, 19 S.W. 737 (1892); Mitchell v. State, 82 Md. 527, 34 A. 247 (1896); McDonald v. Commonwealth, 173 Mass. 322, 53 N.E. 874 (1899); People v. Whitney, 105 Mich. 622, 63 N.W. 765 (1895); State v. Williams, 77 Mo. 310 (1883); State v. Lance, 149 N.C. 551, 63 S.E. 198 (1908); State *ex rel.* Larabee v. Barnes, 3 N.D. 319, 55 N.W. 883 (1893); State v. Sheppard, 54 S.C. 178, 32 S.E. 146 (1899); State v. Becker, 3 S.D. 29, 51 N.W. 1018 (1892); Young v. State, 31 Tex. Cr. R. 24, 19 S.W. 431 (1892); State v. Hodgson, 66 Vt. 134, 28 A. 1089 (1893); State v. Berzaman, 10 Wash. 277, 38 P. 1037 (1894); Johnson v. Waukesha, 64 Wis. 281, 25 N.W. 7 (1885); and *In re* McDonald, 4 Wyo. 150, 33 P. 18 (1893).

27. For others, see People v. Clary, 72 Cal. 59, 13 P. 77 (1887); Griffin v. State, 83 Conn. 1, 74 A. 1068 (1910); Loeb v. Jennings, 133 Ga. 796, 67 S.E. 101 (1910); Hobbs v. State, 133 Ind. 404, 32 N.E. 1019 (1893); Sutton v. People, 145 Ill. 279, 34 N.E. 420 (1893); State v. Hall, 97 Iowa 400, 66 N.W. 725 (1896); Cornelison v. Commonwealth, 84 Ky. 583, 2 S.W. 235 (1886); Lanasa v. State, 109 Md. 602, 71 A. 1058 (1909); Gould v. State, 71 Neb. 651, 99 N.W. 541 (1904); State v. Van Wye, 136 Mo. 227, 37 S.W. 938 (1896); State v. Lance, 149 N.C. 551, 63 S.E. 198 (1908); Ligan v. State, 3 Heisk (Tenn.) 159 (1871); Bennett v. State, 32 Tex. Cr. R. 216, 22 S.W. 684 (1894); and Spencer v. State, 132 Wis. 509, 112 N.W. 462 (1907).

28. Davis v. State, 15 Tex. App. 594, 598 (1884).

29. 72 Cal. 59, 61, 13 P. 77 (1887).

30. See, e.g., Pervear v. Commonwealth, 72 U.S. (5 Wall.) 475 (1866); People v. Stanley, 47 Cal. 113 (1874); Whitten v. State, 47 Ga. 297 (1872); McCulley v. State, 62 Ind. 428 (1878); State v. Hazen, 39 Iowa 648 (1874); Ely v. Thompson, 10 Ky. (3 A.K. Marsh) 70 (1820); Commonwealth v. Hitchings, 71 Mass. (5 Gray) 482 (1855); Cummins v. People, 42 Mich. 142, 3 N.W. 305 (1879); Barker v. People, 3 Cow. 686 (N.Y. 1824); State v. Miller, 75 N.C. 73 (1876); State v. Smith and Lane, 10 Tenn. (2 Yerg.) 272 (1829); Williams v. State, 6 Tex. App. 147 (1879); and Aldridge v. Commonwealth, 4 Va. Cas. 447 (1824).

31. Joel Bishop, *New Commentaries on the Criminal Law* (Chicago: T.H. Flood and Co., 1892, 8th ed.), p. 570.

32. Joseph Magrath, "Cruel and Unusual Punishment," *American and English Encyclopedia of Law*, D. Garland and L. McGehee (eds.), (New York: Edward Thompson Co., 1898), 8: 437.

33. Ho Ah Kow v. Nunan, 12 F. Cas. 252 (No. 6,546) (C.C. D. Cal. 1879); Ely v. Thompson, 10 Ky. (3 A.K. Marsh) 70 (1820); State *ex rel.* Garvey v. Whitaker, 48 La. Ann. 527, 19 So. 457 (1896); State v Driver, 78 N.C. 423 (1878); and State v. Ross, 55 Ore. 450, 104 P. 596 (1909), *aff'd on rehearing*, 55 Ore. 474, 106 P. 1022 (1910), *writ of error dismissed*, 227 U.S. 150 (1913).

34. Ely v. Thompson, 10 Ky. (3 A.K. Marsh) 70, 73-74 (1820). The section referred to provides that excessive bail shall not be imposed, nor excessive fines, nor cruel punishments.

35. State *ex rel.* Garvey v. Whitaker, 48 La. Ann. 527, 19 So. 457, 459 (1896).

36. 144 U.S. 323 (1892).

37. State *ex rel.* Garvey v. Whitaker, 48 La. Ann. 527, 532, 19 So. 457, 580 (1896), quoting O'Neil v. Vermont, 144 U.S. 323, 331 (1892).

38. Ibid., quoting O'Neil v. Vermont, 144 U.S. 323, 338 (1892).

39. Ibid., 533.

40. David Fellman, "Cruel and Unusual Punishments," *Journal of Politics* 19 (February 1957): 35.

41. 240 U.S. 391 (1916).

42. 191 U.S. 126 (1903).

43. Ibid., 135-36.

44. James E. Campbell, "Revival of the Eighth Amendment," *Stanford Law Review* 16 (July 1964): 1009.

45. See, e.g., Weber v. Commonwealth, 303 Ky. 56, 64, 196 S.W. 2d 465 (1946).

46. Hart v. Coiner, 483 F.2d 136 (4th Cir. 1973); Ralph v. Warden, 438 F.2d 786 (4th Cir. 1970); United States v. Pacheco, 18 Phil. 399 (1911); Falkner v. State, 445 P.2d 815 (Alaska 1968); *In re* Lynch, 502 P.2d 921, 105 Cal. Rptr. 217 (1973); Nowling v. State, 151 Fla. 584, 10 So.2d 130 (1942); Kenimer v. State, 83 Ga. App. 264, 63 S.E.2d 280 (1951); Kenimer v. State, 81 Ga. App. 437, 59 S.E. 2d 296 (1950); State v. Evans, 73 Idaho 50, 245 P.2d 788 (1952); State *ex rel.* Bissell v. Devore, 225 Iowa 815, 281 N.W. 740 (1938); Workman v. Commonwealth, 429 S.W.2d 374 (Ky. Ct. App. 1968); People v. Lorentzen, 387 Mich. 167, 194 N.W.2d 827 (1972); Atwood v. State, 146 Miss. 662, 111 So. 865 (1927); Politano v. Politano, 262 N.Y.S. 802, 146 Misc. 792 (1933); State v. Tyson, 223 N.C. 492, 27 S.E. 113 (1943); Cannon v. Gladden, 203 Ore. 629, 281 P.2d 233 (1955); State v. Kimbrough, 212 S.C. 348, 46 S.E.2d 273 (1948); Cason v. State, 160 Tenn. 267, 23 S.W.2d 665 (1930); and People v. Bruinsma, 34 Mich. App. 167, 191 N.W.2d 108 (1971). See also State v.

Longino, 109 Miss. 125, 67 So. 902 (1915); People v. Betts, 142 Misc. 240, 254 N.Y.S. 786 (1932); and Goodwin v. Page, 296 F. Supp. 1205 (E.D. Okla. 1969).

47. Politano v. Politano, 262 N.Y.S. 802, 805, 146 Misc. 792 (1933).
48. Nowling v. State, 151 Fla. 584, 10 So. 2d 130 (1942).
49. State v. Kimbrough, 212 S.C. 348, 353, 46 S.E.2d 273 (1948).
50. Ibid., 357.
51. Workman v. Commonwealth, 429 S.W.2d 374 (Ky. Ct. App. 1968).
52. Weber v. Commonwealth, 303 Ky. 56, 196 S.W.2d 465 (1946).
53. People v. Lorentzen, 387 Mich. 167, 194 N.W.2d 827 (1972).

Chapter 8
Other Challenges Based on the Doctrine
of Excessiveness

1. See "Court Treatment of General Recidivist Statutes," *Columbia Law Review* 48 (March 1948): 238.
2. Daniel Katkin, "Habitual Offender Laws: A Reconsideration," *Buffalo Law Review* 21 (1971): 104.
3. For a list, see Hart v. Coiner, 483 F.2d 136, 143-44 (4th Cir. 1973); or Paul W. Tappan, "Habitual Offender Statutes in the United States," *Federal Probation* 13 (March 1949): 28-31.
4. See, e.g., Graham v. West Virginia, 224 U.S. 616 (1912); McDonald v. Massachusetts, 180 U.S. 311 (1901); and Moore v. Missouri, 159 U.S. 673 (1895).
5. People v. Stanley, 47 Cal. 113, 117 (1874).
6. Kelly v. State, 115 Ill. 583 (1886); People v. Morris, 80 Mich. 634, 45 N.W. 591 (1890); Sturtevant v. Commonwealth, 158 Mass. 598, 33 N.E. 648 (1893); State *ex rel.* Larabee v. Barnes, 3 N.D. 319, 55 N.W. 883 (1893); and State v. Moore, 121 Mo. 514, 26 S.W. 345 (1894).
7. Moore v. Missouri, 159 U.S. 673, 677 (1895).
8. See, e.g., Borck v. State, 39 So. 580 (Ala. 1905); People v. Coleman, 145 Cal. 609, 79 P. 283 (1904); State v. Duff, 144 Iowa 142, 122 N.W. 829 (1909); McDonald v. Commonwealth, 173 Mass. 322, 53 N.E. 874 (1899); State v. Levy, 126 Mo. 554, 295 S.W. 703 (1895); and State v. LePitre, 54 Wash. 166, 103 P. 27 (1909).
9. Graham v. West Virginia, 224 U.S. 616, 623 (1912).
10. 368 U.S. 448, 451 (1962).
11. Oyler v. Boles, 368 U.S. 448 (1962); Robinson v. Warden, 455 F.2d 1172 (4th Cir. 1972); Wessling v. Bennett, 410 F.2d 205 (8th Cir. 1969); Price v. Allgood, 369 F.2d 376 (5th Cir. 1966); Goss v. Bomar, 337 F.2d 341 (6th Cir. 1964); Sanders v. Waters, 199 F.2d 317 (10th Cir. 1952);

Driver v. Hinnant, 243 F. Supp. 95 (E.D.N.C. 1965); Frazier v. State, 480 S.W.2d 553 (Tenn. 1972); Emerson v. State, 476 S.W.2d 686 (Tex. Cr. App. 1972); State v. Polson, 93 Ida. 912, 478 P.2d 292 (1971); Cipolla v. State, 207 Kan. 822, 486 P.2d 1391 (1971); Mottran v. State, 263 A.2d 715 (Me. 1970); Hanson v. State, 48 Wis.2d 203, 179 N.W. 2d 909 (1970); State v. Vale, 252 La. 1056, 215 So.2d 811 (1968); State v. Wishom, 416 S.W.2d 921 (Mo. 1967); State v. Custer, 240 Ore. 350, 401 P.2d 402 (1965); State v. Harold, 74 Ariz. 210, 246 P.2d 178 (1952); Ex parte Zee, 13 N.J. Super. 312, 80 A.2d 480 (1951); State ex rel. Drexel v. Alvis, 153 Ohio 244, 91 N.E.2d 22 (1950); Ex parte Hibbs, 86 Okla. Cr. 113, 190 P.2d 156 (1948); and State v. Scales, 212 S.C. 150, 46 S.E.2d 693 (1948).

12. Katkin, 115.

13. Ibid., 117.

14. Tappan, 28.

15. "Court Treatment of General Recidivist Statutes," 252-53.

16. Hart v. Coiner, 483 F.2d 136 (4th Cir. 1973).

17. Hart could not have been given a life sentence had the check been written for $49.99, because a bad check for that amount was punishable by confinement in the county jail. The statute made life imprisonment mandatory for one convicted of three sentences for which incarceration in the state penitentiary was permitted.

18. Hart v. Coiner, 483 F.2d 136, 141 (4th Cir. 1973).

19. Ibid., 142.

20. Ibid., 143.

21. 18 U.S.C., secs. 471-74 (1952). See "Consecutive Sentences in Single Prosecutions: Judicial Multiplication of Statutory Penalties," Yale Law Journal 67 (April 1958): 916, n. 1.

22. Int. Rev. Code of 1954, secs. 4704-05, 4724.

23. 35 Stat. 614 (1909), as amended, 21 U.S.C. sec. 173 (1952).

24. See, e.g., United States v. Kellerman, 432 F.2d 371 (10th Cir. 1971); United States v. Holman, 436 F.2d 863 (9th Cir. 1970); McWilliams v. United States, 394 F.2d 41 (8th Cir. 1968), cert. denied, 393 U.S. 1044 (1969); and Smith v. United States, 273 F.2d 462 (10th Cir. 1959), cert. denied, 363 U.S. 846 (1960).

25. See Phillip E. Johnson, "Multiple Punishment and Consecutive Sentences: Reflections on the Neal Decision," California Law Review 58 (March 1970): 357-90.

26. State v. Smith, 5 Day (Conn.) 175, 178 (1811).

27. Lillard v. State, 17 Tex. App. 114 (1884).

28. 144 U.S. 323 (1892).

29. Ibid., 331.

30. Ibid., 340 (dissenting opinion).

31. 217 U.S. 349 (1910).

32. See, e.g., People v. Elliot, 272 Ill. 592, 112 N.E. 300 (1916).

33. State *ex rel.* Garvey v. Whitaker, 48 La. Ann. 527, 19 So. 457 (1896).

34. Badders v. United States, 240 U.S. 391, 394 (1916). See, e.g., Manley v. Fisher, 63 F.2d 256 (4th Cir. 1933).

35. See Edward C. Kaminski, "Indeterminate Sentencing–Half Step Toward Science in Law," *Western Reserve Law Review* 10 (September 1959): 576.

36. "Indeterminate Sentence Law," *Harvard Law Review* 50 (February 1937): 677.

37. For a list of the statutes, see ibid., 678, n. 4. For other classification, see Kaminski, 575-76; and Martin S. Bogarad, "Criminal Law–Indeterminate Sentence–Due Process," *Ohio State Law Journal* 16 (Summer 1955): 438.

38. See "Indeterminate Sentence Law," 678. Also see Kaminski, 576.

39. See "Indeterminate Sentence Law," 679, n. 5; and *Ex parte* Lee, 177 Cal. 690, 171 P. 958 (1918).

40. State v. Danforth, 3 Conn. 112, 116 (1819); and People v. Webster, 92 Hun. 878, 36 N.Y.S. 995 (1895).

41. State v. Williams, 77 Mo. 310 (1883).

42. State v. Miller, 94 N.C. 901, 907 (1886).

43. Cornelison v. Commonwealth, 84 Ky. 583, 608-9, 2 S.W. 235 (1886). For later cases, see *In re* Hallawell, 8 Cal. App. 563, 97 P. 320 (1910); State v. Knight, 106 Minn. 371, 119 N.W. 56 (1908); Washington v. Rodriguez, 82 N.M. 428, 483 P.2d 309 (1971); State v. Peters, 78 N.M. 224, 430 P.2d 382 (1967); and State v. Fackler, 91 Wis. 418, 64 N.W. 1029 (1895).

44. People *ex rel.* Bradley v. Illinois State Reformatory, 148 Ill. 413, 36 N.E. 78 (1894).

45. *Ex parte* Farmer, 123 W. Va. 304, 14 S.E.2d 910 (1941). For an analysis, see Benjamin D. Tissue, "Requirement That Penalty be Proportional to Offense," *West Virginia Law Quarterly* 48 (December 1941): 63-67.

46. Commonwealth v. Brown, 167 Mass. 144, 146, 45 N.E. 1 (1896).

47. Miller v. State, 149 Ind. 607, 49 N.E. 894, 896 (1898). For similar decisions, see People v. Cook, 147 Mich. 127, 110 N.W. 514 (1907); William v. State, 91 Neb. 605, 136 N.W. 1011 (1912); State v. Neuman, 108 W. Va. 642, 152 S.E. 195 (1930); and State v. Sullivan, 241 Wis. 276, 5 N.W.2d 798 (1942).

48. Howard J. Alperin, "Length of Sentence as Violation of Constitutional Provisions Prohibiting Cruel and Unusual Punishment," 33 *ALR3d,* p. 376.

49. Jones v. State, 14 Tex. Cr. App. 85, 94 (1883). For a similar ruling, see People v. Huntley, 112 Mich. 569, 71 N.W. 178 (1897).

50. 191 U.S. 126 (1903).

51. Ibid., 136.

52. Chicago and Alton Railroad Co. v. People, 67 Ill. 11, 14 (1873).

53. Borck v. State, 39 So. 580 (Ala. 1905).

54. Krueger v. Colville, 49 Wash. 295, 95 P. 81 (1908).

55. Dinuzzo v. State, 85 Neb. 351, 358, 123 N.W. 309 (1909). Quoting Martin v. Nebraska, 23 Neb. 371, 377, 36 N.W. 554 (1888).
56. Robison v. Miner and Haug, 68 Mich. 549, 563, 37 N.W. 21 (1888).
57. Commonwealth v. Novak, 272 Mass. 113, 116, 172 N.E. 84 (1930).
58. See, e.g., California, *Constitution,* art. 2, sec. 1; Connecticut, *Constitution,* art. 6, sec. 2; Connecticut, *General Statutes Annotated,* secs. 9-46 (1960); New York, *Constitution,* art. 2, sec. 3; New York, *Election Laws,* sec. 152 (1949); Pennsylvania, *Constitution,* art. 8, sec. 9; and Texas, *Constitution,* art. 6, sec. 1 (4).
59. Barker v. People, 3 Cow. (N.Y.) 686 (1824).
60. Ibid., 702.
61. Act of 1817.
62. State v. Smith and Lane, 10 Tenn. (2 Yerg.) 272 (1829).
63. *In re* Henry, 15 Idaho 755, 758, 99 P. 1054 (1909).
64. Green v. Teets, 244 F.2d 401, 403 (9th Cir. 1957).
65. Lathem v. United States, 259 F.2d 393 (5th Cir. 1958).
66. Halprin v. United States, 295 F.2d 458, 461 (9th Cir. 1961).
67. See also Gallego v. United States, 276 F.2d 914, 918 (9th Cir. 1960); and McWilliams v. United States, 394 F.2d 41 (8th Cir. 1968), *cert. denied,* 393 U.S. 1044 (1969).
68. Workman v. Commonwealth, 429 S.W.2d 374 (Ky. App. 1968). For an analysis, see F. Thomas Lewand, "Constitutional Law—Cruel and Unusual Punishment—Eighth Amendment Applied to Sentence Within Valid Statutory Limits," *Wayne Law Review* 15 (Spring 1969): 882-94.

Chapter 9
Deportation, Banishment, and Expatriation

1. For a more detailed explanation, see Henry C. Black, *Black's Law Dictionary* (St. Paul: West Publishing Co., 1958), p. 525.
2. For an illuminating discussion, see David Fellman, *The Defendant's Rights* (New York: Reinhart and Co., Inc., 1958), pp. 248-54.
3. Fong Yue Ting v. United States, 149 U.S. 698, 730 (1893).
4. See, e.g., Harisiades v. Shaughnessy, 342 U.S. 580 (1952); Carlson v. Landon, 342 U.S. 524 (1952); Bilokumsky v. Tod, 263 U.S. 149 (1923); Bugajewitz v. Adams, 228 U.S. 585 (1913): and Quattrone v. Nicolls, 210 F.2d 513 (1st Cir. 1954).
5. *In re* Chin Wah, 182 Fed. 256 (D. Ore. 1910).
6. Soewapadji v. Wixon, 157 F.2d 289, 290 (9th Cir. 1946).
7. For an extremely convincing argument that the courts should hold otherwise, see Victor S. Navasky, "Deportation as Punishment," *University of Kansas City Law Review* 27 (Summer 1959): 213-32.
8. 4 *Com.* 332.

9. Myron C. Banks, "Banishment," *North Carolina Law Review* 32 (February 1954): 221-22; and Gerald R. Miller, "Banishment—A Medieval Tactic in Modern Criminal Law," *Utah Law Review* (Spring 1957): 366 and n. 18.

10. Harry E. Barnes, *The Story of Punishment* (Montclair, N.J.: Patterson Smith, 1972), p. 69.

11. See 16 C.J., sec. 3204 and citations therein.

12. See, e.g., "Massachusetts Body of Liberties," in Bernard Schwartz, *The Bill of Rights: A Documentary History* (New York: McGraw Hill Book Co., 1971), 1:72. See also Navasky, 221.

13. Georgia, *Constitution* (1945), art. I, sec. 1.

14. See, e.g., Kansas, *Bill of Rights* (1861), art. 12; Nebraska, *Constitution* (1875), art. 1, sec. 15; Ohio, *Constitution* (1851), art. 1, sec. 12; Texas, *Constitution* (1876), art. 1 sec. 20; Vermont, *Constitution* (1793), c. I, art. 21; and West Virginia, *Constitution* (1872), art. 3, sec. 5.

15. Alabama, *Constitution* (1901), art. 1, sec. 30; and Georgia, *Constitution* (1945), art. 1, sec. 7.

16. Texas, *Constitution* (1876), art. 1, sec. 20.

17. Maryland, *Declaration of Rights* (1867), art. 23; Massachusetts, *Declaration of Rights* (1780), art. 23; New Hampshire, *Constitution* (1784), part 1, art. 15: North Carolina, *Constitution* (1791), art. 1, sec. 17; and Tennessee, *Constitution* (1870), art. 1, sec. 8.

18. Oklahoma, *Constitution* (1907), art. II, sec. 29.

19. Arkansas, *Constitution* (1874), art. II, sec. 21; Maryland *Declaration of Rights* (1867), art. 23; Massachusetts, *Declaration of Rights* (1780), art. 12; New Hampshire, *Constitution* (1784), art. 1, sec. 15; and Tennessee, *Constitution* (1870), art. 1, sec. 8.

20. Legarda v. Valdez, 1 Phil. 146, 148 (1902).

21. Cooper v. Telfair, 4 U.S. (Dall.) 14, 19 (1800).

22. Aldridge v. Commonwealth, 4 Va. Cas. 447 (1824).

23. 1 Parker Cr. R. (N.Y.) 47, 57 (1846).

24. *In re* Look Ting Sing, 21 Fed. 905, 910-11 (C.C.D. Cal. 1884) (emphasis added).

25. Legarda v. Valdez, 1 Phil. 146, 148 (1902).

26. *Ex parte* Sheehan, 100 Mont. 244, 255, 49 P.2d 438 (1935).

27. United States v. Ju Toy, 198 U.S. 253, 269 (1905).

28. Dear Wing Jung v. United States, 312 F.2d 73, 76 (9th Cir. 1962). The implication is also found in *State* v. *Doughtie,* 237 N.C. 368, 74 S.E.2d 922 (1953).

29. It should be noted that in none of the following cases was the cruel and unusual punishment objection raised. However, the discussion is included to reveal the general trend of legal thinking on the subject.

30. State v. Hatley, 110 N.C. 522, 524, 14 S.E. 751 (1892).

31. Ibid.

32. See, e.g., *Ex parte* Hinson, 156 N.C. 250, 72 S.E. 310 (1911); State v. McAfee, 198 N.C. 507, 152 S.E. 391 (1930); and State v. McAfee, 189 N.C. 320, 127 S.E. 204 (1925). For a note on *McAfee,* see W.T. Covington, Jr., Note, *North Carolina Law Review* 8 (June 1930): 465-67.

33. State v. Doughtie, 237 N.C. 368, 371, 74 S.E.2d 922 (1953).

34. 1 Bailey 283 (S.C. 1829).

35. There is great confusion as to whether banishment was allowed at the common law. The confusion results because transportation was not a part of the common law, but the practice of banishment resulting from sanctuary and abjuration was.

36. People v. Potter, 1 Parker Cr. R. (N.Y.) 47, 56-57 (1846).

37. 81 Okl. Cr. R. 34, 159 P.2d 752 (1945).

38. See Miller, 369 and notes 33 and 44.

39. Commonwealth v. Hatsfield, 1 Clark 177, 2 *Pa. L.J.* 37 (1842), *disapproved in* Commonwealth v. Hoggarty, 4 Brewst. (Pa.) 326 (1869).

40. State v. Hatley, 110 N.C. 522, 524, 14 S.E. 751 (1892).

41. State v. Baker, 58 S.C. 111, 113, 26 S.E. 501 (1900).

42. People v. Lopez, 81 Cal. App. 199, 203, 253 P. 285 (1927).

43. *Ex parte* Scarborough, 173 P.2d 825, 826 (Cal. 1946). For an analysis, see "Banishment," *Minnesota Law Review* 31 (June 1947): 742-44.

44. State v. Kasnett, 30 Ohio App.2d. 77, 283 N.E.2d 636, 643 (1972).

45. 251 Mich. 187, 231 N.W. 95 (1930).

46. Ibid., 189.

47. Ibid. Reaction to the *Baum* decision was mixed. Some scholars apparently approved. See Francis E. Finley, "Punishment—Banishment," *St. Louis University Law Review* 16 (April 1931): 254-55; D.V. Lansden, "Validity of Sentence of Banishment," *Illinois Law Review* 26 (May 1931): 81-82; D.V. Lansden, "Banishment," *Journal of Criminal Law and Criminology* 22 (May 1931): 121-22; Abraham Shapiro, "Sentence to Banishment," *Boston University Law Review* 11 (April 1931): 278-81; and "Validity of Sentence Banishing Accused From State for Period of Probation," *Law Notes* 34 (February 1931): 212. Others apparently disapproved. See "Cruel and Unusual Punishment—Leaving the State as a Condition of Probation," *Columbia Law Review* 30 (November 1930): 1056-57; and Herbert Horn, "Probation on Condition Prisoner Leave State," *Dickinson Law Review* 35 (March 1931): 167-70.

48. State v. Doughtie, 237 N.C. 368, 371-72, 74 S.E.2d 922 (1953). For an analysis, see Myron C. Banks.

49. State v. Kasnett, 30 Ohio App.2d 77, 283 N.E.2d 636, 648 (1972).

50. Dear Wing Jung v. United States, 312 F.2d 73 (9th Cir. 1962).

51. See generally the discussion of Miller, 370-73.

52. Black, p. 685.

53. See John P. Roche, "The Laws of American Nationality—The Development

of Statutory Expatriation," *University of Pennsylvania Law Review* 99 (October 1950): 26-27; and David Nelson, Jr., "Loss of Citizenship—Statutory Expatriation," *Vanderbilt Law Review* 12 (June 1959): 872-73.

54. For a comprehensive history, see Leonard B. Boudin, "Involuntary Loss of American Nationality," *Harvard Law Review* 73 (January 1960): 1510-31.

55. 34 Stat. 1228 (1907); 54 Stat. 1137 (1940); 68 Stat. 1146 (1954). For a thorough analysis, see "The Expatriation Act of 1954," *Yale Law Journal* 64 (July 1955): 1164-1200.

56. See Robert J. Hoerner, "Power of Congress to Effect Involuntary Expatriation," *Michigan Law Review* 56 (May 1958): 1147-57; 15 Stat. 223 (1868); and Shanks v. Dupont, 28 U.S. (3 Pet.) 242, 246 (1830).

57. Trop v. Dulles, 356 U.S. 86 (1958). There have been other successful constitutional attacks however. See Daniel Klubock, "Expatriation and the Constitution," *Law in Transition Quarterly* 1 (Winter 1964): 25-48.

58. Trop v. Dulles, 239 F.2d 527 (2d Cir. 1956). For an analysis, see Theodore D. Fisher, "Congressional Expatriation of Natural Born Citizens," *University of Pittsburgh Law Review* 18 (Summer 1957): 816-20.

59. Trop v. Dulles, 356 U.S. 86, 92 (1958).

60. Ibid.

61. 356 U.S. 44 (1958), *overruled,* Afroyim v. Rusk, 387 U.S. 253, 268 (1967).

62. Trop v. Dulles, 356 U.S. 86, 97 (1958). For an analysis of this aspect of the decision, see John G. Hall, "Loss of Citizenship Upon Conviction of Wartime Desertion," *Villanova Law Review* 4 (Fall 1958): 132-34.

63. Trop v. Dulles, 356 U.S. 86, 101 (1958).

64. Ibid., 124 (dissenting opinion).

65. Ibid., 125 (dissenting opinion).

66. See, e.g., *New York Times,* 1 April 1958, p. 22; "The Non-Americans," *Nation,* 19 April 1958, pp. 334-35; and "From the Supreme Court: New Rulings, New Puzzles," *United States News and World Report,* 11 April 1958, p. 75.

67. *Journal of International Law* 52 (October 1958): 777-85.

68. See, e.g., Ray Besing, "Constitutional Law—Citizens—Denationalization," *Southwest Law Journal* 12 (Fall 1958): 511-14; Robert G. Dorsey, "Involuntary Expatriation," *West Virginia Law Review* 61 (December 1958): 51-53; George Rossman, "Review of Recent Supreme Court Decisions," *American Bar Association Journal* 44 (June 1958): 565, 566; "The Supreme Court, 1957 Term: Loss of Citizenship," *Harvard Law Review* 72 (November 1958): 166-72; and Thomas R. Wilks, "Involuntary Expatriation for Wartime Desertion is Cruel and Unusual Punishment," *University of Detroit Law Journal* 36 (June 1959): 88-91.

69. See, e.g., "Expatriation as Punishment for Desertion," *Minnesota Law Review* 42 (January 1958): 486-90; Robert E. Goostree, "The Denationalization Cases of 1958," *American University Law Review* 8 (June 1959):

87-99; and Eleanor M. Kraft, "Constitutional Law: Citizenship: Statutory Expatriation," *Cornell Law Quarterly* 44 (Summer 1959): 593-600.

70. Cort v. Herter, 187 F. Supp. 683, 687 (D.D.C. 1960).
71. The case was appealed. The Supreme Court joined the case with others and affirmed. Rush v. Cort. 372 U.S. 144 (1963). For an analysis, see John P. Roche, "The Expatriation Decisions: A Study in Constitutional Improvisation and the Uses of History," *American Political Science Review* 58 (March 1964): 72-80.
72. Afroyim v. Rusk, 250 F. Supp. 686 (S.D. N.Y. 1966).
73. Perez v. Brownell, 356 U.S. 44 (1958).
74. Afroyim v. Rusk, 250 F. Supp. 686, 689 (S.D. N.Y. 1966).
75. Afroyim v. Rusk, 361 F.2d 102 (2d Cir. 1966).
76. Afroyim v. Rusk, 387 U.S. 253 (1967). For an analysis, see Donnie R. Duplissey, Note, *Texas International Law Forum* 3 (Summer 1967): 350-58; Warren B. Etterman, "An Expatriation Enigma: *Afroyim* v. *Rusk,*" *Boston University Law Review* 48 (Spring 1968): 295-303; and Frederick W. Marsh, Jr., "The Supreme Court and the Power of Congress to Expatriate," *Southwest Law Journal* 22 (August 1968): 466-81.
77. 401 U.S. 815 (1971). See Justice Black dissenting (ibid., 837). See also Donald R. Jacobs, *"Rogers* v. *Bellei,* Loss of Citizenship," *Williamette Law Journal* 8 (March 1972): 124.
78. For an analysis, see Keith Woodley, "Expatriation and *Rogers* v. *Bellei,"* *Baylor Law Review* 23 (Summer 1971): 494-98.

Chapter 10
Status Statutes and Cruel and Unusual Punishment

1. Forrest W. Lacey, "Vagrancy and Other Crimes of Personal Condition," *Harvard Law Review* 66 (May 1953): 1203-26.
2. The states with statutes in each category are listed in ibid., 1208-09, notes 20-23, and 30.
3. See, e.g., Illinois, *Revised Statutes* (1963), c. 38, sec. 22-23.
4. See also People v. Kelley, 99 Mich. 82, 57 N.W. 1090 (1894).
5. 16 App. D.C. 229 (1900).
6. Ibid., 236.
7. Robinson v. California, 370 U.S. 660 (1962).
8. California, *Health and Welfare Code* (1954), sec. 11721 (emphasis added).
9 Robinson v. California, 370 U.S. 660, 666 (1962).
10. Ibid., 674 (concurring opinion).
11. Ibid., 682 (dissenting opinion).
12. Ibid., 686 (dissenting opinion).
13. Ibid., 689 (dissenting opinion).

14. During 1962 and 1963 approximately twenty journals carried articles on the Robinson decision. See, e.g., "Criminal Penalties for Drug Addiction," *Harvard Law Review* 76 (November 1962): 143-47; "Criminal Penalty for Narcotic Addiction is Cruel and Unusual Punishment," *Minnesota Law Review* 47 (January 1963): 484-93; "Criminal Prosecution for Addiction A Cruel and Unusual Punishment Violating the Eighth and Fourteenth Amendments," *Vandervilt Law Review* 16 (December 1962): 214-20; "Imprisonment for the Crime of Narcotic Addiction Held Unconstitutional as Cruel and Unusual Punishment," *University of Pennsylvania Law Review* 111 (November 1962): 122-28; and Ralph A. White, Jr., "Criminality of Status," *North Carolina Law Review* 41 (Winter 1963): 244-53.

15. "The Cruel and Unusual Punishment Clause and the Substantive Criminal Law," *Harvard Law Review* 79 (January 1966): 646, suggests three possibilities.

16. Walter J. Gorski suggests three alternatives: "Eighth Amendment: Cruel and Unusual Punishment: A Vehicle for Reappraising the Application of the Criminal Law to the Individual," *Connecticut Bar Journal* 40 (1966): 524.

17. See, e.g., J.M. McWilliams, "Cruel and Unusual Punishment: Uses and Misuses of the Eighth Amendment," *American Bar Association Journal* 53 (May 1967): 453.

18. See, e.g., "*Robinson* v. *California* Revisited," *Northwestern University Law Review* 59 (May-June 1964): 271-77.

19. Robert T. Enloe, III, "Criminal Sanctions for the 'Status' of Narcotics," *Southwest Law Journal* 17 (March 1963): 134.

20. "Legal Implications of Viewing Narcotics Addiction as a Disease Rather Than a Crime," *Northwestern University Law Review* 57 (November-December 1962): 618-26.

21. Calvin E. Robinson, "Statute Making the Status of Being a Drug Addict a Crime Held Unconstitutional," *Nebraska Law Review* 42 (April 1963): 685-96.

22. See Michael Asimow, "Punishment for Narcotics Addiction Held Cruel and Unusual Punishment," *California Law Review* 51 (March 1963): 219-28.

23. See, e.g., H.R. Manes, "*Robinson* v. *California*: A Farewell to Rationalism," *Law in Transition* 22 (Winter 1963): 240.

24. See, e.g., John E. Bagalay, Jr., "Penal Sanctions Applied to Narcotics Addiction are Unconstitutional as Cruel and Unusual Punishment," *Texas Law Review* 41 (February 1963): 448.

25. See, e.g., McWilliams, 454.

26. Bagalay, 447.

27. See John B. Neibel, "Implications of *Robinson* v. *California*," *Houston Law Review* 1 (Spring 1963): 5. See also Fred L. Lieb, "Cruel and Unusual Punishment and the Durham Rule," *Journal of Criminal Law and Criminology* 59 (June 1968): 230.

28. *In re* De La O, 59 Cal.2d 128, 278 P.2d 793 (1963).

29. Browne v. State, 24 Wis.2d 491, 129 N.W.2d 175 (1964), *cert. denied,* 379 U.S. 1004 (1965). See also United States *ex rel.* Swanson v. Reincke, 344 F.2d 260 (2d Cir. 1965).

30. 347 F.2d 492 (D.C. Cir. 1965), *cert. denied,* 381 U.S. 929 (1965). For an analysis, see Richard P. Knutsen, Note, *American University Law Review* 14 (June 1965): 243-44.

31. 345 F.2d 964 (D.C. Cir. 1965), *cert. denied,* 322 U.S. 894 (1965). See also Normand v. People, 165 Colo. 509, 440 P.2d 282 (1968), People v. Borrero, 19 N.Y.2d 332, 280 N.Y.S.2d 109, 227 N.E. 2d 18 (1967); and State v. James, 3 Ore. App. 539, 474 P.2d 779 (1970).

32. State *ex rel.* Blouin v. Walker, 244 La. 699, 154 So.2d 368 (1963). See also State v. Bruno, 253 La. 669, 219 So.2d 490 (1969); and Bruno v. State, 316 F. Supp. 1120 (E.D. La. 1970).

33. State v. Margo, 40 N.J. 188, 191 A.2d 43 (1963). For a slight variation, see Salas v. State, 365 S.W.2d 174 (Tex. Cr. App. 1963).

34. 27 Ill.2d 57, 188 N.W.2d 255 (1963).

35. State v. Bridges, 360 S.W.2d 648 (Mo. 1962).

36. Commonwealth v. Hall, 394 S.W.2d 448 (Ky. 1965).

37. 356 F.2d 761 (4th Cir. 1966). But see Sweeney v. United States, 353 F.2d 10, 11 (10th Cir. 1965). For a thorough analysis of *Driver,* see Charles A. Evans, "Imprisonment of Chronic Alcoholic is Not Cruel and Unusual Punishment," *Georgia State Bar Journal* 2 (November 1965): 239-42; Note, *Duke Law Journal* 1966 (Spring 1966): 545-61; and Thomas S. Smith, "Cruel and Unusual Punishment—Chronic Alcoholism," *North Carolina Law Review* 44 (April 1966): 818-23.

38. Ibid., 764.

39. 361 F.2d 50 (D.C. Cir. 1966). For further analysis, see, e.g., Nolan Atkinson, et al., "Cruel and Unusual Punishment and Criminal Responsibility," *Howard Law Journal* 13 (Spring 1967): 402-13; Bill Faller, "Culpability of the Chronic Alcoholic," *Louisiana Law Review* 27 (February 1967): 340-47; John A. Lowe, "The Criminal Responsibility of Chronic Alcoholics," *Cornell Law Quarterly* 52 (Winter 1967): 470-78; Robert S. Moraff, "Chronic Alcoholics Not Criminally Responsible for Their Public Intoxication," *American University Law Review* 16 (March 1967): 295-301; and Joseph F. Ricchiuti, "Conviction of a Chronic Alcoholic for Public Intoxication Violates the Eighth Amendment," *Villanova Law Review* 11 (Summer 1966): 861-69.

40. 3 Mich. App. 666, 143 N.W.2d 577 (1966).

41. 435 P.2d 692 (Wash., 1967). See also Doughty v. Beto, 396 F.2d 128 (5th Cir. 1968).

42. Ibid., 699.

43. Budd v. California, 385 U.S. 909, 911 (1966) (dissenting opinion).

44. Powell v. Texas, 392 U.S. 514 (1968). For further analysis, see, e.g., George F. Bason, Jr., "Chronic Alcoholism and Public Drunkenness," *American*

University Law Review 19 (December 1969): 48-66; Gary V. Dubin, "The Ballad or Leroy Powell," *University of California Law Review* 16 (November 1968): 139-54; Herbert Fingarette, "The Perils of Powell: In Search of a Factual Foundation for the 'Disease Concept of Alcoholism,' " *Harvard Law Review* 83 (February 1970): 793-812; Lynd K. Mische, "Chronic Alcoholism as a Defense to a Charge of Public Intoxication," *Missouri Law Review* 34 (Fall 1969): 597-604; and "The Supreme Court Term, 1967 Term," *Harvard Law Review* 82 (November 1968): 103-11.

45. Texas, *Penal Code* (1952), art. 477.
46. Powell v. Texas, 392 U.S. 514, 532 (1968).
47. Ibid., 534
48. Ibid., 550 (concurring opinion).
49. Ibid., 558 (dissenting opinion).
50. Subsequent to Powell there have been few lower-court decisions bearing directly on the subject. But see Vick v. State, 453 P.2d 342 (Alaska 1969); and Burger v. State, 118 Ga. App. 328, 163 S.E.2d 333 (1968). See also City of Portland v. Juntunen, 6 Ore. App. 632, 488 P.2d 806 (1971).
51. For the statutes see Lacey, 1207 and n. 17. See also Gary V. Dubin and Richard H. Robinson, "The Vagrancy Concept Reconsidered: Problems and Abuses of Status Criminality," *New York University Law Review* 37 (January 1962): 102-36; and Gerald E. Magaro, "Criminal Penalties for Vagrancy— Cruel and Unusual Punishment Under the Eighth Amendment," *Western Reserve Law Review* 18 (May 1967): 1309-29.
52. See, e.g., Papachristou v. Jacksonville, 405 U.S. 156 (1973); Alegata v. Commonwealth, 353 Mass. 287, 231 N.E.2d 201 (1967); Baker v. Binder, 274 F. Supp. 658 (D. Ky. 1967); and Hayes v. Municipal Court of Oklahoma City, 487 P.2d 974 (Okl. Cr. 1971).
53. Hicks v. District of Columbia, 383 U.S. 252, 257 (1966).
54. City of Reno v. Second Judicial District Court, 83 Nev. 201, 427 P.2d 4 (1967).
55. Parker v. Municipal Judge of the City of Las Vegas, 83 Nev. 214, 427 P.2d 642 (1967).
56. 295 F. Supp. 897 (D. Colo. 1969).
57. Ibid., 899.
58. Ibid., 907.
59. Ibid., 908.
60. 306 F. Supp. 58 (W.D. N.C. 1969).
61. The police misbehavior is described in detail by the district judge in *Wheeler v. Goodman,* 298 F. Supp. 935 (W.D. N.C. 1967).
62. Similar statutes have been declared unconstitutional on essentially the same grounds in Hawaii and Texas. See State v. Grahovac, 52 Haw. 527, 480 P.2d 148 (1971); and Baker v. State, 478 S.W.2d 445 (Tex. Cr. App. 1972).
63. State v. Anderson, 280 Minn. 461, 159 N.W.2d 892 (1968).

64. Perkins v. State, 234 F. Supp. 333, 337 (W.D. N.C. 1964).
65. It should be noted that the court vehemently opposed the length of the sentence but refused to declare it cruel and unusual punishment as excessive because it was within the statutory limits. It should also be noted that McCorkle received only five-to-seven years imprisonment.
66. People v. Roberts, 64 Cal. Rptr. 70 (1967).
67. People v. Frazier, 64 Cal. Rptr. 447 (1967).
68. People v. Griffes, 13 Mich. App. 299, 302, 164 N.W.2d 426 (1968).
69. Ibid., 303.
70. People v. Jones, 43 Ill.2d 113, 251 N.E.2d 195 (1969).
71. People v. Stevenson, 28 Mich. App. 538, 541, 184 N.W.2d 541 (1970).
72. *In re* Jones, 432 Pa. 44, 246 A.2d 356 (1968).
73. Maatallah v. Warden, 86 Nev. 43, 470 P.2d 122 (1970).
74. People v. Thomas, 67 Cal. Rptr. 234, 237 (1968).
75. United States *ex rel.* Wolfersdorf v. Johnston, 317 F. Supp. 66, 67 (S.D. N.Y. 1970).
76. Ibid.
77. Ibid., 68 (emphasis added).
78. United States v. Pardue, 354 F. Supp. 1377 (D. Conn. 1973).
79. Ibid., 1377–78.
80. State v. Myers, 6 Wash. App. 557, 494 P.2d 1015 (1972).
81. Ibid., 566.

Chapter 11:
Prison Rules and Practices

1. See Charles E. Friend, "Judicial Intervention in Prison Administration," *William and Mary Law Review* 9 (Fall 1967): 179, n. 7; and Philip J. Hirschkop and Michael A. Millemann, "The Unconstitutionality of Prison Life," *Virginia Law Review* 55 (June 1969): 812, n. 92.
2. 172 F.2d 330, 331 (10th Cir. 1949). See also, e.g., Childs v. Pegelow, 321 F.2d 485 (4th Cir. 1963); Tabor v. Hardwick, 224 F.2d 526 (5th Cir. 1955); and Dayton v. McGrenery, 201 F.2d 711 (D.C. Cir. 1953).
3. Stroud v. Swope, 187 F.2d 850, 851–52 (9th Cir. 1951). See also, e.g., Eaton v. Bibb, 217 F.2d 446, 448 (7th Cir. 1955); Banning v. Looney, 213 F.2d 771 (10th Cir. 1954); and Shepherd v. Hunter, 163 F.2d 872, 874 (10th Cir. 1947).
4. Prisons and Prisoners Act, 18 U.S.C., sec. 4001 (1964).
5. See, e.g., Edmondson v. Warden of Maryland House of Detention, 194 Md. 707, 69 A.2d 919 (1949); and cases cited in "Beyond the Ken of the Courts: A Critique of Judicial Refusal to Review the Complaints of Convicts," *Yale Law Journal* 72 (January 1963): 508, n. 12.

6. See, e.g., State *ex rel.* Jacobs v. Warden, 190 Md. 755, 59 A.2d 753 (1948); and State *ex rel.* Renner v. Wright, 188 Md. 189, 51 A.2d 668 (1946).

7. 180 F.2d 785, 788 (7th Cir. 1950). See also, e.g., United States *ex rel.* Atterbury v. Ragen, 237 F.2d 953 (7th Cir. 1956), *cert. denied,* 353 U.S. 964 (1957); and Swanson v. McGuire, 188 F. Supp. 112, 115 (N.D. Ill. 1960).

8. See, e.g., Sostre v. McGinnis, 334 F.2d 906, 908 (2d Cir. 1964); and United States *ex rel.* Atterbury v. Ragen, 237 F.2d 953, 955 (7th Cir. 1956).

9. For discussions of what rights convicts do retain, see Eugene N. Barkin, "The Emergency of Correctional Law and the Awareness of the Rights of the Convicted," *Nebraska Law Review* 45 (1966): 669-89; "Convicts—Loss of Civil Rights—Civil Death in California," *Southern California Law Review* 26 (July 1953): 425-34; "Convicts—Legal Status," *Virginia Law Review* 34 (May 1948): 463-65; and Livingston Fairbanks, Jr., "The Legal Status of Convicts During and After Incarceration," *Virginia Law Review* 37 (January 1951): 105-17. During the nineteenth century the prisoner was viewed as a slave. For example, in 1871 the Court of Appeals of Virginia declared: "The prisoner has as a consequence of his crime, not only forfeited his liberty, but all his personal rights except those which the law in its humanity accords him. He is for the time being the slave of the state." Ruffin v. Commonwealth, 62 Va. 790, 796 (1871). However, by 1944 the courts viewed the rights of prisoners from a different perspective. Instead of losing all rights, the prisoner was viewed as retaining all rights except those specifically taken from him. For example in *Coffin* v. *Reichard,* 143 F.2d 443 (6th Cir. 1944), the Sixth Circuit Court of Appeals stated that a "prisoner retains all the rights of an ordinary citizen except those expressly, or by necessary implication, taken from him by law (ibid., 445).

10. See, e.g., Williams v. Steele, 194 F.2d 32 (8th Cir. 1952); and Snow v. Roche, 143 F.2d 718 (9th Cir. 1944).

11. See, e.g., Sigmon v. United States, 110 F. Supp. 906 (W.D. Va. 1953). See also "Beyond the Ken of the Courts," 516-26.

12. See, e.g., Stroud v. Swope, 187 F.2d 850, 852 (9th Cir. 1951); and Swanson v. McGuire, 188 F. Supp. 112, 116 (N.D. Ill. 1960).

13. 337 F.2d 72, 74 (4th Cir. 1964).

14. See, e.g., Johnson v. Dye, 338 U.S. 864 (1949); Cannon v. Willingham, 358 F.2d 719 (10th Cir. 1966); Pope v. Daggett, 350 F.2d 296 (10th Cir. 1965); Siegel v. Ragen, 180 F.2d 785, 788 (7th Cir. 1950); United States *ex rel.* Wakeley v. Pennsylvania, 247 F. Supp. 7 (E.D. Pa. 1965); and Commonwealth *ex rel.* Thompson v. Day, 182 Pa. Super, 664, 128 A.2d 133 (1956).

15. See "The Role of the Eighth Amendment in Prison Reform," *University of Chicago Law Review* 38 (Spring 1971): 648. See especially Ronald L. Goldfab and Linda R. Singer, "Redressing Prisoners' Grievances," *George Washington Law Review* 39 (December 1970): 175-320.

16. For other analyses not elsewhere cited in this chapter, see George W. O'Lary, "Federal Remedies for Lawfully Committed Prisoners Who Claim Mistreatment," *Journal of Public Law* 2 (Spring 1953): 181-87; Curtis R. Reitz, "Federal Habeas Corpus: Postconviction Remedy for State Prisoners," *University of Pennsylvania Law Review* 108 (February 1960): 461-532; Martin W. Spector, "Constitutional Rights of Prisoners: The Developing Law," *University of Pennsylvania Law Review* 110 (May 1962): 985-1008, and Jerrod L. Strasheim and Donne Davis, "Remedies Available to Validly Sentenced Prisoners Who Are Mistreated By State Penal Authorities," *Nebraska Law Review* 33 (March 1954): 434-50.

17. This threefold categorization is taken from "Beyond the Ken of the Courts," 510.

18. See, e.g., Williams v. Steele, 194 F.2d 32 (8th Cir. 1952); and Snow v. Roche, 143 F.2d 718, 719 (9th Cir.), *cert. denied,* 323 U.S. 788 (1944). See also United States *ex rel.* Knight v. Ragen, 337 F.2d 425 (7th Cir. 1964).

19. See, e.g., Johnson v. Dye, 338 U.S. 864 (1949) *(per curiam)*; and Felix Weill, "Penal Institutions and the Eighth Amendment—A Broadened Conception of Cruel and Unusual Punishment," *Louisiana Law Review* 31 (February 1971): 395-404.

20. See, e.g., McNally v. Hill, 293 U.S. 131 (1934); *Ex parte* Watkins, 28 U.S. 119, 125-26 (1830); Benjamin v. Hunter, 176 F.2d 269 (10th Cir. 1949); and United States *ex rel.* Binion v. United States Marshal, 188 F. Supp. 905, 908 (D. Nev. 1960), *aff'd.,* 292 F.2d 494 (9th Cir. 1961).

21. Coffin v. Reichard, 143 F.2d 443, 445 (6th Cir. 1944).

22. See, e.g., Johnson v. Dye, 338 U.S. 864 (1949) *(per curiam)*; United States *ex rel.* Weybrauch v. Parker, 268 F. Supp. 785 (M.D. Pa. 1967); McCormick v. Heritage, 216 F. Supp. 222 (N.D. Ga. 1962); and Lloyd v. Heritage, 199 F. Supp. 46 (N.D. Ga. 1961).

23. United States *ex rel.* Maricial v. Fay, 247 F.2d 662 (2d Cir. 1957), *cert. denied,* 355 U.S. 915 (1958).

24. 28 U.S.C. 2254 (1958).

25. 252 F. Supp. 783 (M.D. Tenn. 1966), *rev'd.,* 382 F.2d 353 (6th Cir. 1967), *rev'd.,* 393 U.S. 483 (1969). For further analysis, see Andrew R. Hutyera, "Habeas Corpus—Punishment of Criminals—Prison Management," *Western Reserve Law Review* 18 (January 1967): 681-86.

26. The United States Supreme Court affirmed, but did not discuss, the use of habeas corpus. Johnson v. Avery, 393 U.S. 483 (1969). For other examples, see Dowd v. Cook, 340 U.S. 206 (1951); United States *ex rel.* Westbrook v. Randolph, 259 F.2d 215 (7th Cir. 1958); *In re* Ferguson, 55 Cal. 2d 663, 361 P.2d 417 (1961) (dictum), *cert. denied,* 368 U.S. 864 (1961); and *In re* Chessman, 44 Cal.2d 1, 279 P.2d 24 (1955).

27. See, e.g., Barnett v. Rodgers, 133 App. D.C. 296, 410 F.2d 995, 998 (1969) (religion); Landman v. Peyton, 370 F.2d 135 (4th Cir. 1966) (access to the

courts); Jordan v. Fitzharris, 257 F. Supp. 674 (N.D. Cal. 1966) (cruel and unusual punishment); Johnson v. Avery, 252 F. Supp. 783 (M.D. Tenn. 1966) (access to legal information); Fulwood v. Clemmer, 206 F. Supp. 370 (D.D.C. 1962) (religion); and State *ex rel.* Cole v. Tahash, 269 Minn. 1, 129 N.W.2d 903 (1964) (cruel and unusual punishment).

28. Civil Rights Act of 1871, Sec. 1; 42 U.S.C., Sec. 1983 (1964).

29. See, e.g., Hancock v. Avery, 301 F. Supp. 786 (M.D. Tenn. 1969); Sa Marion v. McGinnis, 253 F. Supp. 738 (W.D. N.Y. 1966); and Talley v. Stephens, 247 F. Supp. 683 (E.D. Ark. 1965).

30. See, e.g., Wright v. McMann, 321 F. Supp. 127 (N.D. N.Y. 1970); United States *ex rel.* Mosher v. LaValle, 321 F. Supp. 127, 146 (N.D. N.Y. 1970); and Roberts v. Williams, 302 F. Supp. 972 (N.D. Miss. 1969).

31. See, e.g., Siegel v. Ragen, 180 F.2d 785, 788 (7th Cir. 1950).

32. Earlier cases of course followed the hands-off doctrine and found no cause for action even when basic rights were involved. See, e.g., United States *ex rel.* Atterbury v. Ragen, 237 F.2d 953 (7th Cir. 1956), *cert. denied,* 353 U.S. 964 (1957), and cases cited therein.

33. See, e.g., Cooper v. Pate, 378 U.S. 546 (1964); Knuckles v. Prassee, 435 F.2d 1255 (3d Cir. 1970); Sostre v. McGinnis, 334 F.2d 906 (2d Cir. 1964); and Sewell v. Pegelow, 291 F.2d 196 (4th Cir. 1961).

34. See, e.g., Jackson v. Bishop, 404 F.2d 571 (8th Cir. 1968); Wright v. McMann, 387 F.2d 519 (2d Cir. 1967); Hancock v. Avery, 301 F. Supp. 786 (M.D. Tenn. 1969); Holt v. Sarver, 300 F. Supp. 825 (E.D. Ark. 1969); Jackson v. Bishop, 268 F. Supp. 804 (E.D. Ark. 1967); Jordan v. Fitzharris, 257 F. Supp. 674 (N.D. Cal. 1966); and Talley v. Stephens, 247 F. Supp. 683 (E.D. Ark. 1965).

35. See, e.g., United States *ex rel.* Wakely v. Pennsylvania, 247 F. Supp. 7 (E.D. Pa. 1965). See also Fallen v. United States, 378 U.S. 139 (1964).

36. See, e.g., Hatfield v. Baileaux, 290 F.2d 632 (9th Cir. 1961).

37. See, e.g., Hirons v. Director Patuxent Institution, 351 F.2d 613 (4th Cir. 1965); and Redding v. Pate, 220 F. Supp. 124 (N.D. Ill. 1963).

38. Monroe v. Pape, 365 U.S. 167, 183 (1961). See also McNeese v. Board of Education, 373 U.S. 668 (1963); Rivers v. Royster, 360 F.2d 592, 594 (4th Cir. 1966); Pierce v. LaValle, 293 F.2d 233, 236 (2d Cir. 1961); Sostre v. Rockefeller, 309 F. Supp. 611, 613 (S.D. N.Y. 1969); and Rice v. Schmidt, 277 F. Supp. 811, 813 (E.D. Wis. 1967).

39. 291 F.2d 196, 198 (4th Cir. 1961), quoting United States *ex rel.* Maricial v. Fay, 247 F.2d 662, 669 (2d Cir. 1957), which was a habeas corpus proceeding. See also Sostre v. Rockefeller, 312 F. Supp. 863, 872-73 (S.D. N.Y. 1970). There is some evidence that strain has been placed on the system as a result. See Friend, 189-90; and *Wisconsin State Journal* (Madison), 8 October 1972, pp. 1 and 2.

40. Washington v. Lee, 390 U.S. 333 (1968). See also "Prisoners Rights Under Section 1983," *Georgetown Law Journal* 57 (June 1969): 1270-98.

41. See Bruce R. Jacob, "Prison Discipline and Inmate Rights," *Harvard Civil Rights—Civil Liberties Law Review* 5 (April 1970): 257-58.
42. 295 F.2d 171, 172 (D.C. Cir. 1961). See also Barnett v. Rodgers, 410 F.2d 995 (1969).
43. 28 U.S.C., sec. 1361 (1964).
44. Walker v. Blackwell, 360 F.2d 66 (5th Cir. 1966); and Walker v. Blackwell, 411 F.2d 23 (5th Cir. 1969).
45. 10 N.Y.2d 531, 225 N.Y.S.2d 497, 180 N.E.2d 791 (1962).
46. See, e.g., Hill v. Gentry, 280 F.2d 88 (8th Cir. 1958), *cert. denied,* 364 U.S. 875 (1960). See also "Prisoners Remedies for Mistreatment," *Yale Law Journal* 59 (March 1950): 800-808 and cases cited therein.
47. 28 U.S.C., secs. 1346(d); 2671-80 (1964). See, e.g., James v. United States, 280 F.2d 428 (8th Cir.), *cert. denied,* 364 U.S. 845 (1960); and Jones v. United States, 249 F.2d 864 (7th Cir. 1957).
48. See, e.g., Sigmon v. United States, 110 F. Supp. 906 (W.D. Va. 1953). See also "Denial of Prisoner's Claims Under the Federal Tort Claims Act," *Yale Law Journal* 63 (January 1954): 418-25.
49. Muniz v. United States, 305 F.2d 285 (2d Cir. 1962); and Winston v. United States, 305 F.2d 253 (2d Cir. 1962).
50. Muniz v. United States, 374 U.S. 150 (1963); and Winston v. United States, 374 U.S. 150 (1963).
51. See Friend, 183.
52. See, e.g., Upchurch v. State, 454 P.2d 112 (Haw. 1969).
53. 28 Ariz. 433, 237 P. 203 (1925).
54. See, e.g., Wright v. McMann, 387 F.2d 519, 522-23 (2 Cir. 1967); Hancock v. Avery, 301 F. Supp. 786, 791 (M.D. Tenn. 1969); Levier v. State, 209 Kan. 442, 497 P.2d 265 (1972); and Henry R. Goldberg, "Prisons and Prisoners," *Suffolk University Law Review* 5 (Fall 1970): 268.
55. See, e.g., Friend, 192; Jacob, 248; and Raymond H. Thoenig, "Solitary Confinement—Punishment Within the Letter of the Law, or Psychological Torture," *Wisconsin Law Review* 1972 (1972): 223-37.
56. Sostre v. McGinnis, 442 F.2d 178, 191 (2d Cir. 1971).
57. United States *ex rel.* Miller v. Twomey, 333 F. Supp. 1352 (N.D. Ill. 1971).
58. Cornell v. State, 74 Tenn. 624, 629 (1881).
59. State v. Nipper, 166 N.C. 272, 275, 81 S.E. 164 (1914).
60. State v. Mincher, 172 N.C. 895, 90 S.E. 429 (1916).
61. State v. Revis, 193 N.C. 192, 136 S.E. 346 (1927). See also Westbrook v. State, 133 Ga. 578, 66 S.E. 788 (1909).
62. *In re* Candido, 31 Haw. 982, 992 (1931).
63. Ibid., 1001.
64. O'Brien v. Olson, 42 Cal. App.2d 449, 460, 109 P.2d 8 (1941) (dictum).
65. Nevertheless, it still prevailed until recently in a large number of prisons. See Karl A. Menninger, *The Crime of Punishment* (New York: Viking

Press, 1968), p. 80. As recently as 1965 a Louisiana court awarded damages to the parents of a boy who died from a whipping received in a state correctional institution. See Lewis v. State, 176 So.2d 718 (La. App. 1965).

66. See, e.g., United States v. Jones, 207 F.2d 785 (5th Cir. 1953).
67. See, e.g., Bryant v. Harrelson, 187 F. Supp. 738 (S.D. Tex. 1960).
68. Talley v. Stephens, 247 F. Supp. 683 (E.D. Ark. 1965).
69. See Jackson v. Bishop, 404 F.2d 571, 572 (8th Cir. 1968).
70. Jackson v. Bishop, 268 F. Supp. 804 (E.D. Ark. 1967).
71. Jackson v. Bishop, 404 F.2d 571, 577 (8th Cir. 1968).
72. 356 U.S. 86 (1958).
73. Jackson v. Bishop, 404 F.2d 571, 579 (8th Cir. 1968).
74. Ibid., 580-81.
75. Morales v. Turman, 364 F. Supp. 166, 173 (E.D. Tex. 1973).
76. Nelson v. Heyne, 355 F. Supp. 451 (N.D. Ind. 1973).
77. 404 F.2d 571 (8th Cir. 1968).
78. Nelson v. Heyne, 491 F.2d 352 (7th Cir. 1974).
79. Johnson v. Lark, 365 F. Supp. 289, 299 (E.D. Mo. 1973).
80. *In re* Birdsong, 39 Fed. 599, 602 (1889).
81. State v. Carpenter, 231 N.C. 229, 241, 56 S.E.2d 713 (1949).
82. Landman v. Royster, 333 F. Supp. 621, 647 (E.D. Va. 1971).
83. Collins v. Schoonfield, 344 F. Supp. 257, 278 (D. Md. 1972).
84. Wheeler v. Glass, 473 F.2d 983 (7th Cir. 1973).
85. The first was a device used in which a prisoner's testicles were shocked by electrical impulses. See *New York Times,* 17 January 1968, p. 26. The second was made by nailing two two-by-fours together so that the longer board was on top, and the nails holding the two extended toward the prisoner. If he fell off the board and could not make it balance, he was beaten with a five-foot-long leather strap. See Jackson v. Bishop, 268 F. Supp. 804 (E.D. Ark. 1967); and *New York Times,* 6 September 1966, p. 268.
86. Jackson v. Bishop, 268 F. Supp. 804, 816 (E.D. Ark. 1967) *aff'd*; 404 F.2d 571 (8th Cir. 1968).
87. Inmates of Attica Correctional Facility v. Rockefeller, 453 F.2d 12, 22-24 (2d Cir. 1971).
88. U.S. *ex rel.* Bracey v. Grenoble, 356 F. Supp. 673 (E.D. Pa. 1973).
89. Ibid., 674.
90. Poindexter v. Woodson, 357 F. Supp. 443, 457 (D. Kan. 1973); Beishir v. Swenson, 331 F. Supp. 1227 (W.D. Mo. 1971); and Landman v. Royster, 333 F. Supp. 621, 649 (E.D. Va. 1971).
91. Ibid. See also Morales v. Turman, 364 F. Supp. 166 (E.D. Tex. 1973).
92. As used here, solitary confinement refers to forms of confinement that totally remove the prisoner from inmate society. Various terms have been utilized, such as strip cell, hole, dark cell dungeon, dry cell, strip room, and dry room.

93. See Blake McKelvey, *American Prisons: A Study in American Social History Prior to 1915* (Montclair, N.J.: Patterson Smith, 1968), 120, 163.

94. See Sol Rubin, Henry Weihofen, George Edwards, and Simon Rosenzweig, *The Law of Criminal Corrections* (St. Paul: West Publishing Co., 1963), p. 293; and the President's Commission on Law Enforcement and Administration of Justice, *Task Force Report: Corrections* (Washington: United States Government Printing Office, 1967), p. 50.

95. For refusals to review solitary confinement, see, e.g., Sutton v. Settle, 302 F.2d 286, 288 (8th Cir. 1962) (internal disciplinary matter); United States *ex rel.* Atterbury v. Ragen, 237 F.2d 953 (7th Cir. 1956), *cert. denied,* 353 U.S. 964 (1957) (nearly all the hands-off rationale); Williams v. Steele, 194 F.2d 32, 34 (8th Cir.), *cert. denied,* 344 U.S. 822 (1952) (internal disciplinary matter); Snow v. Roche, 143 F.2d 718, 719 (9th Cir.), *cert. denied,* 323 U.S. 788 (1944) (internal disciplinary matter); Blythe v. Ellis, 194 F. Supp. 139, 140 (S.D. Tex. 1961) (internal disciplinary matter); Thompson v. Cavell, 158 F. Supp. 19, 21 (W.D. Pa. 1957) (exhaust remedies); and Commonwealth *ex rel.* Thompson v. Day, 104 Pittsb. 317, *aff'd.,* 182 Pa. Super. 644, 128 A.2d 133 (1956), *cert. denied,* 355 U.S. 843 (1957) (not exhaust remedies).

96. Howard v. State, 28 Ariz. 433, 237 P. 203 (1925).

97. Ibid., 438.

98. Ibid.

99. Constitutional challenges to solitary confinement were made on other grounds also. See, e.g., Pierce v. LaValle, 293 F.2d 233 (2d Cir. 1961) (religion); Sewell v. Pegelow, 291 F.2d 196 (4th Cir. 1961) (religion); Davis v. Lindsay, 321 F. Supp. 1134 (S.D. N.Y. 1970) (equal protection); Carter v. McGinnis, 320 F. Supp. 1092 (W.D. N.Y. 1970) (procedural due process); Smoake v. Fritz, 320 F. Supp. 609 (S.D. N.Y. 1970) (procedural due process); Dabney v. Cunningham, 317 F. Supp. 57 (E.D. Va. 1970) (procedural due process); Carothers v. Follette, 314 F. Supp. 1014 (S.D. N.Y. 1970) (procedural due process); and United States *ex rel.* Clegget v. Pate, 229 F. Supp. 818 (N.D. Ill. 1964) (Fourteenth Amendment right of access to the courts).

100. Fulwood v. Clemmer, 206 F. Supp. 370 (D. D.C. 1962).

101. Ibid., 379 (emphasis added).

102. Ibid.

103. United States *ex rel.* Mosher v. LaValle, 321 F. Supp. 127 (N.D. N.Y. 1970).

104. Kostal v. Tinsley, 337 F.2d 845 (10th Cir.), *cert. denied,* 380 U.S. 985 (1964).

105. Mahaffey v. State, 87 Idaho 228, 392 P.2d 279 (1964).

106. Jordan v. Fitzharris, 257 F. Supp. 674 (N.D. Cal. 1966).

107. In a 1971 case, Federal District Judge Merhige ruled that his court would

"permit an inmate to be kept nude in his cell only when a doctor states in writing that the inmate's health will not thereby be affected and that the inmate presents a substantial risk of injuring himself if given garments." Landman v. Royster, 333 F. Supp. 621, 648 (E.D. Va. 1971). He was not persuaded, however, that the taking of blankets and mattresses constituted cruel and unusual punishment (ibid., 649).

108. Jordan v. Fitzharris, 257 F. Supp. 674, 680 (N.D. Cal. 1966).
109. Ibid., 683.
110. For a brief note, see "Punishment and Prevention of Crime—Cruel and Unusual Punishment," *Western Reserve Law Review* 18 (January 1967): 724-25.
111. Wright v. McMann, 387 F.2d 519 (2d Cir. 1967).
112. Wright v. McMann, 257 F. Supp. 739 (N.D. N.Y. 1966).
113. Wright v. McMann, 387 F.2d 519, 525 (2d Cir. 1967).
114. Wright v. McMann, 321 F. Supp. 127, 138 (N.D. N.Y. 1970), *aff'd.,* 460 F.2d 126 (2d Cir. 1972), *cert. denied,* 409 U.S. 885 (1972).
115. Knuckles v. Prasse, 302 F. Supp. 1036, 1062 (E.D. Pa. 1969), *aff'd.,* 435 F.2d 1255 (3d Cir. 1970) *(per curiam).*
116. Lollis v. New York State Department of Social Services, 322 F. Supp. 473, 482 (S.D. N.Y. 1970).
117. Inmates of Boys Training School v. Affleck, 346 F. Supp. 1354 (D. R.I. 1972).
118. Nelson v. Heyne, 355 F. Supp. 451 (N.D. Ind. 1973).
119. Morales v. Turman, 364 F. Supp. 166 (E.D. Tex. 1973).
120. La Reau v. MacDougall, 473 F.2d 974 (2nd Cir. 1972). See also *New York Times,* 24 December 1972, p. 34.
121. Poindexter v. Woodson, 357 F. Supp. 443 (D. Kan. 1973).
122. Gates v. Collier, 349 F. Supp. 881 (N.D. Miss. 1972).
123. See, e.g., Novak v. Beto, 453 F.2d 661 (5th Cir. 1971); Adams v. Pate, 445 F.2d 105, 107-8 (7th Cir. 1971); Sostre v. McGinnis, 442 F.2d 178, 192 (2d Cir. 1971); Kostal v. Tinsley, 337 F.2d 845, 846 (10th Cir. 1964); Carlisle v. Bensinger, 355 F. Supp. 1359 (N.D. Ill. 1973); Breece v. Swenson, 332 F. Supp. 837, 842 (W.D. Mo. 1971); United States *ex rel.* Verde v. Case, 326 F. Supp. 701, 704 (E.D. Pa. 1971); Lollis v. New York State Department of Social Services, 322 F. Supp. 473 (S.D. N.Y. 1970); Hancock v. Avery, 301 F. Supp. 786, 792 (M.D. Tenn. 1969); United States *ex rel.* Holland v. Maroney, 299 F. Supp. 262 (W.D. Pa. 1969); Levier v. State, 209 Kan. 442, 497 P.2d 265, 271 (1972); State *ex rel.* Pingley v. Coiner, 186 S.E.2d 220 (W. Va. 1972); Conway v. State, 483 P.2d 350 (Okla. Cr. R. 1971); and State v. Barton, 79 N.M. 70, 439 P.2d 719 (1968).
124. Novak v. Beto, 320 F. Supp. 1206 (S.D. Tex. 1970).
125. The system has also been upheld by the Fifth Circuit Court of Appeals.

See Novak v. Beto, 453 F.2d 661, 670 (5th Cir. 1971). See also Adams v. Pate, 445 F.2d 105 (7th Cir. 1971).

126. See, e.g., Courtney v. Bishop, 409 F.2d 1185 (8th Cir. 1969).

127. United States *ex rel.* Keen v. Mazurkiewicz, 306 F. Supp. 483, 485 (E.D. Pa. 1969). See also, e.g., Adams v. Pate, 445 F.2d 105, 109 (7th Cir. 1971); Ford v. Board of Managers of New Jersey State Prison, 407 F.2d 937, 940 (3d Cir. 1969) (per curiam); Pope v. Hendricks, 326 F. Supp. 699, 700 (E.D. Pa. 1971); and United States *ex rel.* Holland v. Maroney, 299 F. Supp. 262, 263 (W.D. Pa. 1969).

128. See, e.g., Startti v. Beto, 405 F.2d 858, 859 (5th Cir. 1969); Harris v. Settle, 322 F.2d 908 (8th Cir. 1963) (per curiam), *cert. denied,* 377 U.S. 910 (1964); and Roberts v. Barbosa, 227 F. Supp. 20, 22 (S.D. Cal. 1964).

129. See, e.g., Conway v. State, 483 P.2d 350 (Okla. Cr. R. 1971). See also State v. Scott, 17 Ariz. App. 183, 496 P.2d 609 (1972).

130. 321 F. Supp. 523 (C.D. Cal. 1971).

131. See, e.g., Breece v. Swenson, 332 F. Supp. 837 (W.D. Mo. 1971).

132. For an extremely strong case against the use of solitary confinement, see Thoenig. See also Kenneth M. Cole, III, "The Constitutional Status of Solitary Confinement," *Cornell Law Review* 57 (February 1972): 476-89. But see Sheldon Krantz, *Model Rules and Regulations on Prisoner's Rights and Responsibilities* (St. Paul: West Publishing Co., 1973), pp. 130-54.

133. See, e.g., Roberts v. Pegelow, 313 F.2d 548, 550 (4th Cir. 1963); and Bundy v. Cannon, 328 F. Supp. 165 (D. Md. 1971).

134. See, e.g., McBride v. McCorkle, 44 N.J. Super. 468, 130 A.2d 881 (1957).

135. See, e.g., Sostre v. McGinnis, 442 F.2d 178, 194 (2d Cir. 1971); Davis v. Lindsay, 321 F. Supp. 1134 (S.D. N.Y. 1970); Krist v. Smith, 309 F. Supp. 497 (S.D. Ga. 1970); and McBride v. McCorkle, 44 N.J. Super. 468, 130 A.2d 881 (1957). But see Bundy v. Cannon, 328 F. Supp. 165 (D. Md. 1971).

136. See, e.g., United States *ex rel.* Miller v. Twomey, 333 F. Supp. 1352 (N.D. Ill. 1971); and Bundy v. Cannon, 328 F. Supp. 165 (D. Md. 1971).

137. See, e.g., Sostre v. McGinnis, 442 F.2d 178, 192 (2d Cir. 1971); Burns v. Swenson, 430 F.2d 771, 777 (8th Cir. 1970); United States *ex rel.* Miller v. Twomey, 333 F. Supp. 1352, 1354 (N.D. Ill. 1971); Beishir v. Swenson, 331 F. Supp. 1227, 1234 (W.D. Mo. 1971); Clinton v. Swenson, 320 F. Supp. 595 (W.D. Mo. 1970); Holt v. Sarver, 300 F. Supp. 825, 827 (E.D. Ark. 1969); *In re* Henderson, 25 Cal. App.3d 68, 101 Cal. Rptr. 479, 483-84 (1972); and State *ex rel.* Pingley v. Coiner, 186 S.E.2d 220, 234 (W. Va. 1972).

138. For a general discussion, see Correale F. Stevens, "Punitive Segregation

in State Prisons—The Need for Definite Time Limitations," *Dickinson Law Review* 76 (Fall 1971): 125-43.

139. 455 F.2d 1084 (10th Cir. 1972).

140. United States *ex rel.* Miller v. Twomey, 333 F. Supp. 1352 (N.D. Ill. 1971). See also, e.g., Roberts v. Pegelow, 313 F.2d 548, 550 (4th Cir. 1963).

141. Graham v. Willingham, 384 F.2d 367 (10th Cir. 1967) (*per curiam*).

142. See also Beishir v. Swenson, 331 F. Supp. 1227 (W.D. Mo. 1971); and Knuckles v. Prasse, 302 F. Supp. 1036, 1061 (E.D. Pa. 1969), *aff'd,* 435 F.2d 1255 (3d Cir. 1970) (*per curiam*).

143. Krist v. Smith, 309 F. Supp. 497 (S.D. Ga. 1970).

144. *In re* Ronan, 108 Vt. 481, 188 A. 890 (1937).

145. 333 F. Supp. 1258 (W.D. Mo. 1971).

146. Breeden v. Jackson, 457 F.2d 578 (4th Cir. 1972).

147. Sostre v. Rockefeller, 309 F. Supp. 611 (S.D. N.Y. 1969).

148. Sostre v. Rockefeller, 312 F. Supp. 863, 868 (S.D. N.Y. 1970).

149 Ibid., 871. For further elaboration, see Henry R. Goldberg, "Prisons and Prisoners," *Suffolk University Law Review* 5 (Fall 1970): 259-69.

150. Sostre v. McGinnis, 442 F.2d 178, 192 (2d Cir. 1971). For further analysis, see "Prisoner's Constitutional Rights: Segregated Confinement as Cruel and Unusual Punishment," *Washington University Law Quarterly* 1972 (Spring 1972): 347-53; and "Prisons—Civil Rights," *Suffolk University Law Review* 6 (Summer 1972): 1177-89.

151. Ibid., 194. Judge Feinberg, dissenting in part, wanted to place a time limit on the length of stay in punitive segregation (ibid., 207).

152. Holt v. Sarver, 300 F. Supp. 825, 833 (E.D. Ark. 1969).

153. Davis v. Lindsay, 321 F. Supp. 1134 (S.D. N.Y. 1970). The court specifically noted that she had many more rights than prisoners in "solitary confinement."

154. Ibid., 1138.

155. Ibid., 1139.

156. Adams v. Carlson, 368 F. Supp. 1050 (E.D. Ill. 1973).

157. Allen v. Nelson, 354 F. Supp. 505 (N.D. Cal. 1973).

158. Castor v. Mitchell, 355 F. Supp. 123 (W.D. N.C. 1973).

159. Osborn v. Manson, 359 F. Supp. 1107 (D. Conn. 1973).

160. See, e.g., Stevens.

161. The Federal Bureau of Prison Regulations now prohibits bread-and-water diets. See Hirschkop and Millemann, 837.

162. Hughes v. Turner, 14 Utah2d 128, 378 P.2d 888 (1963), *cert. denied,* 374 U.S. 846 (1963).

163. See, e.g., Ruark v. Schooley, 211 F. Supp. 921 (D. Colo. 1962).

164. Landman v. Royster, 333 F. Supp. 621, 647 (E.D. Va. 1971). See also People *ex rel.* Fallon v. Wright, 40 N.Y.S. 285, 291, 7 App. Div. 185 (1896).

165. Ibid., 647.
166. See, e.g., Sullivan v. Ciccone, 311 F. Supp. 456, 457 (W.D. Mo. 1970) (five days a month); and Virginia, *Code Annotated* (1967), sec. 53-213 (ten days for every twenty days of good time).
167. Some successful challenges have been made on other grounds. See, e.g., Landman v. Royster, 333 F. Supp. 621, 657 (E.D. Va. 1971). But see Douglas v. Sigler, 386 F.2d 684 (8th Cir. 1967). The court held that due process standards need not be applied when good time is revoked. The Federal Bureau of Prison Regulations requires hearings before good time is revoked. See Hirschkop and Millemann, 838.
168. Roberts v. Pegelow, 313 F. Supp. 548, 550 (4th Cir. 1963); and Jacob, 248. See also Hirschkop and Millemann, 831-34.
169. Sullivan v. Ciccone, 311 F. Supp. 456 (W.D. Mo. 1970).
170. O'Neill v. United States, 315 F. Supp. 1352 (D. Minn. 1970). See also Williams v. Patterson, 389 F.2d 374, 375 (10th Cir. 1968); and Walker v. Taylor, 338 F.2d 945 (10th Cir. 1964).
171. Morales v. Turman, 364 F. Supp. 166 (E.D. Tex. 1973). See also Wheeler v. Glass, 473 F.2d 983 (7th Cir. 1973).
172. See, e.g., United States *ex rel.* Schuster v. Herold, 410 F.2d 1071, 1088 (2d Cir. 1969); United States v. Fitzgerald, 466 F.2d 377 (D.C. Cir. 1972); Tijerina v. Ciccone, 324 F. Supp. 1265, 1268 (W.D. Mo. 1971); Sawyer v. Sigler, 320 F. Supp. 690, 694 (D. Nebr. 1970); Owens v. Aldridge, 311 F. Supp. 667, 669 (W.D. Okl. 1970); Ramsey v. Ciccone, 310 F. Supp. 600, 605 (W.D. Mo. 1970); Ayers v. Ciccone, 300 F. Supp. 568 (W.D. Mo.), *aff'd.,* 413 F.2d 1049 (8th Cir. 1968) *(per curiam);* and State v. Driver, 262 N.C. 92, 136 S.E.2d 208 (1964). See also, John W. Palmer, *Constitutional Rights of Prisoners* (Cincinnati: W.H. Anderson, Co., 1973), chapter 9.
173. Tijerina v. Ciccone, 324 F. Supp. 1265, 1268 (W.D. Mo. 1971). On the right to treatment, see especially Barney Sneidman, "Prisoners and Medical Treatment: Their Rights and Remedies," *Criminal Law Bulletin* 4 (October 1968): 450-66.
174. Ramsey v. Ciccone, 310 F. Supp. 600, 604 (W.D. Mo. 1970).
175. See, e.g., Owens v. Aldridge, 311 F. Supp. 667, 669 (W.D. Okl. 1970); Peek v. Ciccone, 288 F. Supp. 329 (W.D. Mo. 1968); and Veals v. Ciccone, 281 F. Supp. 1017 (W.D. Mo. 1968).
176. Haynes v. Harris, 344 F.2d 463, 465 (8th Cir. 1965); Owens v. Aldridge, 311 F. Supp. 667 (W.D. Okl. 1970); Peek v. Ciccone, 288 F. Supp. 329 (W.D. Mo. 1968); and Veals v. Ciccone, 281 F. Supp. 1017 (W.D. Mo. 1968).
177. See, especially, Glenn v. Ciccone, 370 F.2d 361, 363 (8th Cir. 1966) *(per curiam)*; United States *ex. rel.* Knight v. Ragen, 337 F.2d 425, 426 (7th Cir. 1964); Sutton v. Settle, 302 F.2d 286, 288 (8th Cir. 1962) *(per curiam)*; Eaton v. Ciccone, 283 F. Supp. 75, 76 (W.D. Mo. 1966); Blythe

v. Ellis, 194 F. Supp. 139, 140 (S.D. Tex. 1961); Feyerchak v. Hiatt, 7 F.R.D. 726 (M.D. Pa. 1948); *Ex parte* Barnard, 52 F. Supp. 102 (E.D. Ill. 1943); State *ex rel.* Baldwin v. Superintendent, 192 Md. 712, 713, 63 A.2d 323 (1949) (*per curiam*); State *ex rel.* Jacobs v. Warden, 190 Md. 755, 756, 59 A.2d 753 (1948) (*per curiam*); State *ex rel.* Renner v. Wright, 188 Md. 189, 192, 51 A.2d 668 (1946); Commonwealth *ex rel.* Smith v. Banmiller, 194 Pa. Super. 566, 568, 186 A.2d 793 (1961); and Chapman v. Graham, 2 Utah2d 156, 159, 270 P.2d 821 (1954). For a detailed review, see Sneidman.

178. Mayfield v. Craven, 433 F.2d 873 (9th Cir. 1970) (*per curiam*).

179. Reyes v. Hauck, 339 F. Supp. 195 (W.D. Tex. 1972).

180. Austin v. Harris, 226 F. Supp. 304, 308 (W.D. Mo. 1964). But see People *ex rel.* Brown v. Johnston, 9 N.Y.2d 482, 174 N.E.2d 725, 215 N.Y.S.2d 44 (1961) (confinement of sane prisoner with mental defectives and insane persons is cruel and unusual punishment).

181. Sutton v. Settle, 302 F.2d 286 (8th Cir. 1962) *(per curiam).*

182. *In re* Berry, 113 Cal. App.2d 613, 248 P.2d 420 (1952).

183. *In re* Pinaire, 46 F. Supp. 113 (N.D. Tex. 1942).

184. Fraught v. Ciccone, 283 F. Supp. 76 (W.D. Mo. 1966); and Ayers v. Ciccone, 300 F. Supp. 568 (W.D. Mo.), *aff'd.,* 413 F.2d 1049 (8th Cir. 1968) (*per curiam*).

185. Several early decisions held that prisoners alleging a denial of medical treatment must be granted hearings. See, e.g., Edwards v. Duncan, 355 F.2d 993 (4th Cir. 1966) (*per curiam*); Hirons v. Director, 351 F.2d 613 (4th Cir. 1965) (*per curiam*); Coleman v. Johnston, 247 F.2d 273 (7th Cir. 1957); Austin v. Harris, 226 F. Supp. 304 (W.D. Mo. 1964); and Redding v. Pate, 220 F. Supp. 124 (N.D. Ill. 1963).

186. Roberts v. Pepersack, 256 F. Supp. 415, 426 (D. Md. 1966).

187. Talley v. Stephens, 247 F. Supp. 683, 687 (E.D. Ark. 1965).

188. Black v. Ciccone, 324 F. Supp. 129, 133 (W.D. Mo. 1970).

189. Sawyer v. Sigler, 320 F. Supp. 690, 694 (D. Neb. 1970).

190. Ibid.

191. Nelson v. Heyne, 355 F. Supp. 451 (N.D. Ind. 1973).

192. Nelson v. Heyne, 491 F.2d 352 (7th Cir. 1974).

193. Knecht v. Gillman, 488 F.2d 1136 (8th Cir. 1973).

194. Ibid., 1140.

195. Newman v. Alabama, 349 F. Supp. 278 (M.D. Ala. 1972).

196. In *Collins* v. *Schoonfield,* 344 F. Supp. 257 (D. Md. 1972), delay in treating an inmate for hepatitis was deemed cruel and unusual.

197. Rodriguez-Sandoval v. United States, 409 F.2d 529 (1st Cir. 1969).

198. United States *ex rel.* Gallagher v. Daggett, 326 F. Supp. 387 (D. Minn. 1971).

199. Lindsay v. Mitchell, 455 F.2d 917 (5th Cir. 1972) (*per curiam*).

200. Rodriguez-Sandoval v. United States, 409 F.2d 529, 532 (1st Cir. 1969).

201. See Hoitt v. Vitek, 361 F. Supp. 1238 (D. N.H. 1973); and Gomes v. Travisono, 353 F. Supp. 457 (D. R.I. 1973).

202. 313 F. Supp. 158 (D. Kan. 1970).

203. Hawthorne v. People, 68 Misc.2d 858, 328 N.Y.S.2d 488 (1971).

204. United States *ex rel.* Wolfersdorf v. Johnston, 317 F. Supp. 66, 68 (S.D. N.Y. 1970). See chapter 10.

205. People *ex rel.* Brown v. Johnston, 9 N.Y.2d 482, 215 N.Y.S.2d 44, 174 N.E.2d 725 (1961).

206. Challenges to the rules regulating shaving and hair length have also been brought on First Amendment grounds. See, e.g., Brooks v. Wainwright, 428 F.2d 652 (5th Cir. 1970) (*per curiam*); and Brown v. Wainwright, 419 F.2d 1376 (5th Cir. 1970) (*per curiam*).

207. But see Seale v. Manson, 326 F. Supp. 1375 (D. Conn. 1971); and the suggestions of Krantz, pp. 30-32.

208. Rinehart v. Brewer, 360 F. Supp. 105 (S.D. Iowa 1973); Blake v. Pryse, 315 F. Supp. 625 (D. Minn. 1970); and Zeigler v. Riley, 67 Misc.2d 82, 323 N.Y.S.2d 589, 594 (1971).

209. Tarlton v. Clark, 441 F.2d 384 (5th Cir. 1971) (*per curiam*), and Wilkinson v. McManus, 214 N.W.2d 671 (Minn. 1974). Mississippi does allow conjugal visiting, and California has experimented with the idea. See Columbus B. Hopper, "Conjugal Visiting at the Mississippi State Penitentiary," *Federal Probation* 29 (June 1965): 39-46.

210. Shaw v. Beto, 318 F. Supp. 1215 (S.D. Tex. 1970).

211. Howard v. Swenson, 314 F. Supp. 883 (W.D. Mo. 1969).

212. 349 F. Supp. 575 (S.D. N.Y. 1972).

213. Ibid., 585.

214. Morales v. Turman, 364 F. Supp. 166 (E.D. Tex. 1973).

215. Nelson v. Heyne, 491 F.2d 352 (7th Cir. 1974). See also Inmates of Boys Training School v. Affleck, 346 F. Supp. 1354 (D. R.I. 1972).

216. State *ex rel.* du Pont v. Ingram, 293 A.2d 289 (Del. 1972).

217. Martarella v. Kelley, 349 F. Supp. 575, 595-96 (S.D. N.Y. 1972).

218. Brown v. State, 264 So.2d 529, *reversed*, 264 So.2d 549, on *remand*, 264 So.2d 552, *affirmed*, 264 So.2d 553 (Ala. 1972).

219. Ibid., 538.

220. See R.B. Wright, "Discipline or Corporal Punishment," *Education*, September 1969, pp. 69-71, 86.

221. See J.G. Brown, "Law and Punishment: Status of State Statutes," *The Clearing House*, October 1971, pp. 106-9; and Abraham Pallas, "Corporal Punishment: Ancient Practice in Modern Times," *The Clearing House*, January 1973, pp. 312-15.

222. Ware v. Estes, 328 F. Supp. 657, 658 (N.D. Tex. 1971), *aff'd.*, 458 F.2d 1360 (5th Cir.) (*per curiam*), *cert. denied*, 409 U.S. 1027 (1972). For a

comment, see Samuel M. Francis and Emma J. Hirschberger, "Corporal Punishment in School: 1973," *Educational Leadership,* April 1973, pp. 591-95.

223. Ware v. Estes, 458 F.2d 1360 (5th Cir.) (*per curiam*); *cert. denied,* 409 U.S. 1027 (1972).

224. Sims v. Board of Education of Independent School District Number 22, 329 F. Supp. 678 (D.N.M. 1971).

225. 404 F.2d 571 (8th Cir. 1968).

226. Sims v. Board of Education of Independent School District Number 22, 329 F. Supp. 678, 690 (D.N.M. 1971).

227. Glaser v. Marietta, 351 F. Supp. 555 (W.D. Pa. 1972).

228. Gonyaw v. Ladue, 361 F. Supp. 366 (D. Vt. 1973).

229. See, e.g., Breen v. Kahl, 419 F.2d 1034 (7th Cir. 1969).

230. Ferrell v. Dallas Independent School District, 261 F. Supp. 545 (N.D. Tex. 1966), *aff'd.,* 392 F.2d 697 (5th Cir. 1968); Westley v. Rossi, 305 F. Supp. 706 (D. Minn. 1969); and Richards v. Thurston, 304 F. Supp. 449 (D. Mass. 1969), *aff'd.,* 424 F.2d 1281 (1st Cir. 1970).

231. Ferrell v. Dallas Independent School District, 261 F. Supp. 545 (N.D. Tex. 1966), *aff'd.,* 392 F.2d 697 (5th Cir. 1968); and Leonard v. School Commission of Attleboro, Massachusetts, 349 Mass. 704, 212 N.E.2d 468 (1965).

232. Richards v. Thurston, 304 F. Supp. 449 (D. Mass. 1969), *aff'd.,* 424 F.2d 1281 (1st Cir. 1970); and Breen v. Kahl, 296 F. Supp. 702 (W.D. Wis.), *aff'd.,* 419 F.2d 1034 (7th Cir. 1969).

233. Westley v. Rossi, 305 F. Supp. 706 (D. Minn. 1969); Richards v. Thurston, 304 F. Supp. 449 (D. Mass. 1969), *aff'd.,* 424 F.2d 1281 (1st Cir. 1970); and Breen v. Kahl, 296 F. Supp. 702 (W.D. Wis.), *aff'd.,* 419 F.2d 1034 (7th Cir. 1969).

234. Ferrell v. Dallas Independent School District, 261 F. Supp. 545 (N.D. Tex. 1966), *aff'd.,* 392 F.2d 697 (5th Cir. 1968); and Leonard v. School Commission of Attleboro, Massachusetts, 349 Mass. 704, 212 N.E.2d 468 (1965).

235. Rumler v. Board of School Trustees for Lexington County District Number 1 School, 327 F. Supp. 729 (D.S.C. 1971).

236. Press v. Pasadena Independent School District, 326 F. Supp. 550, 564 (S.D. Tex. 1971).

237. Schneider v. Ohio Youth Commission, 31 Ohio App.2d 225, 287 N.E.2d 633 (1972).

Chapter 12
Total Prison Conditions

1. See Commonwealth *ex rel.* Johnson v. Dye, 159 Pa. Super. 542, 543, 49 A.2d 195 (1946).

2. Commonwealth *ex rel.* Johnson v. Dye, No. 3679, Allegheny County
    Common Pleas, April Term, 1946; and 159 Pa. Super. 542, 49 A.2d 195
    (1946).
3. Johnson v. Dye, 71 F. Supp. 262, 265 (W.D. Pa. 1947).
4. Johnson v. Dye, 175 F.2d 250, 253 (3d Cir. 1949). For articles on the
    decision not elsewhere cited, see Arthur S. Bell, Jr., "Application of Cruel
    and Unusual Punishments Clause of the Eight Amendment to the States
    Through Due Process Clause of the Fourteenth Amendment—Habeas
    Corpus," *Southern California Law Review* 23 (December 1949): 86-89;
    "Cruel and Unusual Punishment Provision of Eighth Amendment as
    Restriction Upon State Action Through the Due Process Clause,"
    Minnesota Law Review 34 (January 1950): 134-37; John P. Frank, "The
    United States Supreme Court: 1949-1950, The Writ of Certiorari,"
    University of Chicago Law Review 18 (Autum 1950): 39-40; "Guaranty
    of Eighth Amendment Against Cruel and Unusual Punishments Read
    into the Fourteenth Amendment as a Fundamental Right," *Virginia Law
    Review* 35 (October 1949): 787-88; and John E. Lindberg, "Cruel and
    Unusual Punishment—Effect of the Fourteenth Amendment," *Notre
    Dame Lawyer* 25 (Fall 1949): 153-55.
5. "Georgia Prisons," *Life,* 1 November 1943, pp. 93-99.
6. "Georgia's Middle Ages," *Time,* 13 September 1943, pp. 23-24.
7. "Leg picks" were two-foot-long iron bars locked over the ankle.
8. Johnson v. Dye, 175 F.2d 250, 254 (3d Cir. 1949).
9. Ibid.
10. Ibid., 255.
11. Ibid., 255-56.
12. This fact is overlooked by Judge Henley in *Holt* v. *Sarver,* 309 F. Supp.
    362 (E.D. Ark. 1970), *infra.*
13. See, e.g., Rodney W. DeVillers, "Constitutional Law: Due Process: Habeas
    Corpus in Extradition Proceedings," *Oklahoma Law Review* 3 (August
    1950): 307-11.
14. See Bernard L. Shaprio, "Constitutional Law—Extradition—Due Process,"
    Temple Law Quarterly 23 (January 1950): 234-36; and Arthur E. Suther-
    land, Jr., "Due Process and Cruel Punishment," *Harvard Law Review* 64
    (November 1950): 271-79.
15. "The Case of the Fugitive From the Chain Gang," *Stanford Law Review*
    2 (December 1949): 174-83.
16. Johnson v. Dye, 338 U.S. 864 (1949). See Kenneth Levin, "Habeas Corpus
    in Extradition Proceedings Involving Escaped Convicts," *Journal of Criminal
    Law and Criminology* 40 (November-December 1949): 484-89; "Prisoners
    Remedies for Mistreatment," *Yale Law Journal* 59 (March 1950): 800-8;
    and Sutherland.
17. It will be recalled he omitted appeal to the Suprene Court of Pennsyl-
    vania.

18. See, e.g., Sweeney v. Woodall, 344 U.S. 86 (1952); and Johnson v. Matthews, 182 F.2d 677 (D.C. Cir. 1950).

19. Harper v. Wall, 85 F. Supp. 783, 787 (D. N.J. 1949).

20. *Ex parte* Marshall, 85 F. Supp. 771 (D. N.J. 1949).

21. People *ex rel.* Jackson v. Ruthazer, 90 N.Y.S.2d 205 (1949), *aff'd.,* 181 F.2d 588 (2d Cir. 1950), *cert. denied,* 339 U.S. 980 (1950).

22. *Application of* Middlebrooks, 88 F, Supp. 943, 946–47 (S.D. Cal. 1950).

23. See McLamore v. South Carolina, 257 S.C. 413, 186 S.E.2d 250, *cert. denied,* 409 U.S. 934 (1972). However, Justice Douglas did dissent from the denial. He wished to examine two questions: (1) Does the chain gang fit into our current concept of penology? (2) If not, does it violate the Eighth Amendment? Ibid., 936. See also Wilson v. Kelley, 294 F. Supp. 1005 (N.D. Ga. 1968).

24. See, e.g., Alan J. Davis, "Sexual Assaults in the Philadelphia Prison System and Sheriff's Vans," *Transaction* 6 (December 1968): 8-16; and Philip J. Hirschkop and Michael A. Millemann, "The Unconstitutionality of Prison Life," *Virginia Law Review* 55 (June 1969): 795-839.

25. *In re* Ellis, 76 Kan. 368, 375, 91 P.2d 81 (1904).

26. *Ex parte* Pickens, 101 F. Supp. 285, 287 (D. Alaska 1951).

27. Ibid., 189.

28. Ibid., 290.

29. Beard v. Lee, 396 F.2d 749 (5th Cir. 1968) (*per curiam*).

30. Inmates of Cook County Jail v. Tierney, No. 68 c504 (N.D. Ill. 1968). The opinion is also found in Richard P. Berg, et al. (eds.), *Prisoners' Rights and Jail Conditions* Los Angeles National Conference on Police-Community Relations, 1970), pp. 111-24.

31. Reported in Richard G. Singer, "Prison Conditions: An Unconstitutional Roadblock to Rehabilitation," *Catholic University Law Review* 20 (Spring 1971): 391. See also "Prisoners Rights Under Section 1983," *Georgetown Law Journal* 57 (June 1969): 1270.

32. Curley v. Gonzales, Civil No. 8372 (D. N.M., February 12, 1970).

33. Reported in Singer, 390-91.

34. Hamilton v. Schiro, 338 F. Supp. 1016 (E.D. La. 1970). See also David F. Edwards, "Conditions in Prison System Render Confinement Unconstitutional," *Tulane Law Review* 45 (February 1971): 403-07; and Felix R. Weill, "Penal Institutions and the Eighth Amendment—A Broadened Conception of Cruel and Unusual Punishment," *Louisiana Law Review* 31 (February 1971): 395-404.

35. For another examination of overcrowding, see Landman v. Royster, 333 F. Supp. 621 (E.D. Va. 1971).

36. Hamilton v. Love, 328 F. Supp. 1182 (E.D. Ark. 1971).

37. Ibid., 1191.

38. Ibid., 1194.

39. Roberts v. Williams, 302 F. Supp. 972, 989 (N.D. Miss. 1969).

40. See, e.g., Bethea v. Crouse, 417 F.2d 504 (10th Cir. 1969).

41. See, e.g., Williams v. Field, 416 F.2d 483 (9th Cir. 1969); and Parker v. McKeithen, 330 F. Supp. 435 (E.D. La. 1971).

42. Jones v. Wittenberg, 323 F. Supp. 93, 99 (N.D. Ohio 1971).

43. Jones v. Wittenberg, 330 F. Supp. 707 (N.D. Ohio 1971). See also "Prisons—Civil Rights of Detainees," *Suffolk University Law Review* 6 (Summer 1972): 1138-47.

44. Commonwealth *ex rel.* Bryant v. Hendrick, 444 Pa. 83, 86, 280 A.2d 110 (1971).

45. Ibid., 98.

46. Jackson v. Hendrick, 40 *U.S.L.W.*, 2710-11, May 2, 1972.

47. Hendrick v. Jackson, 309 A.2d 187 (Pa. 1973).

48. Anderson v. Nosser, 438 F.2d 183 (5th Cir. 1971).

49. Ibid., 189.

50. Ibid., 193.

51. Brenneman v. Madigan, 343 F. Supp. 128, 132 (N.D. Cal. 1972) (emphasis added).

52. Ibid., 133.

53. Johnson v. Lark, 365 F. Supp. 289, 302 (E.D. Mo. 1973).

54. See also Wayne County Jail Inmates v. Wayne County Board of Commissioners, Civil No. 173-217, Cir. Ct. Wayne County, Mich., May 18, 1971, where pretrial detainees were also successful in gaining relief. For an analysis, see Penelope D. Clute, "Criminal Procedure—Pretrial Detainment—The Jailer's Duty to Provide Jail Inmates 'Reasonable Protection' and Facilities Conforming to State and Local Housing Codes," *Wayne Law Review* 18 (September 1972): 1601-18.

55. Singer, 372-73. See also Richard G. Singer, "Bringing the Constitution to Prison: Substantive Due Process and the Eighth Amendment," *University of Cincinnati Law Review* 39 (Fall 1970): 650-84.

56. Holt v. Sarver, 309 F. Supp. 362 (E.D. Ark. 1970), *aff'd.*, 442 F.2d 304 (8th Cir. 1971).

57. Several challenges to specific practices were reviewed in the last chapter. See Jackson v. Bishop, 404 F.2d 571 (8th Cir. 1968) (whipping); Holt v. Sarver, 300 F. Supp. 825 (E.D. Ark. 1969); Jackson v. Bishop, 268 F. Supp. 804 (E.D. Ark. 1967) (crank telephone and teeter board); and Talley v. Stephens, 247 F. Supp. 683 (E.D. Ark. 1965) (hard labor by the physically unfit). For a complete account of the scandal surrounding the Arkansas penal system, see Thomas Murton, *Accomplices to the Crime* (New York: Grove Press, 1969).

58. Holt v. Sarver, 309 F. Supp. 362, 372-73 (E.D. Ark. 1970).

59. See also Roberts v. Williams, 302 F. Supp. 972, 989 (N.D. Miss. 1969).

60. Holt v. Sarver, 309 F. Supp. 362, 375 (E.D. Ark. 1970).

61. See also Holt v. Sarver, 300 F. Supp. 825, 828-31 (E.D. Ark. 1969).
62. Holt v. Sarver, 309 F. Supp. 362, 379 (E.D. Ark. 1970).
63. Ibid., 381.
64. Ibid.
65. *Ex parte* Pickens, 101 F. Supp. 285 (D. Alaska 1951).
66. Holt v. Sarver, 309 F. Supp. 362, 383 (E.D. Ark. 1970).
67. Ibid., 385.
68. *New York Times,* 19 February 1970, p. 32
69. See, e.g., Thomas Murton, "One Year of Prison Reform," *The Nation,*
     12 January 1970, pp. 12-17; and Robert Pearlman, "The Arkansas Prison
     Farm," *The Nation* 26 December 1966, pp. 701-04.
70. "Vindication for Murton," *The Nation,* 30 March 1970, p. 357.
71. Arkansas, *Acts* (Special Session, 1970), act 17.
72. Arkansas, *Acts* (Special Session, 1970), act 7.
73. See, e.g., "Conditions and Practices of the Arkansas Penal System Viola-
     tive of the Eighth and Fourteenth Amendments," *Kansas Law Review* 19
     (Fall 1970): 139-45; "Constitutional Law—Cruel and Unusual Punish-
     ment—Arkansas State Penitentiary System Violates the Eighth Amend-
     ment," *Harvard Law Review* 84 (December 1970): 456-63; "Cumulative
     Impact of Deplorable Conditions of Confinement in the State Prison
     Constitutes Cruel and Unusual Punishment, Even Though Inmates Were
     Subjected Incidently Rather Than in Deliberate Retribution for Criminal
     Conduct," *Alabama Law Review* 23 (February 1970): 143-56; "Entire
     Prison System Found Unconstitutional Contravening Eighth Amendment,"
     New York Law Forum 16 (1970): 659-65; George S. Kopp, "Prison
     Reform Through Judicial Fiat," *Arkansas Law Review* 24 (Winter 1971):
     477-500; Dennis G. Linder, "Conditions and Practices of the Arkansas
     Prison System Constitute Cruel and Unusual Punishment Prohibited by
     the Eighth Amendment of the Constitution of the United States,"
     Drake Law Review 20 (September 1970), 188-95; Stacy L. Moore, Jr.,
     "Arkansas State Penitentiary Transgresses Constitutional Proscription
     Against Cruel and Unusual Punishment," *Seton Hall Law Review* 3 (Fall
     1971): 159-67; Richard B. Scherrer, "The Arkansas Prison System—An
     Unconstitutional Outrage," *Missouri Law Review* 36 (Fall 1971): 576-85
     Paul D. Schoonover, "Judicial Supervision of Prisons Via the Eighth
     Amendment," *Southwestern Law Journal* 24 (December 1970): 844-52;
     and Michael L. Wolfram, "Because of Conditions and Practices in Arkan-
     sas Penitentiary System, Imprisonment Therein Constitutes Cruel and
     Unusual Punishment Prohibited by the Eighth Amendment," *Texas Law
     Review* 48 (June 1970): 1198-1206.
74. Holt v. Sarver, 442 F.2d 304, 307-08 (8th Cir. 1971).
75. Gates v. Collier, 349 F. Supp. 881 (N.D. Miss. 1972).
76. Ibid., 887.

77. In 1973 the Fourth Circuit Court of Appeals held that a prisoner could challenge his confinement as cruel and unusual although he himself had not been attacked. Woodhaus v. Virginia, 487 F.2d 889 (4th Cir. 1973).

78. In another case, Judge Allen of the Federal District Court for Kentucky intimated that conditions in the Jefferson County Jail inflicted cruel and unusual punishment on juveniles placed there for "shock value." See Baker v. Hamilton, 345 F. Supp. 345 (D. Ky. 1972).

79. Inmates of the Boy's Training School v. Affleck, 346 F. Supp. 1354 (D. R.I. 1972). For an analysis, see Ronald H. Rosenberg, "The Eight Amendment and Prison Reform," *North Carolina Law Review* 51 (October 1973): 1539-50.

80. Martarella v. Kelley, 349 F. Supp. 575 (S.D. N.Y. 1972).

81. Morales v. Turman, 364 F. Supp. 166 (E.D. Tex. 1973).

82. *Ex parte* Pickens, 101 F. Supp. 285 (D. Alaska 1951).

83. Hamilton v. Schiro, 338 F. Supp. 1016 (E.D. La. 1970).

84. Hamilton v. Love, 328 F. Supp. 1182 (E.D. Ark. 1971).

85. Commonwealth *ex rel.* Bryant v. Hendrick, 444 Pa. 83, 280 A.2d 110 (1971).

86. Jones v. Wittenberg, 330 F. Supp. 707 (N.D. Ohio 1971).

87. 326 F. Supp. 681 (S.D. N.Y. 1971).

88. 186 S.E.2d 220 (W. Va. 1972).

89. Holt v. Sarver, 309 F. Supp. 362 (E.D. Ark. 1970).

90. Commonwealth *ex rel.* Bryant v. Hendrick, 444 Pa. 83, 280 A.2d 110 (1971).

Chapter 13
Conclusion

1. Furman v. Georgia, 408 U.S. 238 (1972).

2. Weems v. United States, 217 U.S. 349 (1910).

3. 370 U.S. 660 (1962).

4. Jacobellis v. Ohio, 378 U.S. 184, 197 (1964) (concurring opinion).

5. 408 U.S. 238 (1972).

6. 438 F.2d 786 (4th Cir. 1970).

7. 100 Cal. Rptr. 152, 6 Cal.3d 628, 493 P.2d 880 (1972).

8. 356 U.S. 86 (1958).

9. 392 U.S. 514 (1968).

Table of Cases

Adair v. Maryland, 231 Md. 255, 189 A.2d 618 (1963), 77.

Adams v. Carlson, 368 F. Supp. 1050 (E.D. Ill. 1973), 129, 212.

Adams v. Pate, 445 F.2d 105 (7th Cir. 1971), 210, 211.

Afroyim v. Rusk, 387 U.S. 253 (1967), 95, 170, 198, 199.

Afroyim v. Rusk, 361 F.2d 102 (2d Cir. 1966), 95, 199.

Afroyim v. Rusk, 250 F. Supp. 686 (S.D. N.Y. 1966), 95, 199.

Aldridge v. Commonwealth, 4 Va. Cas. 447 (1824), 89, 184, 189, 190, 196.

Alegata v. Commonwealth, 353 Mass. 287, 231 N.E.2d 201 (1967), 202.

Allen v. Nelson, 354 F. Supp. 505 (N.D. Cal. 1973), 129, 212.

Alspaugh v. State, 133 So.2d 587 (Fla. 1961), 77.

Anderson v. Nosser, 438 F.2d 183 (5th Cir. 1971), 149-150, 219.

Anthony v. United States, 331 F.2d 687 (9th Cir. 1964), 82.

Application of Middlebrooks, 88 F. Supp. 943 (S.D. Cal. 1950), 14, 144, 170, 218

Atwood v. State, 146 Miss. 662, 111 So. 865 (1927), 191.

Austin v. Harris, 226 F. Supp. 304 (W.D. Mo. 1964), 132, 214.

Ayers v. Ciccone, 413 F.2d 1049 (8th Cir. 1968), 213, 214.

Ayers v. Ciccone, 300 F. Supp. 568 (W.D. Mo. 1968), 213, 214.

Ayers v. State, 25 Ala. App. 469, 148 So. 875 (1933), 35, 177.

Badders v. United States, 240 U.S. 391 (1916), 71, 81, 194.

Bailey v. United States, 284 Fed. 126 (7th Cir. 1922), 169.

Baker v. Binder, 274 F. Supp. 658 (D. Ky. 1967), 202.

Baker v. Hamilton, 345 F. Supp. 345 (D. Ky. 1972), 221.

Baker v. State, 478 S.W.2d 445 (Tex. Cr. App. 1972), 202.

Balser v. State, 57 Del. 206, 195 A.2d 757 (1963), 56, 185.

Banning v. Looney, 348 U.S. 859 (1954), 203.

Banning v. Looney, 213 F.2d 771 (10th Cir. 1954), 203.

Barker v. People, 3 Cow. (N.Y.) 686 (1824), 13, 85-86, 170, 190, 195.

Barnett v. Rodgers, 133 App. D.C. 296, 410 F.2d 995 (1969), 205, 207.

Barron v. Baltimore, 32 U.S. (7 Pet.) 243 (1833), 170.

Bartholomey v. State, 260 Md. 504, 273 A.2d 164 (1971), 41, 180.

Beard v. Lee, 396 F.2d 749 (5th Cir. 1968), 145-146, 218.

Beishir v. Swenson, 331 F. Supp. 1227 (W.D. Mo. 1971), 208, 211, 212.

Benjamin v. Hunter, 176 F.2d 269 (10th Cir. 1949), 205.

Bennett v. State, 32 Tex. Cr. R. 216, 22 S.W. 684 (1894), 168, 190.

Bethea v. Crouse, 417 F.2d 504 (10th Cir. 1969), 219.

Billingsley v. State, 287 Ala. 634, 254 So.2d 333 (1971), 180.

Bilokumsky v. Tod, 263 U.S. 149 (1923), 195.

Black v. Ciccone, 324 F. Supp. 129 (W.D. Mo. 1970), 133, 214.

Blake v. Pryse, 315 F. Supp. 625 (D. Minn. 1970), 215.

Blythe v. Ellis, 194 F. Supp. 139 (S.D. Tex. 1961), 170, 209, 213-214.

Boerngen v. United States, 326 F.2d 326 (5th Cir. 1969), 82.

Borck v. State, 39 So. 580 (Ala. 1905), 84, 192, 194.

Boykin v. Alabama, 395 U.S. 238 (1969), 34, 177.

Boykin v. State, 281 Ala. 659, 207 So.2d 412 (1968), 34, 176, 177.

Branch v. State, 447 S.W.2d 932 (Tex. Cr. App. 1969), 46, 179, 182.

Breece v. Swenson, 332 F. Supp. 837 (W.D. Mo. 1971), 210, 211.

Breeden v. Jackson, 457 F.2d 578 (4th Cir. 1972), 127, 212.

Breen v. Kahl, 419 F.2d 1034 (7th Cir. 1969), 216.

Breen v. Kahl, 296 F. Supp. 702 (W.D. Wis. 1969), 216.

Brenneman v. Madigan, 343 F. Supp. 128 (N.D. Cal. 1972), 150, 219.

Brookman v. Commonwealth, 145 S.E. 358 (Va. 1928), 177.

Brooks v. Wainwright, 428 F.2d 652 (5th Cir. 1970), 215.

Brown v. State, 266 P. 491 (Okla. 1928), 34.

Brown v. State, 264 So.2d 553 (Ala. 1972), 215.

Brown v. State, 264 So.2d 552 (Ala. 1972), 215.

Brown v. State, 264 So.2d 549 (Ala. 1972), 215.

Brown v. State, 264 So.2d 529 (Ala. 1972), 137, 215.

Brown v. Wainwright, 419 F.2d 1376 (5th Cir. 1970), 215.

Browne v. State, 379 U.S. 1004 (1965), 201.

Browne v. State, 24 Wis. 2d 491, 129 N.W.2d 175 (1964), 100, 201.

Bruno v. State, 316 F. Supp. 1120 (E.D. La. 1970), 201.

Bryant v. Harrelson, 187 F. Supp. 738 (S.D. Tex. 1960), 170, 208.

Buck v. Bell, 274 U.S. 200 (1927), 57, 186.

Buck v. Bell, 143 Va. 310, 130 S.E. 516 (1925), 57, 58, 186.

Budd v. California, 385 U.S. 909 (1966), 101, 201.

Bugajewitz v. Adams, 228 U.S. 585 (1913), 195.

Bundy v. Cannon, 328 F. Supp. 165 (D. Md. 1971), 211.

Burger v. State, 118 Ga. App. 328, 163 S.E.2d 333 (1968), 202.

Burns v. Swenson, 430 F.2d 771 (8th Cir. 1970), 211.

Calhoun v. State, 85 Tex. Cr. App. 496, 214 S.W. 335 (1919), 179.

Callins v. State, 500 P.2d 1333 (Okla. Cr. 1972), 77.

Campbell v. State, 491 P.2d 1385 (Colo. 1971), 84.

Cannon v. Gladden, 203 Ore. 629, 281 P.2d 233 (1955), 191.

Cannon v. State, 55 Del. 597, 196 A.2d 399 (1963), 185.

Cannon v. Willingham, 358 F.2d 719 (10th Cir. 1966), 204.

Carlisle v. Bensinger, 355 F. Supp. 1359 (N.D. Ill. 1973), 210.

Carlson v. Landon, 342 U.S. 524 (1952), 195.

Carothers v. Follette, 314 F. Supp. 1014 (S.D. N.Y. 1970), 209.

Carter v. McGinnis, 320 F. Supp. 1092 (W.D. N.Y. 1970), 209.

Carter v. State, 500 S.W.2d 368 (Ark. 1973), 77.

Cason v. State, 160 Tenn. 267, 23 S.W.2d 665 (1930), 191.

Castor v. Mitchell, 355 F. Supp. 123 (W.D. N.C. 1973), 129, 212.

Castle v. United States, 381 U.S. 929 (1965), 201.

Castle v. United States, 347 F.2d 492 (D.C. Cir. 1965), 100.

Chambless v. State, 46 Tex. Cr. R. 1, 79 S.W. 577 (1904), 189.

Chapman v. Graham, 2 Utah2d 156, 270 P.2d 821 (1954), 214.

Chicago and Alton Railroad Company v. People, 67 Ill. 11 (1873), 84, 194.

Childs v. Pegelow, 321 F.2d 485 (4th Cir. 1963), 203.

Cipolla v. State, 207 Kan. 822, 486 P.2d 1391 (1971), 193.

City of Portland v. Juntunen, 6 Ore. App. 632, 488 P.2d 806 (1971), 202.

City of Reno v. Second Judicial District Court, 83 Nev. 201, 427 P.2d 4
    (1967), 103, 202.

City of Seattle v. Hill, 435 P.2d 692 (Wash. 1967), 169.

Clellans v. Commonwealth, 8 Pa. 223 (1848), 68.

Clinton v. Swenson, 320 F. Supp. 595 (W.D. Mo. 1970), 211.

Cobern v. Alabama, 273 Ala. 547, 142 So.2d 869 (1962), 34, 177.

Coffin v. Reichard, 143 F.2d 443 (6th Cir. 1944), 112, 204, 205.

Cole v. State, 262 So.2d 902 (Fla. App. 1972), 82.

Coleman v. Johnston, 247 F.2d 273 (7th Cir. 1957), 214.

Collins v. Johnson, 237 U.S. 502 (1915), 170.

Collins v. Schoonfield, 344 F. Supp. 257 (D. Md. 1972), 119, 208, 214.

Commonwealth v. Brown, 167 Mass. 144, 45 N.E. 1 (1896), 83, 194.

Commonwealth *ex rel.* Bryant v. Hendrick, 444 Pa. 83, 280 A.2d 110 (1971),
    149, 156, 219, 221.

Commonwealth *ex rel.* Johnson v. Dye, 159 Pa. Super. 542, 49 A.2d 195
    (1946), 141, 216, 217.

Commonwealth *ex rel.* Johnson v. Dye, No. 3679, Allegheny County Common
    Pleas, April Term, 1946, 141, 217.

Commonwealth *ex rel.* Smith v. Banmiller, 194 Pa. Super, 566, 186 A.2d 793
    (1961), 170, 214.

Commonwealth *ex rel.* Thompson v. Day, 355 U.S. 843 (1957), 204, 209.

Commonwealth *ex rel.* Thompson v. Day, 182 Pa. Super. 644, 128 A.2d 133
    (1956), 209.

Commonwealth *ex rel.* Thompson v. Day, 104 Pittsb. 317 (1956), 209.

Commonwealth v. Hall, 394 S.W. 2d 448 (Ky. 1965), 100, 201.

Commonwealth v. Hatsfield, 1 Clark 177, 2 *Pa. L.J.* 37 (1842), 197.

Commonwealth v. Hitchings, 71 Mass. (5 Gray) 482 (1855), 190.

Commonwealth v. Hoggarty, 4 Brewst. (Pa.) 326 (1869), 197.

Commonwealth v. Novak, 272 Mass. 113, 172 N.E. 84 (1930), 85, 195.

Commonwealth v. Wyatt, 27 Va. (6 Rand.) 694 (1828), 55, 168, 184, 188.

Conway v. State, 483 P.2d 350 (Okla. Cr. R. 1971), 210, 211.

Cooper v. Pate, 378 U.S. 546 (1964), 206.

Cooper v. Telfair, 4 U.S. (Dall.) 14 (1800), 89, 196.

Cooper v. United States, 403 F.2d 71 (10th Cir. 1968), 78.

Cornelison v. Commonwealth, 84 Ky. 583, 2 S.W. 235 (1886), 82, 168, 190, 194.

Cornell v. State, 74 Tenn. 624 (6 Lea.) (1881), 68, 115-116, 184, 189, 207.

Cort v. Herter, 187 F. Supp. 683 (D. D.C. 1960), 94-95, 199.

Courtney v. Bishop, 409 F.2d 1185 (8th Cir. 1969), 211.

Craig v. State, 383 U.S. 959 (1966), 179.

Craig v. State, 179 So. 2d 202 (Fla. 1965), 179.

Crutchfield v. Commonwealth, 248 Ky. 707, 59 S.W.2d 983 (1933), 178.

Cummins v. People, 42 Mich. 142, 3 N.W. 305 (1879), 76, 168, 190.

Curley v. Gonzales, Civ. No. 8372 (D. N.M., February 12, 1970), 146, 218.

Dabney v. Cunningham, 317 F. Supp. 57 (E.D. Va. 1970), 209.

Davis v. Berry, 242 U.S. 468 (1917), 186.

Davis v. Berry, 216 Fed. 413 (E.D. Iowa 1914), 186.

Davis v. Lindsay, 321 F. Supp. 1134 (S.D. N.Y. 1970), 128-129, 209, 211, 212.

Davis v. State, 15 Tex. App. (1884), 69, 190.

Davis v. Walton, 74 Utah 80, 276 P. 921 (1929), 58, 186.

Dayton v. McGrenery, 201 F.2d 711 (D.C. Cir. 1953), 203.

Dear Wing Jung v. United States, 312 F.2d 73 (9th Cir. 1962), 13, 89, 92, 170, 196, 197.

Deeds v. State, 474 S.W.2d 718 (Tex. Cr. App. 1972), 78.

Delnegro v. State, 198 Md. 80, 81 A.2d 241 (1951), 77.

Dinuzzo v. State, 85 Neb. 351, 123 N.W. 309 (1909), 85, 195.

Done v. People, 5 Parker (N.Y.) 364 (1863), 166, 188.

Doss v. Lindsay, 53 F. Supp. 427 (E.D. Ill. 1944), 170.

Doughty v. Beto, 396 F.2d 128 (5th Cir. 1968), 201.

Douglas v. Sigler, 386 F.2d 684 (8th Cir. 1967), 213.

Dowd v. Cook, 340 U.S. 206 (1951), 205.

Driver v. Hinnant, 356 F.2d 761 (4th Cir. 1966), 101.

Driver v. Hinnant, 243 F. Supp. 95 (E.D. N.C. 1965), 193.

Dutton v. State, 123 Md. 373, 91 A. 417 (1914), 38, 170, 173, 179.

Dykes v. State, 64 Ga. 437 (1879), 76, 189.

Easter v. District of Columbia, 361 F.2d 50 (D.C. Cir. 1966), 101.

Eaton v. Bibb, 217 F.2d 446 (7th Cir. 1955), 203.

Eaton v. Ciccone, 283 F. Supp. 75 (W.D. Mo. 1966), 213.

Edmondson v. Warden of Maryland House of Detention, 194 Md. 707, 69 A.2d 919 (1949), 203.

Edwards v. Duncan, 355 F.2d 993 (4th Cir. 1966), 214.

Eilenbecker v. Plymouth County, 134 U.S. 31 (1890), 170.

Eldridge v. Commonwealth, 87 Ky. 365, 8 S.W. 892 (1888), 187.

Ellis v. State, 54 Okla. Cr. 295, 190 P.2d 156 (1933), 171, 176.

Ellison v. State, 419 S.W.2d 849 (Tex. Cr. App. 1967), 34, 177.

Ely v. Thompson, 10 Ky. (3 A.K. Marsh) 70 (1820), 69-70, 168, 184, 190, 191.

Emerson v. State, 476 S.W.2d 686 (Tex. Cr. App. 1972), 193.

Evans v. Moseley, 455 F.2d 1084 (10th Cir. 1972), 126.

Evans v. State, 228 Ga. 867 188 S.E. 2d 861 (1972), 177.

Ex parte Arras, 78 Cal. 304, 20 P. 683 (1889), 187.

Ex parte Barnard, 52F. Supp. 102 (E.D. Ill. 1943), 214.

Ex parte Brady, 70 Ark. 376, 68 S.W. 34 (1902), 189.

Ex parte Farmer, 123 W. Va. 304, 14 S.E.2d 910 (1941), 83, 194.

Ex parte Hibbs, 86 Okla. Cr. 113, 190 P.2d 156 (1948), 193.

Ex parte Hinson, 156 N.C. 250, 72 S.E. 310 (1911), 197.

Ex parte Lee, 177 Cal. 690, 171 P. 958 (1918), 194.

Ex parte Marshall, 85 F. Supp. 771 (D. N.J. 1949), 143, 218.

Ex parte Medley, 134 U.S. 160 (1889), 60, 173.

Ex parte Miller, 89 Cal. 41, 26 P. 620 (1891), 190.

Ex parte Pickens, 101 F. Supp. 285 (D. Alaska 1951), 145, 152, 155, 156, 218. 220, 221.

Ex parte Quirin, 317 U.S. 1 (1942), 36, 37.

Ex parte Scarborough, 173 P.2d 825 (Cal. 1946), 91, 197.

Ex parte Sheehan, 100 Mont. 244, 49 P.2d 438 (1935), 89, 196.

Ex parte Snyder, 81 Okla. Cr. R. 34, 159 P.2d 752 (1945), 90.

Ex parte Watkins, 28 U.S. 119 (1830), 205.

Ex parte Wong Lung, 17 Haw. 168 (1905), 187.

Ex parte Zee, 13 N.J. Super. 312, 80 A.2d 480 (1951), 193.

Falkner v. State, 445 P.2d 815 (Alaska 1968), 191.

Fallen v. United States, 378 U.S. 139 (1964), 206.

Ferguson v. State, 90 Fla. 105, 105 So. 840 (1925), 174.

Ferrell v. Dallas Independent School District, 392 F.2d 697 (5th Cir. 1968), 216.

Ferrell v. Dallas Independent School District, 261 F. Supp. 545 (N.D. Tex. 1966), 216.

Feyerchak v. Hiatt, 7 F.R.D. 726 (M.D. Pa. 1948), 214.

Fisher v. McDaniel, 9 Wyo. 457, 64 P. 1056 (1901), 189.

Fogg v. Commonwealth, 208 Va. 541, 159 S.E.2d 616 (1968), 179.

Fong Yue Ting v. United States, 149 U.S. 698 (1893), 87, 195.

Foote v. State, 59 Md. 264 (1883), 55, 184.

Ford v. Board of Managers of New Jersey State Prison, 407 F.2d 937 (3d Cir. 1969), 211.

Fraught v. Ciccone, 283 F. Supp. 76 (W.D. Mo. 1966), 132, 214.

Frazier v. State, 480 S.W.2d 553 (Tenn. 1972), 193.

Fulwood v. Clemmer, 295 F.2d 171 (D.C. Cir. 1961), 114.

Fulwood v. Clemmer, 206 F. Supp. 370 (D. D.C. 1962), 121-122, 206, 209.

Furman v. Georgia, 408 U.S. 238 (1972), 11, 15-16, 41, 45-53, 56, 159, 160, 166, 169, 171, 181, 182, 183, 221.

Furman v. State, 225 Ga. 253, 167 S.E.2d 628 (1969), 45, 182.

Gallego v. United States, 276 F.2d 914 (9th Cir. 1960), 195.

Garcia v. Territory, 1 N.M. 415 (1869), 55, 168.

Gates v. Collier, 349 F. Supp. 881 (N.D. Miss. 1972), 125, 153-155, 210, 220.

Gibson v. Commonwealth, 209 Ky. 101, 272 S.W. 43 (1925), 176.

Gibson v. Commonwealth, 204 Ky. 748, 265 S.W. 339 (1924), 170, 176.

Glaser v. Marietta, 351 F. Supp. 555 (W.D. Pa. 1972), 138, 216.

Glenn v. Ciccone, 370 F.2d 361 (8th Cir. 1966), 213.

Godwin v. State, 123 Ga. 569, 51 S.E. 598 (1905), 168.

Goldman v. Knecht, 295 F. Supp. 897 (D. Colo. 1969), 103.

Gomes v. Travisono, 353 F. Supp. 457 (D. R.I. 1973), 215.

Gonyaw v. Ladue, 361 F. Supp. 366 (D. Vt. 1973), 138, 216.

Goodwin v. Page, 296 F. Supp. 1205 (E.D. Okla. 1969), 192.

Gordon v. State, 160 So.2d 73 (Miss. 1964), 179.

Goss v. Bomar, 337 F.2d 341 (6th Cir. 1964), 192.

Gould v. State, 71 Neb. 651, 99 N.W. 541 (1904), 190.

Government of the Virgin Islands v. Venzen, 424 F.2d 521 (3d Cir. 1970), 77.

Graham v. West Virginia, 224 U.S. 616 (1912), 78, 192.

Graham v. Willingham, 384 F.2d 367 (10th Cir. 1967), 126, 212.

Green v. Teets, 244 F.2d 401 (9th Cir. 1957), 86, 195.

Griffin v. State, 83 Conn. 1, 74 A. 1068 (1910), 190.

Griggs v. State, 451 S.W.2d 481 (Tex. Cr. App. 1970), 76.

Guerro v. Fitzpatrick, 436 F.2d 378 (1st Cir. 1971), 82.

Halprin v. United States, 295 F.2d 458 (9th Cir. 1961), 86, 195.

Hamilton v. Love, 328 F. Supp. 1182 (E.D. Ark. 1971), 146-147, 156, 218, 221.

Hamilton v. Schiro, 338 F. Supp. 1016 (E.D. La. 1970), 146, 155-156, 218, 221.

Hancock v. Avery, 301 F. Supp. 786 (M.D. Tenn. 1969), 61, 188, 206, 207, 210.

Handy v. State, 46 Tex. Cr. R. 406, 80 S.W. 526 (1904), 76.

Hanson v. State, 48 Wis.2d 203, 179 N.W.2d 909 (1970), 84, 193.

Harisiades v. Shaughnessy, 342 U.S. 580 (1952), 195.

Harper v. Commonwealth, 93 Ky. 290, 19 S.W. 737 (1892), 190.

Harper v. Wall, 85 F. Supp. 783 (D. N.J. 1949), 143, 170, 218.

Harris v. Settle, 377 U.S. 910 (1964), 211.

Harris v. Settle, 322 F.2d 908 (8th Cir. 1963), 211.

Harris v. Stephens, 386 U.S. 964 (1967), 179.

Harris v. Stephens, 361 F.2d 888 (8th Cir. 1966), 179.

Hart v. Coiner, 483 F.2d 136 (4th Cir. 1973), 79, 191, 192, 193.

Hart v. Commonwealth, 131 Va. 726, 109 S.E. 582 (1921), 26, 38, 174, 179.

Hart v. State, 227 Ga. 171, 179 S.E.2d 346 (1971), 34, 177.

Hatfield v. Baileaux, 290 F.2d 632 (9th Cir. 1961), 206.

Hawthorne v. People, 68 Misc.2d 858, 328 N.Y.S.2d 488 (1971), 135, 215.

Hayes v. Municipal Court of Oklahoma City, 487 P.2d 974 (Okla. Cr. 1971), 202.

Haynes v. Harris, 344 F.2d 463 (8th Cir. 1965), 213.

Helms v. State, 456 P.2d 907 (Okla. App. 1969), 84.

Hendrick v. Jackson, 309 A.2d 187 (Pa. 1973), 149, 219.

Hendrick v. United States, 357 F.2d 121 (10th Cir. 1966), 82, 85.

Hendrix v. United States, 2 Okla. Cr. 240, 101 P. 125 (1909), 168.

Herber v. State, 7 Tex 69 (1851), 55, 185.

Hernandez v. Arizona, 43 Ariz. 424, 32 P.2d 18 (1934), 30, 176.

Hester v. State, 17 Ga. 130 (1855), 76.

Hicks v. District of Columbia, 383 U.S. 252 (1966), 103, 202.

Hill v. Gentry, 364 U.S. 875 (1960), 207.

Hill v. Gentry, 280 F.2d 88, (8th Cir. 1958), 207.

Hirons v. Director, 351 F.2d 613 (4th Cir. 1965), 206, 214.

Ho Ah Kow v. Nunan, 12 F. Cas. 252 (No. 6456) (C.C.D. Cal. 1879), 62, 168, 188, 191.

Hoard v. Dutton, 360 F.2d 673 (5th Cir. 1966), 77.

Hobbs v. State, 133 Ind. 404, 32 N.E. 1019 (1893), 55, 169, 185, 187, 190.

Hoitt v. Vitek, 361 F. Supp. 1238 (D. N.H. 1973), 215.

Holt v. Sarver, 442 F.2d 304 (8th Cir. 1971), 153, 219, 220.

Holt v. Sarver, 309 F. Supp. 362 (E.D. Ark. 1970), 151-153, 156, 217, 219, 220, 221.

Holt v. Sarver, 300 F. Supp. 825 (E.D. Ark. 1969), 128, 206, 211, 212, 219, 220.

Howard v. Fleming, 191 U.S. 126 (1903), 71, 83.

Howard v. State, 28 Ariz. 433, 237 P. 203 (1925), 114, 120-121, 209.

Howard v. Swenson, 314 F. Supp. 883 (W.D. Mo. 1969), 136, 215.

Hughes v. Turner, 374 U.S. 846 (1963), 212.

Hughes v. Turner, 14 Utah2d 128, 378 P.2d 888 (1963), 130, 212.

Hurwitz v. State, 200 Md. 578, 92 A.2d 575 (1952), 77.

Hutchenson v. United States, 322 U.S. 894 (1965), 201.

Hutchenson v. United States, 345 F.2d 964 (D.C. Cir. 1965), 100, 169.

Inmates of Attica Correctional Facility v. Rockefeller, 453 F.2d 12 (2d Cir. 1971), 119-120, 208.

Inmates of Boy's Training School v. Affleck, 346 F. Supp. 1354 (D. R.I. 1972), 124, 155, 210, 215, 221.

Inmates of Cook County Jail v. Tierney, No. 68 c504 (N.D. Ill. 1968), 146, 218.

In re Anderson, 69 Cal.2d 613, 73 Cal. Rptr. 21, 447 P.2d 117 (1968), 44, 181.

In re Berry, 113 Cal. App.2d 613, 248 P.2d 420 (1952), 132, 214.

In re Birdsong, 39 Fed. 599 (1889), 11, 119, 168, 169, 208.

In re Candido, 31 Haw. 982 (1931), 116, 207.

In re Chessman, 44 Cal.2d 1, 279 P.2d 24 (1955), 205.

In re Chin Wah, 182 Fed. 256 (D. Ore. 1910), 87, 195.

In re Clayton, 120 Neb. 680, 234 N.W. 630 (1931), 186.

In re De La O, 59 Cal.2d 128, 278 P.2d 793 (1963), 100, 201.

In re Ellis, 76 Kan. 368, 91 P.2d 81 (1904), 145, 218.

In re Ferguson, 368 U.S. 864 (1961), 205.

In re Ferguson, 55 Cal.2d 663, 361 P.2d 417 (1961), 205.

In re Finley, 1 Cal. App. 198, 81 P. 1041 (1905), 37-38, 178.

In re Hallawell, 8 Cal. App. 563, 97 P. 320 (1910), 194.

In re Henderson, 101 Cal. Rptr. 479, 25 Cal. App.3d 68 (1972), 211.

In re Henry, 15 Idaho 755, 99 P. 1054 (1909), 86, 195.

In re Jones, 432 Pa. 44, 246 A.2d 356 (1968), 105, 203.

In re Kemmler, 136 U.S. 436 (1890), 10, 13-14, 23-25, 29, 60, 168, 170, 173, 175, 188.

In re Kemmler, 7 N.Y.S. 145 (1889), 23-24, 173.

In re Lara, 82 Cal. Rptr. 628, 462 P.2d 380 (1969), 82.

In re Look Ting Sing, 21 Fed. 905 (C.C.D. Cal. 1884), 89, 196.

In re Lynch, 105 Cal. Rptr. 217, 502 P.2d 921 (1973), 191.

In re Main, 162 Okla. 65, 19 P.2d 153 (1933), 57, 186.

In re McDonald, 4 Wyo. 150, 33 P. 18 (1893), 169, 187, 190.

In re Opinion of Justices, 230 Ala. 543, 162 So. 123 (1935), 186.

In re O'Shea, 11 Cal. App. 568, 105 P. 776 (1909), 58, 168, 169, 187.

In re Pinaire, 46 F. Supp. 113 (N.D. Tex. 1942), 132, 214.

In re Ronan, 108 Vt. 481, 188 A. 890 (1937), 127, 212.

In re Simpson, 180 N.E.2d 206 (Ohio 1962), 186.

In re Tutt, 55 Kan. 705, 41 P. 957 (1895), 168.

In re Wells, 340 U.S. 937 (1951), 178.

In re Wells, 35 Cal.2d 889, 221 P.2d 947 (1950), 38, 178.

In the Matter of Brown v. McGinnis, 10 N.Y.2d 531, 225 N.Y.S.2d 497, 180 N.E.2d 791 (1962), 114.

Jackson v. Bishop, 404 F.2d 571 (8th Cir. 1968), 117-118, 138, 206, 208, 219.

Jackson v. Bishop, 268 F. Supp. 804 (E.D. Ark. 1967), 117, 119, 206, 208, 219.

Jackson v. Hendrick, 40 *U.S.L.W.*, 2710-2711, May 2, 1972, 149, 219.

Jackson v. State, 225 Ga. 790, 171 S.E.2d 501 (1969), 182.

Jackson v. United States, 390 U.S. 570 (1968), 178.

Jackson v. United States, 102 Fed. 473 (9th Cir. 1900), 190.

Jacobellis v. Ohio, 378 U.S. 184 (1964), 160, 221.

James v. Commonwealth, 12 S. and R. (Pa.) 220 (1825), 58-59, 187.

James v. United States, 364 U.S. 845 (1960), 207.

James v. United States, 280 F.2d 428 (8th Cir. 1960), 207.

Jensen v. Gladden 231 Ore. 141, 372 P. 2d 183 (1962), 84.

Johnson v. Avery, 393 U.S. 483 (1969), 205.

Johnson v. Avery, 382 F.2d 353 (6th Cir. 1967), 205.

Johnson v. Avery, 252 F. Supp. 783 (M.D. Tenn. 1966), 113, 205, 206.

Johnson v. Beto, 337 F. Supp. 1371 (S.D. Tex. 1972), 76.

Johnson v. Dye, 338 U.S. 864 (1949), 143, 204, 205, 217.

Johnson v. Dye, 175 F.2d 250 (3d Cir. 1949), 14, 141-143, 170, 217.

Johnson v. Dye, 71 F. Supp. 262 (W.D. Pa. 1947), 141, 170, 217.

Johnson v. Lark, 365 F. Supp. 289 (E.D. Mo. 1973), 118, 150-151, 208, 219.

Johnson v. Matthews, 182 F.2d 677 (D.C. Cir. 1950), 218.

Johnson v. State, 214 Ark. 902, 218 S.W.2d 687 (1949), 170.

Johnson v. Waukesha, 64 Wis. 281, 25 N.W. 7 (1885), 188, 190.

Jones v. State, 247 Md. 530, 233 A.2d 791 (1967), 179.

Jones v. State, 482 S.W.2d 634 (Tex. Cr. App. 1972), 77.

Jones v. State, 14 Tex. Cr. App. 85 (1883), 83, 194.

Jones v. Territory, 4 Okla. 45, 43 P. 1072 (1896), 76.

Jones v. United States, 249 F.2d 864 (7th Cir. 1957), 207.

Jones v. Wittenberg, 330 F. Supp. 707 (N.D. Ohio 1971), 148-149, 156, 219, 221.

Jones v. Wittenberg, 323 F. Supp. 93 (N.D. Ohio 1971), 148, 219.

Jordan v. Fitzharris, 257 F. Supp. 674 (N.D. Cal. 1966), 122-123, 206, 209, 210.

Kelly v. State, 115 Ill. 583 (1886), 192.

Kenimer v. State, 83 Ga. App. 264, 63 S.E.2d 280 (1951), 191.

Kenimer v. State, 81 Ga. App. 437, 59 S.E.2d 296 (1950), 191.

Kinkaid v. Jackson, 66 Fla. 378, 63 So. 706 (1913), 170.

Knecht v. Gillman, 488 F.2d 1136 (8th Cir. 1973), 133, 214.

Knuckles v. Prasse, 435 F.2d 1255 (3d Cir. 1970), 123, 206, 210, 212.

Knuckles v. Prasse, 302 F. Supp. 1036 (E.D. Pa. 1969), 210, 212.

Kostal v. Tinsley, 380 U.S. 985 (1964), 209.

Kostal v. Tinsley, 337 F.2d 845 (10th Cir. 1964), 122, 209, 210.

Krist v. Smith, 309 F. Supp. 497 (S.D. Ga. 1970), 126-127, 211, 212.

Krueger v. Colville, 49 Wash. 295, 95 P. 81 (1908), 85, 194.

Lambert v. California, 355 U.S. 225 (1958), 15, 171.

Lanasa v. State, 109 Md. 602, 71 A. 1058 (1909), 168, 190.

Landman v. Peyton, 370 F.2d 135 (4th Cir. 1966), 205.

Landman v. Royster, 333 F. Supp. 621 (E.D. Va. 1971), 119, 130, 208, 210, 212, 213, 218.

LaReau v. MacDougall, 473 F.2d 974 (2d Cir. 1972), 124-125, 210.

Lathem v. United States, 259 F.2d 393 (5th Cir. 1958), 86, 195.

Lee v State, 227 Ala. 2, 150 So. 164 (1933), 35, 170, 177.

Legarda v. Valdez, 1 Phil. 146 (1902), 88-89, 196.

Leonard v. School Commission of Attleboro, Massachusetts, 349 Mass. 704, 212 N.E.2d 468 (1965), 216.

Levier v. State, 209 Kan. 442, 497 P.2d 265 (1972), 207, 210.

Lewis v. State, 176 So.2d 718 (La. App. 1965), 208.

Liddell v. State, 287 Ala. 299, 251 So.2d 601 (1971), 180.

Ligan v. State, 3 Heisk (Tenn.) 159 (1871), 69, 190.

Lillard v. State, 17 Tex. App. 114 (1884), 80, 193.

Lindsay v. Mitchell, 455 F.2d 917 (5th Cir. 1972), 135, 214.

Livingston v. Moore, 32 U.S. (7 Pet.) 469 (1833), 170.

Lloyd v. Heritage, 199 F. Supp. 46 (N.D. Ga. 1961), 205.

Loeb v. Jennings, 133 Ga. 796, 67 S.E. 101 (1910), 170, 187, 190.

Lollis v. New York State Department of Social Services, 322 F. Supp. 473
    (S.D. N.Y. 1970), 123-124, 210.
Louisiana *ex rel.* Francis v. Resweber, 329 U.S. 459 (1947), 14, 26-29, 170, 171,
    174.
Lovett v. State, 479 S.W.2d 286 (Tex. Cr. App. 1972), 76.
Maatallah v. Warden, 86 Nev. 43, 470 P.2d 122 (1970), 105-106, 136, 203.
McBride v. McCorkle, 44 N.J. Super. 468, 130 A.2d 881 (1957), 211.
McCarthy v. Clancy, 110 Conn. 482, 148 A. 551 (1930), 170.
McClosky v. Maryland, 337 F.2d 72 (4th Cir. 1964), 112.
McCormick v. Heritage, 216 F. Supp. 222 (N.D. Ga. 1962), 205.
McCulley v. State, 62 Ind. 428 (1878), 190.
McDonald v. Commonwealth, 173 Mass. 322, 53 N.E. 874 (1899), 170, 190, 192.
McDonald v. Massachusetts, 180 U.S. 311 (1901), 192.
McElvaine v. Brush, 142 U.S. 155 (1891), 188.
McGautha v. California, 402 U.S. 183 (1971), 43-44, 50-51, 182.
McGowen v. State, 221 Tenn. 442, 427 S.W.2d 555 (1968), 85.
McLamore v. South Carolina, 409 U.S. 934 (1972), 188, 218.
McLamore v. South Carolina, 257 S.C. 413, 186 S.E.2d 250 (1972), 60, 188, 218.
McNally v. Hill, 293 U.S. 131 (1934), 205.
McNeese v. Board of Education, 373 U.S. 668 (1963), 206.
McWilliams v. United States, 393 U.S. 1044 (1969), 193, 195.
McWilliams v. United States, 394 F.2d 41 (8th Cir. 1968), 193, 195.
Mahaffey v. State, 87 Idaho 228, 392 P.2d 279 (1964), 122, 209.
Mallon v. State, 49 Wis.2d 185, 181 N.W.2d 364 (1970), 84.
Mallory v. State, 56 Ga. 545 (1876), 168.
Malloy v. South Carolina, 237 U.S. 180 (1915), 174.
Manley v. Fisher, 63 F.2d 256 (4th Cir. 1933), 194.
Martarella v. Kelley, 349 F. Supp. 575 (S.D. N.Y. 1972), 136, 155, 215, 221.
Martin v. Nebraska, 23 Neb. 371, 36 N.W. 554 (1888), 195.
Massey v. Smith, 224 Ga. 721, 164 S.E.2d 786 (1968), 179.
Matter of Bayard, 63 How. Pr. (N.Y.) 73 (1881), 168, 169, 187.
Maxwell v. Stephens, 382 U.S. 944 (1965), 179.
Maxwell v. Stephens, 348 F.2d 325 (8th Cir. 1965), 179.
Mayfield v. Craven, 433 F.2d 873 (9th Cir. 1970), 132, 214.
Mickle v. Henrichs, 262 Fed. 687 (D. Nev. 1918), 57, 186.
Miller v. State, 149 Ind. 607, 49 N.E. 894 (1898), 83, 194.
Mitchell v. State, 82 Md. 527, 34 A. 247 (1896), 168, 189, 190.
Mitchell v. Stephens, 384 U.S. 1019 (1966), 179.
Mitchell v. Stephens, 353 F.2d 129 (8th Cir. 1965), 179.
Monroe v. Pape, 365 U.S. 167 (1961), 113, 206.
Moore v. Missouri, 159 U.S. 673 (1895), 75, 192.
Morales v. Turman, 364 F. Supp. 166 (E.D. Tex. 1973), 118, 124, 131, 136,
    155, 208, 210, 213, 215, 221.

Morgan v. State, 47 Ala. 34 (1872), 188.

Mottran v. State, 263 A.2d 715 (Me. 1970), 193.

Muniz v. United States, 374 U.S. 150 (1963), 114, 207.

Muniz v. United States, 305 F.2d 285 (2d Cir. 1962), 114, 207.

N.A.A.C.P. v. Williams, 359 U.S. 550 (1959), 170.

Nelson v. Heyne, 491 F.2d 352 (7th Cir. 1974), 118, 133, 136, 208, 214, 215.

Nelson v. Heyne, 355 F. Supp. 451 (N.D. Ind. 1973), 124, 133, 208, 210, 214.

Newman v. Alabama, 349 F. Supp. 278 (M.D. Ala. 1972), 134-135, 214.

Normand v. People, 165 Colo. 509, 440 P.2d 282 (1968), 201.

Novak v. Beto, 453 F.2d 661 (5th Cir. 1971), 210, 211.

Novak v. Beto, 320 F. Supp. 1206 (S.D. Tex. 1970), 125, 210.

Nowling v. State, 151 Fla. 584, 10 So.2d 130 (1942), 72, 191, 192.

O'Brien v. Olson, 42 Cal. App.2d 449, 109 P.2d 8 (1941), 116-117, 207.

O'Neil v. Vermont, 144 U.S. 323 (1892), 14, 65, 66, 67, 70, 80-81, 170, 189,
191.

O'Neill v. United States, 315 F. Supp. 1352 (D. Minn. 1970), 131, 213.

Osborn v. Manson, 359 F. Supp. 1107 (D. Conn. 1973), 129, 212.

Ownes v. Aldridge, 311 F. Supp. 667 (W.D. Okla. 1970), 213.

Oyler v. Boles, 368 U.S. 448 (1962), 78, 192.

Papachristou v. Jacksonville, 405 U.S. 156 (1973), 202.

Parker v. McKeithen, 330 F. Supp. 435 (E.D. La. 1971), 219.

Parker v. Municipal Judge of the City of Las Vegas, 83 Nev. 214, 427 P.2d 642
(1967), 103, 202.

Parson v. State, 432 S.W.2d 89 (Tex. Cr. App. 1968), 76.

Peacock Distillery Company v. Commonwealth, 25 Ky. L. 1778, 78 S.W. 893
(1904), 168.

Pearson v. Wimbish, 124 Ga. 701, 52 S.E. 751 (1905), 187.

Peek v. Ciccone, 288 F. Supp. 329 (W.D. Mo. 1968), 213.

People v. Adorno, 17 Puerto Rico 1059 (1911), 187.

People v. Anderson, 100 Cal. Rptr. 152, 6 Cal.3d 628, 493 P.2d 880 (1972), 11,
44-45, 47, 169, 181, 182.

People v. Anderson, 51 Cal. Rptr. 238, 64 Cal.2d 633, 414 P.2d 366 (1966), 44,
161, 181.

People v. Baum, 251 Mich. 187, 231 N.W. 95 (1930), 13, 91, 169.

People v. Betts, 254 N.Y.S. 786, 142 Misc. 240 (1932), 192.

People v. Blankenship, 16 Cal. App.2d 606, 61 P.2d 352 (1936), 57-58, 186.

People v. Borrero, 19 N.Y.2d 332, 280 N.Y.S.2d 109, 227 N.E.2d 18 (1967), 201.

People v. Bruinsma, 34 Mich. App. 167, 191 N.W.2d 108 (1971), 191.

People v. Chessman, 52 Cal.2d 467, 341 P.2d 679 (1959), 44, 61, 188.

People v. Clary, 72 Cal. 59, 13 P. 77 (1887), 69, 76, 190.

People v. Coleman, 145 Cal. 609, 79 P. 283 (1904), 192.

People v. Cook, 147 Mich. 127, 110 N.W. 514 (1907), 194.

People v. Cruz, 113 Cal. App. 519, 298 P. 556 (1931), 169, 170.

People v. Daugherty, 346 U.S. 827 (1953), 31, 176.

People v. Daugherty, 40 Cal.2d 876, 256 P.2d 911 (1953), 176.

People v. Davis, 27 Ill.2d 57, 188 N.W.2d 225 (1963), 100.

People v. Dixon, 400 Ill. 449, 81 N.E.2d 257 (1948), 77.

People v. Elliot, 272 Ill. 592, 112 N.E. 300 (1916), 169, 170, 194.

People ex rel. Bradley v. Illinois State Reformatory, 148 Ill. 413 36 N.E. 78 (1894), 82-83, 194.

People ex rel. Brown v. Johnston, 9 N.Y.2d 482, 174 N.E.2d 725, 215 N.Y.S.2d 44 (1961), 136, 214, 215.

People ex rel. Fallon v. Wright, 40 N.Y.S. 285, 7 App. Div. 185 (1896), 212.

People ex rel. Jackson v. Ruthazer, 339 U.S. 980 (1950), 218.

People ex rel. Jackson v. Ruthazer, 181 F.2d 588 (2d Cir. 1950), 218.

People ex rel. Jackson v. Ruthazer, 90 N.Y.S.2d 205 (1949), 143, 218.

People ex rel. Kemmler v. Durston, 119 N.Y.S. 569, 23 N.E. 6 (1890), 24.

People ex rel. Kemmler v. Durston, 55 Hun. 64, 7 N.Y.S. 813 (1889), 24, 168, 169, 173.

People v. Finley, 153 Cal. 59, 94 P. 248 (1908), 38.

People v. Frazier, 64 Cal. Rptr. 447 (1967), 104, 173, 203.

People v. Griffes, 13 Mich. App. 299, 164 N.W.2d 426 (1968), 104-105, 203.

People v. Hanrahan, 75 Mich. 611, 42 N.W. 1124 (1889), 187.

People v. Harmon, 54 Cal.2d 9, 351 P.2d 329, 4 Cal. Rptr. 161 (1960), 179.

People v. Hartung, 22 N.Y. 95 (1860), 22.

People v. Harwood, 286 Mich. 96, 281 N.W. 551 (1938), 170.

People v. Hoy, 3 Mich. App. 666, 143 N.W.2d 577 (1966), 101, 169.

People v. Huntley, 112 Mich. 569, 71 N.W. 178 (1897), 194.

People v. Illinois State Reformatory, 148 Ill. 413, 36 N.E. 78 (1894), 168, 190.

People v. Jones, 43 Ill. 2d 113, 251 N.E.2d 195 (1969), 105, 203.

People v. Kaganovitch, 146 N.Y.S.2d 565 (1955), 84.

People v. Kelley, 99 Mich. 82, 57 N.W. 1090 (1894), 76, 168, 199.

People v. Kemmler, 119 N.Y. 569, 24 N.E. 6 (1890), 23, 173.

People v. Knowles, 340 U.S. 879 (1950), 35-36, 177, 178.

People v. Knowles, 35 Cal.2d 175, 217 P.2d 1 (1950), 35, 177.

People v. Lopez, 81 Cal. App. 199, 253 P. 285 (1927), 91, 197.

People v. Lorentzen, 194 N.W.2d 827, 387 Mich. 167 (1972), 72-73, 191, 192.

People v. Morris, 80 Mich. 634, 45 N.W. 591 (1890), 168, 171, 192.

People v. Murray, 72 Mich. 10, 17 N.W. 29 (1888), 190.

People v. Oppenheimer, 156 Cal. 733, 106 P. 74 (1909), 38, 178.

People v. Potter, 1 Parker Cr. R. (N.Y.) 47, 1 Edm. Sel. Cas. 235 (1846), 89, 90, 197.

People v. Roberts, 64 Cal Rptr. 70 (1967), 104, 203.

People v. Rogers, 30 Mich. App. 582, 186 N.W.2d 840 (1971), 77.

People v. Sly, 180 Misc. 96, 39 N.Y.S.2d 474 (1942), 170.

People v. Smith, 94 Mich. 644 (1893), 76.

People v. Stanley, 47 Cal. 113 (1874), 75, 190, 192.

People v. Stevenson, 28 Mich. App. 538, 184 N.W.2d 541 (1970), 105, 203.

People v. Tanner, 3 Cal.2d 279, 44 P.2d 324 (1935), 35, 177.

People v. Thomas, 67 Cal. Rptr. 234 (1968), 106, 203.

People v. Vaughn, 78 Cal. Rptr. 186, 455 P.2d 122 (1969), 179.

People v. Webster, 92 Hun. 878, 36 N.Y.S. 995 (1895), 194.

People v. Wein, 50 Cal.2d 383, 326 P.2d 457 (1958), 35, 178.

People v. Whitney, 105 Mich. 622, 63 N.W. 765 (1895), 190.

People v. Wilkerson, 2 Utah 158 (1878), 22, 173.

People v. Williams, 4 Ill.2d 440, 123 N.E.2d 326 (1954), 77.

Pependrea v. United States, 275 F.2d 325 (9th Cir. 1960), 82.

Perez v. Brownell, 356 U.S. 44 (1958), 93, 95, 199.

Perkins v. State, 234 F. Supp. 333 (W.D. N.C. 1964), 85, 104, 203.

Perry v. United States, 209 F. Supp. 691 (W.D. Ark. 1962), 77.

Pervear v. Commonwealth, 72 U.S. (5 Wall.) 475 (1866), 170, 187, 190.

Pierce v. LaValle, 293 F.2d 233 (2d Cir. 1961), 206, 209.

Pineda v. State, 157 Tex. Cr. App. 609 (1952), 77.

Plain v. State, 60 Ga. (1878), 187.

Poindexter v. Woodson, 357 F. Supp. 443 (D. Kan. 1973), 120, 125, 208, 210.

Politano v. Politano, 146 Misc. 792, 262 N.Y.S. 802 (1933), 71-72, 191, 192.

Pope v. Daggett, 350 F.2d (10th Cir. 1965), 204.

Pope v. Hendricks, 326 F. Supp. 699 (E.D. Pa. 1971), 211.

Pope v. United States, 392 U.S. 651 (1968), 181.

Powell v. Hunter, 172 F.2d 330 (10th Cir. 1949), Ill.

Powell v. Texas, 392 U.S. 514 (1968), 101-102, 161, 169, 201, 202.

Press v. Pasadena Independent School District, 326 F. Supp. 550 (S.D. Tex. 1971), 139, 216.

Price v. Allgood, 369 F.2d 376 (5th Cir. 1966), 192.

Pulver v. State, 93 Idaho 687, 471 P.2d 74 (1970), 84.

Quattrone v. Nicholls, 210 F.2d 513 (1st Cir. 1954), 195.

Ralph v. Brough, 248 F. Supp. 334 (D. Md. 1965), 179.

Ralph v. Pepersack, 380 U.S. 925 (1965), 179.

Ralph v. Pepersack, 335 F.2d 128 (4th Cir. 1964), 179.

Ralph v. Pepersack, 218 F. Supp. 932 (D. Md. 1963), 179.

Ralph v. Pepersack, 203 F. Supp. 752 (D. Md. 1962), 179.

Ralph v. State, 226 Md. 480, 174 A.2d 163 (1961), 39.

Ralph v. Warden, 390 U.S. 992 (1968), 179, 180.

Ralph v. Warden, 438 F.2d 786 (4th Cir. 1970), 39-41, 43, 160, 179, 180, 181, 191.

Ralph v. Warden, 264 F. Supp. 528 (D. Md. 1967), 179.

Ramsey v. Ciccone, 310 F. Supp. 600 (W.D. Mo. 1970), 131-132, 213.

Raymond v. United States, 25 App. D.C. 555 (1905), 189.

Redding v. Pate, 220 F. Supp. 124 (N.D. Ill. 1963), 206, 214.

Rener v. Beto, 447 F.2d 20 (5th Cir. 1971), 76.

Reyes v. Hauck, 339 F. Supp. 195 (W.D. Tex. 1972), 132, 214.

Rhem v. McGrath, 326 F. Supp. 681 (S.D. N.Y. 1971), 156.

Rice v. Schmidt, 277 F. Supp. 811 (E.D. Wis. 1967), 206.

Richards v. Thurston, 424 F.2d 1281 (lst Cir. 1970), 216.

Richards v. Thurston, 304 F. Supp. 449 (D. Mass. 1969), 216.

Rinehart v. Brewer, 360 F. Supp. 105 (S.D. Iowa 1973), 215.

Rinker v. United States, 151 Fed. 755 (8th Cir. 1907), 190.

Rivers v. Royster, 360 F.2d 592 (4th Cir. 1966), 206.

Robards v. State, 37 Okla. Cr. 371, 259 P. 166 (1927), 176, 177.

Roberts v. Barbosa, 227 F. Supp. 20 (S.D. Cal. l964), 211.

Roberts v. Pegelow, 313 F.2d 548 (4th Cir. 1963), 211, 212, 213.

Roberts v. Pepersack, 256 F. Supp. 415 (D. Md. 1966), 132, 214.

Roberts v. Williams, 302 F. Supp. 972 (N.D. Miss. 1969), 147, 206, 219.

Robinson v. California, 370 U.S. 660 (1962), 11, 97-100, 101, 102, 103, 104,
    105, 107, 159, 171, 199.

Robinson v. Warden, 455 F.2d 1172 (4th Cir. 1972), 192.

Robison v. Miner and Haug, 68 Mich. 549, 37 N.W. 21 (1888), 85, 190, 195.

Rodriguez-Sandoval v. United States, 409 F.2d 529 (lst Cir. 1969), 135, 214,
    215.

Robers v. Bellei, 401 U.S. 815 (1971), 95.

Rosenberg v. Carroll, 99 F. Supp. 630 (S.D. N.Y. 1951), 61, 188.

Ruark v. Schooley, 211 F. Supp. 921 (D. Colo. 1962), 212.

Rudolph v. Alabama, 375 U.S. 889 (1963), 39, 179.

Rudolph v. State, 275 Ala. 115, 152 So.2d 662 (1963), 179.

Ruffin v. Commonwealth, 62 Va. 790 (1871), 204.

Rumler v. Board of School Trustees for Lexington County District No. 1 School,
    327 F. Supp. 729 (D. S.C. 1971), 139, 216.

Rush v. Cort, 372 U.S. 144 (1963), 199.

Salas v. State, 365 S.W.2d 174 (Tex. Cr. App. 1963), 201.

Sa Marion v. McGinnis, 253 F. Supp. 738 (W.D. N.Y. 1966), 206.

Sanders v. Waters, 199 F.2d 317 (10th Cir. 1952), 192.

Saucier v. State, 156 Tex. Cr. App. 301, 235 S.W.2d 903 (1950), 85.

Sawyer v. Sigler, 320 F. Supp. 690 (D. Neb. 1970), 133, 213, 214.

Schneider v. Ohio Youth Commission, 31 Ohio App.2d 225, 287 N.E.2d 633
    (1972), 139, 216.

Seale v. Manson, 326 F. Supp. 1375 (D. Conn. 1971), 215.

Seattle v. Hill, 435 P.2d 692 (Wash. 1967), 101.

Sewell v. Pegelow, 291 F.2d 196 (4th Cir. 1961), 113, 206, 209.

Shack v. State, 288 N.E.2d 155 (Ind. 1972), 61, 188.

Shanks v. Dupont, 28 U.S. (3 Pet.) 242 (1830), 198.

Shaw v. Beto, 318 F. Supp. 1215 (S.D. Tex. 1970), 136, 215.

Shepherd v. Hunter, 163 F.2d 872 (10th Cir. 1947), 203.

Siberry v. State, 149 Ind. 684, 47 N.E. 458 (1897), 168.

Siegel v. Ragen, 180 F.2d 785 (7th Cir. 1950), 111, 204, 206.

Siegel v. Ragen, 88 F. Supp. 996 (N.D. Ill. 1949), 170.

Sigmon v. United States, 110 F. Supp. 906 (W.D. Va. 1953), 204, 207.

Sills v. State, 472 S.W.2d 119 (Tex. Cr. App. 1971), 77.

Sims v. Balkcom, 220 Ga. 7, 136 S.E.2d 766 (1964), 179.

Sims v. Board of Education of Independent School District No. 22, 329 F.
    Supp. 678 (D. N.M. 1971), 138, 216.

Sinclair v. Henderson, 331 F. Supp. 1123 (E.D. La. 1971), 61, 188.

Skinner v. State *ex rel.* Williamson, 316 U.S. 535 (1942), 186.

Skinner v. State *ex rel.* Williamson, 189 Okla. 235, 115 P.2d 123 (1941), 58, 186.

Slaughter-House Cases, 83 U.S. (16 Wall.) 36 (1872), 170, 173.

Smith v. Swenson, 333 F. Supp. 1258 (W.D. Mo. 1971), 127.

Smith v. United States, 363 U.S. 846 (1960), 193.

Smith v. United States, 360 U.S. 1 (1959), 36, 178.

Smith v. United States, 273 F.2d 462 (10th Cir. 1959), 193.

Smoake v. Fritz, 320 F. Supp. 609 (S.D. N.Y. 1970), 209.

Snider v. Cunningham, 375 U.S. 889 (1963), 39, 179.

Snider v. Peyton, 356 F.2d 626 (4th Cir. 1966), 179.

Snow v Roche, 323 U.S. 788 (1944), 205, 209.

Snow v. Roche, 143 F.2d 718 (9th Cir. 1944), 204, 205, 209.

Soewapadji v. Wixon, 157 F.2d 289 (9th Cir. 1946), 87, 195.

Sostre v. McGinnis, 442 F.2d 178 (2d Cir. 1971), 115, 116, 207, 210, 212.

Sostre v. McGinnis, 334 F.2d 906 (2d Cir. 1964), 204, 206.

Sostre v. Rockefeller, 312 F. Supp. 863 (S.D. N.Y. 1970), 127, 206, 212.

Sostre v. Rockefeller, 309 F. Supp. 611 (S.D. N.Y. 1969), 127, 206, 212.

Southern Express Company v. Commonwealth, 92 Va. 59, 22 S.E. 809 (1895),
    170.

Spencer v. State, 132 Wis. 509, 112 N.W. 462 (1907), 61-62, 188, 190.

Startti v. Beto, 405 F.2d 858 (5th Cir. 1969), 211.

State v. Anderson, 280 Minn. 461, 159 N.W.2d 892 (1968), 104, 202.

State v. Apple, 121 N.C. 584, 28 S.E. 469 (1897), 187.

State v. Atkinson, 278 N.C. 168, 179 S.E.2d 410 (1971), 180.

State v. Baker, 58 S.C. 111, 36 S.E. 501 (1900), 91, 197.

State v. Barber, 278 N.C. 268, 179 S.E.2d 404 (1971), 180.

State v. Barton, 79 N.M. 70, 439 P.2d 719 (1968), 210.

State v. Becker, 3 S.D. 29, 51 N.W. 1018 (1892), 170, 171, 190.

State v. Berzaman, 10 Wash. 277, 38 P. 1037 (1894), 190.

State v. Blake, 157 N.C. 608, 72 S.E. 1080 (1911), 170.

State v. Borgstrom, 69 Minn. 508, 72 N.W. 799 (1897), 169.

State v. Brice, 214 N.C. 34, 197 S.E. 690 (1938),176.

State v. Bridges, 360 S.W.2d 648 (Mo. 1962), 100, 201.

State v. Bruno, 253 La. 669, 219 So.2d 490 (1969), 201.

State v. Burdette, 135 W. Va. 312, 63 S.E.2d 69 (1951), 174.

State v. Burrell, 106 Ariz. 100, 471 P.2d 712 (1970), 82.

State v. Burris, 194 Iowa 628, 190 N.W. 38 (1922), 22, 173.

State v. Butchek, 121 Ore. 141, 253 P. 367 (1927), 173.

State v. Cannon, 55 Del. 587, 190 A.2d 514 (1963), 56, 166, 185.

State v. Carpenter, 231 N.C. 229, 56 S.E.2d 713 (1949), 119, 208.

State v. Chance, 279 N.C. 643, 185 S.E.2d 227 (1971), 180.

State v. Colcord, 170 Minn. 504, 212 N.W. 735 (1927), 173.

State v. Crook, 253 La. 961 221 So.2d 473 (1969), 179.

State v. Custer, 240 Ore. 350, 401 P.2d 402 (1965), 193.

State v. Danforth, 3 Conn. 112 (1819), 194.

State v. Dickerson, 298 A.2d 761 (Del. 1973), 51, 184.

State v. Dixon, 238 Ore. 121 (1964), 84.

State v. Doughtie, 237 N.C. 368, 74 S.E.2d 922 (1953), 90, 91, 196, 197.

State v. Driver, 262 N.C. 92, 136 S.E.2d 208 (1964), 78, 213.

State v. Driver, 78 N.C. 423 (1878), 168, 191.

State v. Duff, 144 Iowa 142, 122 N.W. 829 (1909), 190, 192.

State v. Durham, 89 Tenn. 723, 18 S.W. 74 (1891), 187.

State v. Durston, 52 Iowa 635, 3 N.W. 678 (1879), 76.

State v. Eckenfels, 316 S.W.2d 532 (Mo. 1958), 84.

State v. Evans, 73 Idaho 50, 245 P.2d 788 (1952), 15, 171, 191.

State *ex rel.* Baldwin v. Superintendent, 192 Md. 712, 63 A.2d 323 (1949), 214.

State *ex rel.* Bissell v. Devore, 225 Iowa 815, 281 N.W. 740 (1938), 191.

State *ex rel.* Blouin v. Walker, 244 La. 699, 154 So.2d 368 (1963), 100, 169, 201.

State *ex rel.* Cole v. Tahash, 269 Minn. 1, 129 N.W.2d 903 (1964), 206.

State *ex rel.* Drexel v. Alvis, 153 Ohio 244, 91 N.E.2d 22 (1950), 193.

State *ex rel.* du Pont v. Ingram, 293 A.2d 289 (Del. 1972), 215.

State *ex rel.* Garvey v. Whitaker, 48 La. Ann. 527, 19 So. 457 (1896), 70, 81, 168, 191, 194.

State *ex rel.* Jacobs v. Warden, 190 Md. 755, 59 A.2d 753 (1948), 204, 214.

State *ex rel.* Larabee v. Barnes, 3 N.D. 319, 55 N.W. 883 (1893), 190, 192.

State *ex rel.* Nelson v. Smith, 114 Neb. 653, 209 N.W. 328 (1926), 62, 188.

State *ex rel.* Pingley v. Coiner, 186 S.E.2d 220 (W. Va. 1972), 156, 210, 211.

State *ex rel.* Renner v. Wright, 188 Md. 189, 51 A.2d 668 (1946), 204, 214.

State v. Fackler, 91 Wis. 418, 64 N.W. 1029 (1895), 194.

State v. Farrington, 141 N.C. 844, 53 S.E. 954 (1906), 187.

State v. Feilen, 70 Wash. 65, 126 P. 75 (1912), 57, 171, 186.

State v. Gamble, 390 U.S. 927 (1968), 179.

State v. Gamble, 249 S.C. 605, 155 S.E.2d 916 (1967), 179.

State v. Gedicke, 14 N.J.L. 86 (1881), 189.

State v. Gee Jon, 46 Nev. 418, 211 P. 676 (1923), 29-30, 31, 175, 176.

State v. Gillmore, 88 Kan. 835, 129 P. 1123 (1913), 187.

State v. Grahovac, 52 Haw. 527, 480 P.2d 148 (1971), 202.

State v. Griffin, 190 N.C. 133, 129 S.E. 410 (1925), 187.

State v. Gros, 208 La. 135, 23 So.2d 24 (1945), 187.

State v. Hall, 97 Iowa 400, 66 N.W. 725 (1896), 76, 190.

State v. Harold, 74 Ariz. 210, 246 P.2d 178 (1952), 193.

State v. Hatley, 110 N.C. 522, 14 S.E. 751 (1892), 90, 91, 196, 197.

State v. Hazen, 39 Iowa 648 (1874), 76, 190.

State v. Hodgson, 66 Vt. 134, 28 A. 1089 (1893), 170, 190.

State v. Hogan, 63 Ohio St. 202, 58 N.E. 572 (1900), 168, 187.

State v. Huffstetler, 213 S.C. 313, 49 S.E.2d 585 (1948), 187.

State v. James, 3 Ore. App. 539, 474 P.2d 779 (1970), 201.

State v. Jochim, 55 N.D. 313, 213 N.W. 484 (1927), 169.

State v. Jones, 200 La. 809, 9 So.2d 42 (1942), 174.

State v. Kasnett, 30 Ohio App.2d 77, 283 N.E.2d 636 (1972), 91, 197.

State v. Kearney, 8 N.C. 53 (1820), 55, 184.

State v. Kilpatrick, 206 Kan. 6, 439 P.2d 99 (1968), 179.

State v. Kimbrough, 212 S.C. 348, 46 S.E. 2d 273 (1948), 72, 187, 191, 192.

State v. Knight, 106 Minn. 371, 119 N.W. 56 (1908), 194.

State v. Lance, 149 N.C. 551 63 S.E. 198 (1908), 190.

State v. LePard, 270 N.C. 157, 153 S.E.2d 875 (1967), 187.

State v. LePitre, 54 Wash. 166, 103 P. 27 (1909), 192.

State v. Levy, 126 Mo. 554, 295 S.W. 703 (1895), 192.

State v. Longino, 109 Miss. 125, 67 So. 902 (1915), 191-192.

State v. McAfee, 198 N.C. 507, 152 S.E. 391 (1930), 197.

State v. McAfee, 189 N.C. 320, 127 S.E. 204 (1925), 197.

State v. McCauley, 15 Cal. 429 (1860), 168, 187.

State v. McNally, 152 Conn. 598, 211 A.2d 162 (1965), 82.

State v. Manuel, 20 N.C. 20 (1838), 168, 187.

State v. Margo, 40 N.J. 188, 191 A.2d 43 (1963), 100, 169, 201.

State v. Miller, 94 N.C. 901 (1886), 82, 194.

State v. Miller, 75 N.C. 73 (1876), 190.

State v. Mincher, 172 N.C. 895, 90 S.E. 429 (1916), 116, 207.

State v. Moore, 121 Mo. 514, 26 S.W. 345 (1894), 192.

State v. Myers, 261 La. 100, 259 So.2d 27 (1972), 41, 180.

State v. Myers, 6 Wash. App. 557, 494 P.2d 1015 (1972), 107, 203.

State v. Nance, 20 Utah2d 372, 438 P.2d 542 (1968), 77.

State v. Neuman, 108 W. Va. 642, 152 S.E. 195 (1930), 194.

State v. Nipper, 166 N.C. 272, 81 S.E. 164 (1914), 116, 207.

State v. O'Brien, 106 Vt. 97, 170 A. 98 (1934), 167.

State v. Painter, 135 W. Va. 106, 63 S.E.2d 86 (1950), 174.

State v. Peters, 78 N.M. 224, 430 P.2d 382 (1967), 194.

State v. Polson, 93 Ida. 912, 478 P.2d 292 (1971), 193.

State v. Price, 8 N.C. App. 94, 173 S.E.2d 644 (1970), 78.

State v. Pulley, 216 S.C. 552, 59 S.E.2d 155 (1950), 78.

State v. Reid, 106 N.C. 714, 11 S.E. 315 (1890), 168.

State v. Revis, 193 N.C. 192, 136 S.E. 346 (1927), 116, 207.

State v. Rodman, 58 Minn. 393, 59 N.W. 1098 (1894), 189.

State v. Rogers, 396 U.S. 1024 (1970), 179.

State v. Rogers, 275 N.C. 411, 168 S.E.2d 345 (1969), 179.

State v. Ross, 227 U.S. 150 (1913), 191.

State v. Ross, 55 Ore. 474, 106 P. 1022 (1910), 191.

State v. Ross, 55 Ore. 450, 104 P. 596 (1909), 168, 191.

State v. Sanders, 68 S.C. 138, 47 S.E. 55 (1903), 168.

State v. Scales, 212 S.C. 150, 46 S.E.2d 693 (1948), 193.

State v. Scott, 17 Ariz. App. 183, 496 P.2d 609 (1972), 211.

State v. Sheppard, 54 S.C. 178, 32 S.E. 146 (1899), 190.

State v. Smith, 1 Bailey 283 (S.C. 1829), 90.

State v. Smith, 5 Day (Conn.) 175, 5 Am. Dec. 132 (1811), 9, 80, 167, 188, 193.

State v. Smith and Lane, 10 Tenn. (2 Yerg.) 272 (1829), 86, 190, 195.

State v. Stubblefield, 157 Mo. 360, 58 S.W. 337 (1900), 168, 176, 177.

State v. Sullivan, 241 Wis. 276, 5 N.W.2d 798 (1942), 169, 194.

State v. Taylor, 82 Ariz. 289, 312 P.2d 162 (1957), 171.

State v. Teague, 215 Ore. 609, 336 P.2d 338 (1959), 82, 171.

State v. Thomas, 224 La. 431, 69 So.2d 738 (1953), 76, 170.

State v. Tomassi, 75 N.J.L. 739, 69 A. 214 (1908), 26, 60, 171, 174, 188.

State v. Troutman, 50 Idaho 673, 299 P. 668 (1931), 186.

State v. Tyson, 223 N.C. 492, 27 S.E. 113 (1943), 191.

State v. Vale, 252 La. 1056, 215 So.2d 811 (1968), 193.

State v. Van Wye, 136 Mo. 227, 37 S.W. 938 (1896), 190.

State v. Waddell, 194 S.E.2d 19 (N.C. 1973), 51, 184.

State v. White, 44 Kan. 514, 25 P. 33 (1890), 169, 187, 189.

State v. Williams, 12 Mo. App. 415 (1882), 76, 187.

State v. Williams, 77 Mo. 310 (1883), 82, 168, 169, 171, 190, 194.

State v. Williams 40 S.C. 373, 19 S.E. 5 (1894), 187.

State v. Wishom, 416 S.W.2d 921 (Mo. 1967), 193.

State v. Woodward, 68 W. Va. 66, 69 S.E. 385 (1910), 171.

State v. Youman, 66 N.D. 204, 263 N.W. 477 (1935), 169.

Storti v. Commonwealth, 178 Mass. 549, 60 N.E. 210 (1901), 26, 60, 174, 188.

Stoutenburgh v. Frazier, 16 App. D.C. 229 (1900), 11, 97, 169.

Stroud v. Swope, 187 F.2d 850 (9th Cir. 1951), 111, 203, 204.

Sturtevant v. Commonwealth, 158 Mass. 598, 33 N.E. 648 (1893), 188, 192.

Sullivan v. Ciccone, 311 F. Supp. 456 (W.D. Mo. 1970), 131, 213.

Sutton v. People, 145 Ill, 279, 34 N.E. 420 (1893), 168, 190.

Sutton v. Settle, 302 F.2d 286 (8th Cir. 1962), 132, 209, 213, 214.

Swanson v. McGuire, 188 F. Supp. 112 (N.D. Ill. 1960), 204.

Sweeney v. United States, 353 F.2d 10 (10th Cir. 1965), 201.

Sweeney v. Woodall, 344 U.S. 86 (1952), 14, 170, 218.

Tabor v. Hardwick, 224 F.2d 526 (5th Cir. 1955), 203.
Talley v. Stephens, 247 F. Supp. 683 (E.D. Ark. 1965), 117, 132, 206, 208, 214, 219.
Tarlton v. Clark, 441 F.2d 384 (5th Cir. 1971), 215.
Taylor v. State, 251 Ind. 236, 236 N.E. 825 (1968), 84.
Territory v. Ketchum, 10 N.M. 718, 65 P. 169 (1901), 33-34, 171, 176.
The John and Winthrop, 182 Fed. 380 (9th Cir. 1910), 62, 188.
Thogmartin v. Moseley, 313 F. Supp. 158 (D. Kan. 1970), 135.
Thompson v. Cavell, 158 F. Supp. 19 (W.D. Pa. 1957), 209.
Thompson v. State, 251 S.C. 593, 164 S.E.2d 760 (1968), 77.
Thompson v. State, 91 Tex. Cr. 234, 237 S.W. 926 (1922), 34, 177.
Tijerina v. Ciccone, 324 F. Supp. 1265 (W.D. Mo. 1971), 213.
Tomlinson v. Commonwealth, 261 Ky. 186, 87 S.W.2d 376 (1935), 37, 178.
Toomer v. State, 112 Md. 285, 76 A. 118 (1910), 168, 177.
Trevino v. State, 380 S.W.2d 118 (Tex. Cr. App. 1963), 76.
Trezza v. Brush, 142 U.S. 160 (1891), 188.
Trop v. Dulles, 356 U.S. 86 (1958), 13, 15, 40, 43, 92-95, 117, 161, 170, 171, 181, 198.
Trop v. Dulles, 239 F.2d 527 (2d Cir. 1956), 93, 198.
Ughbanks v. Armstrong, 208 U.S. 481 (1908), 170.
United States v. Collins, 25 Fed. Cas. 545 (Dist. Ct. R.I. 1854), 184.
United States v. Coon, 385 U.S. 873 (1966), 178.
United States v. Coon, 360 F.2d 550 (8th Cir. 1966), 178.
United States v. Coon, 242 F. Supp. 483 (N.D. Iowa 1965), 178.
United States v. Cruikshank, 92 U.S. 542 (1875), 170, 173.
United States v. Edmo, 456 F.2d 240 (9th Cir. 1972), 85.
United States ex rel. Atterbury v. Ragen, 353 U.S. 964 (1957), 204, 206, 209.
United States ex rel. Atterbury v. Ragen, 237 F.2d 953 (7th Cir. 1956), 204, 206, 209.
United States ex rel. Binion v. United States Marshall, 292 F.2d 494 (9th Cir. 1961), 205.
United States ex rel. Binion v. United States Marshall, 188 F. Supp. 905 (D. Nev. 1960), 205.
United States ex rel. Bracey v. Grenoble, 356 F. Supp. 673 (E.D. Pa. 1973), 120, 208.
United States ex rel. Clegget v. Pate, 229 F. Supp. 818 (N.D. Ill. 1964), 209.
United States ex rel. Darrah v. Brierly, 290 F. Supp. 960 (E.D. Pa. 1968), 82.
United States ex rel. Eggleston v. Snow, 219 F. Supp. 417 (S.D. N.Y. 1963), 170.
United States ex rel. Gallagher v. Daggett, 326 F. Supp. 387 (D. Minn. 1971), 135, 214.
United States ex rel. Holland v. Maroney, 299 F. Supp. 262 (W.D. Pa. 1969), 210, 211.

United States *ex rel.* Keen v. Mazurkiewicz, 306 F. Supp. 483 (E.D. Pa. 1969), 125, 211.
United States *ex rel.* Knight v. Ragen, 337 F.2d 425 (7th Cir. 1964), 205, 213.
United States *ex rel.* Maricial v. Fay, 355 U.S. 915 (1958), 205.
United States *ex rel.* Maricial v. Fay, 247 F.2d 662 (2d Cir. 1957), 113, 205, 206.
United States *ex rel.* Miller v. Twomey, 333 F. Supp. 1352 (D.C. Ill. 1971), 115, 126, 207, 211, 212.
United States *ex rel.* Mosher v. LaValle, 321 F. Supp. 127 (N.D. N.Y. 1970), 122, 206, 209.
United States *ex rel.* Schuster v. Herold, 410 F.2d 1071 (2d Cir. 1969), 213.
United States *ex rel.* Swanson v. Reincke, 344 F.2d 260 (2d Cir. 1965), 201.
United States *ex rel.* Verde v. Case, 326 F. Supp. 701 (E.D. Pa. 1971), 210.
United States *ex rel.* Wakeley v. Pennsylvania, 247 F. Supp. 7 (E.D. Pa. 1965), 204, 206.
United States *ex rel.* Westbrook v. Randolph, 259 F.2d 215 (7th Cir. 1958), 205.
United States *ex rel.* Weybrauch v. Parker, 268 F. Supp. 785 (M.D. Pa. 1967), 205.
United States *ex rel.* Wolfersdorf v. Johnston, 317 F. Supp. 66 (S.D. N.Y. 1970), 106, 136, 203, 215.
United States v. Fitzgerald, 466 F.2d 377 (D.C. Cir. 1972), 213.
United States v. Fleish, 90 F. Supp. 273 (E.D. Mich. 1949), 82.
United States v. Holman, 436 F.2d 863 (9th Cir. 1970), 193.
United States v. Jackson, 390 U.S. 570 (1968), 43.
United States v. Jones, 207 F.2d 785 (5th Cir. 1953), 208.
United States v. Ju Toy, 198 U.S. 253 (1905), 89, 196.
United States v. Kellerman, 432 F.2d 371 (10th Cir. 1971), 193.
United States v. Pacheco, 18 Phil. 399 (1911), 191.
United States v. Pardue, 354 F. Supp. 1377 (D. Conn. 1973), 106-107, 203.
United States v. Rosenberg, 344 U.S. 838 (1952), 37, 178.
United States v. Rosenberg, 195 F.2d 583 (2d Cir. 1952), 36, 178.
United States v. Royall, 27 F. Cas. 906 (No. 16, 202) (C.C. D.C. 1829), 59, 187.
Upchurch v. State, 454 P.2d 112 (Haw. 1969), 207.
Veals v. Ciccone, 281 F. Supp. 1017 (W.D. Mo. 1968), 213.
Vick v. State, 453 P.2d 342 (Alaska 1969), 169, 202.
Walker v. Blackwell, 411 F.2d 23 (5th Cir. 1969), 207.
Walker v. Blackwell, 360 F.2d 66 (5th Cir. 1966), 114, 207.
Walker v. State, 186 Md. 440, 47 A.2d 47 (1946), 38, 179.
Walker v. Taylor, 338 F.2d 945 (10th Cir. 1964), 213.
Warden v. Ralph, 408 U.S. 942 (1972), 180.
Ware v. Estes, 409 U.S. 1027 (1972), 138, 215, 216.
Ware v. Estes, 458 F.2d 1360 (5th Cir. 1972), 138, 215, 216.
Ware v. Estes, 328 F. Supp. 657 (N.D. Tex. 1971), 137-138, 215.
Washington v. Lee, 390 U.S. 333 (1968), 113, 206.

Washington v. Rodriguez, 82 N.M. 428, 483 P.2d 309 (1971), 194.

Washington v. State, 2 Md. App. 633, 236 A.2d (1967), 84.

Wayne County Jail Inmates v. Wayne County Board of Commissioners, Civil No.173-217, Cir. Ct. Wayne County, Mich., May 18, 1971, 219.

Weber v. Commonwealth, 303 Ky. 56, 196 S.W.2d 465 (1946), 191, 192.

Weems v. United States, 217 U.S. 349 (1910), 9, 15, 40, 62, 65-71, 81, 121, 159, 167, 171, 176, 182, 188, 189, 221.

Weincke v. State, 34 Neb. 14, 51 N.W. 307 (1892), 168.

Werner v. State, 44 Ark. 122 (1884), 184.

Wessling v. Bennett, 410 F.2d 205 (8th Cir. 1969), 192.

Westbrook v. State, 133 Ga. 578, 66 S.E. 788 (1909), 207.

Westley v. Rossi, 305 F. Supp. 706 (D. Minn. 1969), 216.

Wheeler v. Glass, 473 F.2d 983 (7th Cir. 1973), 119, 208, 213.

Wheeler v. Goodman, 306 F. Supp. 58 (W.D. N.C. 1969), 104.

Wheeler v. Goodman, 298 F. Supp. 935 (W.D. N.C. 1967), 202.

White v. State, 495 S.W.2d 903 (Tex. Cr. App. 1973), 76.

Whitten v. State, 47 Ga. 297 (1872), 168, 169, 186, 190.

Wilkerson v. Utah, 99 U.S. 130 (1879), 22-23, 168, 169, 171, 173.

Wilkinson v. McManus, 214 N.W.2d 671 (Minn. 1974), 215.

Williams v. Field, 416 F.2d 483 (9th Cir. 1969), 219.

Williams v. Patterson, 389 F.2d 374 (10th Cir. 1968), 213.

Williams v. State, 125 Ark. 287, 188 S.W. 826 (1916), 16, 188.

Williams v. State, 91 Neb. 605, 136 N.W. 1011 (1912), 194.

Williams v. State, 6 Tex. App. 147 (1879), 190.

Williams v. Steele, 344 U.S. 822 (1952), 209.

Williams v. Steele, 194 F.2d 32 (8th Cir. 1952), 204, 205, 209.

Wilson v. Kelley, 294 F. Supp. 1005 (N.D. Ga. 1968), 60, 187, 218.

Winsley v. Walsh, 321 F. Supp. 523 (C.D. Cal. 1971), 125.

Winston v. United States, 374 U.S. 150 (1963), 114, 207.

Winston v. United States, 305 F.2d 253 (2d Cir. 1962), 114, 207.

Witherspoon v. Illinois, 391 U.S. 510 (1968), 43.

Woodhaus v. Virginia, 487 F.2d 889 (4th Cir. 1973), 221.

Workman v. Commonwealth, 429 S.W.2d 374 (Ky. Ct. App. 1968), 72, 86, 191, 192, 195.

Workman v. Commonwealth, 309 Ky. 117, 216 S.W.2d 45 (1948), 176, 178.

Wright v. McMann, 409 U.S. 885 (1972), 210.

Wright v. McMann, 460 F.2d 126 (2d Cir. 1972), 210.

Wright v. McMann, 387 F.2d 519 (2d Cir. 1967), 123, 206, 207, 210.

Wright v. McMann, 321 F. Supp. 127 (N.D. N.Y. 1970), 123, 206, 210.

Wright v. McMann, 257 F. Supp. 739 (N.D. N.Y. 1966), 123, 210.

Young v. State, 31 Tex. Cr. Rptr. 24, 19 S.W. 431 (1892), 190.

Zeigler v. Riley, 67 Misc.2d 82, 323 N.Y.S.2d 589 (1971), 215.

Index

Index

Abortion, 33, 73
Act of George II, 60
Addicts. *See* Narcotics
Adultery, 76
Alcoholism, 13, 99, 107, 162; status of, 101-102. *See also* Drunkenness
Alimony, nonpayment of, 71
Allen, Judge, 221n
Alvey, Judge, 97
Andrews, William, 4
Arson, 33, 34, 51, 69, 76, 160
Articles of Confederation, 6
Articles of War, 22
Asimow, Michael R., 99
Assault, 37-38, 41, 68, 76, 77, 82, 84, 91, 115, 126, 160; by a life prisoner, 33, 35, 37-38
Atomic Energy Act, 33

Baldwin, Simon E., 55
Balick, Jacob, 29
Banishment, 13, 87-92, 161, 165n, 197n; as condition of pardon, 88, 90; as condition of release, 89-90; as public policy, 13, 90-92; as punishment, 89; by statute, 88
Bank Robbery Act, 43
Barnes, Harry E., 88
Battery, 52, 84
Beating, 120, 172n
Becker, Judge, 131, 132
Becker, Tracy C., 24
Bedau, Hugo Adam, 33
Begging, 97, 99
Beheading, 4, 172n
Biggs, Judge, 142
Bill of Attainder, 88, 92
Bill of Rights, American 5, 7, 13, 14, 59, 67, 142
Bill of Rights, English, 3, 5, 7, 48, 65, 159
Bishop, Joel, 69
Black, Justice, 37, 101
Black United Front, 126
Blackjacks. *See* Whipping
Blackmun, Harry A., 39, 47, 48, 51, 117, 118
Blatchford, Justice, 24, 80
Blowing from a cannon's mouth, 10
Boiling, 4, 10, 172n

Bombing, 106
Bonynge, Justice, 72
Boreman, Justice, 22
Branding, 4
Bread-and-water diets. *See* Diets, restricted
Breaking and entering, 77, 78
Breaking on the wheel, 4, 10, 24, 58, 148, 172n
Brennan, Justice, 15, 16, 17, 39, 46, 47, 48, 49, 50, 102, 160
Brewer, Justice, 14, 65, 89
Brown, Judge, 125
Bryan, Judge, 95, 101
Bug-out rooms. *See* Solitary confinement
Burger, Warren, 5, 48, 50
Burglar tools, possession of, 78
Burglary, 33, 51, 72, 76, 78, 82, 103, 187n
Burning: at the stake, 4, 10, 24, 58, 166n, 172n; of women, 3, 4
Burton, Justice, 14, 28, 94
Burying alive, 126, 172n
Butzner, Judge, 40

Cadena temporal, 62, 66
California Rehabilitation Center, 100
Campbell, James, 71
Capital punishment, 11, 160-161; aggravating and mitigating circumstances, 51-52; challenged as excessive, 33-42; challenged as per se cruel and unusual, 43-54; goals of, 44, 45, 47; methods of inflicting, 19-32, 174n
Carnal knowledge, 52
Carter, Judge, 129, 144
Carter, Justice, 31, 35
Castration, 10, 55, 187n
Cates, Justice, 137
Cat-o-nine tails. *See* Whipping
Catron, Justice, 86
Chain gangs, 59, 141-144, 162, 187n, 188n
Chaining, 62, 66, 118-119, 162
Checks: passing forged, 77; writing without sufficient funds, 77, 79
Childs, Judge, 23
Chinaman's cue, the cutting of, 62
Chinese toilets. *See* Solitary confinement
Chinese water torture, 148

Christenberry, Judge, 146, 155
Civil Rights Act of 1871, 113, 150
Clark, Justice, 94, 98, 99
Clay, Chief Justice, 37
Clifford, Justice, 22, 23
Close confinement units. *See* Restricted
   confinement
Coleman, Justice, 29, 31
Collar of torment, 4
Common scold, 58, 59
Conjugal visitation, 136, 215n
Constitutional Convention, 6
Constitutional conventions, 5-7
Continental Congress, 6
Control cells. *See* Restricted confinement
Control units. *See* Restricted confinement
Conway, Justice, 135
Corporeal punishment, 4, 5, 19-63 passim,
   116, 117, 118, 137, 138, 143, 160, 161,
   166n
Counterfeiting, 80
Crank telephone, 119
Craven, Judge, 79
Crime against nature, 52
Cruel and unusual punishment: early history,
   3-8; early judicial interpretation, 9-10;
   recent judicial interpretation, 9-17
Crucifixion, 10
Cucking stool. *See* Ducking stool

Dark cell dungeon. *See* Solitary confinement
Day, Judge, 24
Day, Justice, 66
Death penalty. *See* Capital punishment
Death row, 61
de Blanc, Bertrand, 27
Declaration of Independence, 21
Declaration of Rights of Florida, 72
Delinquency, contributing to, 84
Denationalization. *See* Expatriation
Deportation, 87, 91
Desecration of a grave, 33
Desertion, 93, 187n
Destierro, 88
Deterrence, 44, 45, 47, 48
Diamond, Judge, 145, 152
Diets, restricted, 161, 162; administrative
   imposition of, 120, 125, 130; statutory
   imposition of, 61-62, 188n
Disbarment, 86
Disembowelling, 10
Dishonorable discharge, 93, 94
Dismemberment, 10, 165n
Disorderly conduct, 76, 98, 103
Disorderly house. *See* Prostitution
Disparate sentences. *See* Unequal sentences

Disproportionate punishments. *See* Excessive
   punishments
Dissection, 3
Double jeopardy, 75, 80
Douglas, Justice, 14, 28, 39, 46, 50, 98, 101,
   102, 103, 171n
Draft card mutilation, 78
Draper, Justice, 104
Drawing and quartering, 4, 10, 166n, 172n
Dress codes. *See* Personal appearance codes
Drowning, 172n
Drugs. *See* Narcotic addiction, narcotic
   offenses
Drunkenness, 99; common drunk, 97; drunk
   driving, 84; in public, 78, 101. *See also*
   Alcoholism
Dry cell or room. *See* Solitary confinement
Ducking stool, 4, 58, 59
Due process clause, 14, 15, 25
Dueling, 85
Dung cart, 4
Dwight, Charles C., 24
Dynamiting, 33, 52

Eagen, Justice, 149, 156
Earle, Alice, 5
Ears: cut off 4, 166n; nailed, 166n
Eastland, James O., 49
Edward the Confessor, Laws of, 3
Edward VI, 4
Eisele, Judge, 146, 147, 148, 156
Electrocution, 10, 11, 21, 23-29, 160, 174n
Elkington, Justice, 104
Embezzlement, 86
Engine of correction. *See* Ducking stool
Enhanced punishment statutes. *See* Habitual
   offender statutes
Enloe, Robert, 99
Escape, 82, 126, 127, 142
Espionage, 33, 36-37, 160
Espionage Act, 36
Eubanks, Judge, 138
Excessiveness, doctrine of, 63-86
Excessive punishments, 3, 5, 13, 121-122,
   150, 159, 161, 167n, 187n, 203n
Exclusion, 87
Exile, 88, 90
Expatriation, 13, 92-95, 161
Ex post facto clauses, 75
Expulsion. *See* Deportation

Farber, Robert, 153
Federal Bureau of Narcotics and Dangerous
   Drugs, 134
Federal Bureau of Prisons, 112
Feinberg, Judge, 212n
Fellman, David, 70

Field, Judge, 62
Field, Justice, 14, 65, 66, 70, 80, 81
Fifth Amendment, 80, 139
Finnegan, Judge, 111
First Amendment, 136, 139
Flag: defiling of, 91; insulting of, 78
Flaying alive, 172n
Flogging. *See* Whipping
Foley, Judge, 122, 123
Forcing a woman to marry, 33
Foreman, Judge, 129
Forfeiture: of civil rights, 85-86; of licenses,
    84-85; of payment allowances, 93
Forgery, 65, 76, 77, 79, 82
Fortas, Justice, 101, 102
Fourteenth Amendment, 13, 14, 15, 25, 39,
    50, 65, 98, 104, 117, 120, 122, 132, 133
    137, 139, 142, 143, 144, 146, 159
Fourth Amendment, 136
Frank, Judge, 36, 37
Frankel, Judge, 106
Frankfurter, Justice, 14, 28, 29, 94
Fraud, 76, 81, 82, 187n
Froman, Judge, 143
Fuller, Chief Justice, 10, 25, 66, 75

Gallows. *See* Hanging
Gambling, 85, 97, 104; convicted of, 86;
    offenses, 77
Gaseous asphyxiation, 11, 21, 29-31, 160
Gauntlets, running of, 120, 172n
Gerry, Elbridge (founding father), 166n
Gerry, Elbridge, 25
Gibbeting, 3, 4, 10, 24, 166n, 167n
Goldberg, Justice, 39, 150
Good time, 126, 131, 213n
Grant, Judge, 118, 124
Grooming regulations. *See* Personal appear-
    ance codes
Guards, 142, 147, 148, 151, 154-155
Guillotine, 25

Habitual offenders, 99; punishment of, 56;
    statutes, 75-79, 161
Hair cutting. *See* Personal appearance codes
Hale, Justice, 101
Haley, John H., 153
Hammer, Justice, 143
Handcuffing. *See* Chaining
Hands-off doctrine, 11, 111-112, 113, 115,
    117, 120, 125, 130, 131, 132, 135, 138,
    150, 160
Hanging, 10, 11, 21-22, 23, 24, 25, 26, 31,
    33, 160, 176n
Hanging in chains. *See* Gibbeting
Hard labor, 59-60, 66, 93, 161, 218n
Harlan, Justice (grandfather), 14, 65, 66

Harland, Justice (grandson), 15, 94, 101
Harris, Judge, 117
Harrison Act, 80
Hartmann, Robert, 30
Hatch, Charles, 23
Henley, Judge, 117, 132, 151, 152, 153
Henry, Patrick, 6
Hill, David B., 23
Hippies, 104
Hole. *See* Solitary confinement
Holmes, Justice, 26, 57, 71, 167n
Holohan (warden), 176n
Homosexuality, 104-105, 107, 119, 161, 162
Honeycutt, H.A., 31
Hospitals: Alabama Medical and Diagnostic
    Center, 134; Iowa Security Medical Facil-
    ity, 133; Matteawan State Hospital (New
    York), 106; Nevada State Hospital, 105;
    United States Medical Center (Springfield,
    Missouri), 106, 131, 132, 135, 136
House Judiciary Committee, 49
Humane Death Bill, 29

Incorporation of Eighth Amendment, 13-15,
    159
Incorporeal punishments, 5, 63-109 passim,
    160-161
Increased sentence statutes. *See* Habitual
    offender statutes
Indecent exposure, 104
Indenturing, 88
Indeterminate sentences, 81-83, 84, 161
Insanity. *See* Mental illness
Insurrection, 33
Isolation units. *See* Restricted confinement

Jails, 144-151, 162; Central Jail (Los
    Angeles), 97; City Jail of Anchorage, 145;
    Cook County Jail (Chicago), 146;
    Jefferson County Jail (Kentucky), 221n;
    Lucas County Jail (Ohio), 148, 156;
    Manhattan House of Detention for Men
    (New York), 156; Minneapolis Work
    House (Minnesota), 104; New York City
    Women's House of Detention, 128;
    Oreleans Parish Prison (Louisiana), 146;
    Pulaski County Jail (Arkansas), 146, 148;
    St. Louis Jail (Missouri), 118, 150
Jefferson, Thomas, 6
Johnson, Judge, 134
Justice, Judge, 118, 124, 136
Juvenile detention facilities, 155; Boys
    Training School (Rhode Island), 124;
    Gatesville (Texas), 118; Indiana Boy's
    School, 118; Manida (New York), 155;
    Mountain View (Texas), 118
Juveniles, 123-124, 136, 221n

Katkin, Daniel, 78
Kaufman, Irving R., 36, 119, 128
Keady, Judge, 125, 154
Kennedy, Edward, 49
Kidnapping, 33, 35-36, 43, 52, 106, 160
Kidnapping Act, 36
Kiley, Judge, 133
King Alfred, 159
Kleindienst, Richard G., 49
Kleptomaniacs, 99

Larceny, 76, 78, 82
Lasker, Judge, 123, 136, 155
Laurence, John, 21
Lead, pouring on, 172n
Lee, Richard Henry, 6
Leg irons, 142, 143
Leg picks. See Leg irons
Lethal gas. See Gaseous asphyxiation
Life without parole, 86
Lipscomb, Justice, 55
Liquor: concealing of, 72; possession of, 62,
　131; selling of, 65, 80, 84-85 , 145, 187n
Littleton, Justice, 60
Lockwood, Justice, 121
Los Alamos Project, 36
Lottery, 77, 79, 86
Lynching, 33

McAlister, Justice, 31
McCafferty, James A., 33
McKenna, Justice, 15, 66, 67, 71
Mackle, Barbara Jane, 126
McVicar, Judge, 141
Madison, James, 5, 7
Magna Carta, 3
Magrath, Joseph, 69
Manacles. See Leg irons
Manslaughter, 65, 73, 76, 84
Marijuana. See Narcotic offenses
Marshall, Justice, 46, 47, 101, 171n
Mason, George, 5, 166n, 167n
Massachusetts Body of Liberties, 4, 159
Massachusetts Declaration of Rights, 26
Matthews, Judge, 94, 121
Maximum security units. See Restricted
　confinement
Mazzatello. See Beating
Medical treatment, 119, 131-135, 147, 148-
　149, 154-155, 162, 214n
Mental defectives. See Mental illness
Mental illness, 44, 99, 105-107, 123, 136,
　161, 162, 214n
Merhige, Judge, 130, 209n
Model Penal Code, 40
Moody, Justice, 189n
Moral turpitude, 86, 103

Morrison, R.S., 26
Mosk, Stanley, 171n
Multiple offender statutes. See Habitual
　offender statutes
Multiple sentences in single prosecutions,
　80-81, 161
Murder, 33, 42, 51, 52, 77, 82, 84, 86, 106
Murphy, Christian, 3
Murphy, Justice, 14, 28
Mutilation, 4, 10

Narcotic addiction, 13, 97-100, 103, 106,
　161, 162
Narcotic Drug Act, 86
Narcotic offenses: possession of, 16, 80, 100;
　sale of marijuana, 72, 76, 82; selling
　generally, 73, 80, 82, 86, 98; selling to a
　minor, 33. See also Medical treatment
National Commission of Reform of Federal
　Criminal Laws, 40
National Firearms Act, 82
Newman, Judge, 129
Nixon, Richard M., 49
Nonintervention. See Hands-off doctrine
Northrop, Judge, 132
Northwest Territory, 6

O'Brien, Justice, 24
Outlawry, Justice, 88

Paddling, 137-138
Paine, Andrew, 4
Pandering, 103
Parliament, 3, 4, 88
Parole revocation, 131
Peckham, Justice, 89
Penitentiaries and prison farms, 151-155,
　162; Arkansas State (Cummins and
　Tucker), 128, 132, 151, 152, 153;
　Atmore-Holman Complex (Alabama),
　134, 145; Attica State Prison (New York),
　119; Camp Hill (Pennsylvania), 120;
　Central Prison (North Carolina), 30;
　Clinton State Prison (New York), 123;
　Connecticut Correctional Institution
　(Somers), 124; Danbury (Connecticut),
　106; Federal Penitentiary (Atlanta), 135;
　Federal Penitentiary (Sandstone, Minne-
　sota), 135; Federal Penitentiary (Terre
　Haute, Indiana), 135; Folsom Prison
　(California), 37; Green Haven (New York),
　127; Holmesburg Prison (Pennsylvania),
　149; Illinois State (Joliet), 126; Kansas
　State, 125; Kilby (Alabama), 137; Maples-
　ville (Alabama), 143; Mississippi State,
　125, 149, 153-155; Moundsville (Virginia),
　156; New Haven Correctional Center

(Connecticut), 129; Richmond County Prison Farm (Georgia), 143; San Quentin (California), 38, 57, 129; Sing Sing (New York), 61; Soledad (California), 122; Tennessee State Prison, 61

Penn, William, 59

Perjury, 33, 52, 65, 79, 120

Personal appearance codes, 125, 136, 138-139, 162, 215n

Petition of Right, 3

Pettine, Judge, 124, 155

Phebe, Hanford A., 55

Picks. *See* Leg irons

Pillory, 5, 166n

Pillorying, 4, 58, 119

Piracy, 33

Plants, destroying of, 70, 81

Poe, Edgar Allen, 30

Poisoning, 172n

Powell, Justice, 48, 51

Pressing, 4, 165n, 172n

Prison conditions, 141-156

Prison rules and practices, 111-140, 160, 162

Prison transfer, 135-136, 162

Prisons. *See* Penitentiaries and prison farms

Privileges and immunities clause, 13, 14, 25, 65

Proportionality. *See* Excessive punishments

Prostitution, 77, 89-90, 97, 99, 103, 104-105, 107, 161, 162

Public penance, 5

Punitive segregation. *See* Restricted confinement

Pyromaniacs, 99

Quagmire, pushed into, 172n

Quartering. *See* Drawing and quartering

Quinn, Justice, 101

Racks, 167n

Radzinowicz, Leon, 3

Rape, 33, 39-41, 51, 52, 57, 72, 76, 77, 84, 86, 160, 161

Recidivist statutes. *See* Habitual offender statutes

Reed, Justice, 14

Rehnquist, Justice, 47

Remedies for relief, 112-115; Civil Rights Act of 1871, 113; contempt proceedings, 114; Federal Tort Claims Act, 114; habeas corpus, 112-113, 122, 141; injunction, 119, 122, 124, 125; mandamus, 114

Restricted confinement, 120-130, 152, 155

Rioting, 68, 120

Robbery, 33-34, 37, 41, 69, 76, 77, 82, 83, 84, 106, 160, 187n

Robinson, Calvin E., 99

Robinson doctrine, 101, 106

Rock, throwing from, 172n

Rolph, Governor, 86

Rose (cook), 4

Ross, Judge, 133

Rush, Benjamin, 21

Rutledge, Justice, 14, 28

Sanctuary and abjuration, 87-88, 92, 197n

Santa Rita Rehabilitation Center (California), 150

Scarlet letter, 5

Schatz, Norman, 29

Seals, Judge, 125

Segregated confinement, 115

Segregated confinement units. *See* Restricted confinement

Segregation wings. *See* Restricted confinement

Senate Judiciary Committee, 49

Sex offenders and offenses, 55, 77, 99, 104-105, 152

Sexual delinquent person, 105

Shackles. *See* leg irons

Shackling. *See* Chaining

Sherman, Roger, 166n

Shooting, 10, 11, 21, 22-23, 160, 187n

Shrady (doctor), 25

Sixth Amendment, 47

Slap jack. *See* Whipping

Slittings, 10, 172n

Smith (warden), 176n

Smuggling, 115

Sobeloff, Judge, 113

Sodomy, 77, 84, 104, 105

Solitary confinement, 11, 38, 68, 113, 114, 115, 161, 208n; administrative imposition of, 120-126, 162; statutory imposition of, 60-61

Spearing, 172n

Speer, Judge, 119

Spitzka, E.A., 26

Spitzka, E.C., 25

Stanley, Judge, 135

Star Camber, 3

Starving, 172n

Status offenses, 11

Status statutes, 97-108, 161

Stealing, 80, 83, 99

Stephenson, Justice, 91

Sterilization, 11, 17, 55-58, 99, 161

Stewart, Justice, 46, 49, 50, 98, 102, 160, 171n

Stocks, 5

Stolen property, receiving, 76, 82

Stoning, 172n

Strangling, 10, 172n

Straps. *See* Whipping
Strip cell or room. *See* Solitary confinement
Suicide, 44
Suspicious person, 97
Sweatboxes, 142

Tappan, Paul W., 79
Taylor, Judge, 137
Taylor, Justice, 55
Tearing to death, 172n
Teeter board, 119
Teeters, Negley K., 21
Texas Youth Council, 155
Theft, 84, 103
Tier bosses. *See* Guards
Timber, Judge, 125
Tombs, 156
Tongues bored through, 4
Torture, 3, 4, 10, 25, 29, 45, 46, 57, 119, 120, 139, 165n
Train wrecking, 35
Tramps, 99
Transportation, 88, 89, 92, 197n
Treason, punishment for, 3, 35, 36, 37, 52
Trusty guards. *See* Guards
Tumbrell, 4

Unequal sentences for codefendants, 83, 161
United States Board of Parole, 131
United States Bureau of Prisons, 148
United States Department of Health, 134
United States House of Representatives, 7

United States Senate, 7
Urbom, Judge, 133
Uttering of checks. *See* forgery

Vagrancy, 13, 97, 107; status of, 102-104, 161, 162
Van Oosterhout, Judge, 153
Virginia Declaration of Rights, 5, 7

Warren, Chief Justice, 15, 43, 93, 101
Webster, Judge, 118, 150
Weems doctrine, 65-74
Weis, Judge, 138
Whipping, 4, 11, 17, 68, 69-70, 142, 165n, 172n; as administrative action, 115-118, 128; blackjacks, 143; in the colonies, 5; provided by statute, 55-56, 161; straps, 143; of women, 4
Whipping post, 55
Whittaker, Justice, 15
White, Chief Justice, 67, 68
White, Justice, 46, 47, 48, 49, 98, 101, 171n
Whitehall, Robert, 6
Williams, David W., 125
Witches. *See* Burning
Wright, J. Skelly, 27
Wyman, Louis C., 49

Young, Judge, 117, 148, 156

Zampano, Judge, 106
Zirpoli, Judge, 150

About the Author

Larry C. Berkson is assistant professor of political science at the University of Florida. He received the B.A. cum laude from Doane College in Crete, Nebraska. He received the M.A. from the University of South Dakota and the Ph.D. from the University of Wisconsin. Dr. Berkson has contributed articles to several law reviews and political science journals.

Related Lexington Books

Bowers, William J., *Executions in America,* 528 pp., 1974

Chappell, Duncan, and Monahan, John, *Violence and Criminal Justice,* 176 pp., 1975.

Drapkin, Israel, and Viano, Emilio, *Victimology: A New Focus,* vols. I-V, 1974 and 1975

Ellis, Desmond, *Violence in Prisons,* In Press

Gardiner, John A., and Mulkey, Michael, *Crime and Criminal Justice,* 224 pp., 1975

Meyer, Peter, *Experiments on Prisoners: Some Economic Considerations,* in Press

Smith, Joan and Fried, William, *The Uses of American Prisons,* 192 pp., 1974

Steadman, Henry J., Cocozza, Joseph J., *Careers of the Criminally Insane: Excessive Social Control of Deviance,* 224 pp., 1974